ISBN 978-1-330-82413-9
PIBN 10110202

1 MONTH OF
FREE
READING

at

www.ForgottenBooks.com

By purchasing this book you are eligible for one month membership to ForgottenBooks.com, giving you unlimited access to our entire collection of over 700,000 titles via our web site and mobile apps.

To claim your free month visit:

www.forgottenbooks.com/free110202

Similar Books Are Available from
www.forgottenbooks.com

---◈---

Modern Painting, Hardwood Finishing and Sign Writing

PAINTS AND PAINTING

This important subject is thoroughly covered with full explanations of how to test paints for adulterations, causes of blistering, colors, brushes, calcimining, carriage painting, color harmony, color mixing, color testing, exterior painting, gilding, graining, house painting, marbling, oils and driers, etc., including valuable hints on scene painting.

WOOD FINISHING

Under this head is treated the subject of filling, staining, varnishing, polishing, gilding and enameling woodwork of all kinds of woods, both hard and soft. It also treats on renovating old work.

MODERN UP-TO-DATE ARTISTIC SIGN PAINTING

Describing Plain and Ornamental and Ancient and Mediæval Lettering from the Eighth to the Twentieth Century, with Numerals. Including German, Old English, Saxon, Italic, Perspective, Initials, Monograms, Etc.

FULLY ILLUSTRATED

By ARMSTRONG, HODGSON AND DELAMOTTE

SPECIAL EXCLUSIVE EDITION
PRINTED BY
FREDERICK J. DRAKE & CO.
EXPRESSLY FOR
SEARS, ROEBUCK & COMPANY
CHICAGO, ILL.
1914

INTRODUCTION

The Modern Painter's Cyclopedia is not merely the compiling and putting together the stale writings and antiquated methods which have been put to use by many persons to make up a book to sell, but has been completely rewritten and the subject matter handled in such a way as to describe the latest methods used in performing the work. Owing to the great number of subjects handled the descriptions given are necessarily brief. The more important ones will be treated more at length than those of minor interest to the general reader, as for instance "China painting," etc; to treat the subject in a thorough manner would of itself fill a good sized volume, while the majority of readers would probably pass it by as of no interest to them, while they would naturally look for at least concise, full information on colors, house, carriage or sign painting and kindred subjects in which the big majority of readers are interested.

The alphabetical arrangement of the "Painter's Cyclopedia" has been preserved and the subject matter described will be found thus more readily. While this arrangement has many advantages, it must be admitted that it has its faults in that the various operations in painting are rather scattered without regard to sequence or any gradation upward from the simpler to the more difficult parts.

This defect has been greatly minimized by numbering each paragraph and to keep them sufficiently pointed to differ from the preceding or succeeding ones. Throughout the work wherever the necessitv occurs, reference by number will be made to such paragraphs in other parts of the book; this will make the subject matter more easily understood without the necessity of repeating; saving much space. Thus operations which are common to many branches of painting are only described once and the reader will be referred by number to where the additional information can be found. This it is hoped will reduce the defect mentioned above to its lowest limits.

Besides a very copious index has been prepared which will enable the reader to find readily every phase of any subject treated.

To enable students to memorize or recollect the subject matter of each heading, a series of questions will be found at the end numbered to correspond to that of the paragraphs containing the answer. This will enable the student to determine for himself the correctness of his own answer.

As many persons no doubt will buy this book with a view to educating themselves upon one or more branches of the trade—in a manner it will take the place of the correspondence school to such—at a greatly reduced cost.

In organized, practical trade schools, it is hoped that it may prove a valuable help, not only to the students but also the instructors—in that under classified head ings any or at least most of the subject matter relating to the branches taught will be found treated and the questions which are added at the end of each heading will permit its use as a text book in such schools.

It makes no claim to be able to lead the student along as fast nor as well as he would under the personal surveillance and advice of a capable instructor who can demonstrate an error in a practical way—but where it is used as an adjunct to his oral instruction and as a book of reference by the student, it will greatly facilitate the acquiring of knowledge.

The lack of such a book for the purpose indicated above, is one of the main reasons for its publication—aside from the need of a manual covering the ground and subject matter treated in a late and up-to-date manner.

Again it is repeated that many branches of painting require appliances, tools, colors, etc. To save repetition, each of these are treated fully but once, under their several headings, and if the reader will care to inform himself more fully in regard to any of these, he can readily do so by referring to the paragraph number indicated as describing such.

With the above synopsis of the scope and manner of handling the subject matter of the book, it is presented to the world—not as the acme of perfection, which unfortunately is unattainable, but as a helping hand to the student or others seeking general information on the paint and kindred trades—with the hope that many may be benefitted by its perusal, study, or use as a reference book.

F. MAIRE.

ADULTERATION

1. There is much less need of an extensive knowledge of the "how to detect" adulteration in painting material today than was necessary only a decade ago. Thanks to the wise action of the general government and that of many of our state legislatures, the gross adulterations to which all such material had been subjected then, has been greatly curtailed since. At the present time it is possible for one to know to a certainty the composition of any color, or what are the contents of any barrel, can or other package containing paint, varnishes, vehicles, etc. The law in many of our states forcing the manufacturer to state upon the label the name of every ingredient entering into the composition of the contents. So if the name of a desired color, say Chrome yellow, medium, is printed upon the label as pure, and the name of the manufacturer appears upon it too, one may be safe in buying it for what it is. The greatest danger is in the buying so-called second quality goods. In the above instance suppose the label said "Chrome yellow—medium. Contents, chrome yellow and barytes. Of course this indicates that it is not pure—but how much pure? It may contain 25% pure

chrome yellow and 75% barytes which is about the average in the better grade of off colors, or it may be 10% chrome yellow, and even much less, and the rest barytes. And in the dry colors many run as low as 3% actual colors to 97% barytes chalk or other adulterants.

2. In colors or pigments dry or ground in oil, water or japan, there is a possibility of greatly adulterating most of these without any remarkable change in the looks of the goods themselves, so that it requires a knowledge of the principal ingredients used in adulterating to understand *how* to detect them.

3. Heavy weight colors are usually adulterated with some substance of as near the bulk or weight as their own; besides the adulterant must be as clear or colorless as possible, so as not to change materially the color or tone of the pigments they are added to. If much lighter in weight the usual size package used to pack the pure color would have to be greatly increased to accommodate the larger bulk of the adulterant needed to make up the weight. This would at once give it away in the mind of one who is at all familiar with the customary packaging of pure goods.

4. *a.* What is known as Barytes or Barium Sulphate is the most common adulterant used in the sophistification of all heavy colors. This substance seems eminently well fitted for this purpose as when mixed in oil it is so very transparent that it may be painted over new wood in several coats without hiding the grain of the wood much more than so many oilings would have

done. This great transparency enables the color(?) manufacturer to add it in nearly any proportion desired to colored pigments. But it is after all mainly as an adulterant of white lead and zinc white, that it shows up to the best advantage—as an adulterant. It is the nearest substance in weight to white lead, being very heavy, and known as heavy spar in lead mines where it is frequently found. This great density permits the use of a package for the adulterated lead little greater than that used for the strictly pure article. It is said nearly—but not quite. An expert will detect even the slight enlargement of the package necessary to contain a given weight.

b. Some of the colored pigments themselves are adulterated with barytes to an extent and degree incredible to the uninitiated. Some of the stronger ones are frequently met with—especially in the dry state, containing as much as ten or twelve times their own weight of barytes, while in such pigments ground in oil the proportion ranges from 75% to 500% in extreme cases.

c. The pure food laws, so called, are of doubtful utility in that in most states the percentage of each substance or ingredient in a compound is not stated, but the adulteration is only indicated by the mention of its presence. So one is left to guess at it. In the preceding paragraph 4 *b.* it is stated that the proportion may be anywhere from 75% to 500%. Seventy-five per cent., high as that may sound (1 part color to 3 parts adulteration) is legitimate for many colors that are very strong and which cover well in the self color, or which are very seldom used for tinting purposes. Chrome green and all the fancy named proprietary greens, by common consent and custom have sanctioned it, are all made on that basis. The pure color used in painting in its self color will cover very little more surface than the commercial, which is adulterated in the proportion stated of 3 to 1. In that it cheapens the cost of the goods, it really becomes a benefit to the consumer, that is when confined to the well known trade custom limits —but unfortunately it is not always done, and in the dry colors especially, the coloring matter contained in some goods is little more than that used in the preparing of colored chalk.

5. To detect the amount of adulteration present is not so difficult as may be supposed it is. There are two very distinct methods of doing this. First, by a chemical analysis (quantitative) which, if properly made, will give a complete tale of the quantity of each ingredient entering into the compound. As most of the readers of this book are not chemists and as the cost of an analysis properly made will usually cost far in excess of the value of the material under examination, it must be waved aside as impracticable to most people.

While without question a chemical analysis is the most satisfactory, and only correct manner of determining adulteration accurately, fortunately there is a way of approximatively fixing the amount of it in any goods that no one need buy adulterated goods without knowing very nearly just what he is paying for; nor has one any need of a knowledge of chemistry in making the test.

6. This test is called the "Scale test." To make the test all the implements required is an accurate pair of scales with weights in grains or grammes. What are known as army surgeon's scales or any of the apothecaries' pocket scales will do. A few sheets of waxed paper. A few pieces of glass, well cleaned, to lay the colors upon. A palette knife to triturate the colors with and some blotting paper to absorb the oil out of colors so that each may have the same consistency. The above or equivalents are all the appliances needed to equip one for testing.

7. The testing is made in the following manner· The person wishing to make a test should have a sam ple which is well known to be genuine to use as a stand ard to judge of the value of a similar color about to be tested. These standard colors can easily be procured at any color or painter's supply store, by procuring tubes of Windsor and Newton's artist colors in tubes. These are standard colors of known purity and while there may be a number of others as good as they, none will surpass them and they will be found better, while many will be found inferior to them. So that if W. & N.'s are not procurable any other made by a reputable house will be found sufficiently good for the purpose.

Now it stands to reason that if two similar colors to

be tested are equally pure that an equal weight of each color when triturated with two batches of white lead both also of an equal weight it follows that when the two colors have been mixed each one separately with the lead—that the tint made will be very nearly of the same strength of tone if both are equally pure, but that if one has been adulterated then it must lack in coloring matter to about the same quantity or percentage as had been added of adulteration to the pure color in the first place.

Thus if one grain or gramme of say—chrome yellow, is carefully placed upon a small square of waxed paper (about ¾ inch square) and afterward weighed carefully upon the balances, then placed upon a piece of glass, rubbing the waxed paper over the glass to remove all traces of color from it; then triturated with say 50 grains or grammes of white lead, also placed on waxed paper and carefully weighed, the tint resulting from the triturating should be spread out on the glass, bringing it quite to one edge of it on one side, so as to permit of an easy inspection of each sample when placed side and side together; then afterward doing the same with the other color in each case in like manner, that if there be no adulteration that there will be but very little dif ference in the tints made.

If the color examined has been adulterated, the tint it will make with white lead will be much weakened as stated before. Now to determine in a sufficiently accurate manner what the proportion of adulterant has been added to it—all that will be necessary will be to add more white lead to the tint made by the stronger color until it is reduced to the strength of the tint made by the weaker color. The tint made by the addition of more white lead should be reweighed.

Thus if one grain of color and 50 grains of white lead produced a tint that is fully equalled by one grain of another color and 250 grains of white lead, it must be that the color which is the weakest has been adulterated with four times its own weight of some kind of an adulterant which has lessened the proportion of coloring matter to the same proportion that the adulterant contained in it bears to the pure.

This test is especially valuable for all chemically made colors having well known formulas. It is useful, however, to determine the relative value of most all the earth colors also with the exception of some very few transparent ones whose chief value consist in this very transparency and their brilliancy of tone. In the latter case the mere strength test is of little value. Under the subject head of colors by referring to paragraphs 61 to 74, fuller information is given regarding their value and really substitution takes the place of adulteration for such.

8. To test adulteration in white lead made by the Dutch process or the hyd.-carb. of lead, a very simple test is made use of to detect such. Place a small bit of the lead to be tested upon a sliver of pine wood, light a match, bring the flame from it in contact with the lead

on the stick. In a very short time, if the lead is pure, some very fine globules of metallic lead will appear upon it. It may possibly take a couple of matches to make the test satisfactory, if one has been careless in not getting the full force of the flame in the first one.

The blow pipe test is more satisfactory but it somewhat more difficult to make; requiring also a blow pipe which is a tube curved at one end and a piece of charcoal. A candle is also necessary. Place some lead in a small cavity prepared in the charcoal, put the charcoal with the lead on it in the left hand and near the candle, then blow the pipe upon the flame of the candle in such a way as to deflect the blue flame resulting from the blowing upon the lead. This will burn up the oil and in a minute the lead, if it is pure, will have resolved itself into a small metallic globule of pure lead.

If the lead has been adulterated with as small a quantity as 10% of barytes zinc clay or silicate earth, it will not reduce to the metallic state and as no one would undertake to adulterate lead with as small a quantity of barytes as that for it would not pay, it will be easily understood that if it will not reduce, it is surely adulterated much more than that.

It may be well to state here that the above tests will not apply to any other form of white salts used as paint which are derived from lead. Sublimed lead, for instance, will not be reduced by it, being a basic sulphate of lead. It would need fluxing and a very high degree of heat to reduce it and such a test is not to be thought of to a novice or others unfamiliar with the process nor equipped for it.

The described scale test reversed will give a fair indication of the amount of adulteration in any sample of white lead. To make the test—only the one color must be used taken from the same can. Weigh one grain of color, which place on glass—repeat this and place the color upon another glass; then weigh 50 grains of lead which place with the first grain of color weighed out; repeat this but use 50 grains of the white lead you wish to test. The first having been taken from a keg which is known to be pure; the other being the suspicioned one. Triturate each upon their separate pieces of glass, if one has been adulterated, it will lack in opacity and body and the color will be able to tint it to a very much deeper tone than it has been able to do with the pure lead, which being more opaque, will hide the coloring matter much more than the adulter ated sample has been able to do. In other words the stronger the lead—the less will a given weight of color change its color.

Now to return to the practical side of the test; if one grain of Venetian red has been able to color 50 grains of lead known to be pure then it will be safe to infer that the first contains 33 1/3% of white lead and 66 2/3 barytes or other adulterant; or 1 part lead, 2 parts adulteration.

While the above tests are all approximative, they are practical and easily made, being within the possibility of everyone, requiring no knowledge of chemistry and while not conclusive as to what the adulterant really consists of, in reality this knowledge is not very important to the purchaser of color. It shows him how much valuable material is contained in the various samples tested and after all that is the main thing for him to know. He can know to a certainty whether he is paying a right price for his goods or whether he wants them at all or not.

QUESTIONS UPON ADULTERATION.

1.   What can be said generally about the adulteration of colors, etc., at the present time?

2.   Are adulterated colors readily distinguished from those that are pure?

3.   What kind of an adulterant is required for heavy and light colors respectively?

4a.   What adulterant is mainly used in white lead?

b.   Is barvtes used in adulterating colored pigments?

c.   Are the pure food laws a complete protection against the adulteration of color?

5.   How is the amount of adulteration detected?

6.   What is needed in making the scale test?

7.   Describe the manner of making the test.

8.   How can strictly pure white lead be tested for purity?

THE BLISTERING OF PAINT.

9.   There are several causes which produce the blis-

tering of paint, but only two principal ones are worthy of any attention, as all the others are variations of the following two agents, to-wit: Moisture and heat.

10. *Moisture* is the principal direct cause producing nine-tenths of all the blistering of paint on the outside of buildings.

11. But it cannot really produce a blistering of paint without the concurring assistance of *heat.*

12. With the numberless essays which have been written and the endless discussions which have taken place at Painters' Conventions and elsewhere relating to the blistering of paint, it must be acknowledged that there are many points involved in this relation which are as yet but improperly understood.

MOISTURE.

13. Some parts of its action upon paint is very plainly to be seen, so that nearly every one who has given the subject a thought, one would suppose some uniform explanation would be given of it, yet upon the very plainest action of moisture many intelligent men differ materially in explaining its action upon paint.

Moisture in the paint itself very rarely injures the painting done with it, however strange it may sound for one to make the statement. Thus emulsated paints *properly prepared* will last fully as long as paints which have not been prepared by emulsion—but they must have been prepared scientifically or they usually will be found short lived enough.

a. If moisture is present in the wood over which paint is applied or that can be sucked up from the earth by capillary attraction as in stone, brick and cement structure, then there is great danger that the paint will blister sooner or later.

b. As stated before there must be heat present to help moisture in producing a blister. Heat acts upon it in this way: Moisture may and does remain confined for a long time when there is no way opened for it to escape. So long as it remains in the state of water it will never produce a blister. For this reason one never hears of blistering in late autumn, winter or early spring.

c. But when that water becomes heated by the hot sun it is turned into steam; as it is prevented from evaporating by the impervious coat of paint. In expanding itself into steam it forms a blister large enough to hold it under the paint which has been softened by the heat of both steam and sun from both sides.

d. This skin may or may not break out so as to let the steam escape into the atmosphere. When it does not do so, as soon as the atmosphere becomes cooled the steam is condensed into water again. Anyone can easily prove this to his perfect satisfaction by pricking the bubble with a pin when the water will at once run out.

e. It is very seldom that blisters caused by moisture can ever be seen except upon the south side of buildings, the west and the east but mostly on the south, then next in number on the west and least on the east with none on the north. This order verifies the theory advanced that moisture without the aid of heat will not cause blistering of paint as the south which receives the sun's rays nearly all day shows the most blisters, the west next and the east its weakest äs it receives early morning rays and the intense ones only for a short time about 10 to 12 noon exhibits the smallest number of blisters

The above applies to wood, brick, stone, or cement buildings alike, if they absorb moisture—the wooden from imperfectly seasoned lumber and the others by capillary attraction from the earth or by defect in the roof or eaves, causing moisture to run down behind the paint.

HEAT.

14. We have seen its action in the foregoing paragraphs in conjunction with moisture.

a. Heat alone, if it be great enough, will blister paint and the best proof of it is: That most of all old paint removed from overpainted surfaces, is chiefly taken off by the aid of the paint burners which heats it and softens it into heat blisters.

b. There are other instances where blisters are produced directly by the action of heat without the aid of moisture: 1st where a very dark paint has been applied to a surface which before had been coated over with a very light tint. It is explained in this way: Light is reflected by white and all light tints, and absorbed by all dark ones; therefore the dark coat will absorb the sun's rays readily, but it stops at the light color underneath and instead of further penetration the reverse takes place—it is there reflected. The heat having softened the linseed oil contained in the upper coat which from its having been put there more recently is yet full of elasticity, will swell out from the pushing away influence it receives from the heat and light re flected by the light under coat and gradually loosen itself from it far enough away that there is no more expansion needed. These bubbles or blisters are always dry when pricked through, showing no moisture and are always seen *above* the light tinted coat underneath, leaving that intact upon the building. This class of blisters are very similar to the ones formed upon painted surfaces too near a stove and other places subject to overheating.

c. There is another instance where an upper paint coat will separate from an under one—this is due to the action of moisture—not in the wood, brick, stone or cement—but from its development in the under coats of paint. It can be traced as readily as the former and as easily understood.

It is a well known fact that clay will absorb and give out moisture. Some pigments like our American ochres, for instance, are composed mainly of alumina (clay) colored by ferric hydroxides. They may have been very thoroughly dried before grinding in oil and all the care possible taken to have the article in good condition and as the oil used as a vehicle remains sound and impervious there will be no trouble between the clay ochre priming or sub-coats and the superadded ones, as in that condition an air-tight overcoating of the upper layers of paint protect it from moisture; but as soon as the natural decay of the linseed oil has fairly commenced, then the trouble commences, although it is imperceptible at first. The oil having lost all its glycerides, their place forms very fine pores or conduits through which the moisture will find its way to the clay based ochre underneath and as it, too, has felt the effects of the decay in its own coat of oil, this moisture is absorbed by the clay in wet weather and as freely parted with in dry hot weather. The sun soften ing the oil of the upper coat makes it impervious again, its action upon the moisture contained in the clay ochre is to turn that into steam—that of steam is to expand and to vaporize and become absorbed by the atmosphere but being prevented by the softened coats of paint above it, it expands itself into a blister large enough to hold it. Then either of two things happen: 1st the blister will burst and the condensed steam in the shape of water will run out; 2nd, or it will not burst and the condensed steam water will be held a prisoner under the blister till released by the breaking of the bubble or reabsorbed by the undercoat of clay ochre.

This is a form of blistering well known to every experienced painter in the land, but frequently misunderstood by them. They know the effect, but many are not aware of the cause of it. It has led many to reject ochre altogether for priming. For a more extended notice of this peculiarity of ochres the reader is referred to paragraph 79. The above two *reasons why* under which 99% of all cases of blistering can be traced will suffice to explain the troublesome phenomena of blistering. As to the remedy, alas! there is none but a removal of the cause.

QUESTIONS ON BLISTERING OF PAINT.

9.   How many principal causes why paint blisters?

10.   Name the principal one.

11.   Name its accessory.

12.   Are the causes of blistering well understood?

13.   Describe how moisture affects paint in sub-sections, *a, b, c, d* and *e*.

14.   Describe how heat affects paint in sub-sections *a, b* and *c*.

BRUSHES.

15.   Brushes are one of the most important line of implements used by the paint trade in all its branches, from the coarsest down to the finest of artists' work and next to skill in guiding them take the lead as helpers to users of paint.

In the description of all the various brushes used by the paint and paper hangers' trades which follows in the course of this heading, precedence is given to the larger, which will be reviewed first and downward to the smaller ones and this will be the case for each one of the raw material from which they are made—as bristle brushes are those which are used the most of all, brushes made from that material will be reviewed first from the largest to the smallest and the same course will be taken with all the other sorts as much as possible, giving those which are mostly used in sequence.

It is lucky that under the alphabetical arrangement of the subject matter of this book that brushes come in at the beginning of this manual, as there will be no need of any explanation under the various headings other than a reference to the figures and their number, thus showing at a glance the particular tools each branch requires.

It will be in order here to state that the manufacturing of brushes has progressed along and kept up with advances made by other lines toward perfection, which, however, it has not yet attained—but great improvments have been made over the past.

It is not intended to go very deeply into details concerning the manufacture of brushes. This would lead into an infinity of details requiring full and minute description to be intelligently understood and really belongs to a treatise devoted entirely to that industry. Nor would such details be of much interest to the users of brushes.

16. The material from which brushes are made consists of the hair and fur of various animals, usually set in cement or in glue or in rubber, and bound onto the

head which is usually of wood by either thread, cord wire or nailed metal strips or leather or a solid metal casing or vulcanized rubber.

As has already been stated the brushes will be classed and described according to the raw material that they are made from and as near as possible in the order of their greatest usefulness.

BRISTLES.

Boar or hog bristles being by far the most important of all the raw material used in brush making, is entitled to being noticed first of all. It enters into the manufacture of nearly all the brushes used in general painting.

All the larger brushes flat, round or oval, are made of the very highest priced Russian bristles for the first qualities. It is claimed that the best of these are procured from the wild boar. There is no doubt but that some bristles are obtained from that animal, but it seems doubtful if the crop of bristle from that source would go very far in supplying the quantity required for the consumption of the whole world.

The semi-tamed Russian hog produces, fortunately, bristles that are little inferior to that of the wild hog. Those borne upon the crest of the neck of the animal being the most valuable, being strong, elastic and longer than upon other parts of the body, although the other parts also produce very good but shorter bristles. Their market value diminishes according to length from the longest to the shortest. But even in the smaller sizes the Russian hog bristles are superior to all others in elasticity and wearing qualities.

The so-called French bristles into which class nearly all other European bristles may be placed, furnish a very good next quality to that of the Russian and for the purpose of making varnish brushes or fine brushes to lay color for the carriage trade, they even surpass the Russian on account of their greater fineness and smoothness. The black bristles known as Chinese bristles, do not all come from the Orient as their name would indicate, but most of it comes from many other countries in Asia and Europe, beside what is furnished by our own packing houses where everything belonging to the hog is carefully saved excepting the squeal it is said.

Our own packing houses furnish the bulk of the bristles used in making brushes and their output is not confined to black bristles only, but to all the colors which the many breeds are characterized with. But while some very good bristles are originated here, it must be admitted that they are few and come from that now nearly extinct specimen—the razor back. High breeding seems to deteriorate the bristle so that while the flesh and fat producing has greatly improved, the hair is much inferior to the old native and the great bulk of American bristle is inferior to the European importations.

SIBERIAN OX HAIR.

18. Siberian ox hair of the best quality is said to be the clippings of hair from the inside of the ears of the Siberian ox. Whether other parts of the growth on the body is not also used seems doubtful as the quantity of brushes which are sold under the name would indicate that if only the inner part of the ear produces all that is used then they must have enormous herds of oxen in that country. The probabilities are that not only Siberia but America as well is called upon to furnish the material required for the brush matter sold under that name.

The best quality is unusually springy and varnish brushes made from it are very highly prized by the furniture wood finishing trades for certain kinds of work. The sign painter also uses them largely in both the quill bound and flat sizes for the one stroke letter shape so much in demand now days.

BADGER HAIR.

19. Badger hair is the product of several animals belonging to the same family, "the marmotte' or "mar mouse" to which the badger and our famous weather prophet "the ground hog" belongs. It is long and while soft, it preserves its shape well. Finishing and flowing varnish brushes for both the wood finishing and carriage trades are made from it. Gold tips and gold dusters for gilders. Blenders for the graining and marbling trades all prize it highly; nothing has been

devised for that purpose that is anywhere equal to badger hair.

20. These two may be bracketed together as both are used mainly for the purpose of making flowing varnish brushes. They make most excellent brushes for the purpose either alone or mixed together in certain proportions which is thought to make them better by some wood finishers. Many carriage painters having become used to sable hair claim them to be better than anything else.

21. Sable hair of both the *red* and *black* variety are very highly esteemed by artists, decorators, sign writers and stripers. They are rather expensive but as they are much more durable and for the laying of heavy bodied colors are so much better adapted to the work than camel hair brushes are that the latter are losing ground for use in heavy weighted pigments with all discriminating users.

22. Camel hair is a misnomer as the squirrel furnishes the bulk of it, however, as it is known only under that name, it is likely to stick as long as the English language lasts.

It is very soft and lays color very smoothly and when carefully done little if any brush mark will show. The better made brushes of that material are excellent and it would be a sad day for many workmen if the supply should suddenly be stopped as many would be completely lost to know what to do in replacing them. They as well as all good things have a great fault in that being very soft, they have little elasticity and if used in heavy colors they are likely to bend and become deformed. The carriage trade, the wood finisher, sign writers, stripers, decorators, enamelers, lacquerers, artists, etc., all use them to a greater or lesser extent.

23. This concludes the list of raw material from which brushes are made for the paint trade with the possible exception of "Tampico," which may be considered as an adulterant and which is used chiefly in making up the cheaper grades of bristle brushes. It possesses not an atom of value other than to fill up a given space and takes up that which should be occupied by better material. It can scarcely be called a fraud because such brushes are made for a class of trade who want to buy something for nothing and they must be accommodated. But the advice given to those who buy brushes is *to buy the best only.* The first cost of a brush may be large in comparison to the poor tool, but it is actual economy to buy the best, as they last much longer and enable the workman to do his work in a creditable manner, which is nearly impossible to do with poor tools.

BRISTLE BRUSHES.

24. Under this head all bristle brushes made for the general paint trade, including the decorators, etc., will be reviewed and an illustration of each kind given,

Fig. 1—Kalsomine Brush.

which will show the shapes. As, however, all or most of them are made in several qualities and sizes, it will be impossible to give all these in *"illustrations."* In the description the various sizes that each is made up in will be given.

a. The calcimine brush is probably the largest and most expensive brush made for the paint trade. The best are made from long springy Russian stock and on downward to clear Tampico. They are made on a flat wooden head with a wooden handle and are bound in metal nailed on to the head, usually galvanized iron is used for the purpose. They are made in three sizes: 6, 7 and 8 inches wide. See Fig. 1.

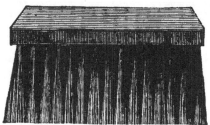

Fig. 2—Extra Wall Stipplers.

b. Wall stipplers are long bristle brushes made upon an oblong square head usually in two sizes, 3½x 8 and 3½x9 inches. These brushes are used only in following up wall painting to obliterate brush marks and producing a uniform grained finish to the work, by beating the painting evenly all over. The head is a wooden one and the finished tool looks like a mam moth cloth brush. See Fig. 2.

c. Flat wall brushes are made up in all qualities

and widths of head from 3 to 5 inches wide, and are bound to a wooden head and handle by a metallic band or by a leather binding when they are then known being set in a rubber head and vulcanized. This pre-

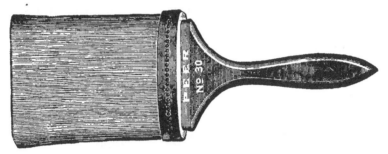

Fig. 3—Stucco Wall Paint Brush.

vents the losing of hair. See Fig. 3 for the shape of as "stucco wall" brushes. Some are also made by

Fig. 4—Stucco Wall Paint Brush.

metal bound wall, and Fig. 4 for the "stucco or leather bound."

d. Round bristle paint brushes are made in many qualities, weights and lengths of bristles; in open centers, semi-open centers or full stock, besides a number of patented arrangements each claiming to be *"it."* The binding is usually wire or cording or set in a solid

rubber head. The sizes run by o from 1.o the smallest
to 8.o the largest. See Fig. 5.

e. *Oval bristle paint brushes* only differ from the
above by the shape of the make up which as the name
indicates is oval instead of round. In qualities and sizes
they are similar to the round brush described in the
preceding sub-section. See Fig. 5, which also repre-
sents it fairly well only that the handle is flatter than
in the round brush.

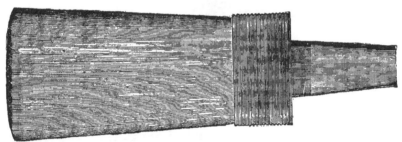

Fig. 5.

f. Painters' dusters, either round or flat, and in
many qualities of white or black bristles. The best
quality is that known as the coach painter's duster and
are made in white bristles only. The length and thickness of hair make the selling price higher and lower
running from 3½ to 5 inches long. See Fig. 6 for the
round. The flat is shaped like Fig. 3 only more loosely
put together.

g. Before closing up on the large bristle brushes it
will be well to note *"the whitewash heads"* as sometimes the painter is called upon to do that kind of work;
besides being an excellent tool to do calcimining with

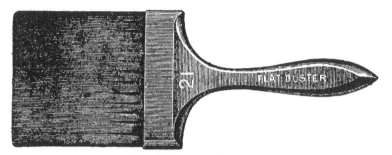

Flat Painter's Duster.

Round Painter's Duster.
Fig. 6.

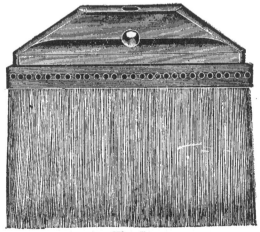

Fig. 7.

also in apartments where furniture, carpets, etc., encumber a room so that stepladders and scaffolding is not to be thought of, a long handle can be set in the whitewash head and the work of calcimining a ceiling done from the floor. They come in widths ranging from 6 to 9 inches. They are bound to the wooden head by either metal bands or leather. The illustration shows the leather bound. See Fig. 7.

h. Sash tools are made either round or oval full length of bristle or chisel edge. They are bound by cording, wire, a solid metal head or set in a hard rubber head and in many qualities of material. They come in numbered sizes, No. 1 being the smallest, to No. 10 the largest. See Fig. 8 for the full·length hair and Fig. 9 for the chisel edge shapes.

i. Coach painters' spoke brushes run in sizes from No. 1 to 3 and are used chiefly by the carriage trade, but they are also very useful for a number of purposes in general painting where a long but slim brush is to be used. Decorators in water colors will also find them a handy tool for coves, etc. See Fig. 10.

j. Glue brushes are usually metal bound and well set. They run in sizes from 000 to No. 4 or from $\frac{5}{8}$ inch to $1\frac{1}{2}$ inch in diameter. See Fig. 11. They are also made flat, metal bound, and from 1 inch to 6 inches wide. The flat brushes are also made chisel edged. See Fig. 12.

k. Painter's car scrub brushes are made from very stiff bristles and run in sizes from No. 4 to No. 6. It

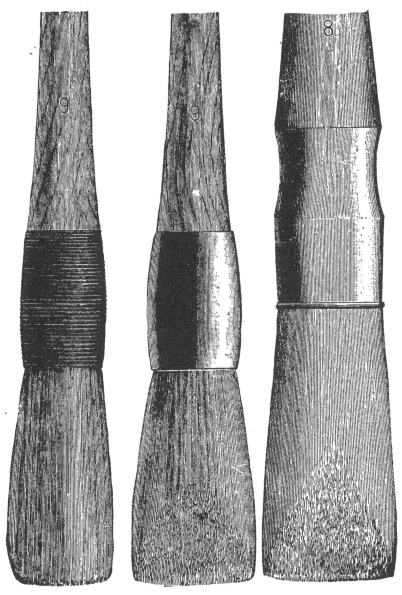

Fig. 8—Sash Tool.   **Fig. 9**—Sash Tool, Chisel Edged.

is a very useful tool to the carriage painter.   See
Fig. 13.

BRÍSTLE VARNISH BRUSHES.

l.   Bristle varnish brushes are usaully made oval

Fig. 10—Coach Painters' Spoke Brushes.

and are bound with wire or by solid metal heads and
with full length of bristle or chisel edged in many qual⁻

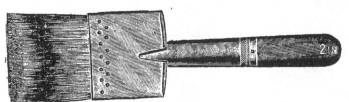

Fig. 11—Round Glue Brushes, Gray Bristles.

Fig. 12—Flat Glue, Gray Bristles.

ities and sized by o from 1.0 the smallest, to 8.0 th
largest.   All have flattened wooden handles, Fig. 1
showing the full length and Fig. 15 the chisel edg
shapes.   Fig. 15 also shows the solid metal head.

There are also a number of different qualities of fl

varnish bristle brushes from very good to very poor single thick, double thick, full length bristle to chiseled edge. The shapes vary very much as well as that of

Fig. 13—Painters' Car Scrubs.

the handles. The two Figs. 16 and 17 will suffice to show the leading shapes. Like all flat brushes they are sold by the inch, being made from 1 inch to 4 inches, graded by half inches between.

Coach painters and many others use a brush made up very much like the one shown in Fig. 15, and which is known as a coach painter's color brush.

m. Stencil brushes are used for the purpose indicated by their name. Like all the rest there are many

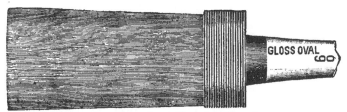

Fig. 14—Gloss Oval Varnish Brushes.

qualities. They are bound with wire or set in a solid metal head or band. In size they run from 1 inch to 2½ inches in diameter. Figs. 18 and 19 illustrate the two bindings.

n. Artists and decorators in both water and oil colors use a number of round, flat and triangular shaped

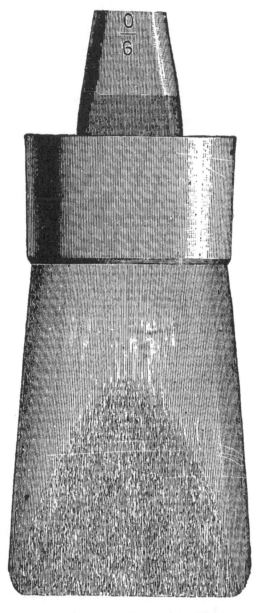

Fig. 15—Oval Chiselled Varnish Brush.

small brushes with either short, medium or long bristles. According to what they have been designed for they are called a multitude of different names, as marking brushes, artists' round and flat bristle, fresco round

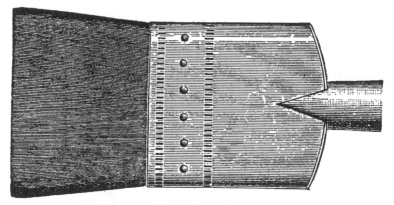

Fig. 16—Fitch Varnish Brush.

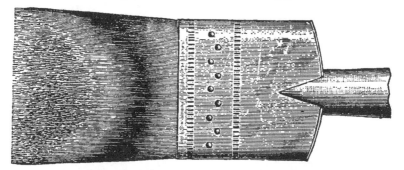

Fig. 17—Badger Hair Flowing Brush.

and flat, these cover about all the varieties. They are all metal ferruled with a long slim handle. They usually run in numbers from 1 to 10 for the round and from ¼ inch to 1¼ inch wide for the flat ones, bv ⅛ inch gradations. Fig. 20 illustrates the round and Fig. 21 the flat sorts.

o.　Weighted brushes for polishing waxed floors for or waxed varnished ones, are extensively used at the present to imitate dead rubbed polish. They are shown in Fig. 22.

p.　The wood finishing trade uses many of the bris-

Fig. 18.　　　　　　　　Fig. 19.

Stencil Brushes.

tle brushes which have been described for filling, shellacing, etc.　They buy those under the special names that they are wanted for, but differ so slightly from many of the flat stucco wall brushes that Fig. 4 will give one

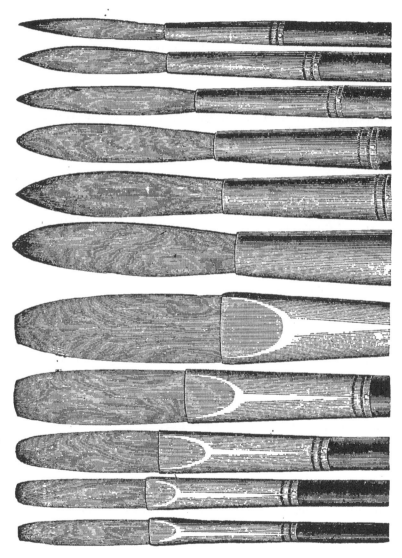

Fig. 20—Fresco Bristle Brushes.

a good idea of their shapes and sizes. However, the furniture trade uses a brush known as rubbing brushes which is illustrated in Fig. 23. This brush comes in many shapes or forms with enough variations to suit all the views of the finishers.

The *brick liner,* a tool used to color the mortar line on painted brick being shaped very nearly as the above only that it contains only a very thin row of hair, it will not be necessary to describe it more.

PAPER HANGERS' BRISTLE BRUSHES.

q. *The paper hanger's paste brush* is specially made so as to rub out paste easily, but many paper hangers use a worn out calcimine brush instead. It is illustrated in Fig. 24.

r. *Paper hangers' smoothing brushes* are made from one to four rows of stiff bristles, wire drawn, in several qualities and are sized according to the length of head from 10 to 14 inches wide. Fig. 25 shows the ordinary smoothing brush and Fig. 26 the combination smoothing brush and seam roller.

GRAINERS' BRISTLE TOOLS.

s. Grainers use a few bristle brushes which are shown by the following illustrations: Fig. 27 shows the stippler used in putting in an all over coarse grain as in walnut, chestnut, etc. Fig. 28 shows the fantail overgrainers which are sized according to width of head from 1 inch up to 4 inches wide by half inch grad-

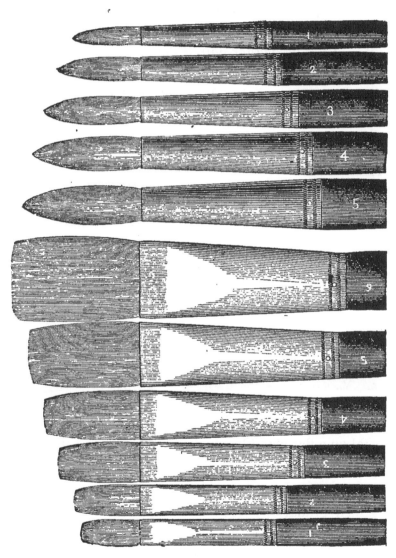

Fig. 21—Artist's Bristle Brushes.

ations.   Fig. 29 shows a grainer's mottler and Fig. 30
a bristle piped overgrainers, etc.

BADGER HAIR BRUSHES.

25.   *a.   The badger haired flowing varnish brushes*
are the principal ones used by the carriage and car
painting trades and are also well liked by some wood
finishers.   They are all made chisel edged and bound in

Fig. 21a.

metal on a flat wood head or a continuation of the metal
binder into a head with wooden handle attached.   They
are made single and double thick, ranging in sizes by
½ inch gradations from ½ inch to four inches wide.
Fig. 31 shows both the single and double shape.

b.   Gilders' tips are made from either badger or
camel's hair or a mixture of both as the squirrel is usually too flimsy by itself.   See Fig. 32.

c. The knotted bonehead badger hair blender of the grainer's trade, is an indispensable tool; it is used also by marblers and all painting requiring good blending.

Fig. 22—Angular Bristle Fresco Brushes.

It is sized according to width by half inch gradations from 2 to 5 inches wide. See Fig. 33.

d. Round badger haired blenders are used princi-

Fig. 23—Furniture Rubbing Brushes.

pally by artists and as a duster by gold leaf workers. They are bound in quill and of various sizes grading by numbers from No. 1 to No. 12. See Fig. 34.

OX HAIR BRUSHES.

26. *a. Ox hair flowing varnish brushes* are very highly prized by many wood finishers. They are made single and double and come in sizes and shapes same as Fig. 31, which see.

b. Ox hair flat sign writers' brushes are made to
supply the demand for a one stroke letter in a cheaper

Fig. 24—Paperhanger's Paste Brush.

material than sable capable of carrying heavy colors.
The size ranges by ¼ inch gradation up to 1 inch wide.

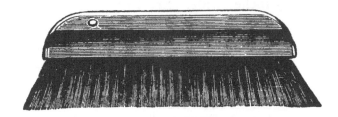

Fig. 25—Paperhanger's Smoothing Brush.

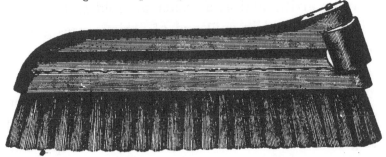

Fig. 26.

See Fig. 35, which also illustrates all other makes from other material.

c. Ox hair is also used in the make up of full lines of lettering and striping brushes, either bound in quill or metal. The illustrations shown below will also illus-

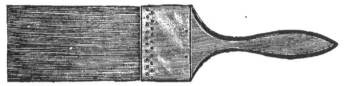

Fig. 27—Walnut Stipplers.

trate all other makes as shapes and bindings are about the same. See Fig. 36 for lettering and Fig. 37 for striping brushes, and Fig. 38 for metal bound handled.

Fig. 28.

The sizes in all kinds are numbered alike from No. 1 up to No. 12. Many kinds are only numbered to No. 6.

RED AND BLACK SABLE BRUSHES.

27. *a. Black and red sable brushes* to all intents

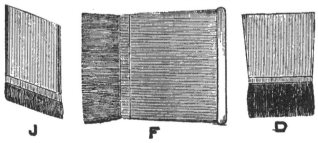

Fig. 29—Mottlers.

and purposes may be classed together, as they are nearly alike in working qualities.   As they are very springy and soft at the same time, they make up a very valuable

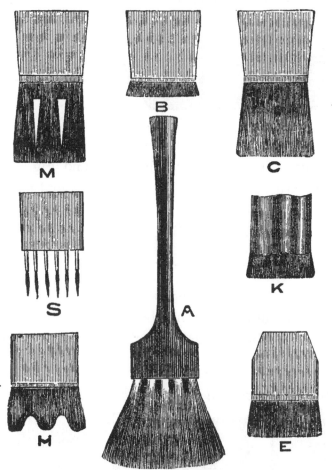

Fig. 30—Piped Overgrainers, Etc.

flowing varnish brush which is highly prized by coach painters and wood finishers.   They are made up in same sizes and shape as shown in Fig. 31, which see.

b. Black and red sable sign writers, flat one stroke lettering, are the best of the kind for heavy colors.

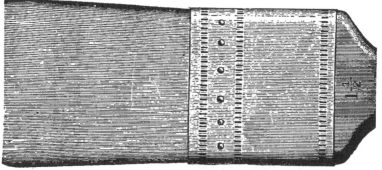

Fig. 31—Badger Hair Flowing.

While costing more than any other, they last so much longer in good condition if taken care of that they are the cheapest in the end. Same sizes and shape as shown in Fig. 35, which see.

c. Sign writers' quilled and ferruled letterers are the same in size and shapes as shown in Fig. 36.

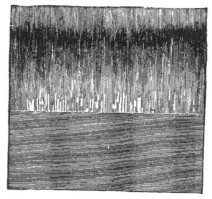

Fig. 32—Gilder's Camel-Hair Tips.

d. Striping brushes of this material are indespensa ble for use in heavy colors. See Fig. 37 for shape and sizes.

e. Red sable artists' brushes are well known the world over. No other material could well replace it for use in heavy colors. They come both round and

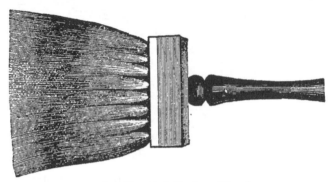

Fig. 33—Flat Knotted Badger Blender.

flat, ranging in number from No. 1 the smallest, to No. 12 the largest. See Fig. 39, illustrating both.

FITCH BRUSHES.

28. *The Fitch flowing varnish brush* is the only valuable brush which comes under that name. It is well liked by some carriage painters and to some extent

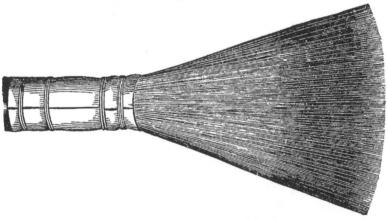

Fig. 34—Round Badger Blender.

by some wood finishers. See Fig. 31 for shape and sizes.

29. *Bear's hair flowing varnish brushes* are very valuable either when made up of that material alone or when mixed with some other material, which is too

Fig. 35—Flat Black Sable Lettering Brushes.

stiff by itself as a corrective. The wood finishing trade especially the better class of furniture manufacturers use it in great quantities. It is made up in same sizes and shape as shown in Fig. 31, which see.

CAMEL'S HAIR BRUSHES.

30. *a. Camel's hair varnish brushes* are used for many purposes and by nearly all branches of the painter's trade. They are very soft and lay varnish very smoothly. They all are made flat on somewhat variously shaped heads with shorter length hair than varnish brushes from other material are usually made as otherwise they would work too flabby. Their sizes are numbered according to width in ½ inch gradations from ½ to 4 inches. See Fig. 40.

b. The camel's hair mottler is a somewhat similar brush, but longer haired and thicker than the varnish brush. The mottler is used by many carriage painters as a color brush, but is specially made up then with thicker hair than the ordinary mottler used by grainers, stainers and others. They are metal bound and sized

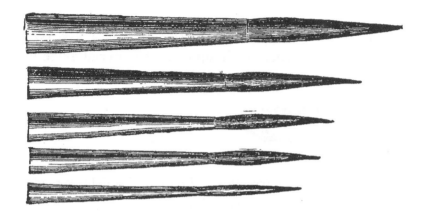

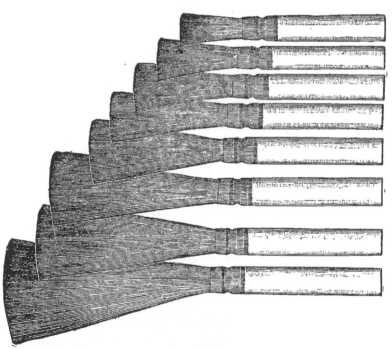

Fig. 36—Lettering.

according to width from 1 to 3 inches by ½ inch gradations. See Fig. 41.

c. Camel hair lacquering brushes are used by all
trades where lacquering is done. They come both

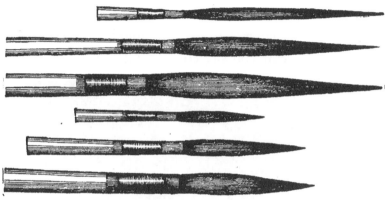

Fig. 37—Striping Pencils.

round and flat. Both are metal bound. The round are
sized from No. 1 to No. 6. The flat according to width
by ⅛ inch gradations up to 1 inch wide. See Fig. 42.

*d. The camel hair quill bound and ferruled letter-
ing*—the flat one stroke letterer and the striping brushes

Fig. 38—Round.

of that material, are excellent tools to work in the
lighter weight colors. See Figs. 35, 36, 37, 38 and 39
to illustrate the shape and sizes of the several brushes
mentioned.

e. The camel hair dagger striping brush is a shape

well liked by many stripers, as much longer lines can be carried through without filling than with other shapes. See Fig. 43. They come numbered from No. 1 to No. 4.

QUESTIONS ON BRUSHES.

15. Generalities?
16. What material is used in making brushes?
17. What can you say concerning hog bristle?

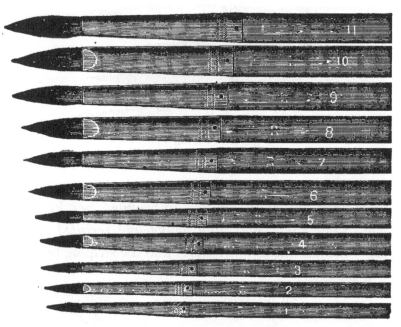

Fig. 39—Artists' Red Sable Brushes.

18. What can you say regarding Siberian ox hair?
19. What can you say regarding badger hair?
20. What are bear and fitch hair brushes mainly used for?
21. What kind of brushes are made from red and black sable?

22. What can you say regarding camel hair?

23. Is Tampico useful as brush making material?

24. *a.* What kind of brushes are made from bristles? *b, c, d, e, f, g, h, i, j, k, l, m, n, o, p, q, r,* and *s*?

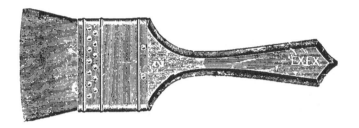

Fig. 40—Camel's Hair Mottler.

25. *a.* Describe the flowing varnish brushes.

    b. Describe the gold tip.

    c. Describe the knotted bonehead badger blender.

    d. Describe the rounded blenders.

Fig. 41.

26. *a.* Describe the Siberian ox hair flowing varnish brushes.

    b. Describe the ox hair flat sign lettering brushes.

    c. Describe the quilled and ferruled ox hair lettering brushes.

27. *a.* Describe black and red sable flowing varnish brushes.

  b. Describe the sable one stroke lettering
brush.

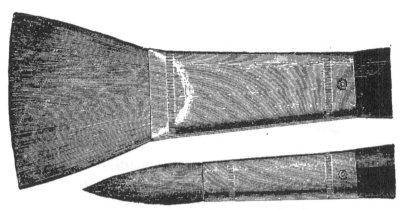

Fig. 42—Camel's-Hair Lacquering Brushes.

  c. Describe the quilled and ferruled sable letterers.

  d. Describe the striping sable pencils.

  e. Describe the sable artists' brushes.

Fig. 43—Champion Sword Stripers.

28. Describe the Fitch flowing varnish brush.

29. Describe bear's hair flowing varnish brushes.

30. *a.* Describe the camel hair flowing varnish
brush.

  b. Describe the camel hair mottler.

  c. Describe the camel hair lacquering brushes.

  d. Describe the camel hair lettering brushes.

e. Describe the camel hair striping brushes.

f. Describe the camel hair striping dagger.

CALCIMINING.

31. Under this appellation will be considered all plastered wall painting done in water colors and distemper, except the more artistic and difficult section better known under the name of fresco painting.

There are several ways of spelling the name used in describing the process such as: kalsomine, calsomine, distemper work and so forth, but all are one and the same thing. The root word calc—being taken from the Latin for *chalk,* which is the main material used in preparing it.

Calcimining in one form or another has been used from time immemorial, probably ever since walls have received coats of plastering to make them more level and pleasing to the eye than the naked rough stone finish did. As this of itself was already a step towards embellishment it is but fair to infer that the same desire for the beautiful must have prompted the uniform coloring of the plastering at nearly about the same time for the purpose of still further embellishing the interior of dwellings.

Walls covered with coatings of water colors and lime are and have been unearthed in Asia Minor and Egypt, which are nearly as old probably as the beginning of civilization in man. One must look for prehistoric remains where everything is blank for a time when painting in some form with water colors was unknown as remains of it are to be found with the oldest records existing of all the ancient civilizations. Nor is the old world the only place where such records exist for the Aztec civilization existing in America previous to its discovery by Columbus is particularly rich in fairly well designed and colored remains of its most ancient periods.

At the present time fully 98 per cent of all wall color ing and embellishments consist of water color painting or printing which are either used upon the walls direct or pasted upon them in the shape of wall paper, which after all, is but—watercolored paper.

Many persons become confused by the same thing being called by so many different names. The decorator hardly likes to have his work known under the name of calcimine (which is all it is in fact) as the name sounds too common, so he dubs it fresco, which it is not, or distemper or watercolor painting, which it is in common with plain everyday calcimining; but the other names sound more aristocratic and under those names he can command a very much larger price than he could under the other and he can hardly be blamed for it.

The name distemper is taken from the French "d'étrempe" or colors mixed with water (drenched). The name is certainly very appropriate for the French at least; but why should English speaking nations call it that when the words "water color" are well understood to mean the same thing and are never misunderstood by anyone.

It is hoped the above will remove any misapprehensions any one may have had as to these various names meaning different sorts of wall painting—they are all one and the same.

TOOLS NEEDED FOR CALCIMINING.

32. *a.* Galvanized pails holding about 12 qts. can be found at any hardware store. A strip of tin or wire should be soldered across the top about 2/3 of the distance of its diameter, this simple contrivance will be found very convenient for the purpose of removing any surplus color not wanted on the brush, it will also act as a support for the brush when not in use, keeping it flat and in good shape. However, it is only a convenience but not a necessity. Besides there are many specially contrived pails for sale at the supply stores which are tony looking affairs, but none will be found much superior to a good galvanized pail with a wire soldered across its face and these will cost much less.

b. An iron stand to rest the pail upon in order to raise it to a convenient height to dip the brush into when working on a scaffold is a necessity, and will quickly pay for itself in time saved bending down to the floor each time color is wanted and will save many a backache. A fair but a much more clumsy substitute can be made by using a wooden box of about the proper height.

c. The calcimine brush (see Fig. 1). Buy only the best—others are mere makeshifts. The first cost of a brush, well made and fitted to this work, will more than be repaid over the price of an inferior one in a single day's work by the increased amount of work that can be done with it—to say nothing of the ease of spreading the calcimine and the certainty of a good looking job when done and of the cleanliness made possible by their use. A good workman can take a high grade calcimine brush and work over carpets without dropping any color upon them—if careful. This, of course, is not advisable and carpets, furniture and everything that could possibly be injured should either be removed or at least covered over—but it is within the possible to not drop anything upon them.

d. A number of smaller flat and round brushes will be needed by the decorator in lining off his work and in hand work decorating also for reaching into coves and mouldings where his larger brush could not be made to reach. For shapes and sizes of these see Figs. 10, 16, 18, 19, 21, 22.

e. Step ladders (see Fig. 78).

f. Tressles and planks (see Fig. 79).

g. Chalk line and plumb bob to lay out work with.

h. A small portable stove to warm or boil water upon to melt glue with. In fact all paint shops need one as there are many uses to which they can be put. A small gasoline stove is probably as convenient and as cheap as any thing that could be got.

Plate I.

i. A glue pot to melt glue in although it is not a necessity especially if the glue has been soaked up in cold water some time before, as when it is swelled up warm water will quickly dissolve it without bringing it to a boil.

j. A T-square, some lining straightedges, a 2-foot rule and an awl to hold the chalk line are needed wher ever any attempts are made at decorations.

The above comprises about all the most essential tools needed in applying calcimine. A number of others will be needed by the decorator in water colors, and will be treated more fully under several headings where water colors are employed in the more artistic branches of distemper work.

33. *a.* The material required for calcimining is fully described under the heading of colors (see paragraphs 61 to 84) it will only be necessary to state that whiting is the mostly used base upon which are added the coloring pigments necessary to produce the tints required. Under heading of color mixing (see paragraphs 61 to 84) full directions are given for making them. It will be useless even to name over the colors which are used in water color painting as nearly every pigment known can be mixed for use in water color painting. The base is the most important of all. The whiting should be of good quality, well washed of sediments and the colors of pure tone, so as to produce clean looking tints. Some prefer to mix their tints on a zinc white base, claiming that the tints so mixed are

clearer toned and cover better in one coat. It increases the cost somewhat, but that will not count on first class work.

b. Glue is used more extensively than any other substance to bind the colors with, for it is both cheap and convenient to handle. Some of the decorators use gum arabic to mix the higher priced colors used on the finest work. There are also a number of patented sizes on the market for which superlative excellence is claimed, which probably will be found convenient but none so far have been able to supplant good glues for general use.

THE WALLS.

34. Calcimining or water color painting is chiefly done on plastered walls. To a great extent it depends upon their being in a proper condition as to whether the work shall look good or bad when completed.

An ideal wall to work upon is one that will be sufficiently hard to have but little suction, nearly but not quite non-absorbent. The patent plastered walls left either in a stipled rough state or covered over with a skim coat of plaster paris make an excellent surface to calcimine upon.

But—alas! all walls are not in such a condition. With all the cheap John sort of plastering that is being done by contractors at a price which would mean a sure loss to them if they used good material, but which must be done so as to make a profit anyhow, many of the surfaces the calciminer has to deal with will be found very porous and absorbing, having a great deal of suction; in many instances so much so that the calcimine will be absorbed from the brush as soon as it is laid upon the wall so that it will not be possible to spread it any distance from where the brush first touched it. Such walls are called in the vernacular, *"hot walls"* They constitute the most troublesome and disagreeable feature of any of the ills belonging to the calcimining trade.

35. The only sure way to enable one to do good work upon such walls is to stop this suction. There are several methods employed to do this. The old timers used to do this by using sizing, double sizing, etc., but it never was an entire success in that glue absorbs and gives out moisture with the result that decay of the glue soon commences and cracking of the glue underneath the calcimine which is soon followed up by the scaling of the whole thing in flakes like bark coming off a sycamore tree. This will not always follow sizing, but the chances are that it may, so that today there is but little sizing of walls being done with glue.

The better way is to give the walls a coat of what is known to the trade as a *surfacer*.

36. A surfacer in reality is a varnish specially prepared with a view of filling and stopping suction. It enters the porous plaster, forming an impervious coating upon them over which one good coat of calcimine usually makes a good looking even finish.

Many surfacers are placed upon the market with

astounding claims and loaded down with superlatives and adjectives sufficient to cause an ordinary circus poster to blush; nevertheless they usually do the work of stopping the suction and that is the main thing required.

Any quick, hard drying varnish will do the same thing and it is even intimated by some that gloss oil will do so. While this may be true in some instances, no one should be advised to put their trust in it and at best it should not be used if anything better can be had. Furniture, No. 1 coach and the cheaper so called "hard oil" varnishes will be found much safer than gloss oil.

37. The surfacing coat being thoroughly dry, which requires from 10 to 24 hours according to the composition of the surfacer, the walls are ready for the calcimine. (For its preparation see paragraph 96.)

If the rooms or halls are large and high ceiled, it will be much better to have tressles of the proper height with a flooring of 2-inch walking boards across them, sufficiently close together that the workmen will not have to waste any of his precious time shifting the boards about while he should be at his work busy on fresh edges upon which he can join before they have set, thus preventing an ugly lap line, showing at the end of every stretch. It should be remembered that the quicker the work can be done and finished from the time it has commenced to completion the better the job will look and the less likelihood of the surface showing brush marks and laps.

Plate II.

The calcimine need not be rubbed out and laid off like oil paint. It will be sufficient that the color be laid on so as to cover every portion of the work without skinning it or leaving any holidays upon it (holidays in painters' parlance means a spot left untouched by paint). To insure having gone all over the surface of the wall, the better way is to first lay the color all over cross ways of the stretch then to brush it the long way of it. In this manner should there be any pin holes or places left untouched by the first cross brushing, the second will be almost sure to catch it unless the work is done in some very dark place where it is impossible to see what is being done.

If the suction has been properly stopped and the calcimine properly mixed the job will present an even and perfectly covered appearance of a beautiful flat finish entirely free of brush marks and laps; but it sometimes happens that the suction has not been perfectly stopped or that the calcimine has been imperfectly mixed. In that case it will be necessary to give the job another coat. To give this second coat one should proceed in exactly the same manner as has been described for the putting on of the first coat.

Where there has been no stoppage of the suction of the plastered walls and they are "hot" or in an absorbing condition, it is possible to go over them in a "way" which reduces the suction trouble to a minimum. It is this: to calcimine mixed in the ordinary way add about 4 ounces of glycerine to the gallon pail. One ounce of powdered alum previously dissolved in warm water with just enough of that to dissolve it added for each gallon of calcimine, will also help. Some add a ½ pint of molasses to the gallon. The idea in all these additions is to retard the drying in of the water paint on the plaster long enough that the next brushfull applied will still find the spot covered by the previous one wet enough to blend in with it without rubbing up. Glycerine has a great affinity for moisture and will retain it, so has molasses to some extent, but in a much lessened degree. A little soft soap is also of good benefit in retarding the drying in, beside giving to the calcimine much easier spreading properties.

38. It is usual to count all ornamental work even that done in stencils over distemper painting as "fresco painting," but it is hardly proper to call by that name a paneled ceiling or walls stenciled with some simple designs or even with a stenciled center piece, corners and brakes. While properly speaking there is no fresco painting done in the United States, the name stands for a higher and more artistic class of work than that spoken of above. Every calciminer should be able to do this simple ornamentation without trouble.

To lay out a ceiling with a center panel with stiles surrounding it in different color requires but little skill. A chalk line should be used to mark out the outlines accurately and the various colors carefully cut in up to the line. When dry it is ready to be lined up with such line work as is necessary and stenciled in appropriate colors.

Under the heading of stencils a full description is given of the "how to make them" beside the proper way of using and taking care of them. (See paragraphs 290 to 302.)

QUESTIONS ON CALCIMINING.

31. What is calcimine and calcimining?
32. *a.* What kind of pails are necessary?
    b. What support is required for them?
    c. What is the main brush used in laying it on walls?
    d. What other brushes are necessary?
    e. How is the work reached?
    f. What other means?
    g. How is work laid out?
    h. What are the best means of heating water
    i. What is required to melt glue in?
    j. What other tools are useful?
33. What material is employed in mixing calcimine?
34. What has been said regarding walls?
35. How can suction be stopped in hot walls?
36. What is a surfacer?
37. How is calcimine applied?
38. How are walls and ceilings laid out into panels, stiles, etc.?

CARRIAGE PAINTING, CAR AND COACH PAINTING.

For all practical purposes, all the above stand upon one and the same footing. The underlying principles and the reasons why of everything connected with them all being the same and having the same foundation.

Why is it that carriages, cars, coaches, and all vehicles, delivery wagons, automobiles, in fact all vehicles making any attempt at brilliancy by a polished varnish surface and which are used out of doors for a great part of the time, subject to all the vicissitudes and hardships, great changes of temperature resulting from the inclemencies of the weather, why is it that such vehicles are painted in an entirely different manner than that used for the painting of buildings which have to be out in the weather all the time, summer and winter when the heat will almost boil water or get down below the o mark until mercury will freeze solid?

At first sight one would think that what was good enough for the painting of buildings which have to stand so much more hardships from the weather than vehicles usually do, that the same treatment applied to vehicles would be just the right thing for them.

All are well aware that house painting is chiefly done by using linseed oil as a binder and vehicle of the pigments used in doing the work and really it is bv this use only that a lasting job of painting can be done at all upon these while in the painting of carriages and other vehicles linseed oil is dispensed with in all but the first priming or foundation coats. Even if that first priming coat could be put on with any other liquid vehicle that would do the same good that is expected of it—it is more than likely that there would be none used at all.

Plate III.

This seeming inconsistency and variance is due to the fact that a perfectly level surface has to be made up for a carriage before it is colored and varnished, which is non-elastic or very slightly so or at least no greater than that of the varnishes themselves is. It is necessary that all coatings going onto the vehicle conform themselves to this end: the making of all the coats as near as possible, of each being as near like the others in contraction and expansion. Now if after the priming, linseed oil was used instead of japan and varnish as binder and vehicles, the varnish, which is composed mainly of hard gums would be unable to follow the greater expansion and contraction of the under-coats where the linseed oil was used with the consequence that it would have to give or crack, which means the same thing, to accommodate itself to its more pliable neighbor and the job would soon be an eyesore—besides oil coats have usually the very bad habit of sweating through the varnish coats and stickiness would ensue, which would catch all the dust and dirt it could carry and hold it there. So that what was once a thing of beauty would soon become an eyesore to look upon.

It can thus readily be seen why it is not emploved in carriage painting.

THE TOOLS REQUIRED.

40. *a.* Round or oval bristle brushes to do the priming with. It does not matter so much about size or shape. It should possess sufficient elasticity and firmness that the oil can be well rubbed in with it.

b. A fair sized flat wall brush rather stiff but elas tic, to put on rough stuff with, with some smaller ones to use in places where the larger ones would not readily reach.

c. Some good heavy camel hair mottlers to lay color coats with somewhat identical in shape to Figs. 31 or 41. Also some oval bristle chiseled edge varnish brushes which are used for the same purpose. (See Fig. 15.)

d. Some badger, fitch and camel hair brushes to use in flowing, rubbing and varnishing running gear parts. (See Figs. 31, 40, 41.)

e. Coach dusters, preferably made of white bristles fine and soft, to clean all dirt and dust with, (See Fig. 6.)

f. Spoke brushes, which are long and slender, to reach down to the hub of wheels. (See Fig. 10.)

g. A number of various sized kinds of lettering, striping and artists' brushes for ornamenting, in both camel hair and sable. (See Figs. 36, 37, 39.)

EQUIPMENT USED IN CARRIAGE SHOPS.

41. *a.* Every shop aims to adapt its contrivances to do work with in accord with its own particular needs and requirements. The ones described below need not be after any set pattern. Almost anything which will answer the purpose intended for will do from the crudest to the very costliest, if they permit the painter to get at his work and do it without loss of time and convenience.

b. The most important are good tressles of proper height or adjustable, to lay bodies upon during the painting and drying operation and some others for carriage parts.

c. Varnishing stands made to tilt are the most convenient and require special mention. They need not be very expensive either, 3 legs and a tilting top 12 inches square is all that is needed. This arrangement permits the workman getting all the way around the job without any hindrance from the tressle legs.

d. Wheel jacks, which may be simply a post with a projecting peg to hang the wheel upon and turn it gradually while it is being painted or varnished.

e. Frames for bodies, gears and seats, each specially designed for the particular parts they are wanted for. .

f. Some good brush keepers—some for color brushes, others for the different brushes used in varnishing, preferably one for each brush to hang in its own kind of varnish. There are a number of very good ones on the market that are patented and in which brushes can be suspended without touching the bottom and with covered tops to prevent dirt or dust entering the keeper. One can make a very good individual brush keeper by going to the refuse heap, picking up some of the smaller sizes of tins wherein fruits and vegetables had been previously packed. Melt the top off, have a wire soldered on long enough to bend it so one end will act as a peg to fit a hole bored in the brush handle so the brush will hang free of the bottom of the can, then put the can into a large glass jar, some of the fruit packing jars will answer, and after the top has been screwed on one has an air tight and convenient brush keeper at small cost. The wire projecting above the tin itself will be found very convenient to lift it by, serving as a handle when it is desired to take it out of the can.

· *g.* Putty knives in various shapes and widths, stiff and flexible square pointed and triangular. Spatulas for triturating and lifting paints and putties; some good paint strainers for straining not only paint but var nishes, compose the most necessary small and large tools of the hardware variety

THE MATERIAL USED.

42. Nearly all the pigments used in painting are available for coloring carriages and wagons, etc., as colors or pigments are fully described in following pages under the heading "Colors," it will be unnecessary here to repeat the same and the reader is referred to paragraphs 61 to 84 for full particulars concerning these.

White lead either ground in oil, japan varnish or dry is probably the most important on the list, ochre and filling material next in preparatory work and blacks by long odds the most important in coloring coats, with a variety covering the whole chromatic scale in wagon and car painting.

Plate IV.

THE WORK PROPER—THE PRIMING.

43. This is the foundation upon which the whole superstructure will either make good or fail, therefore one should well understand its principles and take the utmost care in its performance in a good workmanlike manner.

It has already been mentioned that the priming or foundation coat is the only one in which linseed oil should be used and the reasons therefore given. Under the name of priming, however, it is not meant the first coat (which is merely an oiling) but all coatings of the foundation for rough stuffing must be understood as forming a part of the priming.

The first operation for the priming is the mixing of the color. This should consist of white lead colored to a deep gray with lampblack or white lead and ochre in various proportions also tinted with lampblack, which should be greatly thinned with raw linseed oil to which has been added a little dryer. The pigments themselves are understood as having been finely ground in oil and to have been so thinned, that the application of the priming may be said to be the giving the job a coat of colored oil. While the coating is thin the going over the parts painted must be plainly seen to have been colored by it. The work of its application with the brush must be thorough and put on with plenty of elbow grease, well brushed in—not simply gone over.

The primed parts should be laid aside where they will have a chance to dry well and ample time should be given it for the same. The priming and for that matter all painting done with linseed oil may feel dry and seemingly hard under the touch of the finger, this is not an indication, however, that it is through drying. It is not one day nor two days that it will take for the oil to be dry, but—certainly no less than a week should be allowed and two weeks would be better.

Under the high pressure system in vogue, this is now seldom done, but when it is a well known fact that linseed oil keeps absorbing oxygen from the atmosphere for about 10 days and that during that period it is undergoing changes of both form and bulk—it increases about 10% and it is not to be considered as dry until this change shall have taken place. It must readily be understood that another application of paint over the priming before the changes due to drying are completed that it will be imperfect and incomplete and greatly hindered by the application of another coat from access to air from which it draws oxygen which becomes combined with it and forms a gum resin during the process of drying.

44. *a.* This coat being dry should be followed up by applications which are best known as the lead coats.

THE LEAD COATS.

44. *b.* This is composed of white lead which has been colored with lamp black to a light slate or dark gray. The lead is what in carriage painting is known as keg lead or white lead ground in linseed oil, and

hereafter when that term is used, it means white lead in oil only. This should be thinned with about ¼ linseed oil and ¾ turpentine to a proper consistency for applying with a bristle brush, in a smooth even manner.

Some painters prefer a flat lead coat or one which contains just enough linseed oil to bind it on, the thinner consisting chiefly of turpentine.

THE RUB LEAD.

45.. This is without doubt the better way of preparing the job for further operations. It consists in mixing dry white lead to which a little lamp black has been mixed in about ¾ parts of raw linseed oil to which ¼ part of japan has been added, to a stiff paste and the same ground up in a shop paint mill and afterward thinned in the same proportion of linseed oil and japan. It should be applied as stiff as it can be worked, with a half worn out stiff bristle brush. After it has been spread let it stand a few minutes, just enough to let it take on a *tact,* when the lead rub coat should be rubbed over with the palm of the hand. It is needless to say that this rub lead coat should not be applied over the lead coats mentioned in paragraph 44, but instead it takes their place and should be applied directly over the linseed oil priming first described. This requires some little time to harden sufficiently for further operations, and for that reason is considered too slow in many shops, although it is undoubtedly the "very best way" to proceed in surfacing the priming.

KNIFING IN LEAD.

46. Knifing in lead is a quicker way of surfacing the priming coat. The lead used for this purpose is specially ground in japan for that purpose, but many prefer to mix it themselves from dry white lead mixed in various proportions of rubbing varnish, japan and turpentine. As the name indicates, it is spread with a knife. It requires careful manipulations so as to level up everything perfectly and it should be well pressed into any cavity or depressions. As work which has been "knifed" is seldom rough stuffed afterward it should be done so well that it will in a manner take the place of that operation. In fairly good work it is never used on bodies or wagon beds, but for the cheaper and medium grades even the bodies are "knifed in."

PUTTY AND PUTTYING.

47. The next operation in order after the rub lead has become hardened sufficiently is to putty up the job previous to rough stuffing. It is made by triturating together dry white lead, rubbing varnish and japan in about equal quantities. The consistency is somewhat variable for the different purposes that it may be wanted for, but for general purposes it should be sufficiently thin that it can be made to enter readily into any opening about to be filled, but also thick enough that the putty knife will made a clean level cut over it, as otherwise such parts will be eyesores, especially if the job is not to receive any rough stuffing.

Plate V.

48. After the puttying has dried and hardened sufficiently, the job is ready for the sand papering. This should be very carefully done with fine sand paper to level up any of the putty which rises over the parts surrounding it. Great care should be taken that in using the paper too energetically, the lead coats may not be cut through, therefore it should be confined to the parts where it is needed and the rest very lightly gone over, merely to assure one's self that no roughness has been overlooked.

THE ROUGH STUFF.

49. *a.* It would be impossible to produce that piano-like smoothness of finish which constitutes the chief beauty of a carriage body, without rough stuffing it. Therefore the operation of rough stuffing consists in the perfect leveling of the surface over which it is applied. It fills up whatever inequalities may be upon it, small pores, etc., until it is as level as a slab of polished marble.

b. The material used consists mainly of coarse mineral paints which all the supply stores sell under the name of fillers, and these are combined with white lead. They are mixed in the proportion of 3 parts of the filler to 1 of keg lead, by weight, into a stiff paste in a thinner composed of equal parts of quick rubbing varnish and japan, thinned to the proper working consistency with turpentine. There are a number of other methods of mixing rough stuff, but the one given is that which is chiefly in use and will be found satisfactory.

c. It should be put on carefully and leveled up with as much attention as in any of the other applications, but somewhat thicker than is required for color coats. While rough stuff should be thicker than those, yet it should be thinned sufficiently so as to allow of the proper brushing it out without dragging, and a good chiseled edge bristle varnish brush should be used which has been broken in but not much worn. (See Fig. 15.)

It is a much better policy to give the job 3, 4 or even 5 coats of rather thin coats than to try to accomplish the came object with two coats which are too heavy.

The mixing formula given requires 24 hours drying before a next coat be applied.

d. When giving the job the last coat of rough stuff, the latter should have a little Venetian red mixed up with it and should be thinned more liberally with turpentine than was used in the preceding coats.

RUBBING THE ROUGH STUFF.

50° *a.* If the rough stuff coats have been carefully put on, the work will now be in proper shape for "rubbing down."

There is nothing better for the purpose than the rubbing brick which may be found in all the supply stores in the United States, ready prepared. The fine Italian natural blocks of pumice stone, well leveled, is still used where an extra fine job is desired.

b. While the rubbing is being done the surface should be kept well wetted with clean water and often sponged off to keep it from gumming.

c. And here is where the last guide coat prepared with Venetian red puts in its good end. If the work of rubbing the rough stuff has been carefully and systematically done by rubbing the surface with strokes leading in one direction back and forth, without wiggling or going over the surface in a haphazard way, when the guide coat has been cut through the surface will be level. Yet the cutting through of the guide coat is not always an indication that the work has been properly done or leveled. The skilled workman however can readily ascertain this by passing the palm of his hand over it, and his fine sense of touch will readily give him notice of any imperfectly leveled parts. Time and experience alone will enable one to become a good judge as to whether the work has been well done or not.

THE COLORING AND GLAZING COATS.

51. *a.* Generally speaking concerning the application of the color coats, it must here be stated that it requires a good degree of workmanship to do it well.

b. As to the tools used, nothing but a camel hair mottler or color brush should be used, (see Fig. 41) as the color should be laid very evenly and without brush marks. One thing the novice should learn to guard against is the brushing his work crossways at the ends. This should be avoided and it should be done by working the brush back and forth in one direction only and with an easy and even motion.

b. Each color requires a somewhat different manner of handling, but on the whole this much can be said: never to put them on too thickly, and if the color is very transparent it is better to give the job more coats than to risk spoiling the smoothness of the surface of the job produced upon it by the rough stuffing process.

c. It goes without the saying it again that no linseed oil is permissible in the application of color coats and that the thinner used for binding them should be varnish thinned with turpentine.

d. While jobs require special treatment of their own from the ground up, they should first be cleaned of all dirty marks on the bare wood, then carefully oiled over with clear linseed oil, sand papered and painted over with a keg lead coat, thinned with 1 part of raw linseed oil with 3 parts turpentine. The puttying should be done on this coat, then it should be followed up with another thinned with only half as much raw linseed oil as the first had, with a corresponding increase of turpentine; then after lightly sand papering it, apply a coat of flake white thinned sufficiently to work freely under the brush. This flake white coat should be thinned with hard drying finishing varnish. These coats should be very smoothly and evenly put on and should be followed up with hard drying finishing varnish in which a little of the flake white has been added to hide the yellow tinge of the varnish. When dry rub with

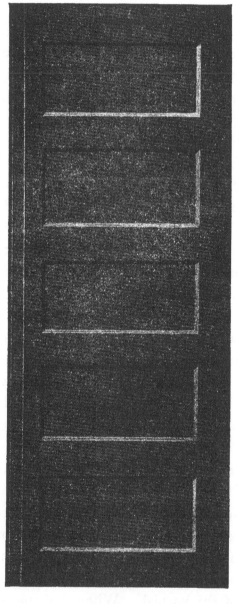

Plate VI.

pumice stone and apply another coat of the same varnish, which should be treated as before.

THE ORNAMENTATION.

52. *a.* Some coach painters do the ornamentation and striping upon the last coat of color, but it is much better and safer to first give the job a coat of quick drying rubbing varnish and to lightly rub it down with pumice stone, being careful not to cut it through into the color. This will act as a protection and prevent fatal results upon the surface as mistakes can be cleaned off the varnish coating which it would be impossible to do over the color coat itself.

The ornamentation consists in fine, medium and broad lines or striping, scroll work, coat of arms and other ornaments, lettering, etc., etc., according as to what the job is; each having its own fashions as to the decoration, be it a coach, carriage. car, business wagon or whatever other name and kind the vehicle may be.

b. The striping requires skill, so a novice will do well to acquire considerable of that before he undertakes the striping upon a good job, for he must have that and a good amount of confidence in himself to make a success of it. For the tools needed to do the work with the reader is referred to Fig. 37 for the shape of quill bound striping brush and to Fig. 43 for the sword striper, which is used in making fine lines.

Colors for striping should be mixed with varnish, japan and turpentine, tempering these to suit the job and color used upon it, some colors requiring a little more of one and less of another than some others would.

 c. A great deal of the ornamentation done upon vehicles is by means of *transfers*. These transfers are printed in colors upon a specially prepared paper which is applied face downward upon tacky varnish on the job, or sometimes the varnish is applied to the ornament itself and then applied to the place wanted. After smoothing over the transfer, the paper is sponged on the back with clean water which it will absorb and swell, when it can be slipped about and off the job, leaving the ornament upon it held tightly by the varnish under it.

 d. Hand ornamentation requires both skill and time. Only such as possess the first should undertake it, as an eyesore and loss of reputation would surely result from a botched job. All colors used in ornamentation require the same thinning and treatment as was described in Sec. B of this paragraph.

Sign writing upon vehicles, aside from the fact that it is done in coach colors thinned in the same manner as stated in section *b* of this paragraph is done in very much the same manner as is fully described under the heading of Sign Painting, so the reader is referred to paragraphs 260 to 277 for fuller information.

THE VARNISHING.

 53. *a.* The varnishing of vehicles is a very particular branch of the coach painter's trade. It is almost

needless to have to warn against varnishing a job where it will be subjected to dust, changes of temperature and the thousand and one other causes which will make varnish go wrong. Only those who are familiar with the host of "make-varnish-go-wrong-agencies" have any idea of their multitude and extent. It also seems as needless to say that it requires skill and experience. Under the heading of varnishing, fuller directions are given as to the "how to do the work" and the reader is referred to.paragraphs 312 to 317 for fuller information, but there are some peculiarities about the varnishing of vehicles which are their own and which are noted below

The skimpy, skinny manner of putting on varnish some workmen have who are always afraid of putting on too much and who brush out the little they put on to the last limit, will never make good carriage varnishers. Even the rubbing coats are the better for hav ing been flowed on, and they should be so put on especially in shops where jobs can be tipted.

It is necessary to caution especially against doing the varnishing in any place where dust cannot be kept out and where the temperature be regulated with uniformity in cold weather.

THE RUBBING COATS.

54. *a.* The job should receive two heavy coats of rubbing varnish which is much better than double that number of coats put on thinly. As soon as dry, which will require two days, the rubbing may be done.

b. The needed material consists in a rubbing pad of felt which can be bought ready made at supply stores. These pads are prepared specially for all sorts of purposes in varnish rubbing. It is made of felt of different degrees of hardness and texture and varies in thickness from ¼ to 2 inches. Chamois skins, sponges, pails for water and o or oo pumice stone. The Italian kind is much the best, running even and free of grit. Some of the American is very poor and especially gritty, for that reason it should not be employed in carriage rubbing as it would scratch the life out of a job.

c. The job should be washed perfectly clean and dried by rubbing it over with a chamois skin, then it is ready to be rubbed. This operation is done by first dipping the pad into clean water then into the box holding the pulverized pumice stone; then proceeding to rub the mouldings and outside edges of panels, then proceeding towards the center where the rubbing should end. The rubbing should all be done in one direction, or as much as possible at least, and should be very carefully made. After the operation has been completed the job should be well washed and cleaned of the pumice stone and again dried with chamois skin. When all moisture has been completely dried it is then ready for the flowing finishing coats.

THE FLOWING FINISHING COATS.

55. As the name indicates these coats should be *"flowed"* on for good results, or the mirror like surface which all the previous operations have led to step by

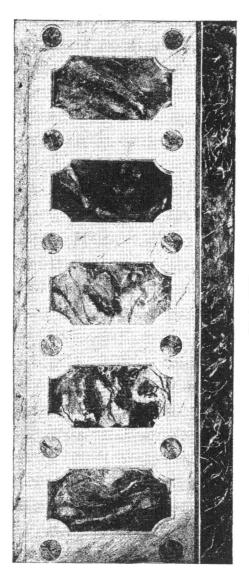

Plate VII.

step, will have been done to no avail. In putting on the flowing coats do all the parts adjacent to the panels first, finishing the wide panels last. The brush should always be loaded full of varnish for in that condition the job can be gone over more quickly and easily. It should be cross brushed lightly before finally laying it off. See paragraph 312 to 317, under the heading "Varnishing," for fuller information.

56. The varnishing of running gears is somewhat easier to do properly than that of bodies, but requires skill too. Only a small surface should be gone over at a time before laying off and it takes a watchful workman to put it on. Much care should be taken to prevent dust and good cleaning done before and after each operation. In putting on rubbing varnish on the wheels always lay it off after having gone over half a dozen spokes or so.

QUESTIONS ON CARRIAGE, CAR OR COACH PAINTING.

39. Give a synopsis of the difference between carriage painting and ordinary out door oil painting.

40.   *a.*   What kind of brush is used in priming?

    b.   What kinds of brushes are used in rough stuffing?

    c.   What kinds of brushes are needed for color laying?

    d.   What kinds of brushes are used for varnishing?

    e.   What kind of brush is used for cleaning?

f. What tool is used in painting spokes?

g. What brushes are needed in striping and ornamenting?

42. What is said regarding the material used?

43. What is priming?

44. *a.* What are the lead coats? *b.* What is a flat lead coat?

45. What is a rub lead coat?

46. What is knifing in lead?

47. How is carriage putty made and applied?

48. How is the sandpapering done?

49. *a.* What is rough stuff?

    b. What material is chiefly used in mixing rough stuff?

    c. How should it be put on?

    d. What is a guide coat?

50. *a.* How is rough stuff rubbed?

    b. How is rough stuff made?

    c. How is it performed?

51. *a.* What is said in a general way concerning the color coats?

    b. Are all colors used in color coats to be used in the same manner?

    c. Should linseed oil be used in the painting of color coats?

    d. How would you proceed to paint a white job?

52. *a.* What is said regarding ornamentation?

    b. How is striping done?

  c.   What are transfers?

  d.   What is said of hand decoration?

  e.   What is said of sign work on vehicles?

53.   What is said generally of varnishing?

54.   How is rubbing done?

55.   How is flowing varnish put on?

56.   How are running gears varnished?

CHINA PAINTING.

57.   China painting differs radically from any othei sort in a number of ways.

It is of course out of the question to think of using linseed oil and ordinary artists' colors mixed with it, as then the painting would be subject to many vicissitudes, it would be easily scratched, marred and even rubbed off, besides it would be impossible to use them upon the table as food carriers or holders, for many of the colors are poisonous and none of them very appetizing, and most persons would as soon have them remain upon the platters or plates, much rather than having them mixed up with their food. At best such painting would render the article so painted good for show only, but unfitted for use; to be hung upon the wall or placed on a shelf to look at, the same as any other oil painting done on canvas.

The requirements of china painting are that both the colors and the medium used in their application shall be *vitrifiable* and assimilate or be capable of being incorporated with the blank china upon which the painting is done that the two shall form but one inseparable whole and become one integral part of it.

Therefore to accomplish this the colors must be either vitrifiable of themselves or be made so by a flux mixed with them that will attach them with an artificial coating under the influence of a high degree of heat which melts it.

As the coloring matter of many of the colors used in china painting are not developed until the china has been fired (put into a kiln and burned) it can easily be understood that in that alone it would differ from any other painting and must cause a novice some anxiety at first as to just what will be the results of his labor, as he cannot always perceive what progress has been made or whether the painting has been rightly or wrongly done. At best he is likely to spoil a few pieces in learning by experience just how to handle these changeable undeveloped colors. This is probably the most troublesome point of difference between china painting and any other.

MATERIAL REQUIRED.

58. There are to be found at the present time a great number of ready prepared colors with plates showing the exact coloring of each, just as they will appear after the firing. This simplifies the otherwise difficult task of knowing what color one must select for obtaining certain results. These ready prepared colors have the flux ready mixed with them or are in the shape of

Plate VIII.

powders to which the flux must be added. Upon the whole it will be best for novices, as well as others, to use moist vitrifiable colors in tubes. These are nearly all the go now among amateur and professional china painters. They save the tedious and annoying methods of goneby days when it was necessary to prepare the medium by the slow processes of evaporation of spirits of turpentine and of oil of tar to make the fat oils of each. Everything can be bought ready prepared and ready to use. It has rendered a great service to the many who have taken up the painting of china as a pastime and for the many who now find pleasure from this employment of their spare time who would have been deterred from the undertaking but for this saving of drudgery.

Small slabs with depressions upon them to lav colors upon and to hold fluxes, mediums, etc., should be procured. Gold, platinum, etc. Gold and other metals used in decorating china can also be bought ready for use in all the shades of the metal and the different alloys.

One should also be well supplied with many different sizes of camel's hair brushes to lay the colors with; a list of useful accessory tools and appliances would make up a fair sized pamphlet. As the description without the illustration of such by cuts would be more likely to be misunderstood than otherwise, the reader is advised to send to some of the art stores in our larger cities for an illustrated catalogue which will give him, for the asking, a very full understanding of all the tools, brushes and appliances needed in china painting, besides giving him the price at which each is sold.

THE PAINTING.

59. Either outline the design upon the china with a lithographic pencil or with black leads. Some use India ink in outlining as it burns out entirely during the firing process, leaving the design painted free of outline marks and for that reason it is preferred by many.

After the design has been laid out, proceed to paint it on by mixing the colors needed with the medium and applying them with a brush.

The powder colors should be laid on a slab and be worked into a stiff paste with the fat oil which is afterward reduced to the proper working consistency by thinning with spirits of turpentine.

Those in tubes should be thinned according to directions.

60. After the ware has been painted it is necessary that it should be fired in an oven to vitrify the colors and bind them to the china. These ovens are portable, many of them, and are made small enough to suit the requirements of those who do not paint china in a commercial way. Again as in all our larger cities persons are found who fire china for an amateur clientele, many of these prefer to patronize them to save the expense and trouble of owning a furnace.

QUESTIONS ON CHINA PAINTING.

57. What is said about china painting in general?
58. What material is required?
59. How is the painting done?
60. What must be done to vitrify the colors?

COLORS.

61. Colors or pigments are of the utmost importance to the paint trade and it should be a subject of great interest to every one who handles a brush. They should be well understood by men who make daily use of them, for without an intimate knowledge of their properties and peculiarities the painting done with them may or may not be all that it should be. Manv a good job well brushed on has gone wrong because of the ignorance of the painter who mixed the paint.

It will be impossible in a work of this size to devote as much space to the subject as it requires, but of all the most important at least, an explanation of their derivation, composition, manufacture and uses will be given. Their chief properties will be considered and warning given of their antipathies for other pigments.

For the purpose of examination the colors will be placed in groups—not because of nearness of relation to each other, nor of their chemical composition, because colors with but little difference in their chemistry may be of an entirely different color as the ferric oxide colors show—ochre being yellow, while the Venetian reds are red. So the colors will be grouped according to their coloring regardless of their composition.

62. Pigments are derived from each of the various kingdoms according as they are most important to the trade. First, those derived from the metals, as the leads, the ferric oxides, the zinc whites, those of copper origin, etc. Second, that numerous branch derived from the mineral kingdom, as the ochres, umbers, siennas, whiting, gypsum, etc.

Third, those derived from the vegetable kingdom, as most of the lakes.

Fourth, those of animal origin, as carmine, etc.

63. While pigments can thus be classed according to their origin, they must be reclassed again for the purpose of examination and grouped together not according to their formation but according to their color.

This will not only greatly facilitate the work but a comparison with others of the same color can be made more readily. Therefore they will be placed together into seven general groups. In each group the pigments which come nearest to its color will be classed. It is true that a few pigments will seem out of place as they border so near to another group that it is hard to tell which has the most claims for it, but only very few such cases will need bother one—the orange chrome yellows—some of the deeper one are really more red than yellow—and but for the fact that under the name of chrome yellow remarks are made which belong to the whole range of color of those yellows, no matter what their tone may be, they would have been included in the red—but for reasons stated they are best placed with the yellows. It saves useless repetition or the need of referring the reader to the proper paragraphs giving the explanations.

64. *a.* For convenience sake then, the various pigments of real value to the painter have been classed in the seven following groups:

1. The whites.
2. The reds.
3. The yellows.
4. The blues.
5. The greens.
6. The browns.
7. The blacks.

b. As each pigment varies in character from others and better adapted to some uses than to others—some being worthless in oil, while they may be invaluable as water colors and vice-versa, they must not be judged by their unfitness for work to which they are not adapted.

THE WHITES.

65. *a.* As the whites are by far the most important of all the pigments used in painting, it is fitting that they should be placed at the head of the list. This is due to them, not only because of their self color, in which they are used in enormous quantities, but also because they are the dominant pigment or base upon

which all light tints made by the addition of other coloring pigments are effected.

b. Whites are chiefly the products of the salts of the metal lead and that of zinc (its oxide and only white form). The rest of the whites being natural earths of various composition and extraction. In examining them the metallic whites being the ones mostly used will be placed at the head of the list.

THE METALLIC WHITES.

66. *a. White lead* heads the list by undisputed right, it being heads and shoulders ahead of any of the other whites, many times over more than all the others put together for out and indoor oil painting and well it deserves it. Its great covering power due to its opacity, (when the word covering is used in connection with a pigment it does not mean its spreading capacity so much as its opaqueness in hiding the coats of paint over which it is applied)

b. Its peculiarities are that it forms a linoleate lead soap with linseed oil which renders it smooth and easy of application. This saponification does not extend to all the oil necessary to its application and it is a pity that it does not, as when dry the lead soap thus formed is insoluble.

White lead should never be used where sulphurous fumes are generated, especially where sulphuretted hydrogen gas is developed, as it greedily assimilates it and is turned into a black sulphide of lead. This change will sometimes occur, over night. The atoms composing the lead seem to have no affinity for one another and·it is no doubt due to this reason that whenever the linseed oil commences to decay that having nothing to hold them on they dust or chalk off, as under the name this peculiarity is best known. It is true that white lead, even the best of it, chalks, but if the painting has been done with good linseed oil the chalking will not commence so soon, nor really is this peculiarity worth mentioning as a fault. A good coat of paint given soon after the lead is noticed to chalk will rebind on all these particles and the surface even when let go for sometime after that will always be in a good condition for repainting as white lead never scales off that has been applied with raw linseed oil.

c. The best qualities of the white lead of commerce known to the paint trade as "strictly pure" is that corroded by the "Dutch. Process." This means that dilute acetic acid, carbonic acid, oxygen and hydrogen are furnished to the lead in more or less ingenious ways and that those agents corrode and combine with the lead and that the product of the combination is what is known as white lead. White lead is a basic carbonate of lead, or to be more correct, an hydrate oxide carbonate of lead. The proportion may vary somewhat, but that agreed upon as being the best is about 1/3 hydroxide of lead and 2/3 carbonate of that metal—more of the hydrate means better opacity but more chalking propensity. More carbonate means less opacity but also less chalking.

d. There are two methods of corroding lead under the "Dutch Process" so called system, the *stack* and the *cylinder* methods.

The *stack* method consists in placing what are known as buckles (these are thin perforated discs of metallic lead) into porous earthenware pots of somewhat the same texture as flower pots. These have a space at the bottom to hold dilute acetic acid of the strength of ordinary vinegar and, along the sides are projections serving to keep the buckles apart. This and the perforations in the disc permits the acetic vapor and the carbonic acid gas to come into contact with the lead. First a floor of manure or tan bark or a combination of the two is laid down at the bottom of the stack, then a row of empty jars which are afterward filled with buckles to nearly the top, then dilute acetic acid is furnished to each jar through a hose with a nozzle. Then the tier is covered over with boards which again are covered with manure or tan bark and the same operations are repeated until the stack is completed to the top. The stack starts from the ground upward to what might be called the second story, but which in corroding houses is known as the working alley, as all the material is first received there to be placed in the stacks, a row of these extending on both sides of it to any length desired. The compartments called stacks being about 8 or 10 feet wide by about 12 to 16 feet long. There are stacks in the corroding houses in all stages of completion. Some finished and the jars containing corroded lead being taken out, others being filled, and so on. It requires about three months to complete the corrosion, which goes on as long as any acetic acid remains and enough heat in generated by the manure to evaporate it and furnish carbonic acid, the main element absorbed by the lead to make itself what it is—a basic carbonate of lead. Were it not for carbonic acid being present and the lead having more affinity for it than for the acetic, then it would simply become an acetate of that metal—of no value whatever as a pigment.

c. The *cylinder* method is an entirely different system of applying the same elements entering into the lead corrosion, i. e., acetic acid, carbonic acid, oxygen and hydrogen, than that of the stack system, and produces a lead of the same chemical composition.

The lead in place of being cast into buckles is melted and while it is being poured out, a jet of live steam is played against it, reducing it to very small globules of about the fineness of ordinary sand. This sand is placed in revolving cylinders (hence the name of the system) which are connected with generators which furnish it with acetic acid vapors, carbonic acid gas, oxygen and the proper moisture for hydrogen. These cylinders revolve slowly all the time and the particles of lead being very fine are soon acted upon and the whole mass becomes pretty thoroughly corroded inside of three to six days. Besides the corrosion is nearly complete, there being very little if any uncorroded blue or metallic lead remaining after the operation is over— which cannot be said of the stack process.

f. Space forbids giving an extended description of the various handlings of the lead after it is corroded, before it is finally ground and packed ready for consumption in the way the painter is accustomed to buy it. There is no material difference between the two leads produced by either system. The difference is in the application of the corroding agents and time required with which operations the manufacturer is more concerned than the painter. The cylinder system does away with the application of manure, heat and carbonic acid being furnished from other sources. This manure, or rather fine particles of it, are very hard to keep out entirely in the *stack* system of corrosion. It is true that infinite pains are taken by conscientious manufacturers by repeated washings in water and fine silk gauze straining to get all such out, but even with such precautions, either through neglect or the human depravity of some of the workmen, it is not unusual to find little specks of it occasionally in some of the lead corroded bv that system of which the cylinder lead is entirely free.

No one should be deterred from using either as the difference is immaterial; it is of course possible to make very poor pure lead by both systems and to have it off color and badly ground or packaged, but of that neither methods are responsible for.

SUBLIMED LEAD.

67. *Sublimed lead* is white and but that it would create confusion in calling it "white lead" because it would then be confounded with what has become a well known article, which, when it has been labeled "strictly pure" is supposed to mean, "hyd-carb. of lead" and nothing else, but for confusing the two it would be entitled to the name. But it would be unwise to open up a door which would break up the distinction between the two and to return to that state of uncertainty which in the past was so annoying and which it took so much fighting for, to establish upon the firm foundation it stands upon today.

Sublimed lead is a basic sulphate of lead containing in its composition some lead oxide with a small percentage of zinc oxide. It has much to recommend it for many purposes to which it is well adapted. It is extremely fine, so much so, that its particles float in oil without readily settling, making it an ideal dipping white paint. It is not affected by sulphureted hydrogen gas, fatal to most all other salts of lead. It is somewhat less opaque than Dutch process white lead, therefore does not cover quite so well. It is produced by the vaporisation of lead ore. These vapors are conducted to chambers above where they come in contact with oxygen contained in atmospheric air, combining with it, form the oxy-sulphate of lead. This transformation takes place in a somewhat similar manner as that which is described for the manufacture of zinc white (see paragraph 69). At the present time it is being used in large quantities by manufacturers of ready mixed paints and color grinders, but so far it has not appeared under its own name in its white state, but is found in many of the compound whites manufactured by color grinders.

68. There are several other salts of lead that are white, such as the white oxide of lead and some other compound salts of that metal, none of which, however, have proven themselves formidable rivals of "white lead" all having so many faults that the ones related as appertaining to Dutch process white lead seem "venial" when compared to theirs.

ZINC WHITE.

69. *a.* Is the white and only oxide of that metal. For painting material it is a very valuable pigment and after "white lead" is next to that, the most extensively used of all the white pigments by all classes of painters with the exception of the carriage trade.

Its peculiarities are all its own and differ widely from those of white lead. It has more spreading power and absorbs more oil. It is not so opaque and in consequence does not cover so well as that pigment, but if its spreading power be taken into consideration, a given weight of it would probably cover over as much and as well as the same quantity of white lead would if thinned out sufficiently to cover as many square feet of surface as the zinc did. Zinc white cannot be applied with the same amount of linseed oil as would suffice to render the white lead thin enough to wcrk well with the brush, as it is much lighter in weight.

One of its peculiarities, is the great affinity. existing between its atoms for each other, it is so great that after the oil has decayed they will hang together into a scale but never chalk off. In this respect it is the very opposite of white lead whose atoms we have seen have no affinity and which fall singly in what is known as chalking when the oil holding them together has de cayed. But while this great adherence of its particles is good in some ways it has its faults too, in that when the oil has decayed instead of falling off single or chalking they hold together until they fall off as scales.

Zinc white therefore is a good corrective to combine with white lead for outside painting while the lead itself is a good corrective for the too great affinity of its own particles. The zinc preventing the chalking off of the lead and the lead its scaling propensities.

b. Zinc white is a very fine pigment to use in distemper, covering well and the tints made with it when used as a base are invariably cleaner and purer toned than those made with any other white as a base. The above also holds true for any tint made from it as a base with colors in oil.

It is invaluable for all enamelling work when ground in varnish. Some of the better kinds of French process made zinc whites are so very white in tone that ordinary white lead shows a yellowish tone when placed side by side together.

Zinc white is the oxide of that metal and is made in two different ways—but by the same process of oxidation. These two methods are known as the *"French"* and as the *"American."* The zinc white made by the so called French process is manufactured from the metal, while that named American from the zinc ore instead.

THE FRENCH PROCESS.

c. Zinc white made by the French process is produced by placing metallic zinc in retorts or ovens where it is vaporized by heat—this vapor is conducted to upper chambers which are supplied with fresh atmospheric air for which the zinc has a great affinity in the state of vapor and with which it instantly combines when it comes in contact with it. From the ceilings of these chambers hang long sacks with their mouths opened and closely fitted together into which the floculent feathery oxide rises up and is caught up in these. The oxide which is caught the farthest away from the openings through which the zinc vapor arises from the retorts is the whitest and best—that which is caught nearest the openings usually containing more or less of foreign matter in the shape of dust, etc., which finds its way from the retorts into the chamber. This feathery mass is next subjected to a powerful compression when it is then ground up and packaged ready for the market in a dry state or to be ground up in oil or varnish.

THE AMERICAN PROCESS.

d. The American process of making zinc white is essentially the same as that related for the French, differing from it only in the shape of the raw material. Instead of using the metallic zinc, zinc ore becomes the provider. That is placed in the retorts and vaporized in the same manner as related for the French process. However, as the ore contains so much more foreign matter and impurities the zinc white thus ob tained is inferior in whiteness and quality to the first and is sold for less money than the other.

e. The name of French zinc has lost its significance as to being an index as to the source of supply of that article as today there is as good a quality of French process zinc made in America and which commands as good a price as any zinc white imported from Europe.

In both the French and American zinc white the first and second qualities are designated as green and red seal respectively. The green denoting the best quality—the red the second.

THE EARTH WHITES.

70. *a.* *Earth whites* so called are all of mineral origin and according as they contain as a base either lime, clay, or sand are known as cretaceous, aluminous

or silicious. All possess somewhat different properties, each being better than any of the others for certain specific purposes.

b. Cretaceous earths are chiefly used in water colors and for that matter all earth whites are at their best in distemper and have that much in common, excepting when they are used in oils as adjuncts, correctives or adulterants for the metallic whites or any of the coloring pigments where each differ materially from the other.

The principal pigment with a cretaceous base is *whiting* or the carbonate of line, all others being simply variations of it more or less impure. Whiting is used in immense quantities as a base upon which to make the tints used in the printing of wall paper. As the main base in mixing tints for calcimine or in its self color, it reigns supreme and nearly all the ready prepared calcimine found on the market contain it as the main ingredient in their preparation. As an adjunct to graining colors in oil it is highly valued as it enables the grainer to reduce the strength of his colors so they can be thinned much more than would be possible but for the addition of the whiting.

The only other cretaceous pigment of value which differs from whiting materially is *Gypsum* or the sul phate of lime. It does not work quite so well as whit ing in water colors and is seldom used as such without a special preparation which is patented and too intri cate for use by the general painter. It is the base used in all the so called anti-kalsomine paints patented preparations. It is too transparent in oil to be of any use as a self paint but is valuable in the preparation of Venetian red where it becomes its base. It is also useful as a corrective in many of the other colors and in the compounding of white paints.

There used to be a number of whites in the markets some years ago such as Spanish white, London and other fancy named whites, which were prepared from whiting and from which they differed only in the form given it of pyramidal drops or cakes.

c. The only pigment with an aluminous base is *"China clay"* which is worth mentioning. It possesses more body in oil than those of the preceding class and when well cleaned of foreign matter makes a good water color paint. On account of its body, if such may be called a semi-transparent muddy looking stuff in its self color in oil it is used as an adjunct and corrective in many white paints which come ready prepared but it is used most frequently as an adulterant.

d. The silicious whites are represented by the *white silicate* earths. Some are found that are of a clean white but most of them are generally off color. The white ones are used in the preparation of "English kalsomine" and used as water colors but they are very inferior to whiting for such a purpose. Their greatest utility as pigments lays in the silicate earth's use as correctives to the white metallic pigments and as such also for several other colors. For such a purpose they are used in very large quantities by the paint grinders, but are seldom bought as such and compounded by the consumer.

BARYTES.

71. *a.* Last but not least among the whites comes *Barytes.* Barytes in its native state is better known as heavy spar. This is ground, washed and is prepared for market according to the qualities it may possess. It is very heavy and in its natural state as clear as quartz.

b. Its utility as a pigment is, to say the least, "questionable" From its transparency one may infer that as an oil color it would cover very little better than the linseed oil used in spreading it and for water colors it is inferior and more costly than whiting. It is true that when it has been prepared to the condition when it takes the name of "Blanc-fixe" it is highly prized by artists for use as an indestructible white in water colors —but then it is not in the same shape as the barytes of commerce. In the latter shape barytes is an intimate friend of almost every color and every package of adulterated color or cheap ready mixed paint contains a good proportion of it. Its great clearness and transparency permits its use in almost any percentage that the greed of the manufacturer would suggest to him that it should be used or that the ability to unload it upon an unsuspecting public would permit.

THE REDS.

72. The red constitute a numerous class of pigments. They are derived from the metallic, mineral, vegetable and animal kingdoms. They comprise a range of color tones varying from a red brown to the most brilliant scarlet reds bordering on the yellow.

They will be reviewed according to their origin as derived from a metallic, mineral or vegetable kingdom.

THE METALLIC REDS.

73. *a. Red oxide* is the most common form of the red pigments derived from iron. It enters into the make up of a number of various reds and in its pure state all by itself is most excellent. It is seldom sold under that name in a pure state nor is it necessary that it should when it is considered that 20 to 25% of the pure color when added to any transparent base will cover solidly over any color black or white. It is so strong that unless it should be used for tinting it will bear reducing very much and still cover well. This addition of a cheaper material is legitimate under such a circumstance when it is known to the buyer and the cost of the paint reduced to him.

b. Venetian red is supposedly a natural color, but that which is found upon the market today is certainly not of that character. It is made artificially and is much better for it, as then it can be made uniform in tone and texture which is not the case with any natural earth color. It is made upon a base of various kinds, the chief of which are barytes, whiting and gypsum to which red oxide of iron has been added. That made with a gypsum base is much the best and the qualities known under the name of English Venetian red are usually of that quality. It contains about 25% of iron oxide and that is enough to enable it to cover over anything. That made upon a gypsum base is very permanent and the change noticed in pure red oxide due to a tendency to become hydrated making it more yellowish, is reduced to the minimum. Thus made it is permanent.

Turkey red, Pompeian reds of some, with others of many names really are only brighter specimen having been made by the addition of some very bright toned oxide of iron on bases similar to Venetian red and they should all be classed under that head and name. Besides the names are used by some manufacturers to designate an entirely different class of pigments especially that known as Turkey red which is a dark purplish red of a rich lakey tone.

All the reds derived from red oxide of iron made on a gypsum base are permanent or so nearly so as to warrant their being so called. All are useful in oil, japan and water colors and are used by all painters, decorators and artists.

c. The *Indian reds* derive their coloring matter from the peroxide of iron. At one time they used to be imported but now they are altogether of home manufacture, being much more even in texture and coloring matter than those which were mined and prepared from the Asiatic ore. Indian reds have a range of tones of an entirely different order from that of the Venetian reds, being of a purplish shade of red ranging from pale to dark. They are very useful in producing tints with white. The light toned Indian red producing tints of rosy lilac while the dark produce tones of a violet lilac. They can be used in oil coach and water color work. They and their shades are permanent.

These are all the red pigments derived from iron. It is true that there are a number of reds for sale in artists' colors especially which owe their coloring matter to either ferric oxide or the peroxide but notwithstanding their high sounding name they can all be classed as shades of either Venetian or Indian reds.

d. The *Tuscan reds* are included with the metallic reds because their base is usually Indian red plus some of the whites. They owe their beautiful tones to a dye in which they are plunged and which they absorb. If they have absorbed much of it they are classed afterward as deep Tuscan—if less as light Tuscan reds. It depends upon what the dyeing agent is, as to the beautiful tone being permanent or not. If made rich by a cheap aniline dye they will fade quickly—if from an alizarin one they will be permanent. They, like the Indian red, of whose nature they mainly partake, are useful for all sorts of painting in oil, japan or distemper but unlike the Indian red they do not produce very good tints with the whites.

THE RED PIGMENTS DERIVED FROM LEAD.

74. *Red lead* is the bi-oxide of that metal. It is made by roasting in retorts either the monoxide of lead or white lead or even the metal itself. They are kept in those revolving retorts until they acquire the proper amount of oxidation. Red lead while permanent in its constituent parts, fades to a lighter tone of yellow red as it has a tendency to return to a monoxide—its more natural condition. It is one of the best pigments known for the priming of iron and all metals and for such a purpose is used in enormous quantities.

75.   *a. Orange mineral* is the ter-oxide of iron and is usually made from white lead which is off color from one cause or another. It carries more oxygen in its composition than red lead and is of a richer tone, but it alsc is not permanent, and will loose its extra oxidation and return to the monoxide. Both are subject to that foe of all lead salts except the sulphate —*sulphureted hydrogen gas.*

b. American vermillion is a pigment made from white lead and bichromate of potash. It is crystallic in form and should not be ground fine as that destroys the color Since the advent of the vermillion reds it has lost ground until it is little known to the present generation of painters.

ENGLISH VERMILLION OR QUICKSILVER VERMILLION.

76. *a.* English or quicksilver vermillion in the shape of native cinnabar which is a sulphuret of mer-

cury is found in all parts of the world where quicksilver is mined. Yet little if any ever finds its way to the market as such. All the quicksilver vermillion is artificially made. The process while easy to understand is nevertheless somewhat intricate and too lengthy to describe fully enough to be understood in the space available. It is first made into a black sulphuret by the addition of eight parts of sulphur to one of mercury which turns it into a black sulphuret which is its natural condition and afterwards it is sublimed when it is changed into the red which is an artificial condition for it, hence its tendency to darken as it seeks to return to its natural condition and it will quickly do so if left unprotected by varnish from atmospheric air.

b. It is used for a great many purposes but not to the same extent today that it was previous to the introduction of the para reds and other imitation vermillion reds. None can compare with it for richness or brilliancy of tone—but for its fugitiveness it would be the king of the reds. There are two varieties of it, one called the pale which is of a bright scarlet tone and the deep which has a bluish tinge and is of the amaranth order. The pale has a much better body or opacity than the deep and cannot be replaced by any other red for striping as it will cover solid over black which no other scarlet red will do in one coat. It is used chiefly by the carriage trade in a self color or as a ground to be glazed over with a carmine glaze. When well covered over by varnish and ground up in it, it will preserve its beautiful tone a long time before changing its color.

THE IMITATION VERMILLIONS OR VERMILLION REDS.

77.   *a.   Imitation vermillions,* or *vermillion reds* as some know them, must not be confounded with American vermillion as some erroneously call them. (See paragraph 75 *b.*) They are not chromates of lead, but are made some of them at least upon a white lead or a chromate of lead base upon which is thrown a dye from which the base absorbs the rich coloring matter giving them the rich tones which make them near rivals of quicksilver vermillion; but there the resemblance ends. The dyes used in giving them their tones vary very much—some of the cheaper reds being colored with the cheapest of aniline dyes, which are fugitive while the better grades are colored with cosine and the best with alizarin. In the best of the vermilion reds such an excellence has been attained that they are much more permanent than quicksilver vermilion, if not quite so rich nor opaque.

b.   These reds are used for an infinity of purposes especially by coach painters, by agricultural implement manufacturers and all builders of machinery. They are as well adapted to water colors as they are to oil and japan work. They are known under an infinity of proprietary names and come in all qualities as well as tones from scarlet to purple red.

THE RED LAKES.

78. a. Lakes usually are transparent colors thrown upon a transparent base. They are chiefly used as glazing colors by artists and coach painters. Some of the lakes are only semitransparent and are used as self colors or in tinting—only more coats are required to cover solidly with them.

It depends upon the bases used in some degree and to a greater degree still to the coloring agent used in giving them their color as to whether the lakes are good or bad, permanent or fugitive. The range of tone for the red lakes is great varying from a scarlet and carmine down the scale to a reddish brown. Carmine itself is derived from coloring obtained from cochineal, an insect. It is too fugitive for work requiring permanency and has become supplanted by alizarin made lakes which are much more permanent and which equal the ones derived from madder

THE YELLOWS.

78. a. The family of yellows is about of equal importance and to the house painter of greater value than the reds. The various yellow pigments are derived from the metallic, mineral and vegetable kingdoms while some are derived from a combination of these.

THE OCHRES.

b. Ochres while not the brightest in tone of the yellow pigments are by long odds the most useful of that color. They are permanent and are used in their self color or combined with the whites to make a wide range of tints from an ivory or cream to a buff and combined with other colors to make an infinity of tints. They may be placed in two general classes: the argillaceous and the silicious according as to which predominates in their base. The first are chiefly derived from America while the second comes from Europe. The argillaceous ochres are best adapted to water color work while the silicious ochres are much the best for oil painting especially if exposed out of doors. All ochres are natural earth products with an earth base colored with hydrate oxide of iron. They vary very much in the quality of this iron hyd-oxide. A volume could be written upon them and their peculiarities without exhausting the subject. The general house painter should never use the American or the argillaceous ochres for solid self painting nor priming for reasons assigned under heading entitled "Blistering of paint" (paragraph 4 *c*, which see). The silicate ochres or the genuine French and English are the only safe ones to use for such a purpose.

CHROME YELLOWS.

79. *a.* *Chrome yellow* or the neutral chromate of lead is the only one of all the shades and tones classed under that name which is really entitled to it as all other shades varying from it are either alkaline on one side or acid upon the other; the canary and range

of tones on the lemon order owing their lighter shade to sulphate of lead or rather to sulphuric acid which turns the lead to a sulphate and the range of the orange toned ones to lime or some other caustic alkali which turns them reddish. All shades owe their yellow tone to bichromate of potash which combines with the lead base to form the neutral and the other shades by the additions mentioned above.

b. Chrome yellows are used in oil, coach or water color painting. It is well adapted to all kinds of painting. The only limitation to their use is that under certain conditions they fade slightly or change their tone. Sulphureted hydrogen gases are as fatal to them as to white lead—that being a part of their make up. The sun's rays too have a tendency to cause them to change somewhat. But with all their faults there are no yellows so useful to the general painting trade. Should they disappear they would be sorely missed.

The chrome yellows with their extended range of shades and tones comprising the whole gamut of yellow tones from the palest of canary to the deepest of orange have nearly driven out of the market a number of other yellows which were extensively used a few years ago such as orpiment, Naples yellow, etc. While fugi tives they are less so than those they have replaced.

80. A simple naming of the other yellows is all that will be necessary as their use has dwindled down to very small quantities and that mainly among artists and decorators of the old school. The only one of any

great intrinsic value is *lemon* or *baryta yellow*. This is permanent and but for its gréater cost and of its being more transparent than the lemon chrome yellow it would be used more than it is.

Aureolin is a cobalt yellow verv transparent even in water and difficult to handle.

Gamboge, an old standard in oil colors, transparent and very fugitive.

Indian yellow is of animal origin and when well prepared is of value to the artist.

Dutch pink. A yellow lake derived from grinding tree barks of various kinds—and dyeing some base with them—of no great value even to the decorator in water colors.

Naples yellow. Not to be relied on, as it is fugitive: besides it is no good as a water color and some varieties of ochre mixed with whites will closely reproduce its tone.

Vanadium yellow—Kings yellow besidçs being poisonous is not permanent.

Yellow lake under which name most anything that is transparent and will do for glazing is sold—all being fugitive and of little value to the general painter.

Under various fancy names the artists' catalogues are burdened with a host of proprietary named yellows belonging really to the ones already enumerated.

THE BLUES.

81. *a.* The blues are derived from metallic, mineral, vegetable and animal sources and combinations of these. Outside of ultramarine blue, no blues are found in a natural state.

b. *Prussian blue* in both the soluble and insoluble form are chemically about the same. The first is better known as *Chinese* and as *soluble blue.* Both are prussiates of iron and are very useful in water or in oil colors. They will loose their color entirely by contact with fresh lime and are not entirely permanent in sunlight. They are very strong in coloring matter.

c. *Ultramarine blue* is the most remarkable blue on the list. As said before it is the only blue found in nature in a developed state, but is difficult of extraction from its matrix "Lapis Lazuli," a semi-precious stone, so it was sold at an enormous price and royalty only could enjoy its use. It is produced artificially at a very low cost fully equal in quality or tone to the genuine. It is entirely permanent in sunlight or in contact with lime and has a range of tones from a greenish blue running to clear blue and on to a purplish cast of blue, the latter being much inferior in tone to the true blue. Ultramarine blue is made use of in all kinds of painting ground in oil, in japan or in water and all painters praise it highly. It is not nearly as strong in coloring matter as Prussia blue.

d. *Cobalt blue* is a very pretty tone of light blue which when pure (which it is difficult to find) is derived from cobalt. It is universally made now by simply mixing enough zinc white to a clear blue ultramarine to reduce it to the tone of the true cobalt blue so that practically it is only a tint of those two pigments. It is so easily made by admixture that few supply stores carry it in stock. It is fully as permanent as its parents.

e. Ceruleum is another cobalt color which can be readily imitated by using the greenish blue ultramarine reduced with zinc white.

f. Indigo blue is derived from a plant and its use in either water colors or oil is confined to a few artists. With so many better blues to choose from, its name as a pigment might as well be forgotten. The scene painters use it mostly.

The above comprise all the useful blues. Yet the manufacturers of artists' colors persist in loading down their catalogues with a long list of names to confuse the public with the false idea that such are distinct pigments when they are not.

THE GREENS.

82. *a.* A wide range of greens are fou.1d in the market but they can be all classed in two groups, those whose tones incline towards the yellows and those which incline towards the blues. Green is a secondary and a compound color made from yellow and blue, so.there is nothing very remarkable in the fact that its tones should incline one way or the other toward the parents.

Greens are all made chemically, yet some dirty greenish black earths are found and classed as greens in some catalogues.

b. *Chrome greens* as they are known in America are by far the most used of any of the greens. They are made by various combinations of Prussian blue and chrome yellow or their chemical equivalents and precipitated. Their range of tone is great from very light tender grass green nearly as bright as Paris green down to the deepest tones bordering on black. While not absolutely permanent, they are fairly so. Of course, lime will destroy the Prussian blue it contains. On the continent and especially in England chrome green is the named applied to the green oxide of chromium, a color little known or used here, but fairly permanent.

c. *Cobalt* or *zinc green,* as some call it, is derived from that metal. It is permanent but as it can be very nearly duplicated by using a good green ultramarine and zinc white one might just as well call it a tint of those pigments and prepare it from them when needed.

d. *Viridian* is an invaluable green to the artist but its great cost will hardly permit its use to the general painter. Much of it is adulterated and it is better to buy it only under the label and name of well known makers of artists' colors.

e. *Paris* or *emerald green* as it is known in England is a very poisonous arsenical product. It is very transparent and only fit to glaze with. It should be discarded entirely.

f. Verdigris. Another poisonous pigment derived from copper. It was used in the past much more than it is today. It is said to possess anti-fouling properties and is used by a few in the painting of boat bottoms. A few old time carriage painters still use it as a glaze but many general painters today die without having, ever seen it and never miss it.

Beside the above are to be found a large number of greens sold under proprietary names—all are various shades of chrome greens to which manufacturers have attached a trade mark name of their own. This creates confusion, leading people to think that such are some different production—besides there is the usual array of fancy named greens of the artists' color catalogue, none better if as good as the well known colors described above.

THE BROWNS.

83. *a.* · The *Browns* are produced in abundance in the natural state by mother earth. There are also to be found of metallic origin. To facilitate the understanding of some of the brown earth pigments, it will be well to note that the burning of them has a tendency to change their tone. Those containing ferric oxide will become redder than they were in the raw state. Those containing manganese will become darker in tone. Nearly all the brown earth pigments are valu able for one purpose or another in water colors to produce neutral tint and for the same purpose in oil paint-

˄ng or in japan for the coach painter. Some are very transparent, others only semi-transparent and such are of value to the grainer or for glazing to the carriage painter, artists and decorators.

b. *Umber, raw* and *burnt,* vary very much in their composition. The best come from Asia Minor and are sold as Turkey umber. The raw is of a greenish brown and by burning is changed into a rich clear toned brown which in good umbers will be free of redness— they are semi-transparent. They are useful in all kinds of painting and in all mediums.

c. *Siennas, raw* and *burnt,* like the umber vary greatly, so much so as to be hardly recognizable as being of the same nature—the poor, showing a muddy brownish red tone in the burnt, while the good has a rich subdued red which has a clear lakey transparency. For this reason the siennas are invaluable to the grainer and artists, who could not get along without it. It is used in oil, japan and water color painting.

The raw owes its yellowish brown tone to its ferric oxide which is hydrated and which looses by burning, becoming red after that.

d. *Vandyke brown* is a natural bituminous color found chiefly in bogs. It is known as Cassel earth, from the town in Germany near which it is produced. It is very transparent. It is useful as a glazing color in carriage painting and as a graining color to the grainer. It is **not** entirely permanent and for that reason, besides of its being a very poor dryer in linseed oil, it **is** not as extensively used now as it was.

e. Asphaltum or mineral pitch, when well refined is useful as a glaze, it being very transparent. As it is liable to crack it is more useful in show card painting or for the painting of iron gratings, heat registers and such than for anything else.

f. Metallic browns. Under that name a number of raw and calcined dark iron oxide paints are marketed, some becoming quite reddish by calcination, some being of that tone naturally. They have an excellent body or opacity but that the tone of their color is not very attractive nor the tints made from them they would be used still more than they are. For freight car painting, bridge work, barns and the cheap outbuildings, roofs and all kinds of structural iron work they are used in immense quantities.

Under the name ought to be included such old time colors as Spanish brown, etc., which designation is still used on the eastern seaboard while it has become obsolete in the middle west.

THE BLACKS.

84. *a.* The blacks play an important role in every department of painting. It is used largely as a self color in the painting of iron work, steam and other ships and carriages, coaches, etc. While as a tinting color with whites and as an adjunct to other colors to darken them they are invaluable as tint producers.

. Most of the blacks are of carbonic composition produced in a natural state in black lead; derived from fats as in lampblack or from the calcination of the bones of animals as ivory black and again the product of the calcination of woods as in Brunswick black.

b. *Lampblack* is produced bv the incomplete combustion of fatty substances. It is very strong in coloring matter, but only moderately black in tone. It produces clean toned grays with whites and is the best black to use for the making of tints with any other colors. It is used more than any of the other blacks by sign and house painters and by the carriage trade for priming coats. It has more opacity than any other black excepting gas black.

c. *Gas black* or *carbon black* is also a black produced by the incomplete combustion of natural gas. It is more intensely black than lampblack and used as a self color it is a close rival to the bone blacks for its jet black tone. As a tint producer it is very poor— the tints being rusty with none of the clearness of lamp black. It is used to improve the tone of that pigment in sign writer's black and since the grinders have dis covered a way of grinding it so that it will not liver with linseed oil, it is highly prized for solid black painting of all kinds. It is also substituted for drop black in the cheaper colors ground in japan as it will bear adulterating 10 to 1 and still be as strong as ivory black.

d. *Ivorv, drop* and *coach blacks* are all one and

the same article under different labels it is true but—
the same. They are bone blacks which vary greatly in
quality according as to the kind of bones, hard or
soft, used in calcination and also in the carefulness in
conducting of the process. All are useful in oil, japan or
water colors. It is used in all kinds of painting, but
the carriage trade consumes the most of it.

e. Brunswick black is the charcoal produced by the
combustion of twigs of trees and vines of various
growths. It is very transparent and useful only in
water colors.

f. Black lead or *plumbago* is a natural carbon produced by nature and it is mined in many parts of the
world. As a pigment it is permanent and but for its
indifferent tone, would be used more extensively than
it is. It is chiefly used in oil for the painting of roofs,
iron structures and out door painting.

This ends the list of useful pigments.

QUESTIONS ON COLORS.

61. What is said regarding colors in general?

62. In how many main classes can pigments be
divided?

63. How are pigments grouped for convenience?

64. *a.* How many groups of colors?

    b. What is said concerning their characters?

65. *a.* What is said of the whites generally?

    b. Give their derivation?

66. *a.* What is said generally of white lead?

b. What are its peculiarities?

c. What is the "Dutch process" or corrosion?

d. What is the "stack" system of corrosion?

e. What is the "cylinder" system of corrosion?

f. Does one system make a better white lead than the other?

67. What is "sublimed lead"?

68. Are any of the other salts of lead that are white useful as paints?

69. *a.* What is said of zinc white and its peculiarities?

b. How many processes are used for making zinc white?

c. Describe the French process?

d. Describe the American process?

e. Are French zinc whites made in France only?

70. *a.* How are the earth whites divided?

b. What are the pigments with a cretaceous base?

c. What are the pigments with an aluminous base?

d. What are the silicious whites?

71. *a.* What is barytes?

b. What are its uses?

72. What is said of the reds generally?

73. *a.* What is said of red oxide of iron?

b. What is said of Venetian red, Pompeian red, Turkish red, etc.?

    c.   What is said regarding the Indian reds?

    d.   What are Tuscan reds?

74. What is red lead and what are its uses?

75. *a.*   What is orange mineral and what are its uses?

    b.   What is American vermillion?

76. *a.*   What is English or quicksilver vermillion?

    b.   Where is it mostly used?

77. *a.*   What are imitation or Vermillion reds?

    b.   What are their uses?

78. What are lakes and what are their uses?

79. *a.*   What is said regarding the ochres?

    b.   What are chrome yellows?

    c.   What are their uses?

80. What other yellows are they?

81. *a.*   What is said of the blues in general?

    b.   What is Prussian blue and what are its uses?

    c.   What are ultramarine blues and what are their uses?

    d.   How is cobalt blue made?

    e.   What is ceruleum and how is it imitated?

    f.   What is said of indigo blue?

82. *a.*   What is said of greens in general?

    b.   What are chrome greens?

    c.   What about cobalt or zinc greens?

        What is said of viridian?

         What of Paris or Emerald green?

83. *a.*   What is said generally of the browns?

b. What about raw and burnt umbers?

c. What about raw and burnt sienna?

d. What is Vandyke brown?

84. *a.* What is said of the blacks generally?

b. What is lampblack and what are its uses?

c. Where does gas black differ from lampblack?

d. What is Brunswick black?

e. What is black lead or plumbago?

COLOR HARMONY.

85. Exterior and even more so interior painting no matter how well it may have been done nor how well planned, the decorations will have that undefinable "gingerbread" look to it as the painters would call it, if the coloring lacks in harmony, and even if well done and harmonious, if the draperies, furniture and carpets are not in harmony with the painting, that will suffer in consequence of the latter inharmonious neighborhood.

It is said that poets are born but not made; this to a certain extent can be said of a good colorist. It is a lamentable fact that 10% of men are at least partially color blind and incapable of judging the effects of true harmony. Some are totally color blind and can only recognize shades of black and white—the latter case is much more rare but railroad companies are forced to reject a large per cent of applicants for positions where the quick recognition of certain colors is a "sine qua non."

But while poets are not made, persons who so desire may educate themselves into certainly not becoming good colorists but into a knowledge of the laws governing coloring and when they understand them fairly well they will be able to design color schemes which will not be an outrage upon the vision of persons of taste who are naturally able to recognize harmonious coloring.

86. The subject of color harmony is too deep a topic to elucidate in even a desultory manner in the small space which can be devoted to it in a manual which is to treat of the whole subject-matter of paint and painting. All that can be done is to point the reader the way to a deeper study of harmony in books devoted to the subject of which many have appeared recently.

To understand how to harmonize colors one must first of all become acquainted with a knowledge of what colors are. These are the result of decomposition of light which is white and which is the result of the perfect union of all colors. The rainbow with its beautiful coloring does on a large scale what a glass prism breaking the sun's rays does on a smaller scale; it decomposes the rays into the various colors of the spectrum.

This decomposition of light shows in reality to the naked eye but three groups of three colors each, the last three but faintly, however, while the first three alone cannot be divided and therefore are called the *rimary colors:* the are: *Red*, *ellow* and *blue*.

87. Secondary colors, also three in number, are formed by the mixture of any two of the primaries, thus: Red and yellow gives *orange,* red and blue gives *purple* and yellow and blue gives *green.* So orange, purple and green are the secondary colors.

88. A third trio of colors is produced by the mixture of any two of the secondaries thus: Orange and green gives *citrine;* green and purple gives *olive* and orange and purple gives *russet.* So citrine, olive and russet constitute the three tertiary colors.

89. The further combination of the tertiaries produce an infinity of neutral grays with an addition of white or black.

It must be born in mind that to produce a perfect harmony that the primaries or their equivalents in secondary or tertiary colors ought to be present to produce a perfect harmony in about the same proportion as they exist in the spectrum and in which they unite to produce perfect light or white.

90. But other harmonies can be produced by graded shades of the same color. Such an harmony is always pleasing to the eye and are always in good taste, so that a person can hardly err in giving satisfactory results if he treats his decorative scheme in this way. This is called harmony by analogy.

91. Harmony by contrast is much more difficult to master, as it is not only the coloring used in the decoration that must be taken into consideration but that of the furniture and draperies. Besides there are a great

many things which must be well understood which enhance or detract from the effects to be had from the use of any color.

A good general rule to follow, is: that the complementary colors (as are called the contrasting opposites) should be used in about the same proportion as the three primary colors themselves stand in the formation of pure white. The primary colors stand in the proportion of three parts red, five parts yellow and eight parts blue in the make up of white light; then if the leading color used in the decoration is blue, it follows that red and yellow or the product of their combination, *orange* is the complementary color of blue and either that or the color value of these in others either secondary or tertiaries must be used in about the proportion needed of the primaries in making them would have stood to make white light. If yellow is the main color ground, blue and red or their tertiary equivalents or secondary, which is *purple,* must be the complementary color to use. If the main color be red then *green,* which is the result of the union of blue and yellow, is the contrasting color of red.

It does not follow however that a pleasing contrast will follow even by a proper use of opposites, unless these are of the right tones and shades and as these depend upon a number of qualifying circumstances which will have great influence in the making of a perfect blend, the laws of color relation to each other and of the effect of neutrals and of black and white must be well understood.

92. The secondary and tertiary colors are simply combinations of the primaries and their source must be carefully noted, so that the equivalent of the opposites may be furnished as they are necessary to form a good harmony by contrast.

93. The rules given are general and must be very incomplete even then as so much must be taken in consideration as influencing the results in the use of color that the reader must be referred to some good treatise on color harmony treating the subject-matter fully. Then only can one understand why it is that after having chosen proper complementary colors, that the contrast seems dull or out of harmony. The knowledge of the effect neutral tones have in heightening or depressing colors or why certain tones should be used instead of others of the same color will then be understood and even a partially color blind decorator will not commit any unpardonable sins—in harmonizing colors.

QUESTIONS ON COLOR HARMONY.

85. What is said of color harmony?
86. What are the primary colors?
87. What are the secondary colors?
88. What are the tertiary colors?
89. What are further combinations called?
90. What is harmony by analogy?
91. What is harmony by contrast?

92.   What is the harmony of contrast of the secondary and tertiaries?

93.   What is further said regarding harmony?

COLOR MIXING.

94.   The mixing of tints requires some care and attention but is not as difficult to understand as many suppose it to be.   If the rules given below are strictly followed, even a novice will come very near to the matching of sample tints—at least of such as are mostly used and with the tones of which he is familiar.

There is a wide difference between mixing tints in oil or in water colors.   In the former a person can see for himself just what the mixture is all through the stages of the mixing but in water colors the tints show so much darker than they will be when dry that somewhat different rules must be adopted to mix the two.

RULES FOR MIXING COLORS IN OIL.

95.   *a.*   The base color is always the most important one.   It may be any color and here is where some good judgment is at times required to determine what that is, when one has to choose it for himself in trying to match certain samples.   Usually it is a white if the tint is at all light in tone.   If it be a dark one, the mixer should be sufficiently well acquainted with colors to judge at a glance which must be used as having the prevailing importance in the make up of the tint and that is the base.

b. This base should be well broken up in linseed oil but not nearly as thin as it should be for application with a brush. If it be white lead, the most usual base for all light tints, it is better to have it well broken up the day before as then all small lumps will be dissolved and when it has been well stirred up, it will be uniform throughout—a very important requisite.

c. The tinting pigments or colors which it will be necessary to add to the base for producing the tint should be pretty well thinned with linseed oil and turpentine half and half. It is of great importance that no lumps or specks remain undissolved in these and they should be thinned somewhat more than stated for that of the lead base. If necessary they should be strained through a fine meshed paint strainer.

d. The pigment entering in the largest quantity in the make up of a tint aside of the base should now be mixed with it—not by pouring it in all at once and thus overshooting the mark, but very gradually and should be well stirred up to insure uniform incorporation. It should not be added to the full extent needed for the tint, but just short of it. Proceed next to add in the other colors needed in the same manner as stated above. When all the pigments required have been well stirred up, if the mark has not been overshot, the resulting tint will be very near to the color wanted and by a further addition of this or that one, the tint will be brought up to just where it is wanted. If too much coloring pigment has been put in however it is easy to understand that it cannot be taken out. Then the only remedy is to add more base to counteract the too great quantity of color used and also of the rest of the tinting colors and this usually means loss of material where too much has been mixed.

e. A list of principal tints is given further on. Many are so very closely related that but some who desire to make them, might be misled, they might as well have been left out. Another word—what one man understands as an apple green may be very different from what another's idea of what an apple green ought to be and so on all through the list. For this and other reasons the quantity of each is not given. The other reasons are that some colors of the same name bought of various manufacturers may be twice, thrice and even four or ten times stronger in coloring than others and a tint would be utterly ruined if quantities were given. The colors are named according to the importance they occupy in making the tints. The more important being named after the base and the least— last.

96. Tints in water colors require about the same coloring pigments to produce any given tint as in oil and the same advice about not overdoing the addition of the pigments to the base is even more needed. The base for tints is usually whiting or some other earth white which has been properly thinned with glue water. But after colors also thinned with glue water have been added, as the tint appears much darker than it really

is, it will be necessary to "try" it. Dip a small piece of paper in it and place it in the sun or upon a stove and dry it. As soon as dry the true tone of the color will show up and any colors lacking can be added— gradually, well stirred up and tried by heat again, being always careful to have it just a trifle under than above the mark. This trying is tedious, it is true, but much less so than having to throw away the whole batch and commence the mixing all over again—and less expensive too.

LIST OF TINTS.

97. *Acacia.* Lampblack for base, colored with Indian red and tinged with Prussian blue.

Acorn brown. See Chocolate as it is nearly the same but lightened up with white lead.

Alderney brown. Lampblack, orange chrome yellow, French ochre, white lead.

Alabaster. White lead for base, add enough medium chrome yellow to very slightly tinge it.

Amaranth. Tuscan red and vermillion for base, add enough ultramarine blue to shade wanted.

Anemone. Vermillion red for base, add Prussian blue to suit shade wanted and a trifle of black and white lead or zinc which is better.

Antique bronze. Orange chrome yellow for base, add ivory black. Lampblack can be used but shade will not be so bright.

Antwerp blue. Ultramarine blue for base, add

chrome green to shade wanted, lighten up with zinc white.

Apple green. White lead for base, add light chrome green and orange chrome yellow.

Apricot. Medium chrome yellow for base; venetian red and carmine lake. If a light shade is wanted lighten it up with zinc white.

Armenian red. Bright venetian red for base, lightened up with French ochre.

Asiatic bronze. Raw umber for base; medium chrome yellow to which add sufficient white lead for shade wanted.

Ash gray. White lead for base; tinge with lampblack; add a bit of French ochre.

Autumn leaf. White lead for base; to which add French ochre, orange chrome yellow, a trifle Venetian red to tinge it to tone of red desired.

Azure blue. White lead for base, but zinc white is better; add Prussian blue to shade of it desired.

Bay. Lampblack for base; add Venetian red and orange chrome yellow.

Begonia. Vermillion red of a good scarlet shade for base; tinge with Prussian blue and lampblack.

Bismark brown. Burnt sienna for base; add burnt umber and orange chrome yellow; lighten slightly with white lead to suit.

Black slate. Lampblack for base; Prussian blue; slightly lighten it up with white lead.

Bordeaux blue. Lampblack for base: Prussian blue, orange chrome yellow.

Bottle green. Lampblack and Prussian blue for base; lemon chrome yellow; to obtain this color at its best glaze it over with a yellow lake.

Brass. White lead for base; add medium chrome yellow and French ochre to shade of it wanted.

Bronze blue. Lampblack for base; tinge with Prussian blue and slightly lighten with white lead.

Bronze green. Extra dark chrome green for base; add lampblack. For a richer tone of it: medium chrome green for base, add ivory black and a trifle of raw umber

Bronze red. Vermillion red for base; add orange chrome yellow and a trifle of lampblack.

Bronze yellow. Medium chrome yellow for base; raw umber, lighten up to suit with white lead.

Brick color. Yellow. ochre for base; add Venetian red to suit; for very light shades add white lead in very small quantity.

Brown stone. Tuscan red for base; add orange chrome yellow; lighten up to suit with white lead. Some shades of it require a bit of ivory black.

Browns and *Brown drabs—all shades.* Venetian red for base; add French ochre and lampblack in various proportion according to shades of brown wanted. For the brown *drabs* add white lead to reduce the above brown tints.

Buttercup. White lead for base; add lemon chrome yellow to suit shade wanted.

Café au lait. Burnt umber for base; add white lead, French ochre and Venetian red.

Cambridge red. Vermillion for base; add Prussian blue to suit.

Canary. Use chrome yellow of that name or lemon yellow for base, lightened up with zinc white.

Carnation. English vermillion for base; add good madder lake or carmine. If wanted very light, add zinc white.

Celestial blue. Prussian blue for base; chrome green and zinc white.

Cerulean blue. Zinc white for base; add ultramarine blue of good tone to suit.

Chamois. White lead for base; add French ochre, medium chrome yellow to suit, redden it with a little burnt sienna.

Chamoline. White lead for base; add raw sienna. lemon chrome yellow to suit.

Chartreuse. Medium chrome yellow for base; add some medium chrome green.

Chestnut. Venetian red for base; add medium chrome yellow, French ochre and lampblack to suit.

Chocolate. Burnt umber for base; add rich crimson vermillion red or lake. Another which is cheaper but not so rich: French ochre for base; add lampblack and Venetian red to suit.

Cinnamon. White lead for base; add burnt sienna, French ochre, medium chrome yellow.

Crimson. Deep English vermillion or any of the crimson shades of vermillion reds. If desired very rich, add some of the crimson lakes or glaze with them.

Claret. Madder lake and ultramarine blue for base, to which add English vermillion and ivory black.

Clay bank. French ochre for base; add orange chrome yellow, lighten up with white lead to shade desired.

Clay drab. White lead for base; medium chrome yellow, raw and burnt umber.

Cobalt blue. This is a solid blue. Good ultramarine blue; lighten up to suit with zinc white.

Cocoanut brown. Burnt umber for base; lightened up with white lead.

Colonial yellow. White lead for base; add medium chrome yellow, tinge with a trifle of orange chrome yellow.

Copper. Medium chrome yellow; tinged with burnt sienna.

Coral pink. Vermillion for base; white lead, medium chrome yellow.

Cotrine. White lead for base; add orange chrome yellow and lampblack.

Cream color and *all the buffs.* White lead for base · add some good French or Oxford ochre to make the shade of them wanted. More or less of the ochre added to the base will make an affinity of shades of that order.

Dove color. White lead for base; add ultramarine blue, Indian red and lampblack.

Dregs of wine. Dark Tuscan red for base; add white lead and a trifle of zinc white.

Ecru. White lead for base; add French ochre, burnt sienna, lampblack. The tint has a wide range of tones.

Electric blue. Ultramarine blue for base; add white lead and raw sienna.

Emerald. Paris green as it is, or better an imitation of it, in very light chrome green.

Egyptian green. White lead for base; add raw umber, lemon chrome yellow, Prussian blue to suit.

Fawn. White lead for base; add medium chrome yellow, Venetian red, burnt umber.

Flesh color. White lead for base; add medium chrome yellow, French ochre and Venetian red.

Fog blue. Burnt sienna for base; add Prussian blue, then lighten up with white lead to suit.

French blue. Ultramarine blue for base; lighten up with zinc white to shade wanted and tinge it slightly with light chrome green.

French gray. White lead for base; add ivory black with a faint tinge of ultramarine blue and madder lake or carmine.

French red. Indian red for base; add English pale vermillion to brighten it, then glaze with madder red or carmine.

Gazelle. French ochre for base; add Tuscan red,

Venetian red, lampblack, lighten up to suit with white lead.

Geranium. Vermillion red for base; add Indian red and a trifle of ivory black.

Gobelin blue. Ivory black for base; add white lead, Prussian blue and a trifle of medium chrome green.

Gold. White lead for base; add medium chrome yellow, some good bright French ochre and a very little English vermillion or vermillion red of good tone.

Golden brown. French ochre for base; add orange chrome yellow, lampblack . Lighten up with white lead to suit.

Grass green. Extra light chrome green just as it comes from the can or lighten up the light chrome green with canary chrome yellow.

Gray green. White lead for base; add ultramarine blue, lemon chrome yellow, lampblack.

Granite blue. White lead for base; lampblack, Prussian blue.

Green stone. White lead for base; add medium chrome green, raw umber, and French ochre.

Gray stone. White lead for base; add lampblack, Prussian blue, Venetian red.

Gray drabs—all shades of them. White lead for base; add lamp or drop black with a little burnt umber in various proportions according to the depth and shade of drab wanted.

Grays, all shades. White lead for base; lampblack in various proportions to suit shade wanted.

Hay color. White lead for base; add orange chrome yellow, light chrome green, Indian red.

Heliotrope. Zinc white for base; add bright Venetian red and ultramarine blue.

Indian pink. White lead for base; add Indian red.

Indian brown. Indian red for base; add lampblack, French ochre.

Iron gray. Lampblack for base; add white lead and a trifle of orange chrome yellow.

Ivy green. French ochre for base; add lampblack, Prussian blue.

Jasper. Lampblack for base; add medium chrome yellow, light Indian red.

Jonquil. White lead for base; add medium chrome yellow to which should be added a tinge of red with English pale vermillion.

Lavender. White lead for base; add ivory black, ultramarine blue, tinge with carmine or madder lake.

Leaf buds. White lead for base; add orange chrome yellow, light chrome green.

Lead color. See *Grays.*

Leather. French ochre for base; add burnt umber. If a warm tone is wanted add Venetian red.

Lemon. Use the chrome yellow of that name.

Lilac. White lead for base; add dark Indian red to suit.

London smoke. Yellow ochre for base; add ultramarine blue, lampblack, lighten up to suit with white lead.

Magenta. Vermillion for base; add carmine or madder lake with a tinge of ultramarine blue.

Manila or *deck paint.* White lead for base; add French ochre, medium chrome yellow.

Marigold. Medium chrome yellow for base; add white lead, orange chrome yellow.

Maroon. Carmine or madder lake for base; add ivory black and a bit of orange chrome yellow. A cheaper way: Tuscan red for base; add orange chrome yellow and some ivory black.

Mastic. White lead base; add French ochre, Venetian red and a trifle of lampblack.

Mexican red. Bright Venetian red for base; add red lead.

Mignonette. Medium chrome green for base; add Prussian blue, medium chrome yellow, lampblack.

Mascot. Lampblack for base; add Prussian blue to suit.

Mauve. Ultramarine blue for base; add zinc white, tint with madder lake.

Methyl blue. Ultramarine for base; add medium chrome green and a tinge of red.

Moorish red. Vermillion red for base; add madder lake.

Mouse color. White lead for base; add lampblack, a tinge of Venetian red and burnt umber.

Moss rose. Lemon chrome yellow for base; add medium chrome green; lighten up with white lead to suit.

Mountain blue. White lead for base; add madder lake, ultramarine blue.

Navy blue. Ultramarine blue for base; add ivory black.

Neutral blue. Prussian blue for base; add raw umber and lighten up with white lead to suit.

Nile blue. White lead for base; add Prussian blue with a trifle of medium chrome green.

Normandy blue. Medium chrome green; ultramarine blue, a trifle of white lead.

Nut brown. Lampblack for base; add Venetian red, medium chrome yellow, French ochre.

Oak color. Light and dark shades of it. White lead for base; add French ochre and a small quantity of Venetian red; vary quantities to suit light or dark shades.

Old gold. White lead for base; add medium chrome yellow, French ochre and a little burnt umber.

Olive. Lemon chrome yellow for base; add about equal parts of Prussian blue and lampblack. Some shades of olive can be made by substituting French ochre for lemon chrome yellow, when, of course, the tone will not be so bright. A trifle of lemon chrome added to the ochre will improve it and still make another variety of it.

Olive brown. Raw umber for base; add lemon chrome yellow. Vary the quantity to suit depth of tone wanted.

Opal gray. White lead for base; add burnt sienna, ultramarine blue.

Oriental blue. White lead for base; add Prussian blue, lemon chrome yellow.

Oriental green. Raw umber for base; add lemon chrome yellow to suit.

Orange. Orange chrome yellow as it comes from the can.

Orange brown. Orange chrome yellow for base; add raw sienna, a trifle of burnt umber.

Peach blossom. White lead for base; add pale Indian red to suit. A tinge of madder lake will enrich it. ʹ

Pearl. White lead for base; add ivory black and a trifle of ultramarine blue and carmine lake. This is a very light shade just off the white. It must not be overdone.

Pca green. White lead for base; add medium chrome green to suit.

Peacock blue. Ultramarine blue for base: add extra light chrome green and zinc white to suit.

Persian orange. Orange chrome yellow for base; add French ochre, white lead.

Pistache. Ivory black for base; add French ochre, medium chrome green.

Pink. Zinc white for base; add madder lake or carmine or the crimson shades of vermillion.

Pompeian red. Vermillion red base; add orange chrome yellow, a bit of ivory black.

Pompeian blue. White lead base; add ultramarine blue, vermillion red, French ochre.

Plum color. White lead for base; add Indian red, ultramarine blue.

Portland stone. French ochre for base; add raw umber; lighten up to suit with white lead.

Primrose. White lead for base; add lemon or medium yellow chrome, according to the shade wanted.

Purple. White lead for base; add dark Indian red and a trifle of light Indian red to suit.

Purple brown. Dark Indian red for base; add ultramarine blue, a trifle of lampblack and white lead to lighten up to suit.

Quaker green. White lead for base; add French ochre, lampblack and burnt sienna.

Roan. Lampblack for base; add Venetian red, Prussian blue; lighten it up to suit with white lead.

Robin's egg blue. White lead for base; add ultramarine until the shade is a deep blue, then add some pale chrome green to suit tone desired of it.

Russet. White lead for base; add orange chrome yellow, a trifle of lampblack and Prussian blue.

Russian gray. White lead for base; add ultramarine blue, pale Indian red and lampblack.

Sage green. White lead for base; add medium chrome green until the tint is nearly but not quite a pea green, then add lampblack to tinge it the sage tint.

Salmon. White lead for base; add French ochre,

burnt sienna, with a trifle of English vermillion or a good vermillion red.

Sapphire blue. Zinc white for base; add ultramarine blue.

Sap green. White lead for base; add medium chrome yellow, lampblack.

Sea green. White lead base; add Prussian blue, raw sienna.

Seal brown. Burnt umber for base; add good French ochre and a trifle of white lead.

Scarlet. Pale English vermillion or any of the scarlet toned vermillion reds.

Shrimp pink. White lead base; add Venetian red, burnt sienna and a trifle of vermillion.

Sky blue. White lead for base; add Prussian blue to suit.

Slate. White lead for base; add raw umber, ultramarine blue, lampblack.

Spruce yellow. French ochre for base; add Venetian red; lighten up with white lead to suit.

Snuff color. French ochre for base; add burnt umber and a bit of Venetian red.

Straw color. Medium chrome yellow for base; add French ochre; a bit of Venetian red; lighten up with white lead.

Stone color and *yellow drabs.* White lead for base; add French ochre; tinge up with medium chrome yellow and burnt umber. By varying quantities all shades of yellow drab can be made.

Tan. White lead for base; add burnt sienna and a trifle of lampblack.

Tally-Ho. White lead for base; add French ochre, Venetian red, dark chrome green with a bit of ivory black.

Terra-cotta. French ochre for base; add Venetian red and white lead. Some shades of it require the addition of Indian red. If some rich shades are wanted use orange chrome yellow in place of French ochre; add Venetian red and a trifle of burnt umber to suit.

Turquoise blue. White lead for base, or better zinc white and cobalt blue; Paris green or pale chrome green.

Vienna brown. Burnt umber for base; add Venetian red, French ochre, and lighten with white lead to suit.

Violet. White lead for base; add pale Indian red, a trifle of dark Indian red.

Willow green. White lead for base; add sufficient medium chrome yellow to make a pretty deep shade; then add a small quantity of raw umber and ivory black.

Wine color. English vermillion or scarlet toned vermillion red for base; add madder lake or carmine, ultramarine blue, lampblack.

Another way: Dark Tuscan red of good quality to which add a trifle of ivory black.

Water green. White lead for base; add raw sienna, dark chrome green.

Yellow bronze. Lemon or medium chrome yellow for base; add French ochre and a trifle of burnt umber.

QUESTIONS ON COLOR MIXING.

94. What is said about color mixing in general?
95. *a.* What is a base for a tint?
    b. How must the base be prepared?
    c. How are the tinting colors prepared?
    d. How must one proceed to mix the tinting colors with the base?
    e. What advice is given in this section?
96. How are tints in water colors made?
97. Pupils should familiarize themselves with the tints given and refer to them when they want to know how to make them.

COLOR TESTING.

98. Under the heading of "Colors," paragraph 71 *b,* the reader will have noticed probably what has been said concerning the chief role played by barytes in the paint world. He may have noticed also what is said in paragraphs 5 to 7 inclusive, under the heading of "Adulterations in relation to the *scale test* as indicating the relative strength of coloring matter contained in pigments." As a fairly full explanation of the test is there given, it may be well to read that portion over again as it is not necessary to repeat it here, and it plays a very important part in testing the value of many pigments.

There is no better test for nearly all manufactured colors having a recognized chemical formula and besides it nearly always indicates (indirectly) the quality of tone in the tints made while making the test; but after all this test does not show everything connected with the testing of colors nor is it applicable to a large number of valuable pigments, therefore the subject matter of this heading will be considered from the several points which have a bearing upon enhancing or depreciating the value of pigments.

The following are points which are recognized universally as having something to do in determining values; some for one class of pigments, others for another class and some are applicable to all:

1. Purity of material.
2. Purity of tone, brilliancy, richness.
3. Fineness of grinding and preparation.
4. Spreading capacity.
5. Its body; applying only to opaque or semi-opaque pigments.
6. Its staining power or tinting strength with white lead.
7. The quality of purity of their tones with whites.
8. If a paste color the consistency of the paste.

PURITY OF PIGMENTS.

99. All chemically prepared pigments which have a well known formula which is recognized among color men as such, have that for a standard of purity. White

lead, zinc white, Prussian blue, the chrome yellows, greens, etc., belong to this class. The word pure here means only this: that they contain no adulteration, but it does not take into consideration, the quality of tone, fineness of grinding, brilliancy, etc., each of which is an important factor in determining the relative value of pigments. The scale test is very valuable in determining the strength of this class of pigments and usually this is the most important point in the judging of values. A color may be very pure and still be very poor, but the above statement applies with more force to the earth or natural pigments than to those that are chemically prepared. Yet it is sometimes necessary to have recourse to all the points named in the preceeding paragraph to fully determine the true value of a pigment.

PURITY OF TONE OF PIGMENTS.

100. This test is applicable to all classes of pigments and the chemically prepared colors should have it applied as well as the others for a Prussian blue or a chrome yellow may have such a poor tone as to be valueless and still be chemically pure and for the natural or earth pigments this test is of the greatest importance and leads all others. In paragraphs 3 to 8, good advice is given in relation to chosing some good standard colors to judge others by. The reader will do well to keep a supply of all such as he is likely to need in testing other colors by and comparing their tones. Brilliancy is as desirable as purity of tone and usually the two are

inseparable for it is inconceivable of a pigment of a good pure tone that it has not brilliancy also, so that there is no need of a separate test for it. Richness is also an inherent quality belonging to purity of tone and it must be inferred as it cannot be separated from it.

FINENESS OF GRINDING.

There are several methods of determining the fineness of grinding of pigments. The fineness of grinding of any color but those of crystallic formation is very important as it gives them more spreading power, makes them more absorbent of linseed oil, which in outside painting means more durability and as finely ground pigments can be spread more smoothly, it also means additional beauty. For the earth colors such as the siennas, the umbers, Vandyke brown, etc., especially if used in their self tones, as they are in graining or in glazing—fineness of grinding is of much importance as it will prevent speckiness, a fault for which the reputation of a carriage painter or grainer using them may suffer much on account of the poor quality of work turned out with such. The following methods may be used in judging the fineness of grinding:

The simplest and easiest of all is to place a little bit of the pigment upon a piece of clean glass and to reduce it with oil until very thin, then to spread it out upon the glass very thinly, then looking through the glass holding it so the light will go through it, it will show any speck or imperfect grinding. Another way is to thin out the pigment with turpentine and paint it out thinly upon the glass and doing the same with some of the standard which is known to be very finely ground and which is thinned with the same quantity of thinner, and which should be painted alongside of the color being tested. When dry the painting will clearly indicate the relative fineness of the two samples.

The following method is probably as good as any or better rather than any, but it requires a little more time to make the test: Weigh out equal parts each of the colors being tested, after having first taken the precaution to place each upon a piece of blotting paper to remove the oil as one might have more than the other, then after weighing place each sample in a graduated test tube, putting in each tube the same quantity of turpentine to thin them, after which shake them up thoroughly. It will be easy to see which precipitates first, as the heaviest will go to the bottom first always and the finest or lightest will be held in suspension the longest. But even this test would become worthless for colors which have been adulterated with a very fine atomed adulterant or for white lead which contains sublimed lead as that is much finer than Dutch process lead. In either case, however, if the scale test has been used, it will have given away the pigment at fault and one can give a pretty good guess as to what the adulterant may be.

SPREADING POWER OR COVERING POWER.

102. The spreading power or covering power of pigments are not controvertible terms and they are not identical, as between zinc and white lead for instance, and one of great opacity may not have much spreading power. But in pigments which are being tested with another of the same name and composition to all intents and purposes, and for comparison it may be assumed that the two are identical and that spreading is due to the opacity of the pigment, and that they should go hand in hand in helping to determine the value of the samples tested. It would not be fair nor conclusive to apply this test to any of the transparent or even the semitransparent pigments, but is applicable only to white lead and other opaque pigments.

THE BODY.

103. The body of a pigment lays in its opaqueness or its capacity to hide from view, the coats of paint over which their covering properties are being tested. It is nearly related to its spreading so that what was said in the preceding paragraph applies to that also. A pigment having a better body than that of another of the same name, can be spread further, to cover as well as one lacking in body, each hiding the surface over which they are applied as well in each case. For instance if to cover over a certain number of square feet of surface painted black requires one pound of white lead to do as well as one and a half pound of white

lead of another sample did, then the first is worth 50% the most and has 50% more body and the spread helps to determine its body.

TINTING OR STAINING STRENGTH.

104. This is determined by the "scale test" which has been explained under the heading "Adulteration" and the reader is referred to paragraphs 5 to 7. This test is an infallible one in detecting the lack of coloring matter in any pigment.

THE PERMANENCY OF PIGMENTS.

105. This is a very important test but it takes a very long time to make it. There is nothing else to do but to wait for results after having painted over two or more pigments being tested for permanency upon a board side by side, the board being the same and the ground coats being alike, and the exposure the same for each. Each pigment has a permanency of its own and therefore the term is only a relative one. White lead should not be tested by the permanency belonging to lampblack for instance, but by that of samples of other white lead and time will decide which of two or more white leads is the most permanent. Under the heading of "Colors" is given their peculiarities and in the leading ones especially a list of conditions under which they should not be applied and which would shorten their permanency.

QUESTIONS TO COLOR TESTING.

98. What is said generally of color testing?

99. What about the purity of pigments?

100. What can you say regarding the purity of tone?

101. How can the fineness of grinding be detected? test is an infallible one in detecting the lack of colorering power of pigments and to what class of pigments is the test applicable?

103. What is the body of a pigment?

104. How do you test for the amount of coloring matter contained in pigments?

105. How is the permanency of pigments tested?

ESTIMATING.

106. There is nothing pertaining to the business of painting or decorating which is more puzzling to the beginner and if you please, to many veterans than "how to proceed in making an estimate upon an architect's specifications or even for the repainting of an old building where all the work is in full sight, just as it is." It requires a minute understanding of everything to be done and of the time that will be required to do it, besides making a liberal allowance for time lost or wasted on account of. delays occasioned by the thousand and one causes which the experienced contractor alone knows of.

Some men go to work with paper and pencil, reduce every board, molding, etc., into inches and square feet, counting parts requiring more time than plain square surfaces 50, 100 or even 200 per cent more than that for the extra trouble. Others again will simply average up the number of plain, molded and transomed doors and their casings; so many windows of various sizes and their casings; base boards, wainscoting, etc. For the outside they square it up adding a fifth for underside of weather boarding, etc. But it seems to be an intuition with some men to know just how much to charge for each job by just "looking it over," without ever so much as taking the pencil out of the vest pocket. Nor will their figures usually vary as much as those of the men who toil and sweat over long rows of additions made necessary by the carefully itemized account they have made of every board in the house.

How it is possible for people who figure a job so closely to vary so much in their estimates is a puzzle for the Philadelphia lawyer to solve. The opening up of the bids is such a joke that one may look out for any kind of a surprise in the figures named for doing the painting. The results would indicate that reckless guessing was more prevalent than sober judgment in naming the figures as these show variations of from 10 to 150 per cent sometimes. Variations of from 10 to 20% are to be expected—but the others?

Common sense and a thorough knowledge of the "How to bid" should be the motto of the contractor. They generally go hand in hand, but this knowledge is gained only by cool, careful comparisons made as to what former jobs of about the same amount of surface have cost and in time a man is able to name a price off hands for nearly all kinds and sizes of ordinary buildings by making a proper allowance for the safe side. But the novice who has no such retrospective experience to lean upon and also the men who do not accumulate experience from past transactions, need to square up everything to be able to bid intelligently.

The National Master Painters' Association some years ago adopted a system of measurement which, while it was not to be binding upon its members, was to be used as a guide in the making of estimates, but more especially to establish a price for all kinds of painting which had to be established by law, where the settlement for the painting of a job had to be done through litigation, but it did not work. The association had it made up into pamphlet form and placed it on sale with its secretary and while it was well ad vertised it took several years before it was sold and given away together. No new edition will ever be made of it.

The Pittsburg local association of Master Painters recognizing the need of a guide in making estimates adopted a price list which is given below. This list is a fairer one than that adopted by the national association, but it is not binding upon the members either. It serves merely as a guide and members can cut it in two if they like.

THE PITTSBURG PRICE LIST.

SQUARE MEASURE.

107. Plain weatherboarding, close fencing, ledge doors, partitions, paling fences, etc., all common colors, viz: White, light yellow, slate, pearl, light buff, light drab or cream color, per yard for each coat....... 8c

Each coat of varnish, per yard................10c

PANEL WORK.

Flush panel work, panel doors, recesses, etc.

All the above colors, for each coat, per yard......10c

The same in two colors, per yard...............12c

The same in three colors, per yard..............14c

Striping after other work is finished, lineal meas
    ure, per foot.......................... 1c

For expensive or unused colors, additional, per yard 1c

For each coat of varnish, per yard..............12c

For each coat of shellac, per yard..............12c

BRICK WORK.

First coat, per yard..........................15c

Second coat, per yard.........................12c

Third coat, per yard..........................10c

Pencilling, per yard..........................15c

Mastic on cement, per yard....................20c

Addition coats on that same as brick.

INSIDE WALL PAINTING.

First coat, per yard..........................12c

Second coat, per yard........................10c

Third coat, per yard........................ 8c

Ordinary puttying, charge price of first coat for the several kinds of work. Puttying longitudinal joints in ceilings, siding, floors, etc., to be charged two to four times the price of first coat for the several kinds of work at the discretion of the measurer.

Each coat of surfacing, per yard...............10c

Each coat of stain, per yard.................. 8c

Each coat of varnish, per yard..... ....12c

Pillasters, architraves, frames, jambs, base moldings, etc.

	Per ft.	Varnish
Girth 1 to 4 inch, each coat,........	½c	¾c
Girth 4 to 6 inch, each coat.	¾c	1c
Girth 6 to 8 inch, each coat. .	1c	1¼c
Girth 8 to 10 inch, each coat........	1¼c	1½c
Girth 10 to 12 inch, each coat........	1½c	1¾c
Girth 12 to 14 inch, each coat........	1¾c	2c
Girth 14 to 16 inch, each coat. .	2c	2¼c
Girth 16 to 18 inch, each coat........	2¼c	2½c
Girth 18 to 20 inch, each coat........	2½c	2¾c
Girth 20 to 22 inch, each coat........	2¾c	3c
Girth 22 to 24 inch, each coat.	3c	3¼c

Larger dimensions taken in square measure.

Column mantle as above.

Panel jambs, door casings, etc., to be measured by the above rule.

Plain rosettes—add one foot to the length.

Carved rosettes—add two feet to the length.

Other carved or ornamental work at the discretion of the measurer.

MODE OF MEASURING.

Begin at wall, press line in all quirks to bead at edge of jamb casing for girth. For jambs, take inner sash rabbet to corner bead, double the height and measure between jambs for length.

STRING BOARDS, ETC.

Plain, each coat, per foot.............. 2c
Bracketed, each coat, per foot........... 3c
Carved, each coat, per foot...................4c
Staff heads, each coat, per foot............... ½c
Edge of shelves, each coat, per foot...... . ¼c

CORNICES AND COLUMNS, PLAIN.

Girth 1 to 2 feet, each coat.....................3c
Girth 2 to 3 feet, each coat............... 4c
Girth 3 to 4 feet, each coat............. 5c
Girth 4 to 5 feet, each coat.............. 6c

Plain caps on columns—add to length two feet.

Ornamental caps on columns—add to length four feet.

CORNICES WITH BRACKETS.

Girth 1 to 2 feet, each coat..................... 4c
Girth 2 to 3 feet, each coat..................... 6c
Girth 3 to 4 feet, each coat..................... 8c
Girth 4 to 5 feet, each coat.....................10c
Girth 5 to 6 feet, each coat.....................12c
    Larger dimensions in proportion.
    Dential cornices same price as brackets.

MODE OF MEASURING.

For girth begin at the top, press line into all quirks and over each member at bottom and to the length add one-half the medium girth of the brackets multiplied by their number.

PRIMING OR TRACING AND GLAZING SASH.

	Priming or Tracing	New Glazing	Old Glazing & Glass S.S.
8 to 10x12 to 14.	1¼c	5c	$0.20 S. S.
8 to 12x16 or 18.	1½c	8c	35 S. S.
8 to 14x24	2c	10c	40 S. S.
8 to 18x24	3c	14c	50 S. S.
8 to 24x30	5c	18c	1.00 D.S.
8 to 26x36	6c	20c	1.30 D.S.
8 to 30x36	8c	25c	1.65 D.S.
8 to 36x40	10c	30c	

8 to 40x44	12c	35c
8 to 40x50	14c	40c
8 to 40x56	16c	50c
8 to 50x60	18c	60c
8 to 50x70	20c	75c

These prices do not apply when called out to glaze one or two lights.

For back puttying add one-quarter and for bedding add one-half to above rates.

In new glazing cost of glass is not included. All breakage at the risk of owners, if glass is furnished by them. To all bills of glass furnished by the trade, 20 per cent will be charged additional.

PLATE GLASS.

Sizes same as table above at same prices. Sizes above up to 90 square feet 5 per cent on net cost delivered; 90 to 108 square feet 8 per cent; 108 square feet and upward 10 per cent.

Removing old glass same as above. The owner to pay cost of taking up large glass above first floor.

Unless otherwise provided for the glazier puts glass in at his own risk of breakage, but cutting will be at owner's risk.

SANDING.

First coat of sand equal to two coats of paint in addition to paint coat.

Second coat of sand equal to three coats of paint in addition to paint coat.

GRAINING—SQUARE MEASURE.

Plain Oak, per yard $0.40
Plain Walnut or Ash, per yard................ .70
Plain Satinwood or Maple, per yard........... .70
Plain Mahogany or Cherry, per yard........... ./0
Shaded Oak, per yard...................... 1.00
Pencilled Oak or Ash, per yard.............. 1.00
Pencilled Chestnut or Cherry, per yard........ 1.00
Pencilled Walnut, per yard.................. 1.00
Rosewood, per yard 1.00
Oak or Walnut root, per yard............... 1.50

LINEAL MEASURE.

	Graining	Varnishing
Girth 1 to 4 inches, per foot.	3c	¾c
Girth 4 to 6 inches, per foot.	4c	1c
Girth 6 to 8 inches, per foot.	5c	1¼c
Girth 8 to 10 inches, per foot.	6c	1½c
Girth 10 to 12 inches, per foot.	7c	1¾c
Girth 12 to 14 inches, per foot.	8c	2c
Girth 14 to 16 inches, per foot.	9c	2¼c
Girth 16 to 18 inches, per foot.	10c	2½c

Other members in proportion.

Graining edges of shelves, per foot, 1½c.

Graining sashes double the price of plain painting.

MARBLING—SQUARE MEASURE.

White Marble, per yard....................$0.75
Other kinds, per yard....................... 1.00
Varnishing, each coat, per yard.............. .12

LINEAL MEASURE.

All members from	Marbl- ing	Varnish- ing
1 to 8 inch girth, per foot....	8c	1c
8 to 10 inch girth, per foot....	12c	1¼c
10 to 12 inch girth, per foot....	16c	1½c
12 to 14 inch girth, per foot....	18c	2c
14 to 16 inch girth, per foot....	20c	2¼c
Larger members in proportion.		

CLEANING AND CALCIMINING.

Ceiling and walls, per yard............. 16c
Plain cornices, 1 to 2 feet girth, per foot. 2c
Plain cornices, 2 to 4 feet girth, per foot. 3c
Add to the above for each color if more than one,
   per foot 1c

QUESTIONS ON ESTIMATING.

106. What is said in a general way of estimating?

107. Tables of reference regarding prices of paint-ing to be referred to when needed.

EXTERIOR PAINTING.

108. The treatment of painting exposed to the tender mercy of the elements such as exterior painting has to go through naturally implies a good understanding of what these conditions are and also a good knowledge of how to adapt the material used in doing it so as to best meet them. Therefore it will be best to first review what these are and this will enable us to be better prepared to devise a suitable remedy, so that whilst decay must in time destroy it, at least that time may be longer delayed.

CAUSES OF DECAY.

109. Nature seems very busily engaged in trying to reduce all compound substances into its simpler constituent elements or in recombining them with others for which they each have a greater affinity and this causes a constant changing or terminating of one partnership and the forming of others. If the reader will remember it was said of red lead and of orange mineral —one being the bi-oxide and the other the ter-oxide of lead that each being overloaded with oxygen had a natural tendency to return to their simpler forms of a monoxide or litharge; also that English or quicksilver vermilion had a tendency to return to its more natural form of a black sulphuret of mercury. These are but samples of what is constantly taking place in nature. The constant changes caused by linseed oil or any of

the other fixed oils coming in contact with the oxygen in the atmosphere will no doubt have been noticed by any one who has taken the pains of so doing. Yet while all this is in plain sight how few who have really thought anything about it or lost a single moment in making any inquiries as to the *why* and *how* these changes occur. The phenomena of oil drying is wonderful and full of interest, yet produces but little interest or inquiry about it from the great army of those who daily use it and the *why* and *wherefore* never bothers them. But there are many who are interested and it is due to these, that experimenting has been carried on and that some progress has been made in the knowledge which the world at large has of it. The ignorance regarding the drying of linseed oil is such as to hardly be thought possible and like as not half of the painters when asked as to the *how* it occurs will likely as not tell you that it evaporates itself dry. Such an explanation of it was once given in a trade paper by a man whose name usully carries some weight when he writes about the technical application of paint which he does know—as he is an expert. When such a man can give such a reason as that, it is not to be expected that the others not nearly as well posted should be so ignorant of it.

The various elements composing the air with which exterior painting is in constant companionship are all invisible, being subtle gases which while when joined together in the proper proportions are endued with life giving properties are deadly to all life when separated and alone.

Oxygen, one of the main constituents of our atmospheric air, is one of the principal component parts of an innumerable number of substances and it combines readily with most other elements to form compound substances. Its action upon the drying of the fixed oils is very beneficial—up to a certain point, but after that point has been reached, then it becomes harmful, as after that point has been past the further action of oxygen upon it causes decay. This action is promoted and also retarded by many accessory agents and greatly accelerated by the presence of another constituent of our atmosphere:

Hydrogen which causes the decay of exterior painting by accelerating the action of oxygen and also by that of its own beside. But moisture alone without air will not cause decay readily nor will it act even in the open air without the aid of heat. We have already seen what its action is when present either in the paint itself or in the surface over which paint is applied; the same being fully explained in paragraph 13 *a* to *e,* which see.

Sunlight and heat may as well be bracketed together as they are usually inseparable. Yet each has its own particular function as destructive agents of painting. Sunlight causes many pigments to fade away but the heat which its rays also produce causes it to act much more quickly, so that sunlight is much less destructive to color in the winter than it is in the summer. *Light* and *heat* and *moisture* are the accessories which help hydrogen accomplish its work of destruction and after *oxygen* are the principal factor which cause paint to decay.

These same agents are also very active in causing the destruction of the fibres of the woods and for this reason it is mainly—after that of beautifying—that the painting of exterior surfaces is used to protect them. "How" it does this will have to be understood in order to apply the remedy more effectually.

It would require a larger volume than this devoted entirely to the subject to enter minutely into a relation of the details which enter into what constitutes the bene ficial action of the elements or their destructiveness of painting material and "how" this beneficial and destructive agency occurs. As much of it could not be understood by the reader who is not familiar with chemistry mere generalities will be all that can be indulged in.

PAINT AS A PROTECTION TO SURFACES.

111. Not only wood fibres but, metals, stone, brick in fact everything movable or immovable is subject to the action of some of the gases which compose atmospheric air and to others also which are disseminated here and there in it. The metal "iron" which is chiefly used in large architectural structures, bridges, ships, etc., eagerly combines with oxygen to form *oxyde of iron or rust.* Limestone, marbles, and other form of

lime are very hungry for sulphurous acid fumes of which moisture carries quantities in solution in certain localities and which combines with them to quicken them on to dissolution. The whole list of stone, including sand or even granite are more or less quickly acted upon by some form of the elements or some gases carried by the air.

As the beauty of uncut or cut stone depends upon its natural setting and dress it will not be necessary to say anything further concerning them as they are seldom painted as it destroys their natural beauty and charm. But *iron* which next to woods is fast becoming the chief material used in house construction and which probably in the near future will become the principal, needs to be well protected in order to prevent as much as possible the injurious action of the elements upon it. Having no beauty of its own to plead, it has to depend upon its protector in a large degree for any artificial beauty which that can impart to it, besides the protection that it gives it.

As the principles upon which paint benefits exposed surfaces generally speaking are the same for all kinds of surfaces let them be iron, steel, wood, brick, stone or cement it will be unnecessary to review them separately as they apply sufficiently near to each of them.

Iron, brick, stone or wood are all porous, some so much so that these pores can be detected by the naked eye. Under a powerful microscope their surfaces appear as a huge sponge. It is through these openings that *moisture,* that greatest enemy of them all—for it is mainly by its aid that other destructive agencies are able to do their worst—enters and with it all the others too. It stands to reason that in order to be able to afford protection to this valuable structural material that these pores must be closed up effectually in order to keep out moisture and the other destructive elements.

This is the protection that is given them by the use of paint properly mixed and applied. The paint itself must be finely ground in order to penetrate with its vehicle into the pores of the surfaces over which it is applied; therefore the practice of many to use dry pigments, such as ochre, Venetian red, etc., is a pernicious one and must be unequivocally condemned. Many painters act upon the theory that anything is good enough for priming; instead of which they should adopt the motto that: *Nothing is any too good* for it nor too finely ground. If any unground pigments must be used upon a job, let its place be upon the finishing coat but *never upon the first.* It is the very poorest, foolishest of economy to use such for the purpose of priming or for any other for that matter as dry pigments soaked up in oil and unground is unfit for any kind of painting. So that while it is said that it is better to use such on the finishing coat rather than the first is to be taken in the sense that such would be less harmful there than in the priming coat, but not as an indorsement of them for that or any other use in painting.

The action of the vehicle is beneficial in two ways,

if it be a proper one well fitted for the purpose. It binds the particles of the pigment together and holds them in its embrace and it penetrates even to where the finest ground pigment could not enter. It must not however be so penetrating that it will filter through out of sight and leave the pigment entirely. Besides it must be able to solidify without any shrinkage of its bulk as that would imply some room left open for the passage of air. It must also be water or moisture proof and that the latter cannot dissolve it nor wash it out. So the reader must see at once that the vehicle even more than the pigment has a mission to fulfil that requires a number of good qualities to fit it for the purpose.

112. Of all the many liquid substances which can be used for the binding of paint or of dry substances which when dissolved in water are used as vehicles for pigments (as gum arabic or glue) none fulfil the conditions enumerated in the preceding paragraph as well as *"Linseed oil,"* the king of the fixed oil and what is of enormous importance—as cheaply as that will. It is the painter's best friend.

Linseed oil in common with all other fixed oils possesses the quality of absorbing some oxygen from the atmosphere and by that subtle gas aid, to solidify after having formed a union with it into a waterproof rubber-like gum which is elastic and which lends itself to the contraction and expansion of the material over which paint has been applied so that while solidificatior takes place, it is not caused by evaporation out rather by absorption without loss of bulk, but rather with a slight increase of it as it actually does so when it combines with oxygen some 8 per cent, thus swelling up tightly into every nook in the side of the pores through which it has become absorbed. So that it not only *binds* but *fills* at the one operation.

The life of linseed oil is prolonged or shortened by the action that is produced upon it by the pigments with which it has been mixed.

Some pigments are neutral; that is, neither acid nor alkaline and such have no effect whatever upon it other than the separation it produces between its atoms. Others again are active in that many of them are alkaline, in such a case the alkali will turn the linseed oil into a soap which when dry may be or may not be soluble and which according as it is one or the other may or may not be beneficial to its longevity.

113. This needs more explanations. Red lead for instance is an active pigment, turning the oil into an oxy-linoleate lead soap, when dry it becomes *insoluble*. This soap becomes the best of cements to join two pieces of glass together and makers of aquariums use it for that purpose. This is certainly a very good proof of its insolubility. Another proof is the use made of it not only as first but as finishing coats for iron ships below the floating line where it remains continually sub merged; it stands that where the neutral pigments would surely fail.

As a primer for iron it stands head and shoulders above any other pigment. It lends itself to all the contractions and expansions of that metal without cracking or checking. So the reader will see that the proper kind of an emulsion is not harmful but the reverse.

An emulsated oil, be that a good one or a bad one, will not be subjected to any other changes but dries out its water of emulsion by evaporation leaving the linoleate soap to dry in its accustomed manner. But it is not iron and steel alone which are benefited by the red lead priming, nearly all other metals needing paint as a protection or as an embellishment are greatly benefited by having been primed with it—when afterward as its color is objectionable for many purposes they may receive over that any other color wanted. Galvanized iron either on plain surfaces or·on cornices which have been primed with the ordinary mixtures of paint used for the rest of the buildings usually scales off in a short while, but let it be painted with red lead for first coat and there is no more danger of paint scaling afterward than upon any other part of the house.

114. For wooden buildings there is nothing better than a coating of white lead or one of half white lead and half French ochre which has been finely ground. Both should be greatly thinned with linseed oil, just enough pigment being added to that to fairly show when applied to the building.

115. For brick, stone and other porous mineral substances finely ground English Venetian red is excellent

as a primer but if the finishing coats are intended to be painted white or in light tints white lead and French ochre half and a half—both being also finely ground in oil will be better. If the brick or stone is soft the color should be as thin as for wood but if the brick or stone is very hard and non-absorbent the color should be mixed with more pigment and well rubbed out to keep it from running.

Cement which has recently become in almost general use in all kinds of house construction and which from its being so well adapted to such use is very likely to grow into becoming the leading material in the near future seems to require a long time to ripen and undergo certain changes during which time it exudes certain salts which have the property of staining through paint, thus greatly damaging not only its appearance but in disintegrating the coating also. Heretofore it has not been considered safe to apply any paint to it until all the deleterious matter it contains had come out or was washed away. Many painters were afraid to undertake the painting until a cement building had been exposed a couple of years at least. Thanks however to Mr. Charles MacNichol of Washington, D. C., who very disinterestedly made known to his brother master painters in convention assembled the results of his experiments which enables him to paint over cement as soon as he would over any other kind of material. It is very simple and consists in dissolving equal parts by weight of sulphate of zinc and water and of painting the surface of the cement with the solution applying it as any other paint. From all reports of those who have tried it it seems to do the work.

THE PAINTING OF EXTERIOR SURFACES.

116. *a.* Considerable space has been devoted to noting the various conditions and building material over which exterior painting is usually done; each kind of material we have seen, having its own peculiarities, in the form of its atoms, their sizes, closeness of adherence together, etc., requiring in some instance a difference in the treatment they should receive in the "priming" as it is the coating which unites the paint to the surfaces any number of subsequent coats may be put on. The importance of its being well done in a workmanlike manner warrants all the space that has been taken up in the telling of it, if it will induce the reader to do it well—and more. As to the manner of the application of the paint, it is supposed that the reader is sufficiently acquainted with the "Modus operandi" of the handling of the brush to need any lengthy advice as to the *how* it should be done; nor would it be very easy to show him how it is done "under printer's type"; but a few words will be said in the following sections regarding priming and the application of the second and third coats of paint upon various surfaces.

PRIMING.

b. *For woods,* use white lead or white lead and

French ochre, both to be finely ground in oil and heavily thinned with raw linseed oil. In cold weather if the oil is at all viscid, it will be well to add as much as ¼ of turpentine or benzine to it as it will be necessary to render it more limpid. It should also have in addition a tablespoonful of some good liquid drier to the quart as otherwise it might take too long to start it to drying and it might become fatty and sticky. No such advice as to adding either is given for priming in warm weather as then neither volatile oil nor drier is needed. Then oil is very fluid and will penetrate into the pores but when cold renders it viscid, it becomes sluggish and is not sufficiently fluid to penetrate as it should. Priming thus treated will penetrate where otherwise it could not and really more linseed oil thus thinned out can be crushed into the pores than would be possible when it is in a viscid condition without the addition.

It is superfluous to say that the surface of the job must be well cleaned and the dust well brushed off before the priming is applied. The lumber should be *dry* also. The pernicious practice of following up the carpenter with a brush and of priming a board as quick as he has hammered in the last nail, may serve his purpose in preventing any shrinkage on his work. Such a practice is all right enough when the lumber is good and dry and when there is little moisture in the atmosphere, but during wet weather it is the reverse. It is better to let the lumber have a day's drying rather than to paint it damp. It may check, that is true, but better

have a few checks which can be puttied up than blisters
and paint cracking.

c. For iron. If the iron is new and free of rust
which is seldom the case, it will be fit to be primed after
a good cleaning of dirt and dust, etc.; it may have
scales and these should be removed with a putty knife
and a stiff wire brush, as otherwise the priming coat
will not penetrate into the main body of the iron and
such unpainted parts would soon rust. If as usual the
iron or steel has already started to rusting, a good free
use of the wire brush will remove it, and a good dusting
from the painter's duster will fit it to receive the priming. As it has been already said, there is nothing
better, if as good, for the priming of iron, steel and
other metals than *red lead.* This pigment cannot be
bought ready ground up in oil and must form an exception to the advice given—never to use colors in a dry
state in the covering of surfaces with linseed oil paint.
Red lead has the property of turning linseed oil into a
soap as noted before, but it has another also
which prevents its preparation in advance by grinding in oil as other pigments in that it has the
property of becoming hardened in it. This would
render it useless for brushing out, this hardness
in time being nearly that of the metal itself.
therefore it is better to mix it up in oil as wanted
on the job and still better after having so mixed it to
run it through a hand paint mill. When put through
the mill more oil can be used with it without its running

than possible by a simple addition of it to the dry pigment. If put on without the grinding it will have to be applied much thicker than any ordinary pigments used for priming would have to be otherwise the lead being coarser and heavy will separate from the oil and run in streaks down the sides of the job. It should therefore be put on thick and rubbed out thin which will if carefully done prevent the separating of the red lead.

d. For brick and stone. If the brick work is in good condition and the mortar lines solidly filled and the sun has been shining good and bright for a few days, so that there is no possibility of any moisture remaining anywhere upon the surface to be painted then it is ready for the priming, after having first been well cleaned up with the duster. But if the building is an old one and has never been painted before it is very likely that some of the mortar joints may have to be filled up to the same level as the rest of it. This should be attended to some few days ahead of the priming in order that the moisture may pass entirely away before it is applied. The job dusted and cleaned proceed to coat it over by a good, faithful brushing in of the priming which for a red brick finish or any other dark colors may consist of good English Venetian red and for light colors of half and have French ochre and white lead; neither should be thinned quite so freely as stated for wood priming—but it should not be nearly so thick as used generally for the finishing coats on wood but more like the consistency of that used for second coating on three coat work on wood; but no very fixed rule can be given for the reason that brick and stone varv greatly in their absorbing power—a soft brick being very much more absorbent than a hard one and the same may be said of stone. The priming will necessarily have to be adapted to suit the particular job it is applied upon and the thinning will need to be much more freely done for the softer surfaces than for the hard ones where there is little absorption and where consequently the priming must be put on thick and rubbed out thin.

e. Cement. After the cement or cemented surface has received its coat of sulphate of zinc and water and the latter has evaporated away as described in the preceding paragraph then it should be primed with a good medium heavy coat of white lead and French ochre half and half of each which must be well rubbed in and brushed out, as cement is not very absorbent being in that respect very similar to a hard burnt brick and there would be some danger of the priming running if put on too thin.

THE SECOND COAT.

117. It is becoming quite a custom to give new wood work only two roats of paint and to wait a year or so before putting on any more paint on the building. This is a very foolish practice to say no more about it and the architects who so specify must be hard up for a place to save their client's money as to want to

mar the beauty of finish of a building they have planned and which would be more creditable to them if turned out with the best looks possible than the measly looking things it is possible to make of them in two coat work. But they have not only hurt the look of it by so specifying but have deliberately planned to ruin all the future painting that may be put on the building.

The reader will remember the reasons given for a thin priming for wood structures. Now if the job is to be finished in two coats such a thin priming as recommended is an impossibility, because if so given the second which is to be the finishing coat on such jobs *will not cover* sufficiently well and both the architect and the owner would make a kick about it, so of necessity the priming coat has to be given too heavy and thus become a pretty sure cause for future trouble. It seems that any one would or should know that in a heavy coat of priming much of the oil used in spreading the pigment will be absorbed away from it by the pores underneath and that what is left has an insufficient quantity of oil which will leave the priming dry and porous. Priming cannot be both a penetrating coat and a binder for a surface coat at one and the same time. But this is what is required of it if the second coat of paint is to be the last. As to the supposed saving, it is not worth considering—the three coats necessary to good work will take but little more material than the two heavy coats given and the saving will be in the application only. But no matter how heavy the first coat may have been applied, it cannot stop the suction evenly and the second coat must dry uneven in appearance over it, as it will sink in, in the soft parts of the wood, and in the parts where there is no suction it will be glossy, giving a sort of arlequin look—anything but what is should be—certainly not a credit to the painter who puts it on.

THE PAINTING OF THE SECOND COAT.

118. *a.* Before proceeding to the painting of the second coat—the *puttying* should be done. It is supposed that a reasonable time to dry has been given the priming coat. The word *dry* means something else. besides that it will not rub off when it is touched. It means that the oil has undergone all the changes during the time it absorbs oxygen. This it does while it *feels dry* and for some days after, so that there should be eight or ten days allowed before it is *real dry.*

b. Nail holes, joints, cracks and checks or any defects in the carpenter's work should be carefully gone over and stopped upon the priming coat and should never be done before the priming has been applied; for then the cracks, nail holes, etc., have been filled up with oil and the putty will stick to it, which it would not do if it had been done before for then the pores, cracks, etc., would have pumped all the oil out of it, leaving it oilless, showing fine lines all around it which could be seen through the several coats of paint applied over it.

c. The painting of the second coat—if that must be the last one, should be as heavy or even heavier than it is usual for the third coat where three coats are given. As the wood is not properly filled up, some of the oil of this second coat will be absorbed by the first coat, especially as that has been put on too heavy and that it has become porous from having its pigment left with an insufficiency of oil. This of course will make the paint flat from having to part with some of its oil to the pigment of the first coat. But as the knotty parts have little absorption, these localities will have a gloss with the result already mentioned that it will not look uniform.

While the above is said concerning wooden buildings, it will also apply to brick and stone structures, as usually they absorb even more oil (being more porous than wood) and if the brick is at all soft it will absorb much more. Cement of course is less absorbent but still even upon that it is not always possible to make a good even looking job in two coats of paint. The puttying, if any be required, should be done before the application of the second coat as was related for that of wood.

The second coat should be about the same as for wood, thinned to suit the job which may be so very porous as to be still absorbent in which case it can be thinned more than if it is to be the last coat; if it is to be followed by a third coat, it should be of nearly the same color as the finishing coat, just a shade darker to serve as a guide for the third coat, as then one can readily perceive if the whole of the surface has been gone over. The above will apply with equal force to all kinds of painting although it is not absolutely necessary. If the weather is cool, a little turpentine added to the second coat of paint will make it work better and will not harm it—but it must not be over done.

THE THIRD COAT.

119. After the second coat has become quite hard which will take about as long as the priming, it will be ready to receive the third or last coat. Before it is applied the surface should be slightly sandpapered to cut down any uneven streaks or dust and dirt which may have blowed against it while it was fresh. This sandpapering can be done as each stretch is being painted and while the ladders or scaffolding is being used for that, as it will save a needless moving of these.

All new work after having received two coats of paint will be well filled and will have become non-absorbent or very nearly so; consequently the third coat will dry upon the surface of the second without parting with any of its oil and will dry with a full uniform gloss. This seals up everything from the injurious action of the elements and will afford the protection that good painting is expected to give the surfaces over which it has been applied.

For third coat the paint should be mixed middling heavy for all kinds of surfaces, wood, brick, stone, cement or iron and the thinner should consist entirely of linseed oil. No turpentine should be used, as it will need all the oil it should carry to bind on the pigment. Being rather thick and heavy it should be well brushed out but it should not be skinned on.

REPAINTING OLD WORK.

120. *a.* All that has been said in the previous paragraphs concerning the painting of exterior surfaces supposed these to be new and to have never been painted before. The painting over of surfaces which have been painted before is somewhat different than that of new work, yet in many respects it is similar to that. The chief difference being in the priming coat, which will not be necessary for old work.

If the repainting has not been delayed too long there will be no difficulties. The linseed oil of the previous painting may have become porous but unless the painting is very old, it will not absorb as much oil as the priming did when first put on.

The surface should be well cleaned up and dusted and puttied up and two coats of paint applied over it which will make the job as good as ever again.

But the paint may not be in good condition. From various causes it may be scaling or may have had so many coats put on it that it would be dangerous to apply any more to it. There is but one thing to do under such circumstances and that is to burn it off with a good gasoline torch following it up with a wide putty knife. Some are afraid to undertake it, but with a little care it is safe enough and much the easiest way to remove old paint upon weatherboarding. Then the job should be sandpapered, primed anew, second and third coated as for new work.

If the job is very old and weatherbeaten it may be necessary to fill it, for it will have become so absorbent that the oil will seem to soak clean through the boards and out again.

b. Such old weatherbeaten surfaces are dreadful and will require more paint and oil than they are worth —if put on in the ordinary way.

They should first be filled. A very good way to do that is to make an emulsion of the first coat of paint in this way: Take 25 lbs. of white lead and add this to 10 lbs. of whiting which has been previously mixed up to a stiff paste with water. Mix the white lead with it, paddling it until it has formed into a stiff paste. In a short time the whiting which is carbonate of lime will have emulsated the oil and the two will mix readily. Now thin this with half linseed oil and half sweet milk —putting in the sweet milk first, a little at a time—so that it may become absorbed before any more goes in when about half a gallon has been absorbed add about the same quantity of linseed oil. This may require a little more thinning for that quantity of material, if needed use more milk and oil in the same proportion. Apply this with a brush as any other paint when it will be found to slide over the old boards with ease, whereas before a brush full of all oil paint would hardly paint a surface larger than where it first touched the board. When gone over the surface will be much smoother than it would have been possible with an oil paint and a good coat of all linseed oil paint given over it will make out of it not only a *nicer* looking job of it but a much *better* one as well, much better in fact than it would if a whole barrel of linseed oil had been wasted upon it.

No one need to be afraid that the above will go wrong with them *for it will not.* The writer is so sure of that that he is willing to stake his last cent on it— as not only being as good but better and that the finish will be smoother. Any one who has had such old jobs to paint will comprehend what is meant by that, especially if he has done the painting in the ordinary way —to such this smooth finish will be a revelation and will astonish them.

As stated before two coats are usually enough for repainting any old work excepting when it has been burned off.

QUESTIONS ON EXTERIOR PAINTING.

108. What is said of exterior painting in general?

109. What are the causes of decay in exterior painting?

110. How does paint protect surfaces?

111. What action performs the vehicle in surface protection?

112. In what way does linseed oil fulfil the require-

ments needed as a vehicle of pigments in exterior painting?

113. What is said of red lead as an iron primer?

114. What is the best wood primer?

115. What pigments are best for priming brick, stone, etc.?

116. *a.* What is said of the painting of outside work in a general way?

b. How should wood buildings be primed?

c. How should iron be primed?

e. How should cement be treated and primed?

117. *a.* What is said regarding finishing the exterior painting on new work in two coats?

b. When should the puttying be done?

118. *a.* When should the second coat be applied?

b. How should the painting of the second coat be done?

119. How should the third coat be mixed and applied?

120. *a.* What is said regarding the painting of old buildings?

b. How would you treat old weatherbeaten buildings?

c. How should paint be mixed for repainting?

ENAMELING.

CHINA OR PORCELAIN FINISH.

121. *China, Porcelain or Enamel* painting are controvertible terms for the same thing. It is a most beautiful way of painting the interior wood work of rooms. It may be done in any self color without ornamentation or it may be used in connection with gold upon some member of the moulding, but it looks best in white or light tints.

In the white or in very tender tints such as ivory white or pearl white only will it show its beautiful effect of solidity yet with an indescribable transparency which is so much admired. The gloss without this transparency would be apt to clog and look heavy when done in dark tints or colors. As 95 per cent of enameling is done in white the process described below is mainly applicable to that and other very light tints. For dark colors the number of coats can be reduced, as no such care will be required to build it up.

122. When the job is new and has never been painted before the wood work should be carefully dusted and the room swept clean of dirt and dust before commencing operations; then it should be primed with white lead and linseed oil, put on somewhat thicker than recommended for the priming of the exterior of wooden buildings.

This priming coat should be allowed fully one week before it is painted over with the second coat. The puttying up of all nail holes, depressions, cracks and any hollow defects should also be done now with putty prepared as described in paragraph 47, which see, as that will sandpaper smooth.

123. *The second coat* should be mixed from flake white and zinc white half and half of each by weight. If flake white is not readily obtainable, some good white lead—that is white may be used instead. This should be thinned with linseed oil and turpentine half and half of each and applied smoothly. When dry which should take another week if the time can be spared, if not then in not less than three days, the coating will be ready for sandpapering and dusting afterward. Should any imperfections have been overlooked in puttying up on the priming coat, it should now be attended to as it is the only time when it can be remedied by leveling up with the same kind of putty as was used before. The second coat should be mixed also a trifle heavier than it is usual to do on outside work which is to be followed up with a third coat.

124. *The third coat* should consist of zinc white ground in poppy seed oil for the best class of finish, although a good green seal French process zinc ground in bleached linseed oil will answer nearly as well. No white lead should be used on this coat. When good genuine French process zinc white has been used and it is thinned with $\frac{1}{4}$ of poppy seed oil or bleached linseed oil and $\frac{3}{4}$ turpentine put on rather thick and well rubbed out, the job should look solidly and uniformly

white carrying a fine semi-gloss. If however for any reason it should not look perfectly white and uniform then give it another coat.

125. *Fourth coat* mixed as described for the third and the job should be gone over with it in the same way. This will assure a full, uniform finish all over the surface alike. It always pays in the end to give this fourth coat even when one feels reasonably certain that the third is all it should be.

126. *The fifth or the flat coat* should be mixed from green seal French process zinc white and should be thinned with turpentine only with just enough very light colored varnish to bind it on and this should be laid with a camel's hair coach color brush—after the previous coat has been carefully sandpaperd and dusted off and the room swept clean, with all windows and doors shut to keep the air out so that the coating may set as slow as possible in order to have time to make joints on the work without doubling up and showing laps. This coat dries rapidly and usually will be ready for the next in twenty-four hours.

127. *The sixth coat* should consist of green seal French process zinc white ground in damar varnish, thinned with half damar varnish and half turpentine and should be very evenly applied with a camel's hair coach color brush.

128. *The seventh and last coat* should be damar varnish of good quality into which just enough zinc white has been added to tinge it slightly—this is done

in order to remove any tinge of yellowishness that might be present in the damar varnish and it will also prevent any cloudiness on the finish, but it must not be overdone as the less color used the better it will be. It goes without the saying it that nothing but a camel's hair brush should be used in applying it. While it must not be flowed on as in finishing carriage work, it should be put on full and not skinned on.

This sort of finish requires seven coats as narrated, but if the third is good enough the fourth may be dispensed with reducing it to six. The extra coat, however, is best to be put on and where economy need not be practiced it is better to always give it to make assurance doubly sure

When tints are used instead of white alone a good copal varnish of pale tone can be advantageously substituted for the damar as that is softer and less waterproof than the other; besides it will stand harder usage in cleaning than that too.

This makes a beautiful finish with a soft porcelain or china look which shows transparency and opaqueness combined—a depth of tone similar to some that are obtained by the coach painter in over glazing and it carries a look which is unobtainable by any other method. The "modus operandi" may be thought irksome, but after all it is not so very difficult as many suppose it to be. Neatness and cleanness throughout all the operations is the main thing and plenty of time so that no part need be hurried onward before it is fit for the next move. When disasters happen and sometimes they do, they can always be traced to the above two causes aside of that of the use of improper material for which there is no excuse. Of course it would be possible for a botch to so apply the china finish that an uneven surface would be produced and that instead of a joy producing affair might be made an eyesore, but no professional painter used to brushing out his paint evenly need be afraid to tackle it.

129. *On old work enameling.* There is but little difference between the manner of doing that except in so far that the filling and priming coats having already been done, this will be unnecessary. If the work has been painted white or very light tints after puttying up, sandpapering and cleaning it up properly a good coat of white lead should be given it thinned with ¼ linseed oil and ¾ turpentine, after which the mixing recommended for third coat for new work should be put on and the flat coat over that as this ought to make it very solid and opaque. Then the rest should be put on just exactly as recommended for the treatment of new wood.

QUESTIONS ON ENAMELING.

121. What is said of enameling?
122. How should the wood work be primed?
123. How is the second coat mixed?
124. How should the third coat be mixed?
125. Is a fourth coat always necessary?

126. How is the fifth or flat coat applied?

127. How is the sixth coat prepared?

128. How would you apply the seventh coat?

129. Wherein does enameling old work differ from new?

FLATTING.

130. The flatting of paint upon wod work at least is usually done upon the inside only. It is by far the prettiest manner of finishing it. Flatting has a softness of finish and reposeful look to it which cannot be obtained from gloss coats such as are given to the outside of buildings. The preceding paragraphs give the method used in painting wood work in enamel which certainly carries a gloss too and the statements made under that head seem at first to be at variance with those made here; but there is a wide difference between a glaring gloss such as linseed oil produces on the outside and the softness of finish of an enamel such a was described—but even the subdued and toned down glare of an enamel coat would pall upon most persons if every room in the house should be done with it. As only a few such are done in most houses the change from the flat to a well done enamel is pleasing by contrast. A whole house alone in enamel would tire out its occupants much quicker than if it had all been done in flat work.

If anything could make a person walk about with a chip on his shoulder looking for some one to touch it in order to find an excuse for knocking him down, that person is surely living in a house where glaring colors on walls and wood work stare him in the face the live long day and it would surely put an average man on the warpath. It acts upon him precisely as a red flag is said to act upon the optics of a bull, rendering them desperate.

While glaring gloss paint possess this exasperating quality—if quality it be; flat or dead painting has just the contrary effect, it produces a quieting effect upon the mind.

131. *To flat wood work* which has been painted before, it should have had at least three coats including the priming.

There is a rule in flatting paint which applies with equal force upon all kinds of material or surfaces over which it is put to wit: That the flat coat should be put on over a gloss coat or that if a gloss coat is desired that it should be put on over a flat one. If the reader will bear this in mind, he will never have trouble in obtaining a good flat or gloss upon any kind of surface.

If the wood work is old and has been already finished flat or semi-flat and it is to be refinished in flatting so much the better as one coat of gloss can be applied over it which will make a good ground for the flat and will help hold it on, if the flatting is not delayed too long.

To produce a *dead flat* the paint must be thinned with turpentine only. Usually most pigment ground in linseed oil contain enough of that to bind them on, but white lead is not ground with enough of it to bind it on as good as it should be and it would soon wash off with the ordinary cleaning painting receives in most households and it is much better to add a trifle of linseed oil to it in order to bind it better. This will make it carry a very slight gloss, barely noticeable, called an egg shell gloss—but it must not be overdone, one table spoonful to the pint of paint will suffice. This is advisable as better than a dead flat for the wood work which is subject to being touched by greasy sweaty hands and what not—in unavoidable accidents.

In warm weather all flat paints being thinned with turpentine evaporate very fast and set quickly so that to do good work, it must be put on very quickly so the painter should be very careful when painting the panels of a door not to run the paint over on the rails or stiles or in painting the rails to square up pretty even to the stiles in order that there may be no set paint upon such parts when he gets to them in the course of his painting. If he accidently does run over them he should wipe it off with a clean rag.

Great care must be taken to close up all openings which might let in the outer air such as windows, doors, etc. This will prevent in a measure the too sudden evaporation of the turpentine and usually will give a person time to do the work before it sets.

132. Flatting walls and ceilings demand exactly the same treatment as is required for wood work, to wit: a good gloss coat for underground. The same

care to keep out drafts of air and air itself as much as possible. One person should never undertake to flat the walls or ceiling of a room alone, but should always have another man to help him.

On the ceilings of most ordinary sized rooms, the work can be divided up in two stretches. The first man commencing the painting at the side of the room on to the center when the other man takes it up on to the opposite side, continuing in this way until the ceiling is done. If the ceiling is very wide, in halls and in stores, three and even four or more men will be needed to carry the full width along through.

On an ordinary sized room the walls can also be divided up in two strips, with one man to take the upper strip from the ceiling down to the middle from a step ladder while the lower man can do the rest of it from the floor. Where the walls are above 10 feet three or more men will be needed according to height.

If the job is to be stippled as it should be, it will be better to have the previous gloss coat also stippled as one coat only is apt to look uneven. On the flat coat the stipplers should be right behind the men who apply the flatting and should never allow the flat paint to become set before the stippling has been done for no good stippling can be done over paint that has set.

133. Brick flatting is not so difficult to execute as the same kind of work on wood or plaster because the painter can stop his painting anywhere, if he squares it up to a brick joint either at the bottom or side of a

stretch. It requires carefulness mainly. The flatting of brick work on outside or exterior surfaces can have but one excuse which is to imitate pressed brick by producing an even dead flat surface. This it very closely does.

Like all flatting the ground to hold it should be pretty glossy and oiled and to have been painted but a couple of days previous to the application of the flat coat for the reason aready given and another very good one besides which is that the gloss coat being still tacky will dry and hold the flat coat very fast and this it sorely needs as the turpentine thinner which was used in its application could not be of any help in holding it on with the battle it must endure against the warring elements which would otherwise make short work of it and wash it off. But if done as recommended before the gloss coat has completely hardened the two practically become one coat only, *drying together.*

QUESTIONS ON FLATTING.

130. What is said of flatting in general?
131. How is the wood work flatted?
132. How is flatting done on plastered walls?
133. How is brick flatting done?

FRESCO PAINTING.

134. True Fresco such as practiced the great masters of the Renaissance period and of which the greatest of them all Michael Angelo has left such numerous and shining examples, may be said to be a dead art today as

few if any practice it even in an amateurish way. This no doubt is due to the fault of this age "Hurry." The present times require speed and to be just—to the many new ways and inventions in pigments as well as in the methods of their application which were unknown in the days when it flourished.

True fresco is very far removed from what is now understood to be that art under the same name. *Fresco* in Italian means *fresh* and it indicates the character of the painting it designated, i. e., painting upon fresh laid plaster. In fact it was a part of the plastering itself as the frescoer in those days had to do it himself and no faster than he could color it and put it on. So the fresh lime and sand served him both as surface and binder. Naturally he was restricted in the use of pigments to such as were not affected by lime and one can well wonder today at the knowledge of effects they must have had to judge of the right mixture to make the variations in their shadings to produce such life like pictures as they did with the limitations of such restricted palettes as they possessed then.

True fresco will have to be dismissed with the few outlines of it that are given above, as such it is now too near obsolete to warrant any more details concerning it. A few artists have tried hard to renew it but its revival never extended beyond a narrow circle and it was not a success. It had its days and our age will have none of its slow methods and limitations of colorings.

135. *Fresco painting* or the decorative painting which is known under that name in America today is of two kinds to wit: 1st. Fresco painting in water colors or distemper. 2d. Fresco painting in oil colors on flattened walls and ceilings.

136. *Fresco painting in water colors* or distemper is very popular and a number of our largest churches, halls, theatres, and private residences as well as public buildings are decorated in that manner. As the preparation of the walls and ceilings is similar to calcimining the reader is referred to what is said in paragraphs 31 to 38 for full information concerning this as it is the same up to the point where the decoration commences. As the decoration and the manner of executing it is very much the same for both water color and oil painting aside of the difference of mixing the colors and their manipulations previous to their application, this will be considered together making due allowance for their difference.

137. *a. Fresco painting in oil* requires a proper preparation of the walls and ceilings with oil paint to fit them for receiving the decorations. Fresco painting in oil is by far the most satisfactory and the most permanent way of doing this work. Unlike water color fresco, the walls can be washed with water and ordinary dirt can be easily cleaned off from them without injury to the decorations therefore it should be encouraged more than it is. It is very true that on account of its better flatting properties that water color frescoing looks

best for a while at least—but when a person takes in consideration the great danger of having the whole work spoiled it is questionable if the difference in looks will warrant one in taking such risks. The superior finish and transparent effects of the decorative painting done in oil colors too, will more than balance the lack of perfection in the flatting of the walls. While the preparation of the walls is much cheaper in water colors than in oil the cost of the decorations which is really the main item of expense to be considered is very nearly the same for both and if this is at all intricate the dif ference will be slight in the making up of the total.

PREPARATION OF THE WALLS FOR OIL FRESCO.

b. There are three methods employed in preparing walls so that they may be decorated in oil fresco, which are as follows:

1st. To size the walls with glue size or a surfacer with a glue size over it and to give them one coat of gloss paint followed by a flat coat upon it.

2d. To paint one coat of linseed oil paint over the walls, then give one coat of glue size over it to be followed with one coat of gloss and another of flat paint over it.

3d. The last is the best way. It consists in painting the walls with three coats of oil paint and to follow this with another of flat paint.

The first method answers fairly well, when there is no danger of moisture or water coming through the plaster. If there is and there always is such a possibility in accidents, the glue will swell and surely crack and peel off.

The second is much less likely to suffer from such a cause, but yet it is not entirely immune from injury from that cause. Water if present for a long time will filter finally through the one linseed oil coating and the sizing will also flake off.

But the third is a dead sure thing and a perfect guarantee can be given with it from any such a cause and that it will last as long as the plaster is not knocked off or other injuries received from the outside.

Some plastered walls have very persistent fire cracks as they are technically called by fresco painters. These fire cracks do not appear usually until after the painting of the first oil coat. They run in all directions and seem to absorb oil "ad libitum" nor to seem to know when they have enough of it. Ordinarily three coats of oil paint plus one flat coat over them suffice to stop this suction but then again sometimes it will not. In such a case there is nothing to do but to give another coat after the third and in some very bad cases even another may be needed to stop this suction as it would mar the finish. This is hardly ever necessary and as said before three coats plus a flat one is usually all that is needed and where so much expense has been incurred an extra coat should not be dispensed with if necessary to insure a good finish.

THE TOOLS NEEDED.

138. Level and plumb, straight edges, T square dividers of various sizes, some long legged wooden ones, chalk lines, etc., a number of various sizes of small bristle brushes of round, flat and triangular shapes (the latter for angles), see Figs. 18 and 19. The large calcimining brush (Fig. 1) and various sizes of water color camel's hair brushes. For very fine work in oil or water colors, a full set of artist's brushes in sable, ox hair and camel's hair will also be needed.

For oil work there will be needed for the preparing of the walls some good wall brushes, as shown in Figs. 3 and 4 and a stippling brush Fig. 2.

Step ladders, trestles and some two inch thick walking boards. Some few 12 quart galvanized pails for use in distempering, some one gallon tin pails for col ors used in painting the walls in oil, and a number of small tins to hold the colors needed for the decorative portion of the work. Glue pot, strainers, etc. These are the principal tools and appliances needed. To these however, every decorator has some pet tool or another that he would wish to add to the list.

MATERIAL USED.

139. *a.* For distempering: Whiting is the principal color used as a base for tinting. For self coloring or for the preparing of tints, all kinds of dry pigments excepting such as are noted as unsafe to use in water colors under the heading of "Colors." Gum arabic

glue, and gold leaf besides all the bronzes, metallics, flitters, etc.

b. For oil work: White lead and zinc white ground in oil. All the various pigments which are to be found ground in oil may be used in decorating.

THE PAINTING.

140. Painting the walls in distemper and preparing the colors for the same is identically the same as fully described under the heading "Calcimining," so the reader is referred to paragraphs 34 to 37 for the information required.

141. This work in oil as it was seen, is entirely different from that done in water colors. See paragraph 125, as that explains the various methods sufficiently and needs not to be repeated here.

THE DECORATING.

142. This is a big subject, so it will be impossible to do it justice in the space available, for it must cover the whole field of designing in lineal, mechanical and free hand drawing, each of which by itself, alone, would more than fill this volume.

For the cheaper work, most of it is done with stencils in one, two, three or more colors, either in distemper or in oil with a few hand painted lines. The ceilings being usually divided in panels and stiles, the latter of a different tint, bordered by a narrow dividing line from the panel. Some small stencil bordering is sometimes used and also in other cases a stenciled center piece with corners and a break between. The walls receive a stenciled border or frieze. The reader is referred to that portion of this manual treating specially upon stencils for fuller information regarding them.

Much hand decoration can be made by persons who know little of drawing, if they buy some of the decorative schemes that are for sale or which they can copy and enlarge from books on decoration, to be had from most art stores. They must not undertake anything too intricate at first but gradually work their way upward. Much of decoration even in hand work is repetitions of a few designs. These can be enlarged to the exact size desired upon a sheet of manilla paper. When the design has been copied to the satisfaction of the decorator, it should be run over all its lines with a tracing wheel or in default of it, pricked through with a coarse needle. The better way to do this is to place the sheet upon a cushion or some blanket or cloth so that the needle will pierce it more easily. When so pricked the holes will not readily clog up. The pounces so prepared can be used to duplicate a design any num-· ber of times wanted. It is held in place upon the ceiling or walls by means of small thumb drawing tacks with wide heads and small short points. A small piece of muslin, not too closely woven, in the center of which has been placed a few spoonsful of powdered charcoal or some dry color which can be seen on the wall, and the side of the rag drawn up tight around it, after tying some string around it, the pricked design is pounced over with this color bag and it will be found that it has sifted through the holes in the design onto the walls and marked out an exact duplicate of the design pricked on the paper, which can be traced out with a brush and colored to suit, in as many colors as desired.

The whole ceiling should be laid out true and squared up for the paneling, center, corners and brakes, and their true position mapped out, and then it is ready for the painting of the decoration.

While the beginner is not advised to undertake to do a class of work which requires much previous training, there is much very pretty, neat decorations which he could do and with some practice gradually grow up into the more intricate parts of the business. He should study drawing and the harmonious use of color, for without that the ability of a Michael Angelo would be of no avail and his best work would look—Bum.

QUESTIONS ON FRESCO PAINTING.

134. What is true Fresco?

135. How many sorts of Fresco (so called)?

136. What is Fresco in water colors?

137. *a.* What is Fresco painting in oil colors?
  b. How are walls prepared for frescoing in oil?

138. What are the tools and appliances needed?

139. *a.* What material is needed for distemper work?

b. What material is used in oil Fresco?

140. How are walls done in water colors?

141. How are they done in oil colors?

142. What is said about the decorating?

GILDING AND BRONZING.

143. *a.* Gilding is the name used to designate the art of laying on of gold leaf and binding it on to surfaces for the purpose of ornamentation. It is not a new art by any means, as it was practiced in very early days. Many persons who will read this have no doubt had the privilege of examining some of the old manuscript books preserved in the larger libraries with so much care, and must have witnessed with astonishment, the wealth of coloring with a profuse use of gold in the illustrations, that the Monks of the middle ages patiently wrought out in the making up of annals, chronicles and especially missals. One can hardly realize that such beautiful capitals and headings could possibly have been done during a period which many of us have been taught that ignorance reigned supreme in the land. The pseudo historians who would have the people believe thus, however, cannot well hide the living witnesses to the contrary, in stone, paintings, gildings, carvings, in the shape of stately cathedrals, churches, castles and public buildings and during that period the handicraft of the gold beater and gilder was probably as much used, according to the wealth of the times, as they are today. Much of the lacelike

tracery of the sculptured woods which then was the covering—with tapestries used in the best rooms over the bare stone walls—were decorated with gilt upon some members of moulding or to emphasize some particular ornament.

The use of gold in decoration is nearly as old as civilization itself and it would be hard to find some of the recently discovered remains of their vanished civilization without also finding that gold was used in some way or another in their ornamentation.

The goldsmith and gold beater no doubt was known hundreds of years before western Europe was more than a vast forest broken up here and there with a little open ground which afforded pasturage to a few herds belonging to the tribal people whose descendants today claim more culture than any other nations of the world.

With the great wealth which has resulted from the discovery of America by Columbus, and from the product of its numerous gold mines, has been continuously adding to that year by year ever since, gold becoming so plentiful, it is little wonder that its employment in decoration has been making a constant gain and that at the present time there are few if any of the dwellers of the land who do not have more or less gilding or gilded objects in their home, let that be as humble as it may. If upon nothing else than a picture frame, or gilt-edged book or china cup. The use of gold leaf is enormous and it is not confined to the decorations of the interior alone by no means, but exterior decorations and embellishments are done with it on an enormous scale. Domes of the largest size are entirely covered with it on statehouses, churches, halls and other public buildings, producing most brilliantly lighted effects which please the eyes and civic pride of the millions who live in the cities containing them. Many private residences decorated with wrought iron crestings have their most prominent parts emphasized with gold leaf, mouldings of outer doors and what not. But the most profuse use made of it upon exteriors is by the sign writer for gilded signs on wood or upon the glass fronts of stores or other public buildings.

There must be some very potent reasons why gold has been employed for so long a time and for that of a constantly increasing use in ornamentation. In the first place, gold being very bright, of a rich tone, it illuminates everything it comes in contact with. It does not oxidize and with aluminum, another metal having the same property, it remains unchanged amidst the constant changing with which it is surrounded on all sides, so that while its first cost appears great when compared with the cheaper metals, its greater durability to say nothing of its embellishing property, reduces this in the end. The cost of application being the same if gold lasts as long as the object over which it is placed does and which would have had to have been done over many times over again with any other finish, the higher first cost will not appear so great after all and may really be the cheapest in the end.

In interior work and ornamentation it is used even more extensively than upon the exterior; all kinds of wall ornamentation being adorned with it, even wall paper of the better sorts has some gold tracery upon it and in the higher grades it is put on by hand. Mouldings and sculptured and carved parts on woodwork especially in the tasty and dainty—white and gold enamel finish. It imparts richness to water and oil color work so that the fresco painter must be a good gilder if he wishes to obtain good results from his work. Even the dinner table bears it up at least as the ornamentations on china platter, plate or cup bears witness.

b. Gold is one of the most ductile of the metals and this is what makes its use possible to the extent it is for if gold could not be beaten out in sheets thinner than iron can be there would be but few persons so fortunately situated as to be able to afford to use it on account of its great cost. But its ductility permits its being beaten to a very remarkable degree of thinness and still leaving it entire and solid. It is possible to beat it so thin that it would take 350,000 sheets placed one upon another to make a pile of them *one inch* in height and one single ounce of gold will beat out into 2,500 leaves 3¼ inches square, besides the tailings cut off to square the sheets and which are remelted again.

144. *a.* Gold is alloyed with many other metals and in many different combinations with them to produce the various colors of it demanded by certain in-

dustries for special objects. The colors of it that are
best known and which all the supply stores handle are
the "pale gold" which as the name indicates is of a
light tone, to "deep" and "extra deep" which give the
rich gold tones and which are mostly used.

Gold leaf comes in books containing 25 leaves 3¼
inches square and a pack contains 40 books or 1,000
sheets. Gold leaf is placed between the paper leaves of
a book hence the name. The leaves having been
rubbed over with red chalk or bole to keep the leaf
from sticking to the paper as otherwise there might be
some greasy spots which might hold the gold when it
would be broken to pieces when an attempt is made
to remove them from the book.

b. All gold leaf manufacturers now also pack it
by first attaching each sheet of gold upon a sheet of
paper just a trifle larger upon which some substance has
been rubbed which gives the paper a slight adherence,
sufficient to hold the gold leaf when these are placed
inside of the books in the same manner as the loose
leaves are. This is a good thing especially so to those
who have to do any outside gilding as one may well
infer, when even indoor the least breath of air will send
it flying about like feathers. If the manufacturers
would only use as good a quality of leaf for what is
known as their "Stuck leaf" it would be all that could
be desired, not only for outside where it can be used
with impunity in any wind, but for inside also—excepting always water and glue sizes for which they would

not answer. The better way is to use paraffine wax to rub over sheets of paper and stick the gold on it that is packed loose, it can then be cut with little or no waste and the leaf will have all the density that the loose leaf has usually to a greater degree than the "Stuck" or "Patent."

145. The term "Gilding" has come to be used indiscriminatively so that now it covers all metal leaves as well as gold, so that silver, aluminum, imitation gold, Dutch metal, etc., are all included in under the title, at least in so far as that title applies to the application of the leaf, so that it is perfectly proper for a man to say that he is about to gild a surface in aluminum, however absurd it may sound to the uninitiated.

146. *a. Gilding in oil on wood and other surfaces* is the method most usually adopted for gilding any kind of a surface exposed to the elements, a size must be used to cover all the parts to be covered with gold. It will depend upon what the size consists of and of how it has been prepared, as to the resulting permanency of the work. Where pure gold leaf is used the size is protected from the injurious effect of the elements by the gold leaf itself, which we have seen, is not acted upon by oxygen.

In order that the gold leaf may be applied easily and preserve its full lustre the sizing must be tacky. Tackiness does not mean stickiness, however, and gold should never be applied to a surface that is still wet or from which the size can be removed by placing a finger upon it and to which it would stick. It is a stage which oil painting acquires just before it becomes hard. In ordinary oil painting that stage is of very short duration and the proper time would be very hard to catch so that unless but a very limited quantity of gilding is to be done, such would become too dry before it could be completed and it would not hold the gold tightly or if the gilding was done just on the border of tackiness, then some parts probably would still be too wet and the oil would come through the gold matting it and causing it to darken.

But linseed oil may be so prepared that it will hold a tack on much longer than it is usual for it to do naturally—even for several days after it has set sufficiently hard to become tacky, thus allowing ample time for the completion of a very large amount of gilding. It is prepared in this way: Take shallow dishes into which pour raw linseed oil, then cover them with cheese cloth to keep out insects and dirt, but not air. Place these dishes upon a shelf inside next to a window where sun and air will have free access to them—but rain must be kept out. A few months of such an exposure will render the oil fatty—in other words, the oil will have been in constant contact with oxygen for so long a time that it has lost its power of absorbing much more and when painted out thin, even when driers are used in combination with it, it will dry as far as to become solid, but it will take a long time before it becomes bone hard.

When a supply of fat oil has been obtained it should be bottled and kept for future use. It should be tried by itself to know how long it remains in good condition for gilding when used alone, than with various quantities of liquid driers to know how long it will take before it is ready for gilding and how long it remains in the proper condition. This description and mode of preparation will hardly suit the man who has a job of gilding to do in the near future, but he should take care to prepare some of it, for if he does not, he will have to depend upon such as all supply stores handle ready prepared and none are as good—certainly none can be any better than that which he can prepare for himself. The ready prepared fat oils of the stores come usually in three varieties: The quick fat oil size that will dry in twenty-four hours ready for gilding and hold a tack five or six hours. The medium fat oil size which suits the majority of gilders best of any, this usually dries in 24 to 30 hours ready for gilding and will hold a tack for twenty-four hours or longer. The slow fat oil size which requires 36 to 48 hours to dry fit for gilding and will hold a tack for several days. This is too slow for any purpose except upon very large surfaces and where the greatest solidity is desirable as the slow fat oil size has but little if any driers added to it and as it dries more naturally, it will have more life and elasticity to resist injury from the action of the elements.

b. The surface to be gilded should have become

very dry by exposure to the atmosphere for several weeks after it has been painted and should be perfectly free from tackiness, for if it is not in such a condition it will probably hold the gold in many places where it is not wanted to stick. The surface should be well cleaned with soap and water and afterward rinsed with clean water to free it of any greasiness which may have gathered upon it from any cause. If it lays with its flat side up it should be sprinkled over with bolted whiting which should be well rubbed over it. Gold will not stick to it and such a surface being flat and whitish makes an excellent ground to size up with size which has not been colored up as that sometimes makes it specky, unless great care has been taken in preparing it. The size will show blackish and shiny. If the ground is very dark or the gilding is done on the side of a wall where the whiting cannot be used, a little chrome yellow medium ground in oil should be added to the size and after having mixed it thoroughly, should be strained through some fine cloth. Previous to sizing such part it will pay well to go over all the parts adjacent to where the gilding is to be done with a freshly cut raw Irish potato, cutting off a fresh surface as needed. There will be a thin film of its juice left to which the gold will not adhere. After this is dry which will require but a few minutes the sizing can proceed. It should be applied with a camel hair brush and laid on evenly; in running lines care should be taken to make them true and even sized without ragged edges and to bring them to the ends perfectly square. It is proper attention to these details that marks the workman from the botch. It is now a matter as to whether the size used was a quick or a slow one as to how long the gilder will have to wait before laying the leaf but under the greatest temptations of hurrying up, he should hold his peace and wait till it has reached the full stage of tackiness as it is then only that he will ex perience no trouble nor difficulties in laying his leaf properly.

c. There can be several quick sizes made which answer the purpose fairly well, especially if the gilding upon it is not expected to last forever. Japan (so called) gold size thinned with half its bulk of turpentine or the same mixture of quick drying varnish and turpentine, can be used for a quick gilding size; but as it has already been stated the gilder is sometimes sorely disappointed in not having caught the very short time when the size was in a proper condition to receive the gilding and then he will have had all his pain and labor for nothing.

After all there is little to be gained and very much to be lost by using any of the quick sizes and nothing but a case of absolute necessity and hurry will justify any one in taking such risks. The fat oil sizes can be quickened so they can be used over twenty-four hours after they have been applied. That is quick enough and then they lay in condition for several days.

147. For gilding in water colors usually one should

prepare two kinds of sizes—one that will permit of *burnishing* and the other which will make the gold look flat or *matt it,* as the gilder's technical name for it.

The *burnishing* size is made from pipe clay and plumbago to which a small quantity of mutton suet has been added while they are ground up on the slab. These sizes require to be prepared as wanted and should be thinned with glue water of medium strength. There is so little gilding been done in water colors at the present time, that it will be better to buy it ready prepared when wanted as it will save the trouble of preparing it every time it is wanted. Those are specially prepared so as to keep and probably have anti septics added to them which prevent the suet from becoming rancid and ill smelling. This size takes on a good polish and will burnish, which operation should be performed with an agate burnisher.

The second or matt size and Armenian bole, and is also thinned with glue water as stated for the previous one. It too can be bought ready prepared for use and this is much more convenient than preparing for one's self every time it is needed. It will not burnish and can be relied upon to dry "matt."

148. More water color gilding is done upon picture frame molding and room molding than upon anything else and all things else put together.

Picture frame makers use whiting sized up with glue for the purpose of filling and surfacing their moldings.

They gve them an indefinite number of coats as some forms require more than others, which they continue until they obtain a good body to rub on and this they proceed to do. This levels up the surface of the moldings smoothly and fits them to be burnished. They use both the burnishing and the matt size and they apply 5 or 6 coats of it, which are rubbed smooth after each coat has dried, when they are ready for gilding by simply applying water to the molding with one hand and with the tip holding the leaf letting it down to where the water, will carry it level on the molding, the water acting in much the same way as when gold leaf is applied to glass in glass gilding. When dry the gold is either burnished or remains matt according as to the size used. It requires a little practice to become efficient as to the proper way to handle gold for this work. One must acquire a certain deftness of motion in order to be able to do the amount of work which is considered a day's work in that trade, and the only way to gain this experience is by constant practice.

GILDING ON GLASS.

149. This kind of gilding is used mainly by sign painters and more will be said under that heading, as there are several ways of using leaf on glass which apply to sign work exclusively. But all styles and modes used for applying gold to glass require the same sizing which is that kind of glue known as *Isinglass.* This glue is very thin and nearly as transparent as glass and as much

at least as mica, so it will not dull the gold when coming between it and the glass. It should not be made too strong either as then the gold will not burnish so well. A small piece the size of a nickel or a quarter of a dollar, should be soaked up in cold water until it has absorbed all of that of which it is capable, then it should be melted in warm, but not boiling, water which should not exceed much over a pint in quantity, to which should be added about a gill of grain alcohol. It should be strained through very fine silk cloth into a bottle which should be labeled and from which it can be used until exhausted, as the alcohol it contains will keep it from souring.

The glass to be gilded should be washed very clean with soap and water, rinsed wth clean water and again sponged with clear alcohol and dried carefully. This will remove any greasiness, fly specks or any other dirt, leaving the glass clean, and through which the gold will appear full of brilliancy and at its best.

The designs to be gilded should be roughly sketched upon the outside so as to act as a guide in applying the gold and to show the gilder if enough has been put on to afterward paint his design upon. Gold leaf is very fragile and much of it, even in the book before touching it, will be found either with small pin holes or even larger ones through which light can be readily seen and through which the paint used in backing it will also show through, for the above reasons it is always best to give a double coat of gold leaf. As soon as the first coat is

dry, which is, say, half a day or more, if there is no
hurry, the second coat can be put on in the same manner
as the first, which is to keep the surface of the glass well
wetted with the isinglass size just ahead of the application of the leaf which should be transferred from the
book with a gilder's tip. (See Fig. 32.) If sufficient
size is on it will flow the leaf perfectly level on to the
surface of the glass. Owing to the much wettings which
the underparts receive, it should always be commenced
at the top and the application continued downward,
taking care to allow about 1/16 of an inch lap to insure
a close fit between the pieces of gold. Where the members
bers of the design are small and not closely clustered together it will be well to cut the leaves up to the required
width with a small margin allowance of it, but if the designs are clustered close, then it will hardly pay to cut
the leaf up and it can be applied in full. The second
coat is applied over the first in the same way.

As glass gilding is usually done inside, there is usually
no difficulty in protecting one's self against draughts of
air, but sometimes it may be necessary to do so and
screens should be put up to prevent it. A gilder's cushion which is simply a board through which a round
handle to hold it up by is nailed some strips of felt should
be glued on the upper side of it and upon that a chamois
skin. All around it except in front a strip of stiff
leather should be nailed on the side and one-third of
the back part of it should be hooded. The gold leaves
can then be stowed away underneath it, protected from

air and can be pulled out with the tip upon the front part where they can be straightened and cut up with a gold knife into the required size. This gold knife need not, in fact should not, be sharp and it need not be pressed down upon hard as that would uselessly injure the chamois skin, it should be used like a saw, with a for ward and backward motion, otherwise the gold will be ragged edged and will stick to the blade.

The gilder's cushion can be bought ready made, but any one can make one for himself without being much of a mechanic, either. It is needless to say that its use is not confined to gilding upon glass, but that it is useful in oil gilding on wood, or in water color work as well.

The design which is desired to appear in gold on glass should have been drawn upon a piece of manilla wrapping paper and holes pricked through it with either a tracing wheel or a needle, so as to allow it to be pounced upon the gold previous to backing it up with paint, as it will furnish the proper outlines for that operation. The paint should be mixed from coach colors ground in japan or varnish, but never from colors ground in oil; they should be thinned with varnish and turpentine about half and half of each. It is best to give two coats of backing and this should be mixed exactly as directed for the first. When thoroughly dry the surplus gold can be washed off the glass. The backing coats of paint preserve the design from the water, but the gold which has not been coated over with it will wash off. If the sizing was strong, the water used in the washing should be warmed and then it will soon soak up the glue sizing so that it will come off. In washing surplus gold off of glass the water should be applied with a soft sponge only, as anything harsh might damage the clean cut edges made with the backing. Many beginners are in too great a hurry to wait until the backing is hard enough and commence the washing too soon, with the universal result that the edges curl and the perfect look of the work is damaged.

BRONZING.

150. Bronzing is not gilding although its main object and purpose is to create an impression in the mind of others that it is. It is a sham, but such a sham as false teeth and other false things which have become so common, that, notwithstand that no one is fooled by them it is broadly done and admitted as a matter of course. It permits the vanity common to human kind, a mild sort of outlet in making believe something that nobody believes. It enables the lady to buy a 10c store plaster of paris statue to be daubed over with another 10c worth of gold (?) bronze, and made to represent an ormolu worth 10c worth $50.00. La Fointaine in one of his fables tells of an ass who thought of scaring all the other animals he was chumming with—taking a lion's skin and dressing himself with it to procure the effect he desired but he had miscalculated the length of his ears nor did his bray correspond to the roarings of the genuine, so that no one was fooled after all.

Bronzes are to be found in all colors imaginable, and in such when used to produce certain metallic reflections in colors otherwise not obtainable in decoration they have a legitimate and even artistic look to them, and the ironical sayings just indulged in at their expense is only directed at their misuse in trying to imitate something which it is not. They are made from all sorts of compoundings of metals, powdered glass and what not. The processes some of them undergo, are carefully guarded, so that the public usually is not invited into the manufacturer's sanctum sanctorum, especially when he has hit upon a happy combination which permits him to control the market upon it after a demand has been created for it. The cheaper inferior sorts quickly tarnish, but the good grades of it are remarkably permanent (some of them) and it is of these and of the manner of their preparation and of fixing the permanency which is kept as secret as possible. Chemists may find out their composition but the manner of keeping the fade out of them, is beyond the power of analysis.

Bronzes are sold according to their fineness at least all the ordinary sorts are. Bronzes sell at from 50c per pound to $8.00. No doubt but that a good portion of the price paid for the higher grades by the consumers goes to the manufacturers to pay for the "know how."

151. Bronzes may be applied with any kind of a size that carries a little tack so as to hold it on. If an object is to be bronzed all over, the size can be put on as a paint coat would be over it and when it has set suf-

ficiently to have a tack, the bronze powder may be dusted on to it or better rubbed over it with a piece of cotton batting which has first been dipped in the bronze powder. In that way there will be little or no waste of the bronze. If only a certain design in bronze is to appear upon the surface the object should be carefully washed and cleaned free of grease spots for if any tack caused by greasiness remains the powder would adhere to it. The oil, japan or varnish sizes must be put on in the same manner as related for gilding. But there is a better way and a much safer way and that is to mix the bronze powder with a good vehicle which will bind it on the same as any other pigment. Many manufacturers put upon the market bronze sizing japans, etc.; some are fair but many worthless. The best known and mostly used bronze sizing to be used for mixing those with it, is called "Banana Oil" of a strong, pungent, disagree able odor of that fruit. For those who can stand that odor it is the best there is, as unlike the japans it leaves the bronze with a full undulled metallic luster which is as bright after mixing as it was before, which cannot be said of the others. In fact it is mainly for that reason that objects which are solidly bronzed are sized all over and the dry powdered bronze applied over it—in order to preserve the full metallic reflection.

QUESTIONS ON GILDING AND BRONZING.

143. *a.* What is said generally of the use of gold?
 b. How is gold leaf made?
144. *a.* How many kinds of gold leaf are there?
 b. How is gold leaf packed?
145. Is the term "Gilding" applicable to gold only?
146. *a.* What is said of gilding in oil?
 b. How is it applied?
 c. How are quick sizes made and used?
147. How are water sizes made and used?
148. How do picture-molding makers prepare them for gilding?
149. How is gilding on glass done?
150. What is said regarding bronzing?
151. How is bronzing applied?

GLAZING.

152. The technical term "Glazing" is in itself a very good description of what the operation it designates consists of, so that its name is appropriate.

Glazing, to painters, has a double signification, especially to such who conduct a general business and who are glaziers as well—but to the coach painter, decorator or artist it has the signification which is given it here. It means with them the application of a coat of paint, giving to an already painted surface an artificial look of transparency and depth which appears somewhat as if the previous coating of paint had been covered over with a sheet of glass—hence the name.

It imparts to pianted surfaces an undescribable look of depth and effect which can be obtained in no other manner. As stated before the glazing coat must have another one of solid color under it. It must be made up with a transparent lake, or some of the transparent colors, or with a solid color which has been made transparent artificially.

These glazing colors need not always be of the same tone as that of the solid color over which they are placed, and some of the richest effects are produced by glazing certain colors with a lake of a widely different tone. But some very pretty effects are obtained by glazing over colors with a glaze coat of a color of the same order, but of a different tone of it; for instance, for a carmine glaze a solid English vermillion coat is given, which when followed with a carmine glaze partakes of the character of both, the vermillion tone being reflected through the transparency of the carmine glaze, but the carmine itself also showing its own particular richness of tone. Thus a double tone is really produced. This is very pleasing to the eye, and this is why this effect is being used upon all first-class carriage work other than black. This is imitated by a blend of solid colors for cheaper work, but, like all imitations, it falls far short of the genuine.

In carriage work the glazing coat follows immediately after the last coat of color has been put on and just previous to the safety coat of varnish used to decorate upon.

Decorators use glazing colors also, and for the very same purpose as the carriage painters do: that of producing certain depth of tones which they could not obtain in any other way.

Artists, likewise, are very familiar with the use of glazng colors and have recourse to it on many occasions.

QUESTION ON GLAZING.

152. Give a description of glazing.

GRAINING.

153. *Graining* is not a very old art and it is very doubtful if it was known at all two centuries ago. It is very true that artists had occasion to represent various woods upon pictures, but only in so far as the wood represented was necessary in the make up of their pictures—not as graining. Graining in a commercial way as it is known today was, therefore, unknown previous to the time related, and the artists who imitated woods upon the canvas had no idea as to how the grainers execute their work, nor of its methods, and such a knowledge would have been useless to them as a picture would have been nofield where such could have been practical.

Graining began to flourish about the commencement of the eighteenth century, and from that period until the middle of the nineteenth it increased greatly until the first class grainer became an mportant character in all communities where such existed, and their renown usually spread all around them. Such as had a wide acquaintance, and grainers were never slow in blowing their horns, were sent for quite long distances from their home towns. The British Isles—England, Scotland and Ireland—seem to have produced the best and most renowned grainers. The Continental countries of Europe, especially the more southern, had the best of Great Britain in the production of good colorists and decorators but that country bore the palm in its graining and the men who did it. The traditions which have been handed down and reached our times give accounts of the feats of the renowned ones who had made enviable reputations during the first three quarters of the last century, which ends the flourishing period of that art. It very suddenly came to an end about the middle of the seventies with an occasional spasmodic revival, which did not last long, however

Without a doubt, this was due to the introduction of hardwoods in house construction. The supply of white pine finishing lumber giving away about that time, its cost began to rise up so high that it became as cheap or cheaper to use hardwoods for the purpose. As the hardwod is usually better than the imitation the skill of grainers became less and less needed, and with the results that the great grainers of the past have few if any successors in the present generation. The discriminating customer of "ye olden times" was willing to pay a pretty good price for the graining of a double front door and vestibule or a library, dining-room, or even a parlor, hall, etc.; that would beat some neighbor because good graining was then regarded as an art—which it really was. It deserved good remuneration and it received it as the artist does—not at so much a day—but for the artistic effects produced, regardless of the time consumed. For no one but an artist could reproduce the woods in such natural imitations that it frequently fooled good judges of woods.

The great diffusion of wealth since that time, too, has been another factor militating against graining because it has enabled the great middle class to procure the genuine wood in place of the imitation. So high priced white pine finishing lumber plus the high prices heretofore paid for artistic graining made the imitation come higher than the natural wood, and the cheap, hurry-up kind of graining could not hold out sufficient inducements to tempt artists to devote their life work to do this cheaper class of work: there is little wonder that such were deterred from adopting it as a calling, and that the field is so bare of really good grainers.

But a reaction is taking place now which promises to advance this branch of work again. It must not be expected that it will ever reach the high planes of the past, but the first class grainer today finds that room for his skill is increasing. This, no doubt, is due to the fact that it is now the universal practice of finishing flats, etc., in varnished yellow pine and that that sort of a finish does not satisfy owners nor tenants after a few years, as they darken and become very dingy. The only remedy is painting them over every year, or graining at a little greater expense at the start, but much cheaper in the end, as it need not be renewed yearly to be in good condition.

There is, therefore, a good future in sght now for good grainers and this art is bound to grow into favor again. Possibly there may not be so much oak done as formerly, although that will still remain at the head of the list, but mahogany and maple for bed rooms, with the former for anywhere, as its place is suitable to any room is even now having quite a run, and while it is a bit dark, its richness of color lightens it up and that is overlooked on that account.

It is not intended to give a lengthy account of "how to do graining," but the subject is of sufficient importance to warrant giving enough details as to the "how" to proceed to grain all the principal woods.

THE TOOLS NEEDED.

154. Oval or flat wall paint brushes to paint the ground coats with (see figs. 3, 4, 5). Some partly used oval varnish brushes or any other fair sized wall brushes, not too nearly worn out to be stiff or scrubby.

Oval varnish brushes 4 to 8° (see fig. 15), some mottlers (see fig. 29), floggers (see fig. 28), fantail over grainers of various sizes (see fig. 27), bone-headed badger hair blenders (see fig. 33), with a good assortment of lettering camel's hair brushes for putting in veins; also a line of various sizes of sable artist's brushes for fine detail work.

Sponges of various sizes and texture.

Rubbers for wiping out.

A set of steel graining combs. Fig. 44.

A set of rubber graining combs. Fig. 45.

A set of three rubber graining cylinders. Fig. 46.

A set of rubber graining rollers or rubber spring. Fig. 47.

Sectional grainers as shown below.

A check roller for putting in weather checks in oil. Fig. 48.

Some clean, soft cotton rags. The above are the essential tools. No doubt the professional grainer may have some pet tool or another of his own invention which he may want to put into the list—but the best of graining can be done without any other. The piped overgrainer, etc., have been cut out of the list as unnecessary; also some forms of mottlers.

THE MATERIAL USED.

155. For paintng the grounds suitable for the graining of the various woods upon the following list of pigments required is given: white lead is usually the principal pigment used for the base of all light-tinted grounds, and to that is added the colored pigments required to produce the right tints. These are: Venetian

red, Vandyke brown, raw and burnt umber, raw and burnt sienna and ivory, all to be finely ground in linseed oil.

For thinning: raw and boiled linseed oil, japans and varnishes.

For graining in oil the above named oil colors thinned properly can be used, or graining colors all prepared, ready for thinning, can be bought for almost any of the woods, and in light or dark tones of them.

PREPARING THE GROUNDS.

156. Break up some white lead ground in oil rather stiff in a little linseed oil, add to that the pigments which are named under each wood for the preparing of the right ground for them. These pigments, finely ground in oil, should be thinned much more than the lead, previous to their being mixed with it; stir the mix ture well to insure the bottom of it being equally as deep toned as the top. Do not add too much pigment all at once, but add them very slowly until the tone wanted is obtained. The ground color being ready, it should be thinned with raw linseed oil and turpentine sufficiently for application. A little drying japan can be used also to insure proper drying. If two coats are necessary, which is usually the case, give the first one with more oil than turpentine, and the last one with more turpentine than oil so as to have it semi-flat. For graining in water colors the grounds of all woods so to be grained should be a little flatter than for graining in oil.

There is a great variation in the same kinds of natural woods as to their color when finished and varnished so that a man can hardly err if he comes anywhere near to what it should be. No two grainers would select from a line of tints the same shades of them for the graining of any given wood. Of course there is a limit —but it would be very hard to define it. In trying to match some natural wood in the same room, always make the ground for graining about as light as the lightest parts of the wood shows, and when the·top graining color is wiped out, it will show an average tone of that of the natural wood it is called upon to imitate. For practice one should have a few sample boards of various toned woods and·by a proper selection of grounds and grainng colors, he will soon be able to judge at sight of the right shade to make for any sort of toned wood.

Below is given a few simple directions for the selection of colors needed in making grounds. The tone and depth of shade must be left to the judgment of the one who prepares them.

LIGHT OAK.

White lead for base. Raw sienna or French ochre.

DARK OAK.

White lead for base; raw sienna; raw umber, some little ivory black if required for as dark a shade as antique oak

GOLDEN OAK.

White lead for base, raw sienna or ochre and a trifle of burnt sienna to redden it.

WALNUT.

White lead for base; Vandyke brown or burnt umber ochre; Venitian red; a trifle of ivory black.

MAHOGANY.

White lead for base; ochre and Venitian red.

CHERRY.

White lead for base; raw sienna, tinged with burnt sienna.

MAPLE.

White lead; add just enough raw sienna to make it an ivory white.

SATINWOOD.

Requires a ground of about the same tone as stated for maple.

ASH, CHESTNUT AND SYCAMORE.

Requires the same kind of a ground as a medium oak does.

ROSEWOOD AND DARK MAHOGANY.

· Venetian red for base; orange chromo, yellow ochre and burnt umber. It may be required to lighten it up with a little white lead.

The above are about all the woods that are imitated; yet it may be necessary sometmes to match something different than the ones named as in a room finished in hard pine, and where a closet or addition is made from white pine or cypress and one has to grain it to match the rest of the room. It will be an easy matter to make the right ground by following the rule given as to the lightest tone shown by the natural wood and the top graining color will be easily picked out.

PAINTING THE GROUNDS.

157. If the house is new, proceed to prime it with an all oil coat with a little white lead in it; when dry putty it up and follow with a coat of color suitable for ground for the wood to be grained over it; this second coat should be middling heavy and well rubbed out. It should be thinned with half oil, half turpentine. When dry, sandpaper it and it will be ready for the third and last coat. This, like the preceding one, should be a suitable tone for the wood to be grained; it should be thinned with $\frac{1}{4}$ linseed oil and $\frac{3}{4}$ turpentine. When dry it should present a smooth, uniform egg-shell gloss or just a trifle more gloss than that.

Old woodwork that has been painted or varnished a reasonable number of coats, not to exceed seven or eight, will be safe enough to work upon, but, if, as is frequently the case, it has had from a dozen to twenty coats or more, as in some tenement houses one finds them, it is better to remove the old paint as there is great danger of blistering if painted, overgrained and varnished. When it is not necessary to remove the paint, two coats of ground color is enough to make a good solid surface to grain upon; otherwise it should be treated as stated for new work.

GRAINING OAK.

158. Oak is one of the most beautiful of our native woods and it has such a wealth of variations that it takes a pretty good head to remember them all. This is the reason why probably so many grainers, without exception, adopt some styles of it; which, while not a single one will be a duplicate of any other which they may have grained before, will have a certain family resemblance with all of them because they cannot help working along certain grooves which are peculiar to themselves only, and which one who is at all familiar with their style of graining will recognize at once, and some will go so far as to infallibly give the name of half a dozen grainers who may have done as many rooms on the same jobs, if acquainted with them. It is the same as a handwriting expert would do and no more. The sign writer cannot hide his style of work either. So, if a good grainer is recognized in his work he need not be ashamed of it.

Oak is grained in water colors and in oil, or in combinations of the two. Some grainers excel in the one or the other, but rarely in both. In either ways of graining it is divided up into *heart growths* and in *quarter-sawed*. In color it varies in the natural tones of it, and greatly so in the many dyes of it, whch are fads, and which the grainer can adapt his colors to—the coloring having nothing to do with the manner of graining it.

Besides the heart growths and quarter-sawed oak, there are some root growths and the pollard oak both of which differ very much from the two first. There is so much variety and choice in these that there is only the embarassment of the choice from such

The beginner who has just started to learn graining should procure as many veneers as possible in all varieties of growths of it to familiarize himself with them by copying them for practice. The above advice holds good and applies with equal force to all other kinds of woods. There is nothing equal to it for the purpose of learning their variations, and a few dollars invested in such will be money put in a savings bank at a high rate of interest.

OAK GRAINING IN OIL COLORS.

159. Under Paragraph 155 the material required for graining oak in oil is given and it is stated there that the colors can be bought ready prepared for thinning, or that they could be prepared from colors in oil by the grainer if he so desired.

The professional grainer who does nothing else can prepare his own megilp, as the old English grainers call the prepared graining color, to better advantage than one who probably may not be called upon to do a job of graining again for weeks; such can use the ready prepared graining colors in oil to better advantage than to make up the little he will use on his one job. As every manufacturer of colors mixes his own graining colors according to his own formulas, for best results in using them the grainer should become well acquainted with their several differences in working so as to know how to use them rightly, and when he has found the one which he can work to the best advantage with, he should *stick to it.*

It requires some little time to prepare them for one's self. The colors should be pure, rich-toned and as transparent and fine ground as possible. Beeswax, which has previously been cut fine and soaked in turpentine for 12 hours, will dissolve it at a very low heat in that and can be incorporated readily with the thinner oil color, which has been warmed also. Take care not to put too much in it, about the value of a teaspoonful of the wax to a half a pint of the thinner color. The color itself should be thin, with ¼ raw linseed oil plus a trifle of driers and ¾ turpentine. Frequently the graining color has to be applied too thin to comb or wipe out well in order that the ground may not be coated over too dark; in order to remedy that, fine, bolted whiting, which has been well triturated with linseed oil should be added to the color, and then it may be applied heavier with little danger of making it too dark as the whiting makes it more transparent.

It is then ready to be *rubbed in,* the technical name used for the aplying of it upon the ground coat. This can be done by the grainer himself, but he will usually prefer to have a man known as the *rubber-in* to go ahead of him and leave him to do the graining. A half-worn, oval varnish brush makes a good tool for its application, but it can also be done with any other kind of brush of fairly good size that is not too new. The rubber-in should put it on equally all over, but not too heavy for it to run when combed or wiped out. Again, it must not be rubbed in too dry as it would not wipe out well. If the colors have been well tempered and thinned there will be no difficulty in so doing. The panels should be done first, then the inner stiles, then the upper, middle or lock rail, bottom rail, finishing a door with the long side stiles.

The grainer will proceed to wipe out and to comb his panels to suit the style of graining he proposes to execute. Directions as to the "how to do that" would never teach one how to proceed. The beginner should at least see some grainer at it to form an idea of how it is done. Some use their thumb, covering it with a clean rag to do their wiping out; others again make an artificial thumb out of rubber, which they also cover with cloth, sliding that along as the work proceeds in order to always present a dry, clean surface to the ground about to be wiped; if this is not done the color will slide along in ridges which will give the graining an unnatural and forced look.

For the cheaper graining the use of graining rollers has largely displaced hand work in graining oak either in oil or water color This, however, applies only to plain growths. Quarter-sawed oak will have to be done by hand as the rollers will not do this right—at best where they are used much of it will have to be finished by hand. These rubber rollers will do the graining wonderfully quick and a great many variations of heart growths can be made with them when they are properly understood and worked.

161. The advice given above as to the rubbing-in of colors and of graining them by wiping or with graining rollers is applicable to all kinds of graining in oil where the graining is done by wiping out; therefore it will not be necessary to repeat it over again under each wood. Should the reader forget let him turn back and read these directions over again.

162. Graining oak in water colors is very much different than the preceding. For the graining colors one should procure them either dry, or, which is preferable on account of their greater firmness, ground in distemper or water. They are found for sale put up in small glass jars with a tin top cover at all supply stores. The color should be taken out of the jar, put into a clean tin can and thinned with beer to a proper working consistency, and they should be frequently stirred up

while being used as they settle much faster than colors in oil do. If beer is not handy a very good binder for them can be made by using ¼ vinegar and ¾ water with a little brown sugar dissolved in it, or a weak glue size; in short, most anything which has a gelatinous, sweetish tack when dissolved.

To grain heart oak growth for the better kinds of graining it should be done by hand. Run the panels over with the check roller, using some dark color— either raw or burnt umber or ivory pink, according to the color of the oak to be grained; then proceed to pencil in the veining with a camel's hair lettering brush of suitable size, taking care to use the badger hair blender freely while the color is still wet or else it will be too late and the unblended veins would be harsh looking. The blender should always be used outwards from the growth lines—never blended inward. Only run a few lines, therefore, before blending them, and proceed thus until all the panels have been done. The rails and stiles can be done plainly combed or veined with a fantail overgrainer, taking a dry one and using it over the lines to split them while wet, instead of a blender. The water color can be sponged on and the rubber combs used on it while wet.

The rubber graining rollers can be used as easily or even better over water colors than over oil. The panels should be sponged over with the color the same as the stiles and rails and the rollers used while wet. A little practice will soon enable the operator to turn out neat work with them.

For quarter-sawed oak, sponge the color over the panels, comb and proceed to wipe out the champs or flakes with a chamois skin doubled over the thumbs or an artificial rubber thumb. This can be as well or better done after the color has set; it will be necessary, however, to wet the chamois skin and to go over with that the flakes which will need finishing with a dampened rag afterward. A very nice effect is to touch up a few with the graining color and to put in a few dark flakes with a camel's hair brush which make a pleasing variation.

The better way is to grain quarter-sawed oak in oil, however, and when dry to overgrain it with water colors, putting in the dark flakings where wanted and in burled and knotty growths, to line up gnarled veilings and emphasize knots.

Some of the finest and most natural-looking graining of quartered oak can be done by combining oil and water color work.

When dry both oil and distemper graining of oak can be improved by judiciously shading the tone of colors used, but it must not be overdone as then it will appear ridiculous.

163.   Oak root and pollard oak graining may as well be bracketed together as to the graining for both are gnarly growths and are best done in water colors. Oak root resembles a hugh sponge full of little round openings or circles with a system of fine veins intermingling among them, some parts being very close together; in

others again being separated from each other by a few inches of vein veinings. Pollard oak is very similar, the unevenness of the surface being caused by cutting over the branches of the trees at the head for a number of years until an abnormal growth of gnarled projections are the result; these sawed into veneer produce what is known as pollard oak. The knots in pollard oak are larger than in the roots where really there are no knots but the appearance of circular openings resembling them where the circling veining has been cut through by the saw. The ground for oak root or pollardized oak is best made in several shades or tones of the ground color as this will greatly help the graining; it should be put in in clumps according to the graining which is to go over it. The grainer who is to do the work should make his own grounds to suit what he has laid out in his mind's eye. The graining is done with a sponge and blended as the work proceeds; most of it can be characterized with the sponge, to be afterwards emphasized with the camel's hair brush and fantailed overgrainers. The colors used should be very near, or at least in touch with that used on the stiles and rails, otherwise if there is too much contrast the work will appear incongruous.

All water color graining should be oiled soon after the completion of the graining as that will preserve it against harm, for after oiling it will be permanently fixed—becoming, in fact, oil graining.

164. What has been said under oak graining re-

garding the use of water colors and their application with a sponge and camel's hair pencils should be remembered as all other woods done in distemper are treated with them in the same manner, barring the differences between them in color and form of veining. This difference the grainer can readily adapt his colors to, and the style of his graining to suit the difference of forms. Where there is a real difference in the manner of using them, this will be noted under each wood and the same explained.

WALNUT.

165. At one time there were few double front doors and vestibules in our Eastern seaboard cities which were not grained in imitation of walnut—usually with burled walnut panels and the rest in plain black walnut with, possibly, the lock rail veined. Halls, libraries and sometimes parlors were also grained in that wood, and then all at once it disappeared. The introduction of hardwood doors did it, and where an imitation in graining was substituted it became golden or some other kind of oak. Walnut, being such a dark wood, is not suited to all places as its somber aspect is not conducive to cheerfullness. The Italian or English walnut is not quite so dark as our American black walnut and the burled markings are so pretty that more of it should be done than is the case today.

166. Walnut is usually imitated in water colors or in a combination of water colors and oil. For either

methods it should be stippled first. This is best done by applying some walnut distemper color (either Vandyke brown or burnt umber), with a brush or sponge, and by beating it upward with the flogger (see fig. 28). This divides the color into little short-like pores, which that wood is filled with in all its growths but the burled and with more prominence in the American than in the Italian. The burled walnut is done in the same manner as related for the graining of oak root and pollard oak, the arrangement being somewhat different, however, and the grainer must know how to bring out the details so as to make the imitation look natural.

CHERRY.

167. There is quite a variation in the coloring of this wood and much more in the colors it is grained in than in the natural wood itself. Some people are not satisfied with its rather plain and non-assuming character, and are not satisfied with anything short of the color of its fruit! This is really ridiculous, but they will tell you: "Why, no more so than masquerading oak with a green or blue stain," and how can one blame them when that is tolerated? The natural cherry wood has a very plain growth with quite a few pores showing through, which should be stippled in with a color composed of raw sienna, burnt sienna and burnt umber, but which should not be made nearly as strong colored as in walnut as they show very much more subdued and lighter. The veining is not very prominent either, the

veins being separated far apart, but are fine-lined, for all such woods it is better to mark out the veinings with a pencil of the right color, which, in this instance, is one made of raw sienna and burnt sienna. These pencils can be bought at most of the supply stores and are catalogued in artist's supply houses. There are some fifteen or twenty different tints made of them. They are encased in wood; the wood being colored with the same color as that inside of them it is easy to pick out the right shade at sight.

MAPLE.

168. Maple is one of our most beautiful woods and well deserves the use made of it in house construction, especially for the wood work of bedrooms, for which it is so well fitted. The veining in plain maple is very thin and simple and it owes its chief beauty to its mottlings. Its pores are very small and not sufficiently prominent as to require them to be taken into consideration in making an imitation of that wood. The veining, as stated for cherry, is fine-lined and of but little prominence, and is made best with a proper colored pencil or with an artist's brush and raw sienna in distemper. The ground should be nearly white.

Curled maple is very richly marked with markings called mottlings, of a rich darker color than the rest of the wood and is done by using the mottler and water colors and blending them with the badger hair blender. It can be imitated in oil but will not look so rich. Bird's eye maple is the richest of all, and it, too, is best imitated in water colors. Raw sienna darkened just a trifle with raw umber to kill its too great yellowness is best for the graining. The mottlings having been put in, it is the practice of some to dip the end of their fingers in the graining color and to put in the eyes by pecking their fingers against the ground. The above is easy but is not nearly as good by long odds as the following: Take a fine-pointed red sable artist's brush and put them in—not by dabbing them in solid but by making small circles with it for the natural bird's eye has usually an open center. After these have been put in their proper places, and this is very important and nothing but a close study of the natural wood will teach one where they really belong, proceed to put in the veining with a proper colored pencil as stated for plain maple when it will be ready for varnishing. Bird's eye or mottled maple might be imitated in oil colors but it takes much more time and is more difficult as well— and when finished would not look as well.

ASH

169. Ash is grained in much the same way as oak heart growth. The color of the ground is very much the same. The growth is more regular and somewhat coarser than that of oak. It is easily imitated with the rubber graining rollers. It can be grained in both oil and water colors—the first by wiping out and the latter by penciling on the veining. The variety of it known as

"Hungarián Ash" has a very peculiar growth which looks as if some one had blowed in the lower part of the log and the veining had been swelled out in circles more or less oblong in form. This wood is the most showy of the family and like the plain heart growth is best imitated in water colors.

SYCAMORE.

170. There is but little of this wood imitated by graining. Why that is so is hard to tell. There are indications that more of it will be done in the future than in the past as sycamore lumber is being used more now in house finishing than formerly, and justly so, for it has fine and peculiar markings all its own. These mottlings are small and irregular all over the growth.

It is easily imitated in water colors with a sponge and blender. The ground coat should be about the same as that of dark oak, just a trifle lighter. The graining colors are raw sienna and raw umber. It can be easily imitated with the rubber graining rollers intended for quarter-sawed oak, rolled over quickly over water colors and well blended, and instead of that name they should be called "sycamore rollers," as they are better fitted for that than for the other.

MAHOGANY.

171. Mahogany is one of the richest of woods and it well deserves the great popularity it now enjoys for both furniture and house finishing. It is the richest

toned wood of them all and while rich it is not loud; even that with the richest of marking is never gaudy or suggestive of vulgarity. In shades and tones it runs from a yellowish buff with darker brown mottlings to a rich burnt sienna red with dark brown and some nearly black featherings of great beauty. A wood having such a range of color can have no set tint for a ground color and as to the tint that the ground should have will depend entirely upon the character of the sort of mahogany that is wanted. If a yellow-toned mahogany is desired the ground will have to be made more yellow and lighter toned than for aged mahogany, which will require a deeper reddish-toned ground. While mahogany can be imitated in oil graining, it is much easier and better done in water colors.

The character of the wood should be sponged in and well blended more strongly than for woods of fine veining; this will feather out the edges in both directions. When blended and dry, the details, if any are desired, can be added with either a camel's hair pencil or a fan tail overgrainer, and well blended, too. When dry it should be coated over with linseed oil and turpentine.

ROSEWOOD.

172. Rosewood is a very dark wood and for that reason is seldom used in such large a quantity as for instance a whole room would demand. It is one of the most expensive of the woods. Its use is chiefly confined to piano cases and small artistic objects, and in

furniture. As its darkness and high cost prevents its being used largely its graining, too, is very limited for the first reason given—too dark. Many small objects are grained in imitation of it, however, which is usually done in factories where they are made. The ground for it is about the same as that of dark mahogany, only more red. The graining is best done in water colors. Drop black applied with a sponge in erratic heavy lines to be blended slightly but not feathered as in mahogany, then followed with a fantail overgrainer filled with the same color; put in the fine lines which nearly cover the whole wood, leaving but little here and there of the ground to show through. It is very easily imitated when one has a good conception of its character in mind; but it is also easily spoiled if its average markings are misrepresented. The greatest trouble with the novice is that he tries to put in too many details, and these in the natural wood never force themselves upon the attention, but they have to be closely looked for to distinguish them.

QUESTIONS ON GRAINING.

153. What is said regarding graining?

154. What are the tools required?

155. What material is used?

156. What is said about preparing the ground?

157. How many coats of ground color should new and old wood receive?

158. What is said in a general way about oak graining?

159. How are graining colors mixed for graining oak in oil?

160. How is the graining color in oil rubbed in and how is the graining done?

161. Is what is related in Paragraphs 159 and 160 applicable to other woods as well?

162. How is the graining color in distemper for oak prepared and how is the work done?

163. How is oak root and pollard oak grained?

164. Is what has been related of the water color graining of oak applicable to other woods?

165. What is said of walnut graining in general?

166. How is walnut grained?

167. How is cherry grained?

168. How is maple grained?

169. How is ash grained?

170. How is sycamore grained?

171. How is mahogany grained?

172. How is rosewood grained?

HOUSE PAINTING.

173. House painting is of two very different kinds —exterior and interior.

Both exterior and interior of buildings are painted for a twofold purpose: first, as a protective covering to the material used in house construction, and secondly, as a means of beautifying its surface.

Under the heading of "Exterior Painting" (see Paragraphs 108 to 120), the reader will find a full explanation as to the best manner of treating all the various material used in the construction of houses, therefore it would be useless to repeat the same here.

174. The painting of interiors has also been fully reviewed in all the several methods used in doing the same, such as in water colors or distemper under the heading of "Calcimining" (see Paragraphs 31 to 38) also the same under the heading of "Fresco Painting" (see Paragraphs 134 to 142), and in oil under the heading of "Flatting" (see Paragraphs 130 to 133), also under the heading of "Enameling" (see Paragraphs 121 to 129), besides such as is finished in "Graining" (see Paragraphs 153 to 172) and "Marbling" (see Paragraphs 173 to 192). The above covering all the various ways used in finishing up interiors will suffice without repeating it and the reader can readily find what he is looking for under the several headings mentioned.

QUESTIONS ON HOUSE PAINTING.

173. What is said of exterior painting?

174. What is said of interior painting?

MARBLING.

175. The imitation of marbles and other variegated stones is a very attractive and interesting section of the painter's trade—one almost feels like saying *art*; for to produce a good imitation of them is artistic. To be able, then, to imitate them the student should have a

good conception of it formed in his mind ready to be transferred by his good right hand by the proper handling of the tools that will reproduce what his head has conceived upon the surface he desires to ornament. Should he spend a whole week in going about from building to building, examining good natural specimens of marble in the great office vestibules, corridors, etc., or in public buildings, churches, in any of our larger cities, it would be time well spent with him as this would do more to fasten up in his mind a good understanding of their forms and the great variations of these in the several marbles which are so profusely used at the present time. Reading about them will not learn him anything, and he might read till he was gray headed before he could have as clear an understanding of them as a good square look would give him—at the marble itself.

Nor need this study be commenced over for every kind of marble he hears about, nor will he need to make a study specially for each kind of marble as the grainer has to do to understand the peculiarities of each kind of wood, for all marbles, while each has some peculiarity too, can be in reality divided into two general groups: Fissured marble and the other—conglomerate marble.

All the fissure marbles have a great family resemblance; the main difference being in the frequency of occurrence and the fineness of the fissures, the more or less of their transparency, and mostly in the coloring itself. There are a great many names given to certain colored marbles, yet as the chief difference lays in the colors used in executing them, this need not worry the marbler very much.

During the week which he has been advised to spend in examination of various specimens of marbles he will have come to a seemingly contradicting opinion "that they are all alike" and "that it is impossible to find two pieces of marble a foot square that are exactly alike," that is in the fissured marbles, for the solidly colored ones need not be considered, so far as being counted in —they are not imitated. This seeming contradiction— as to their being all alike and yet as being all different— lies in that when one color of fissured marbles has been well studied and understood, all the others, barring the color, will be understood also and their minor differences can be readily taken care of. Their variations are infinite, however, so that the statement that no two pieces are alike is true also.

176. To make a good imitation of marbles a person needs to have an intimate knowledge of colors and of the "how to handle them" by blending them properly so as to make them appear transparent if he wants them so, or solid if he desires it. He will find numerous specimens of markings and veinings in the natural marble that he should not try to imitate because if he did he would be laughed at for his pains. Nature misses it at times and produces some unnatural looking specimen but the marbleizer is not supposed to reproduce them.

It is the same in the various woods; only those of pleasing forms are copied and the abnormal should be shunned as no one wants them. The pleasing forms of marbles are so numerous that if a person was to imitate them daily for a lifetime it is doubtful if he would reproduce any former design; yet, as in graining, every person will adopt certain forms and peculiarities and unconsciously he will put on some of this individuality into his work and these "personal marks" will be recognized by other painters who are familiar with his peculiarities, and a look will suffice them to enable them to name the person who did the job.

176. The tools needed for marbling are few. Some brushes to lay colors with; these may be of any shape, but as only rather small surfaces are laid over with colors at one time, they should not be too large. Some few flat and round fresco bristle liners; some camel's hair pointed lettering brushes and a few artists' brushes to put in fine lines and outlining with. Some bristle blenders and some badger hair blenders; some feathers to put in fine veins with. Sponges for water colored work and some soft, clean cotton rags. The material used for marbling in oil is: white lead, which is usually the base or principal color in the foundation of all the lighter tints of marble, and for coloring it or for using singly or in connection with other colored pigments; raw and burnt sienna; raw and burnt umber, Oxford and French ochre; Indian red, Prussian blue, ivory black, etc. As marbles can be found in nearly all colors,

it is hard to say where the naming of the list of colors used should stop as nearly all of them can be put to use.

For marbling in water colors all the same colors, dry or ground in distemper, can be used with the exception of white lead for which whiting must be substituted.

By long odds the better way of imitating marbles is with oil colors—and the easiest, too. The blending of the colors in distemper is very much more difficult to do properly, and usually it is used only upon the very cheapest of wall work that any of it is ever attempted. A person cannot judge rightly of the value of the colors used as they dry so much lighter than when first put on. It requires quite an expert to imitate marbles properly in distemper. Some few do obtain very good results in work done in that way, but mostly in scenic painting, and their work while pleasing at a distance will not usually bear a very close inspection.

DOVE MARBLE.

178. The ground for dove marble should be a warm gray composed of white lead, lampblack and a trifle of red to warm it up. When dry go over it with a transparent gray made of zinc white, black and whiting to give it transparency and further spreading; put in the darker gray tones in places where desired; then blend them in with a bristle blender. Then run in the veining in white, which blend with the badger blender to make them transparent and look as if disappearing be-

low the surface. Then finish up by putting in the high lights on the veining with white. This makes them appear as if they had continued from below to the top of the surface through the transparent ground. The painter will find it one of the easiest to imitate. The broader veins or layers, as some call them, can be put in with the bristle fresco liners and the finer with artists' brushes, or still better with feathers dipped into the color; with the feather can also be applied the network veining in clumps where they usually center and divide out from. It is very quickly done and the quicker the better the work will look as hesitation always causes veining to be harsh. For very good work it is better to accentuate details with a camel's hair artist's brush to put in a trifle of dark shading upon spots on one side and to lighten up on one side the lighter shades. This helps to produce a more transparent effect to the marbling.

As many of the above details are applicable to the imitation of all kinds of marbles it will not be necessary to repeat them again, so the reader should bear them in mind.

BLACK AND GOLD.

179. The ground for this marble is black and the veining is gold colored as the name indicates. Some large veins of straggling character run in zigzag fashion in all directions; these are made of yellow ochre, raw umber and Venetian red and are to be blended in with

the black and gold veining. After the color has set a bit, the high light gold veining is put in again but not over the first ones which were blended and no attention should be paid to them; they appear as if they were below the ground through the transparency of the surface. Only a portion of this last veining must remain as "high lights," the rest must be carefully blended to make them look as if they were gradually disappearing and give still greater transparency to the job.

EGYPTIAN GREEN MARBLE.

180. The ground for this marble is an invisible green made of black and yellow. When the ground is dry, paint over the whole surface with a green which is suitable, putting in the black masses here and there and with a feather putting in some of the green in veins through these which should be blended. When dry run over the work with blocks of black to give it its proper character. The white masses should now be put in and one side of them should be made sharp by touching them up with a camel's hair pencil.

When stones are cut and polished they are frequently so transparent that we seem to look beneath the surface, and crystallized masses may be observed distinct from the substance which forms the matrix. These crystalline bodies may present their sides or may be cut angularly, thus giving a singular variety of form and great transparence to the mass. This is where the painter can display his skill by imitating it. The novice will, no doubt, find it difficult at first but perseverance will reward him with success.

VERD ANTIQUE.

181.   Black is the ground for verd antique marble. Mix in a small can some Prussian blue and yellow ochre so as to form a brownish green.   Then, with feathers, put in the colors—blue and yellow—which blend with a bristle brush, afterwards touching up the same with blue and yellow by means of a camel's hair pencil.

This marble is of the same general character as the Egyptian, its chief distinguishing features being that it is more blotchy.

SERPENTINE MARBLE.

182.   This marble resembles the above, being somewhat more veiny and less blotched.   There is also less conglomeration showing through it.   The green is also lighter toned but otherwise treat it as described for the others.

BROCATELLO.

183.   The ground for brocatello is a light, warm yellow of the same tone as that commonly used for sienna marble and is formed of ochre and white lead. Take raw and burnt sienna and add enough whiting to make them spread out very transparent and glaze over the job with it; when this color has set, sprinkle it over with turpentine, using a sash tool for this pur-

pose. It will cause the color to flow and the yellow ground to show through. Then shade the larger blots with a light yellow ochre to show the angular fragments and to give it greater depth. A suitable color made of Prussian blue and vermillion is then prepared, and with a pencil it is used to put in veins around the angular parts, but care should be taken not to carry the dark lines through the blots.

ITALIAN PINK MARBLE.

184. This marble is somewhat of the same general character as that described under sienna marble, and in reality it is only a variation of that. The chief distinction consists in its being more rosy in tone and of a less yellowish red. The painter can follow directions given below, changing the colors to suit this.

SIENNA MARBLE.

185. This marble has a great variety of character and is also known under a variety of names in many places. The tendency now seems to be the placing of all marbles of that character together under the name of sienna and to designate the color of it wanted. One slab will have a dark hue, tending to an umber tone, and another from the same quarry will be a bright yellow. When it is imitated the ground is made a light yellow. After the ground is dry the work should be gone over with a transparent yellow made so by the addition of whiting. While the color is still wet the character may

be formed with a No. 2 black drawing crayon and the same blended with the color with a badger hair blender. The painter will now display his taste by choosing the proper shades and the placing of his colors which are raw and burnt sienna; raw and burnt umber and Venetian red with which he will fill up the spaces left open by his crayon, when the several colors should be blended together. When this is dry the shades should be put in with a darker color; then the work should be thinly glazed here and there and well blended with a badger blender.

Some painters in finishing sienna spot it with pure white. The novice should study this marble well, as it is one which is suited to many situations and which is nearly always pleasing to look at.

WHITE VEINED MARBLE.

186. This is one of the commonest of the marbles, and the painter has frequent occasion to imitate it, but it does not usually require the services of an expert to distinguish between the imitation and the real article. As simple as it looks, it is the hardest marble to imitate of the whole list of them. The man who can fool anyone into believing that his imitation is genuine marble can turn out to perfection any of the colored marbles.

The ground for this marble is a pure white. When it has been applied and is dry; mix white lead and turpentine, adding some whiting to make it more transparent and with that paint over the work. While the color is wet, form the veins with a black crayon and with a bristle blender soften the veins with the ground. Simple as it is, it is not an easy thing to make it look natural.

FLORENTINE MARBLE.

187. The ground for this marble is white lead, tinted up to suit with Indian red or Tuscan red and black to produce a rather light neutral red tint. Put in the veining with burnt umber and burnt sienna, a few of each, running in all directions without any show of regularity. This veining must be done while the ground is wet. Sometimes these veins run in clumps and seem to break forth, leaving patches here and there nearly free of any veinings, and then suddenly to make a network of them as intricate as those upon the rind of a nutmeg melon.

AGATE.

188. Agate is a conglomerate and really not properly a marble, partaking more of the nature of quartz than it does of lime formation. As it is sometimes imitated it is well to place it with the other stone imitations, along with jasper, porphyry and other forms of granitic formation which the skill of the painter is frequently called upon to imitate. The ground for agate is made of white lead, and the character of the work is put in with a feather, which has been dipped in a transparent crimson lake color and blended. When dry it should be run over with the crimson lake in spots and between

these put in other spots with a medium tone of green made from Prussian blue and yellow ochre, and when the work begins to set, it should be sprinkled with turpentine, whch will cause the three colors to run in all directions and afterward they should be touched up in places here and there with some of each of the colors with a camel's hair pencil.

RED PORPHYRY.

189. Red porphyry is of granite formation; it is of a dark redidsh tone and the ground should be made from vermillion and black. Sprinkle the ground with vermillion, dulled with a little white lead, taking care that it does not run on the ground but present each spot separately and distinctively. This done, the work should be sprinkled in the same way but with a still lighter shade of red.

SWEDISH PORPHYRY.

190. The ground for Swedish porphyry is a grayish stone color, formed of white lead, black and raw umber. The work should be sprinkled in shades of gray in a similar way to that stated for red porphyry.

SWISS PORPHYRY.

191. This is considered the most valuable on the list. The ground is black; sprinkle it with two shades of color made from black and red, but the sprinkling should be done more liberally than in the two former

ones, so that they may run into each other. Afterward sprinkle a litle white over the whole work; the white spots should be small.

JASPER.

192.   Is a fancy stone which is seldom used in large masses except by imitation. The ground may be made in color that is suitable to the style or color of jasper to be imitated or to the situation, but usually it is a gray or a yellowish stone color. The ground being dry, paint over a certain portion of the work with an opaque color, made of burnt sienna and a little Indian red. In about half an hour it will be set and then it should be sprinkled with turpentine and whiting; a clean brush being used for the purpose, and wherever the moisture falls large spots will be formed. Then the character must be laid out. This is done with a yellowish grey color by introducing it among the red masses. The work must be then heightened with a pure white color. The peculiar ribbon structure or waving line must be afterward introduced, which is done with the feather of a quill. It has the effect of uniting the red and the other colors. This is done with pure white lead thinned with turpentine, a little inside varnish being added to give it binding. The work is afterward finished in with a camel's tair pencil in light touches.

GRANITES OF ALL KINDS.

193. Granites of any color can readily be imitated. Proceed as stated under porphyry. Prepare the ground of the predominating color of the granite and then sprinkle on the remaining colors so as to spot large or small, according as it is wished.

QUESTIONS ON MARBLING.

175. What is said of marbling in a general way?

176. What should a person be required to know to become a marbler?

177. What tools and material are needed?

178. How is dove marble imitated?

179. How is black and gold marble imitated?

180. How is Egyptian green marble imitated?

181. How is verd antique marble imitated?

182. How is serpentine marble imitated?

183. How is Brocatello marble imitated?

184. How is Italian pink marble imitated?

185. How is sienna marble imitated?

186. How is white veined marble imitated?

187. How is Florentine marble imitated?

188. How is agate imitated?

189. How is red porphyry imitated?

190. How is Swedish porphyry imitated?

191. How is Swiss porphyry imitated?

192. How is jasper imitated?

193. How are granites imitated?

OILS AND DRYERS.

194. There are several different kinds of oils, each having peculiar properties belonging in general to their class besides each one of the class having some distinguishing traits belonging to them only and not to the others. All classes of oils are useful to man for some purpose or another. For the painter's use, however, there are only two kinds which are of interest to him as related to their business and employed by him in his work, to wit: The *"fixed oils"* and the *"volatile oils."*

THE FIXED OILS.

195. The fixed oils have the property of solidifying during the process of their drying into a rubber-like gum, which is waterpoof. This property is invaluable to the painting of exteriors, as without such a quality in the liquid used in the application of paint, it would be impossible to hold the pigment of the paint upon it and its stay there would be limited to dry weather, as rains, moisture, hail and beating storms would soon make short work of it and wash it off and the pigment having nothing but its own adhesiveness to hold it on, would soon all be at the bottom of the house, leaving the building in no better condition, if as good, as it was before the painting was done. There are no liquids or substances that will render liquids waterproof, known at the present time, with which pigments could be mixed and applied over surfaces with as vehicles of them which will render the hard service which is demanded of them

and which will turn itself into a waterproof covering but—*the fixed oils.*

It is not the purpose of entering into any great details in reviewing the fixed oils, and some of them will not even be mentioned, as they are either too scarce or expensive to be thought of for use in painting. All fixed oils have the same general properties characteristic of their class in a greater or lesser degree—which is, that they absorb oxygen from the atmosphere and that during this absorption they become solidified into a rubber like waterproof gum; but besides this general characterizing property of the class which belongs to this group only, they have each of them their own.

All fixed oils gain in weight from the oxygen which they have absorbed, yet the gain is nearly, but not quite, offset by the evaporation of the moisture contained in them and the loss of some certain volatile ethers which are evolved during the wonderful process of their drying.

The drying of the fixed oils is a very interesting study for those among the painters who have a love for knowledge, and to such the study of such works as "Chevreuil's" on the drying of oils, will well repay them for the trouble. A good knowledge of the material they use will greatly help them to understand the why and wherefore of things and no one can know too much about his own business or any of the material used to carry it on.

LINSEED OIL.

196. Of all the drying fixed oils, no others possess as many of the qualities that are desirable in them for the purpose of a paint vehicle and as a preservative of surfaces nor to as high a degree of perfection as *Linseed oil* does.

Besides that it is so much superior to the others in quality, it is far cheaper than the next one to it in cheapness. All things being equal, that of itself would suffice to make it the most popular, so that when the fact is taken in consideration that its qualities are superior to the others in all but a few immaterial points for outside painting at least, and for interior painting excepting in a very few instances, such as white enameling, etc., it is no wonder that it holds first place and stands far above them all.

It was stated in the preceding few lines that linseed oil was the cheapest of all the fixed oils and so it is. *Linseed* is a Frenchified word for *flaxseed,* which it is, and it is known under that name all through its growth. The change to linseed only occurring after the oil has been expressed from it upon the same principle that a calf becomes veal after its death. Flax is one of the most useful of all the plants to the human family. When it is wanted for its fiber, however, it is grown in a different manner. Then it is sown much more closely together, which prevents it from going to seed properly, and to branch out, when it is pulled and from such no seed is obtained.

For seed it is sown farther apart, which gives each plant a chance to spread and make a good head for seeds and'to become a perfect plant fitted to ripen its seeds properly. This makes its fiber much coarser and it unfits it for all the finer uses made of that raised specially for its fiber, for the weaving of linen cloth, etc. The coarse linen tow which is now extracted from the flax straw is of but little commercial value.

To make good oil—that is to say, to make the very best possible out of it, the flax should not be cut until it has commenced to ripen its seeds and such is the way that it is harvested in India, where labor only costs a few cents per day. In that far-off country the flax is pulled by hand and all the manipulations are hand work. The seed consequently is very plump and rich in oil, the juices having been perfectly elaborated by the natural process of ripening. This seed from India produces an oil that is highly prized by varnish makers and all others who *must have* linseed oil at its best and as good as can be made. It is for this reason that Calcutta seed linseed oil is so highly esteemed and that these varnish men, who are the best judges of linseed oil in the world, are willing to pay more for it than the price asked for the home grown linseed oil.

But the system of harvesting flaxseed in India cannot be practiced here in the United States nor in the South American countries where it is also raised, not even in Russia, where a good quantity of flaxseed is grown. Such slow processes would raise the price of the seed away beyond the limit. With the large acreage which the American farmer devotes to it, the harvesting of flaxseed would be a hard problem to solve, in fact, it is one that bothers them now under the rapid methods they employ, and what would it be, if they were to undertake the slow ways of India? In America the flax is cut by machinery, in the same manner as wheat—but if the farmers waited until the seed had begun to ripen to cut it, much of it would shell out and be scattered over the field and be wasted from the violent shaking it receives when struck by the harvesting machine; so to prevent this loss, it is cut while the seed is in the dough as it is called, just previous to its hardening. There can be no question but that it becomes solid and that it ripens after the cutting, but it is not so good for it as it does not receive the juices which it would have drawn from mother earth during the finishing of its ripening, and much of it is cut so green that it produces an inferior seed. When the season happens to be a dry one, the seed produced is generally fair, but when, as it sometimes happens, it is rainy and muggy, much inferior seed is the result, which contains more than the average of mucilaginous matter and it cannot be as good for painting purposes as it should be. There is no question then that it would pay owners of buildings being painted on the outside, to pay double the price asked for the inferior oil for a *good oil* to spread the paint upon them, than it would to use the poorer—but they will not, and who is to blame if poor painting is done?

It is not intended to convey the idea that *all* American linseed oil is poor; far from it, for some very good oil is made here, but only that much inferior seed is raised and sold and that such will not make good oil.

Much poor painting is done—all are aware of that—some contractors use snide oils knowingly, and again some have doped linseed oil palmed off upon them, and again some careful men have an occasional job go wrong, for which they rack their brains to find a cause for; but seldom do they ever think that it lavs where it really does—the quality of the linseed oil. *Good linseed oil is the life of paint.*

THE MANUFACTURE OF LINSEED OIL.

197. Not so very many years ago, nearly every locality had its linseed oil mill, its wool carding machine, etc.; many other industries that have all taken wings and left for the great cities, and there are still plenty of men who are living to-day who will recollect them. These local presses bought the seed raised in the neighborhood, crushed it, expressed the oil out of it, tanked it and when settled, sold it far and near. The name and reputation for honesty of the manufacturer was one of the biggest assets of the concern—but those days are gone. These old time crushers did not get near as much oil out of the seed then as is done now and if some of them could go to the present day linseed oil factories and see what is done in the way of extraction, they would hardly believe it possible. Then, under their

crude system of crushing the seed under the chasers and of pressing it with little better machinery than that used by the cider mill next door, perhaps.

The principles of making linseed oil is much the same to-day as then, but their application is different. There is no waste of anything under the new system—but that of the quality. We hear and read a great deal about cold pressed oil, etc., but with the powerful hydraulic presses in use it does not matter so much as to whether the flaxseed meal has been slightly heated or not as to the resulting quality. The only real difference will be that heated seed will make a somewhat more highly colored oil from some of its coloring pigments being released by the process, but that this injures the binding quality of the oil is very doubtful and much of this coloring matter is thrown down during the settling process. Considerably more of the mucilagenous parts of the seed is expressed under the new system than under the old and how much more of this is held in solution by the oil or how much of it is precipitated during the settling and clarifying process is the question, and it has not been satisfactorily answered so far.

Linseed oil after having been pressed out in the days that are gone, used to be put into settling tanks and good old father time set to work to do the precipitating of all the impurities to make it limpid and fit for use. This took several months. The foots and settling remained behind and—pure linseed oil was the result— such oil as old time painters loved to work with and they did good work with it—*work that stood.*

These old time retrospects are not colored by fancy or sentiment—no, they are not wanted to come back again and the present has much to be proud of—but its methods certainly do not give us as good linseed oil as into tanks where it is agitated with sulphuric acid as that which we used to get.

Linseed oil today, after it has been expressed, is run into tanks where it is agitated with. sulphuric acid, usually, which hastens the precipitation of its impuri ties. Some mills use chemicals to produce this precipitation and in one week of such treatment, the oil is limpid and ready to be barreled—but is it as good as that settled naturally by 90 days of tanking?

The above is the most usual method of obtaining the linseed oil from flaxseed, but there are other methods, one of which only will be described as it seems to have a sensible way of producing oil, it differing in every respect from that of expressing. It is called the *"perco lation process."*

By the percolation process the oil is not extracted by expression but is dissolved from the seed with a solvent in the following manner: After grinding, the meal is conducted to the top floor of rather high buildings, through the several stories of which to the top floor also, has been built percolators reaching from top to bottom. Into these the flaxseed meal is thrown and solidly packed; then benzine is poured in at the top and percolates through the flaxseed meal, dissolving all the oil in it on its flow downward and holding it in solution carries it down to the bottom with it; there it flows into pipes hich are heated. Benzine being volatile, vaporizes at comparatively low heat, escaping in that shape into condensing pipes and drums where it is cooled and returned to its liquid state to be used again and again in the same manner—as an agent of extraction. The oil itself is entirely freed of benzine and is conducted to clarifying tanks where it receives the usual treatment to clear it. Benzine no doubt dissolves some other substances, such as coloring matter, etc., that is undesirable in a paint oil—but it has no affinity for mucilage and other baneful substances which are expressed by the other methods and no doubt but that during the process of clarifying much of these foreign substances are eliminated. Some claim that some of these remain which is not thrown down and that it injures the oil—it may be so; as most of these statements seem to orginate with people whose interests are connected with linseed oil obtained the other way may it not be possible that many of these may have been sugegsted by self interest? While not Missourians, there are several persons who have used both who affirm that they would have to be shown if there was any material difference between them in the use they have made of them in their practical painting experience.

Linseed oil is at its best in the "raw" state only, and it is only in that condition that intelligent painters use it and that it can be recommended for the painting of exteriors of buildings or even for the interiors. In its raw state it is elastic, which permits it to expand and contract along with any kind of surfaces it is spread over, be they wood, brick, metal or stone. Raw linseed oil is also penetrating, unless in very cold weather, when it is viscid, which enables it to reach down into the pores of any material it is applied upon, with the exception of glass—as all other material used in house construction is more or less porous even to iron and steel. Linseed oil painting thus forms little rootlet like connections with the material it is placed over, which gives it a firm anchorage to its under surface and from which it can be forced only by moisture or the decay of the linseed oil in time. Pigments having a great tenacity between their atoms will usually pull themselves off from surfaces in the shape of scales when they have been used in the priming and these scales will show these rootlet-like projections very plainly.

BOILED LINSEED OIL.

199. *Boiled linseed*—that has been boiled—which is far from being the case always, has lost its elasticity by the process of boiling it and nearly all its penetration. Boiling it, turns it into a varnish and really it partakes more of that character than that which has been described under raw linseed oil. As it cannot contract and expand itself to accommodate the nature of the surface it covers, it must in time give to the strain given it by the contraction of the surface it is painted over, with the result that it cracks to accommodate it. White lead.

which the reader will recollect is not given to scaling on account of its atoms having no affinity for each other, which chalk off with raw oil after that has decayed— will crack and scale when mixed with boiled oil and all painting of any kind done with it will do the same; only more so.

Then again as nothing short of an expensive chemical analysis can possibly determine its purity the door is practically thrown wide open for the possibility of its adulteration. Few retail dealers buy it in a pure state, although they may believe it to be so and buy it for such. Many others, knowing that the probabilities of obtaining it *pure* are rather slim, and that some jobbers dope it or bung hole boil it, conclude that they may as well have a finger in it themselves and to know just how much of it they have in it, so they usually take out 5 or 10 gallons of the raw oil from a barrel usually averaging 50 gallons and fill it up with 10 gallons of benzine dryers, a cheap manganese wash, dear at 25 cents per gallon in barrels lots, which gives the oil the proper color and drying qualities of boiled oil and unconsciously perhaps, but surely, the customer is benefitted thereby as that oil so treated is fully as good, if not better, for painting than pure boiled oil—*that has been boiled*. Bung hole boiling as the above described substitution is called, has become a byword common to every user of linseed oil.

REFINED AND BLEACHED LINSEED OIL.

200. As the refining of oil bleaches it and the bleaching refines it, these two designations should go hand in hand as they practically mean one and the same thing.

Linseed oil contains some coloring matter in solution which is extracted with it from the flaxseed, either by the hydraulic system of pressing or that of percolation, as it was seen. It parts with a portion of it while it is settled but still holds a quantity of it after that. Now certain light tones of colors and especially the zinc whites, which require much more oil to grind them than white lead, are apt to gain a yellowish tinge from ordinary oil. Varnish manufacturers too, who put out efforts on all sides to make as light and clear toned varnishes as possible, must get rid of most, if not all, this coloring matter contained in the oil used in grinding such colors, or in preparing varnishes. Such either buy the oil already refined or refine it themselves.

The process of refining and bleaching linseed oil is simple enough; it is: Further agitation of the oil with sulphuric acid and exposure to sunlight for a few days in shallow vessels covered so as to exclude dirt, but admitting light, but little if any air, as that might have a tendency to *fatten* it.

Linseed oil which has been treated so is nearly as light toned (not quite) as poppy seed oil, but it will not nor cannot take the place of that and nut oil for artists' use because—all linseed oil, no matter how carefully coloring matter may have been extracted out of it—

will darken with time. Even the others do, but not quite to the same extent as it will. This darkening of oil is what causes the darkening of old oil paintings.

Let *linseed oil's* faults be what they may, there is nothing better made for painting purposes, and it is better and stronger than any other of the *fixed oils*.

POPPY SEED OIL.

201. As its name indicates, this oil is the product of the poppy plant. Some varieties of it produce very large seed heads and are raised in fields in a commercial way for its seeds. They are harvested in baskets as the head ripens—which they do not do all at once, so that it requires several goings over the field to get them all in. This is a slow process, hence this paint oil can never be cheap. The seeds are crushed, the oil drawn out by pressure in much the same way as related for linseed oil. The oil produced is very light and clear, and it is highly esteemed by artists as it does not turn dark with age as linseed oil does, although it will too, (in a lesser degree.)

It does not dry very readily, nor has it the tenacity of linseed oil, and as its cost is so much greater, there is little danger of its ever becoming a very dangerous rival and its use is mainly confined to artists.

The main uses are in the grinding of zinc white, but even for the grinding of this the use of it is waning— even artists are beginning to shun it as the cleaner tone obtained from its use applies to whites only, and as with time it darkens also, there is but little gained by its use after all, especially for those who are working for posterity.

NUT OIL.

202. Nut oil is produced mainly from the meats or kernels of the English walnut, so called no doubt because most of them come from Italy, France and Spain. These meats are crushed and the oil expressed in much the same manner as stated before for linseed oil. This oil is very light and clear with just the slighest suspicion of yellow and is the cleanest toned that can be had for mixing with pigments and for that reason is most highly esteemed by artists who cater mainly to the sale of their painting to the present and do not care to have their work endure forever, for unfortunately the old adage holds true for it : "Pretty is who pretty does," it has not got the tenacity of linseed oil and the decay of the oil will in a comparatively short time loosen its hold upon the pigments. So with a prohibitive cost in the first place, which artists only can stand—as a little goes a long ways with them—there is little danger of its ever being as much as spoken of in general paint shops.

THE VOLATILE OILS.

203. These oils are so named because of their having great evaporating qualities. When exposed to air, especially under heat, which accelerates the process of evaporation, they vanish entirely away in vapors. All

the volatile oils have an extremely pungent small which is peculiar to each, and by which each class of them is easily recognized by the nose to any one accustomed to their use. Their action in connection with paint and its application is to render it more fluid. They can be mixed in any proportion with linseed oil and are perfect solvents of it.

204. They are indispensable to the proper mixing of paints and without them it would be impossible to do many kinds of painting. By their admixture they render linseed oil more fluid, more penetrating, helping to make it set more quickly. This quicker setting renders possible the application of heavy pigments which would otherwise quickly separate from linseed oil alone as that would not commence to set for a much longer time.

The volatile oils have no binding properties whatever, and their beneficial use for outdoor painting is altogether mechanical as adjuncts to linseed oil and for specific purposes only. When enough has been used of them to accomplish the purpose intended not a drop more should be added—for then they become harmful instead of beneficial.

205. They are chiefly used for interior painting and it is well that it is so, as being in a manner protected they can be used in much larger quantities than for outdoor painting and for *flatting* instead of being the adjunct to linseed oil, they are the principal thinner and linseed oil enters the compound simply because of its binding property and not because it is desirable. All

through this manual has been given under their proper headings, directions as to how the various coats of paint should be mixed with them.

Volatile oils are extensively used in the preparation of varnishes and for tempering them for application when they need it. They are good solvents of the fixed oils and having detergent properties are useful to clean paint brushes, etc.

TURPENTINE.

206. This is the product of the conifers—all pine and resinous evergreen trees contain it in some form, but our own southern long leaf yellow pine produces more of it than all the other pines of the whole world put together. The trees are scarified and the crude turpentine exudes through the wounds, gathering at the bottom of the cut out and hollowed in grooves called "the box." This crude turpentine solidifies into a soft gum which is distilled when the spirits of turpentine of commerce as we know it is separated from its solid portions which remain behind as *rosin*.

Turpentine is by long odds the most useful of the volatile oils used in painting. Its odor while very pungent is not disagreeable to most persons, and while when it is used in large quantities as in flatting, when a person will absorb large quantities of it by absorption and through inhaling it, it will act excessively upon his kidneys when used in a moderate way or out of doors it will not be very likely to injure him.

BENZINE AND NAPTHA.

207. Benzine and naptha are both volatile oils which are obtained from the distillation of crude petroleum oil. They are so nearly identical in composition, working qualities and everything else, that they are joined together in this review as everything that can be said of the one applies to the other also. Their odor is extremely pungent and disagreeable to most persons. They are very dilutent and their effect and action upon paint is very similar to that of turpentine. Few people can remain shut up in a room where they are used in flatting, for few men can stand their fumes long at a time. This is their worst fault, and after all this is the chief reason why they are not used more extensively than they are—without the having to give any other reasons which usually are not to the point and which cannot be made to stand investigation. The time is near at hand when painters will be *forced* to use them as the turpentine fields are narrowing up every day more and more and in a very few years there will be little more left than will be needed for pharmaceutical preparations in compounding medicine and it will have become so high priced that it will have to be benzine and naptha or *nothing*.

It is hoped that preivous to that time, chemistry will discover some remedy to remove or disguise the "smell." It is to a great extent minimized now, and the barrel heads say: *deodorized* benzine, etc., but there is room for still more of it to kill it entirely and much remains to be done.

OIL OF LAVENDER (OIL OF SPIKE.)

208. . This is used only in china or porcelain painting, where owing to its fatty and lesser volatile condition than the others which have just been noticed—it prevents the colors from running and gives plenty of time for their application. This is never used in general house painting.

DRYERS.

209. Linseed oil, unless under very adverse circumstances, would dry naturally. Some pigments when mixed with it have the property of rendering it more drying and help it to dry more quickly than it would by its lone self—but others again are anti-drying and greatly retard the drying of the oil. Again the weather conditions may not be propitious to the proper drying of the oil, so that when a person has some outdoor painting to do unless the weather is fair, settled and warm, he will need to use some dryers to hasten the drying of the paint as it would not do to trust to luck and the weather and have the painting spoiled.

The above must not be construed as an endorsement of the unlimited use of driers in paint. No, far from it. There is no one cause why so much linseed oil painting goes to pieces in a hurry than can easily be traced to the *abuse* of driers. The word abuse is used purposely and underscored because the proper use of driers is allowable.

Nearl all the driers in the market today are compounded from the oxides of manganese and are naturally dark colored on that account. They are prepared and sold under a great variety of names, as japan driers, liquid driers and with a host of fancy proprietary names and at prices where no painter can afford to fool his time away in preparing them himself.

There is a queer thing in connection with the use of the liquid driers and it is that a small quantity of it will sometimes act quicker than an overdose of it, and that when it is used in overdoses it will retard instead of hasten the drying of oil. One tablesponful of any good liquid drier will be sufficient to dry a quart of paint or more.

There are some special driers prepared for use with zinc white—these too are best bought ready for use, ground up in paste form, as the time required and the special facilities needed for grinding, mixing, etc., are not to be had in every shop.

QUESTIONS IN OILS AND DRIERS.

194. How are oils useful in painting divided?

195. What is said of fixed oils in general?

196. What is said concerning the production of flaxseed?

197. How is linseed oil manufactured?

198. What is said of raw linseed oil?

199. What is said of boiled linseed oil?
200. What is refined or bleached linseed oil?
201. How is poppy seed oil produced?
202. What is nut oil?
203. What are volatile oils?
204. What action do they exert in paint?
205. Where are they most useful?
206. What is turpentine and how produced?
207. What is said of benzine and turpentine?
208. Where is oil of lavender mostly useful?
209. What is said regarding driers?

PAINTING IN OIL ON GLASS.

210. Most of the painting done in oil on glass is that done by "Sign Painters," and as this branch of the business will be treated at length in subsequent pages, the reader is referred to that subject where he will find full directions given for the same. See paragraphs 275 to 276.

There is, it is true, some little amateurish painting in oil upon glass, but such work stands to *true art* in very much the same relation as "doggerel" verse does to poetry.

On account of the difficulty of judging the effects of colors from the back side of the glass where the painting must be done in order to produce the solid and enameled effect which is the only excuse people can have for doing any painting at all upon such fragile material, for if the glass be painted on its front side then it would in no wise differ from any other painting done on canvas or wood and there could be no excuse given for not using those insetad. For painting on glass from the reverse side, the subject must be outlined and all the prominent dark colors must be put on first, for otherwise they would not show if applied over white and other light tints; then when dry the next prominent dark tints and others which must be blended into them to make graded tones. This is where the great difficulty comes in—to blend them properly—even when well done, which is seldom the case, it cannot possibly be done as well as upon surface work and with its outlines, etc., must present a gingerbread appearance which is in bad taste, to say the least, and which will set an artists' teeth on edge. Such attempt must always be crude and unsatisfactory.

QUESTION ON PAINTING ON GLASS.

210. What is said concerning painting in oil on glass?

PAINTING A BATH TUB.

211. The painting of a *bath tub*, or rather the repainting of them, is not a very difficult operation—but the preparing and getting ready for it may be so; especialy if the painting is expected to stand any length of time.

The paint on a bath tub is subjected to considerable more hardship than any other kind of painting has to·

unless it be that done upon steam pipes and radiators. The great heat at which hot water is sometimes turned on and the suddenness with which ice cold water follows it to cool it is very much harder on the paint than anything it would have to stand from the elements out doors; in order to stand all those extremes it must be mixed in an entirely different manner from that in which exterior oil painting is done, as ordinary linseed oil paint would peel off in no time under the strain it would have to bear.

New bath tubs are painted with a specially prepared varnish paint where the pigment is mixed with what is called "baking japan." After the painting they are placed in an oven and subjected to a great heat which causes the japan paint to flow level and this leveling frees it of brush marks and causes it to dry very hard, nearly as hard as the iron over which it is applied. After having gone through this baking process, water and heat—such at least as it is subjected to in a bath room—have no effect upon it.

212. But when a bath tub is repainted the above process cannot be employed unless the tub is returned to some establishment where they are prepared to do such work with ovens sufficiently large to bake the tubs. This would be much the best way—but such concerns are not to be found everywhere and it is well to know what is the "next best" way to effect the repainting of it "where it stands in the bath room." The *"next best"* as in most all other things, is not as good as the origi-

nal but answers the purpose fairly well. It will have to be mixed so that it will *air* dry and as no heat can be applied which will cause it to flow level it can not be as level as in the original painting.

In the first place all the chipped or loose paint must be carefully removed and sandpapered; then the surface should be run over with a very stiff bristle brush to remove any dirt which may have found a lodgment any where, especialy between the chipped places. The whole of the inside of the tub should be now washed with a solution of sal-soda which should be afterward carefully rinsed off with clean water and afterward well dried by friction with dry cotton rags, when it should be left several hours to become free of moisture when it will be ready to receive the paint coats.

This is prepared from white lead and turpentine. The white lead should be ground in japan as no oil at all should be used. Go over the bare spots first of all, in order to level up the surface as much as possible; be careful to wipe off the surplus color which will find its way on the adjoining surface of the paint and would make a ridge if not wiped off. It will take two coats of the filling to fill these places. These coats dry quickly and two or three coats can be given in one day. When the filling to fill these bare places. These coats dry quickly and two or three coats can be given in one day. When the filling up has been completed, give the whole inside of the tub two coats, prepared as for the filling. This should make a pretty fair job if the brushing has been carefully done. It will, however, look flat and a protecting coat of good varnish must be given the paint. It must be a hard drying varnish and moreover it must be of light color. This is sometimes difficult to find in many localities. Upon the whole it will be much better and safer to employ the following system in repainting a bath tub: Clean up in exactly the same way as stated before, then buy some ready prepared bath tub enamel. It is mixed, ready thinned for application with the right kind of varnish by the manufacturers, who are usually better judges of the right sort of varnish to use than the average painter is and these have a reputation to make and sustain and they have to use all possible precaution in preparing them so as to do all that such a paint is expected to do. As some manufacturers prepare these bath tub enamels differently from others, each having their own formula, it will be best to follow the directions printed on the label of each can—and the painting will be the better for it.

QUESTIONS ON PAINTING OF BATH TUBS.

211. What is said about the painting of bath tubs in general?

212. How are bath tubs to be prepared and repainted?

PAINTING OF STATUARY.

213. Few persons have any idea of the extent of this branch of the painter's art—for it is at least a semi

artistic occupation. Statues in city and country churches and statuettes in numberless quantities are used in nearly every home, no matter how humble it may be, either as religious objects or in the bric-a-brac shelf or chimney mantle, besides the ornamentation in bed rooms, etc. Some is done in china factories and the greater part of the statuary painting is done in European establishments. Many have commenced the manufacture of statuary in this country. But it is not so much of the painting required in their manufacture which will be referred to in this article as the repainting of them, as in all our larger cities the repainting has to be done again and again, owing to the smoky atmosphere which soon makes them dingy. This furnishes lucrative employment to many painters aside from what is originally done in factories where statues are manu factured.

214. The statutes are cast in plaster paris from moulds. The plaster having been mixed with fiber very similar to well picked oakum but somewhat coarser and longer; this is done in order that they may not break so readily and upon the same principle that hair is added to mortar for plastering.

After the statue has been cast and well seasoned, they must be filled, but previous to the filling it should be primed inside with linseed oil. The statue should be placed upside down as they are usually cast hollow, they should be carefully propped up and guarded from injury from falling and then linseed oil should be poured into the opening up to the top of it. After an hour the linseed oil should be poured back as the statue will have absorbed all it is capable of in that time.

The above applies to busts and statuettes really more than to statues as the valuable ones of these are frequently cast solidly.

They are then placed upon a receptacle to drip and dry, which will require a week as the linseed oil should be raw and used without any drier.

When dry they should be placed upside down again in the same manner as before, being filled with oil and should be filled with plaster paris made sufficiently liquid to pour out. But little at a time should be added as there is considerable heat evolved during the setting and also some swelling, and the statuette might be cracked from that cause. Pour a little at a time, waiting two hours before pouring in any more and continuing doing so until it is completely filled up. This will make it as solid as if it had been cut out of stone and about as heavy. No more plaster should be mixed up than can be used at one pouring as otherwise it would set very hard and be lost.

According as to the size of the statues it will take from one to three weeks for the plaster to part with all its extra moisture and to become sufficiently dry to begin the painting. If the painting should be commenced before the drying is thoroughly accomplished there would be great danger of its peeling.

215. The statuettes should now be well rubbed

over with a coat of clear linseed oil, brushing them over and over again two or three times as the oil will soak into them quickly. They should now be laid aside to dry and given eight or ten days for the oil to harden up thoroughly, when the painting proper may begin.

The first coat may be thinned with half oil and half turpentine and the coloring should be nearly the same as that intended for the finishing, but no attention need be paid to any of the details.

After two or three days' drying the finishing coat may be applied. This should not contain more than 1/5 linseed oil and 4/5 turpentine for the thinner of the pigment. About ¼ ounce of beeswax (bleached) should have been previously melted for every pint of turpentine used and mixed up with that warmed up. This makes a beautiful, soft flat finish with a delicate transparency of tone unobtainable in any other way. The statues or statuettes are now ready for the details etc.; and the gilding also should be applied as soon as it has well dried, which will take from 24 to 48 hours.

QUESTIONS ON THE PAINTING OF STATUARY.

213.   What is said of painting statuary?

214.   How are statues and statuettes prepared for painting?

215.   How are they painted?

PAPER HANGER'S TOOLS.

216. One of the most important tools to the paper hanger is a good table and supports for it to cut paper upon and to spread the paste on it.

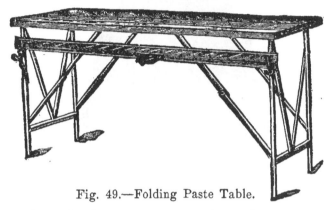

Fig. 49.—Folding Paste Table.

The above is shown not so much as that some other form of pasteboard and tresoles may not answer the purpose; but that this is a very convenient and handy one which folds up into a small space when not in use.

The paste brushes shown below will suit the requirements of any paperhanger. Fig. 50 has a grip

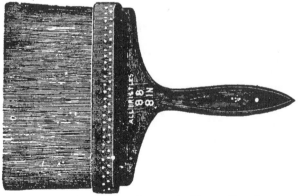

Fig. 50—Paperhanger's Paste Brush.

handle and Fig. 51 a slim, oval handle easy, on the hand.

Fig. 51—Paperhanger's Paste Brush.

Under the heading of "Brushes" see Figs. 25 and 26, which show two styles of smoothing brushes, Fig.

Figs. 52 and 53—Paperhanger's Smoothing Brushes.

26 showing one which is a combination tool, having a seam roller at one end.

Seam rollers are shown below in Figs. 54, 55 and 56 of various forms under the letters A, B, C, D, E, F, G, H, J, K, L, M.

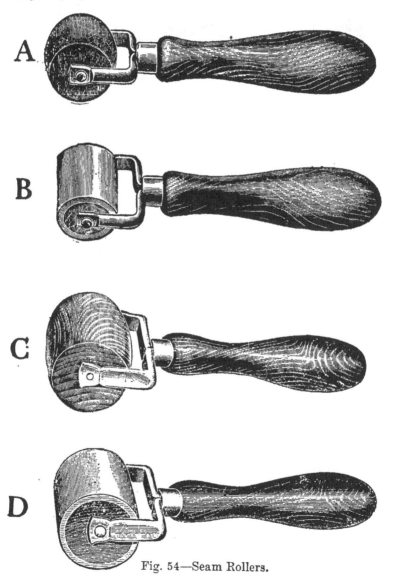

Fig. 54—Seam Rollers.

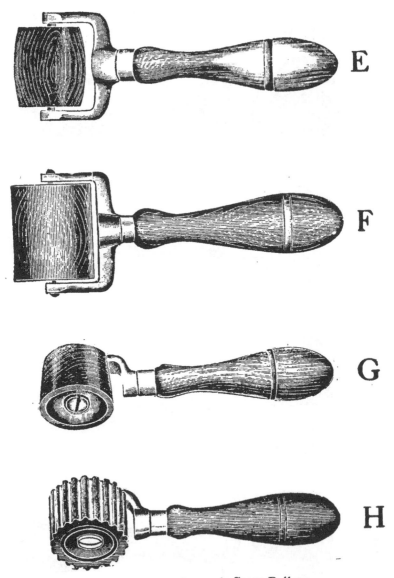

Fig. 55—Paperhanger's Seam Rollers.

J

K

L

M

Fig. 56—Paperhanger's Seam Rollers.

Smoothing rollers are indispensible in smoothing embossed and other high priced paper as the ordinary

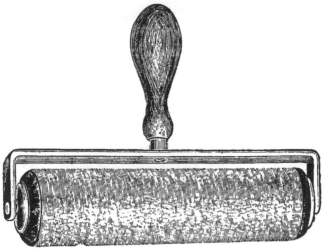

Fig. 57—Smoothing Roller.

smoothing brush would be apt to obliterate the embossing. Two kinds are shown in Figs. 57 and 58.

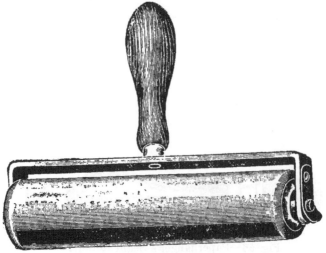

Fig. 58—Smoothing Roller.

A good machine to trim paper is useful for the trimming of all the cheaper papers and can be made to answer fairly well for the better grades also if care is exercised in the trimming with them. Fig. 59 shows how one is operated.

Fig. 59—Machine Trimmer.

Straight edges to trim paper by with the knives, also to split same, are usually made of narrow strips of dif-

No. 1 Brass Bound Trimmer Straightedge
Fig. 60—Straight Edges.

ferent kinds of wood glued together. Fig. 60 shows how they are put together.

Paper hangers as a rule are very fastidious about the shape of the knives they use in the trimming of paper. It is a matter of custom and habit which may be gratified, as our Fig. 61 shows all kinds of shapes of them.

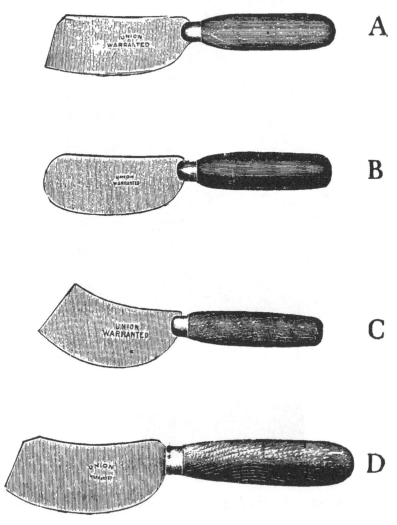

Fig. 61—Paperhanger's Knives.

And of the rotary knives an equally large variety are shown in Fig. 62 under the letters A, B, C, D, E, F, G, H.

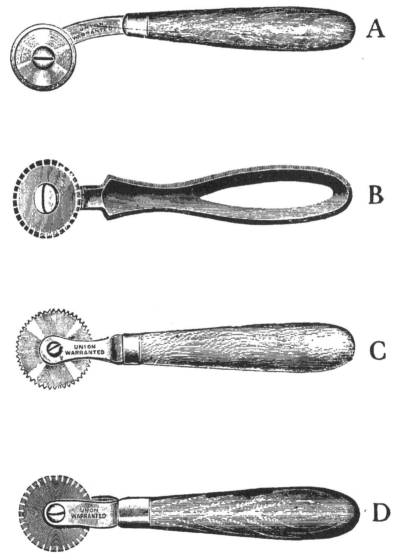

Fig. 62—Paperhanger's Wheel Knives.

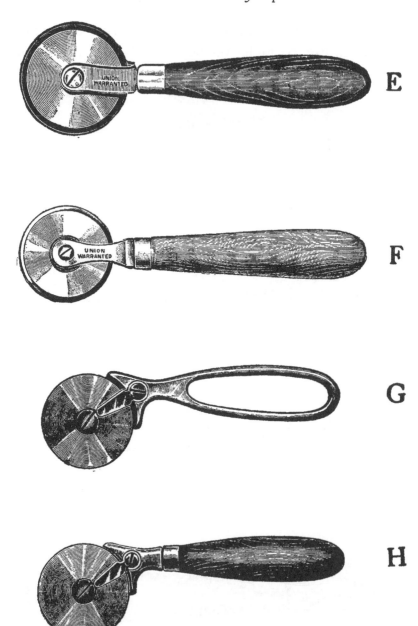

Fig. 62—Paperhanger's Wheel Knives.

An excellent and handy tool to have is a combination casing and corner knife such as is shown in Fig. 63.

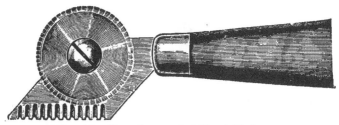

Fig, 63—Paperhanger's Wheel Knives.

Some very handy rotary trimming knives are now made which run in a grooved straight edge, which pre‑vents the wheel from slipping or getting off the track.

Fig. 64—Wall Paper Trimmer.

Fig. 64 illustrates the manner of using them and shows the groove on the straight edge into which they are fastened and held.

Another excellent tool is the graduated plumb and level. Fig 65 gives a good illustration of the tool.

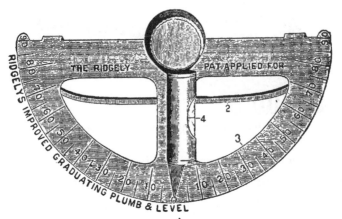

Fig. 65—Graduating Plumb and Level.

The old fashion plumb bob is also very useful and is too well known to need illustrating.

A few twelve or fourteen quarts galvanized iron pails to hold size and paste in, a supply of step ladders, ladder trestles and strong 2-inch walking and scaffold planks complete the list.

QUESTION ON PAPER HANGER'S TOOLS.

216. Use the above to refer to as you have need for the same.

PAPER HANGING.

217. Paper hanging has become such an enormous factor in the decoration of interiors as to be used by every family in the land from the very poorest shack or hut to the palatial residence of the millionaire. It is no wonder, then, that it gives employment to such an army of men. Probably 95 per cent of all painters who call themselves general workmen are paper hangers also.

Wall paper certainly is the poor man's friend as some of it is so cheap as to be next to nothing per roll. This makes it possible for any person having a desire for clean and cheerful looking rooms to indulge the fancy at a cost so small that it is not a burden.

Some years ago there was much space taken up in the papers about persons having been poisoned by sleeping in papered bedrooms and the fault had been laid to the employment of arsenic and other poisons in the printing of the wall paper. One hears but little of this now, so the presumption is that whatever may have been the practice of wall paper manufacturers in the past, that now, at least, there are no poisons used in the colors used by them. As they have always strenuously denied that they used arsenic when they were accused of it, it is a matter of great doubt if they ever did resort to it as the purpose for which it might be used can be supplied at a lower cost by non-poisonous compounds. Human nature is much the same in wall paper printers as it is in any one else. They certainly would be fools to pay more for doing something which they could all know would be hurtful to that business.

Everything under the sun that has ever been used as wall covering is now imitated by wall paper, and that so cleverly as to appear to be the very kind of material they are imitating—tapestries, draperies, canvas, burlap, buckram, laces, leather—there is nothing or no effects which they do not reproduce and the imitative powers of wall paper artists is wonderful to behold!

The wall paper trade has so systematized and arranged things that a good, tasty selection is made possible even for people who are color blind. The arrange ment of sample books which show combinations of ceil ings, walls and frieze, all colored and designed purposely for each other, are all so good that no one can go far wrong in making a selection. Besides these already prepared tasteful combinations there is a limitless quantity of independent designs which give the tasty person a chance to select something which will show individuality of arrangement, and where he can give his own artistic tastes full play in arranging his decorative schemes.

When selecting wall paper several things should be taken into consideration in order that there may not be any incongruities. The location of the room as to light, the character of the house itself, the prevailing tone of the furniture and carpets, and the social position of the occupants of the house, etc., etc.

A sunny room with plenty of light usually requires cool-toned paper as warm-toned hangings have the tendency to add a feeling of increased heat; this is imaginative it is true, but existing just the same, and no amount of reasoning takes it away, either.

Likewise, for the same reason, but reversed, warm toned hangings should be selected for rooms which have no sunshine and are in constant shadow. The warm coloring adds a feeling of warmth. Thus by judicious selection an evenly balanced whole will be secured where the difference in temperature will not be so keenly felt as it would be otherwise. The coloring of the carpets may greatly mar an otherwise prefectly combined scheme for the walls and these should always be considered in making a selection.

Now, as to the social position, many would say: "How can that possibly affect the selection of wall paper?" The right of selecting any kind of wall hangers is not denied to any one for we are all born equal and free(?) but sometimes exercising the right may render people ridiculous. A man has a perfect right to wear a swallow tail dress suit on the street and with that put on a chauffeur's cap, but they seldom exercise it. So a person earning $12.00 per week who would select silk hangings with hand made gold leaf decoration on it to match a 75-cent-a-yard ingrain carpet would have as good a right to it as the man whose weekly income is as great as the first earns in a whole year—the $12.00 man should not exercise his rights, that's all. Happily wall paper has tasteful selections to suit the pocket books and taste of all sorts and conditions of people.

218. The proper conditions for hanging paper upon the walls requires them to be hard and smooth. If they are not so naturally they should be made so—at least as near as it is possible to do so, before the hanging is commenced.

In new houses and for new work everything usually works lovely and easy, seldom presenting any difficulties and so such need no special mention as to how to prepare the walls and are ready for hanging.

219. If the house has been papered before, it is always best to wash off and remove the old paper before applying the next coat of it, yet some people will keep on hanging paper on walls repeatedly without taking off the old. If wall paper is hung anew every year or at most, every two years, it would not be especially hurtful if two thicknesses of it is left on, provided that it be surely 'taken off before the third one goes on—but usually persons who form the bad habit of hanging new paper over old hardly ever stop on two coats and the habit in time becomes incurable—or till the myriads of bacterial colonies breeding all the diseases human flesh is heir to—fastens some deadly disease upon a member of the family and sends him to an untimely grave. No doubt but that decaying wall hanging furnishes a medium through which many a disease germ has been carried to persons who live in houses where coat after coat of paper have been put on, one on top of another,

for years and years. Probably all the poison cases we used to hear about were due to this same cause—decay.

The moral carried by the above is: Always take off the old paper in a room before hanging the new, that is if you value your own or your family's health.

After taking off the paper the walls should be sized over with glue size made antiseptic by the addition of a few drops of carbolic acid. If the smell is objectionable, by the addition of a few grains of corrosive sublimate, which is still better. This protects the underside of the paper from becoming the habitation of visible as well as invisible insects and bacteria.

In very old houses some of the old-time plastered walls can frequently be found which are in such dilapidated condition that one may well wonder why the plasterer had not been called in ahead of the paper hanger to do patching, which, in some instances, amount to as much as a fourth of the whole surface to be papered—but the paper hanger is suposed to cover the old walls and make them look as good as new.

All paper hangers should be at least two-third plasterers, too, and carry a kit of plasterer's tools with them, at least a pointing trowel and even a large plastering trowel will be needed to patch up some of the "grand openings" on the walls. With the ready-to-use prepared plasters, which can now be found everywhere, it is not such a very difficult job to fix up walls, after all, and they can be gone over in a very little time, ordinarilly. Cracks on plastered walls require more time to fill them properly than bigger holes do, especially where they are numerous and small. A preparation of plaster paris thinned with glue water will be found best for all the smaller openings as that will set slowly enough to allow plenty of time to do the work, and there being no caustic lime in it, the color of the wall paper will not be injured. As soon as the cracks and holes in the plastering have been repaired, go over them with the size mentioned before and the room is then ready to be papered.

220.   Sometimes the paper hanger is called upon to hang paper in the back rooms of stores and elsewhere where one or more sides of a room are wooden partitions. Wall paper hung upon bare wood will soon crack, as the paper is inflexible and cannot give with the wood's contraction in cold, dry weather or its expansion during a hot, moist spell. To prepare the wooden surface so the wall paper will stay on it, they must be canvassed over with muslin. The best way to do this is to sew together enough widths to cover the side of a wall to an opening cut to the proper lengths; then it should be tacked first at the top, then at the bottom and sides. Then tack it through the center and elsewhere so that it will not bag anywhere, but lay flat.

Some paper hangers prefer to size the partitions and to paste the muslin, laying it on in strips the same as wall paper. This method has the advantage of making a solid job of it, but the beading of the boards is likely to show through the paper after it is hung over it. It is also more difficult to hang the wet, limp muslin and it will require two men to handle the wet pieces—the extra man to pull the strip of muslin off the boards until the other has brushed it down.

HANGING THE PAPER.

221. The paper which is sent on the job is some· times machine-trimmed at the shop before it is sent out. With a little care in the pasting of it, paper trimmed before hand answers very well for all ordinary work; but much the better way is to paste the wall paper, fold it both ways and trim it with a knife and straight edge. These knives come in all sorts of shapes and are shown in Fig. 61. Some paper hangers prefer a rotary wheel knife and a good' variety of these are shown in Fig. 62. But the surest of these, and the handiest, too, is shown in Fig. 64.

222. There are many different kinds of paste in the market which are offered ready prepared. Some are made from flour, steam cooked, and put up in barrels and half barrels. Some antiseptic preparation is usually added to it to prevent its souring as quickly as it would otherwise. The steam cooked paste is put up very thick and requires thinning with cold water. It works smooth and nice, but it has its faults—the greatest one being that when it has to be shipped from a distance the freight on the water it conains, and he cost of the package, count up heavily, making its cost too high.

The cooked and dried paste in powdered form, only requiring thinning with cold water or even with warm water, are excellent. They keep indefinitely, there is no freight to pay for water. They are handy to send out on a job, being always ready to be thinned as wanted, and enough can be carried in the coat pocket to do an ordinary room.

Then again there are preparations which resemble dextrine somewhat, but which make a stronger paste that dries harder, which are made out of some of the by-products of starch and glucose factories, which come cheap and are very efficient. They do not make as white a paste as flour but they do not strike through the paper, and paper pasted with it will slide better than the ordinary flour paste would permit; they are readily dissolved in cold water and for that reason are preferred by many paper hangers, but warm water is better.

Some, again, prefer to make their paste from starch. This, of course, makes a very nice, clear smooth paste—but it is not considered as strong as flour paste.

While prepared pastes and powdered paste are very handy, etc., it frequently happens that they cannot be bought in certain localities and for that and other reasons every paper hanger should know how to make his own paste from flour, either wheat or rye. The following directions will make good, smooth paste if the directions are carried out; to make an ordinary pail of paste, take 2½ pounds of flour. It need not be the highest quality as the lower grades make a stronger paste than the whitest does, and the color of paste does not hurt it any. Put the flour in the pail you intend to make it and cook it in. Then pour in enough cold water to make it up into a stiff dough as for bread. Stir it up well until you are tired of it and some more. When well worked up pour in a little more cold water, stir as before, only that it will be a little thinner, and keep on adding a little water and stirring well until the whole mass is about of the consistency of thick pancake batter. This batter should be of a uniform texture if it has been properly stirred up. While preparing the flour, plenty of water should have been provided and put on the stove to boil. Then pour some of the boiling water into the batter slowly, stirring it well, and keep on pouring with one hand, stirring it well, and until it is cooked, which you will soon find out as the paste thickens and changes color when cooked. Be sure to have enough boiling water or you may not have enough, and the batch will be spoiled, as it must be cooked then or never. As the paste thickens in cooling, it should be thinned with enough water to make it rather thinner than it needs to be for the pasting on, but even then when it cools it will be likely to be too thick for use and probably will require to be thinned with more water. Should it be lumpy it will show that it has not been properly stirred up in the dough or in the batter before cooking it; in that case strain it through a calcimine strainer or through cheese cloth, and it will then be fit for use.

223. Paste should be applied to the *wrong* side of the paper, never on its *face*. This advice may sound simple and foolish to most persons, but that is where many paper hangers who are good at hanging manage to get more on than they intended. Good pasters among paper hangers are not as plentiful as they ought to be, and many an otherwise well executed job is marred by paste spots showing here and there or along the edges.

In pasting the paper the outer edge is usually easily taken care of by bringing it over the edge of the board beyond the rest of the paper so that the paste brush will not touch the understrips; it is the back edge which gives trouble. The better way is to run the paste brush on the body of the paper to within ¾ of an inch of the edge and when the strip has been all pasted but that to slip the hand under the strip being pasted and to slide it along ahead of the paste brush so that the brush can slide over the edge of the paper while it is lifted by the left hand clear of the board. In the ready trimmed pa per, extra care should be taken that the edges are not given too much paste as it would squeeze over while be ing smoothed on the wall.

When the first half of a strip of paper has been pasted, fold it over carefully and pull up the rest of the strip on the paste board, which proceed to paste the same as directed; then fold it together. Folding it in that way prevents the paster slide coming in contact with the hands while handling it, and makes it easy to carry about as only the dry side shows.

For very long strips the paper may have to be doubled over again and again in order to get it all pasted on the ordinary 7 or 8-foot board. In such cases it must be machine-trimmed beforehand as it would be a very difficult and annoying job to unfold it and trim it piecemeal with a knife, or it may be dry trimmed by hand with shears as is the general practice in England today.

224. For very good reasons ceilings are usually papered first. This can be done in two ways: First, with a scaffold, supporting walking boards, which may be ordinary horses of the right height, which can be pulled along on the floor to the end of the room or from a walking board supported by a couple of ladder trestles. If the room is not square, a chalk line should be used in order to mark out the edge where the first strip of paper is to be placed; this should catch all parts of the ceiling between it and the side wall. If the wall is not true, some portions of the first strip will lap over on the side wall, but that does not matter as the frieze will cover it. Then continue, strip by strip, to the end. The first strip being right, all the others must be, too.

Dropped ceilings are so called in wall paper parlance when the ceiling paper is extended over on the side walls either one-half or the width of a whole strip or more.

Cheap papers are usually trimmed only on one side and lapped over the selvage of the other.

The better grades are usually *"butted,"* or both edges are trimmed off and a joint made, as the name indicates, by abutting the two sides together when they are rolled over with the seam roller, and the rest of the strip with the smoothing roller.

In the hanging of ingrained paper great care must be taken to have the ceiling and walls sandpapered smooth, as a single sand speck will show through it. Also great care must be exercised in trimming the edges for they *must* fit up close or the plaster will show through. If the ceiling is uneven it will be impossible to make a good job with it except by matching up some distemper color as near like it as possible, and painting a strip an inch wide where the seams should meet; then, if, perchance, the perfect fitting of the edges is impossible, the plaster will not show through and nothing but a critical investigation will show it to the observer.

225. As nearly everything said above concerning the hanging of paper upon ceilings applies with equal force to the hanging of paper upon the side walls, it will be unnecessary to repeat it here again. The only difference is in the manner of doing the work of applying it, which for side walls is done from a step ladder. Commencing at a point where, after going around the room should there be a miss-match where the paper comes together, there will be the less likelihood of its being noticed; the work is continued, strip by strip, until one reaches the starting point. Windows and doors should have the design carried through over them, and the windows under them also. All corners

should be cut out, making an allowance of ½ an inch of paper for the lap over.

It is immaterial as to which way a man turns around the room in hanging wall paper, and it is altogether a matter of habit, as it cannot possibly make any difference. The pieces should have been cut long enough so that the border will catch all of it at the top and a trifle over, and that it will reach down on the base board with a little to spare. The paper itself should be hung perfectly plumb. The paper hanger should always carry a plumb bob with him on every job for the purpose of knowing that his work is done properly. A good casing and corner knife will be of great help and a time saver in helping him to fit the end of his pieces. It requires good judgment at times in papering rooms in some of the old houses, where they are not properly trued, and where, sometimes, even the doors and window frames are out of plumb. He has to so plan the hanging of the paper that it may partly hide these defects; as he could not follow the door frames in their wobbling. Under such conditions never use stripe paper nor paper showing a prominent geometrical design, as much as possible select paper having a design with little striking features on it.

226. Borders come in half strips ,whole strips, and again in any number of strips to the width of the roll. These smaller borders are used mainly in decorative paper hanging, in panels, etc. Dropped ceilings usually have a picture molding nailed on at the point of junc-

tion of the side wall paper proper, but there are imitations of these now made in paper and many use it in place of the real molding. In most rooms the wide borders or friezes are usually hung where the ceiling and sidewall come together or on half-strip dropped ceilings, just below that.

There are several ways of hanging borders, the most usual is to cut the border up into lengths just about wide enough for the paper hanger to fit on the last one hung, and to reach as far as his other hand can brush it on the wall with the smoothing brush from the top of a step ladder, which is then moved on for the hanging of the next stretch.

Another way: Where there is a walking board to reach from one side of a room to another, or where a scaffold has been put up permitting to go all round the room, which is to have the border trimmed on both sides with a machine trimmer; to paste it, folding it in short folds six to eight inches wide, one fold on top of another, the folds being carried in the left hand, the right fits the border at its beginning, and with the smoothing brush, brush the border tightly to the wall, the left hand letting out the folds as desired to the end. Where a ceiling is straight and the proper walking facilities exist this is much the best way as no laps are shown—but good work can be done by either way.

227. Hanging burlap requires a little more care all the way through than wall paper does. It is much heavier than the heaviest of paper and *must* be butt-

edged. Both selvedges must be knife-trimmed as they are more or less dirty. This should be done with a very sharp knife in order to get a clean cut, without ragged edges, which would prevent the two edges coming closely together. It will be well to read over the directions given in Paragraph 224 as to the painting of a strip under the junction point where the two edges come together so as to prevent any of the plaster showing in places where an imperfect union is made, either through carelessness or, sometimes, unavoidably on account of imperfect walls.

The walls should be sized with glue size in which a little brown sugar has been dissolved, or with some of the prepared glue sizes made especially for the purpose. A strong paste should be made into which about one ounce of glue to the ordinary pail has been dissolved.

228. It frequently happens that the ceilings and walls of a room become very dirty and smoky, especially in our larger cities; where illuminating gas is used, the ceilings will surely become blackened by it and elsewhere the smoke nuisance from the factories will find its way to the interior so that in a comparatively short time the paper begins to show signs of dinginess.

Such can be readily cleaned and restored to their original brightness nearly by the *"cleaning"* process given below: Take flour and mix it with water to the consistency usual for dough for bread; then knead into it enough plaster paris to make it up into a stiff dough, which will not leave any traces of its component parts on the walls. Then go over these with a back and forth motion, overlapping each time so that no parts may be left untouched. This must be done in a thorough manner, the hand kneading the dough all the time in order to incorporate the dirt on the wall into it. The ball will become pretty black in time, but as long as the dirt is well worked into it, it will not soil the paper. If the rooms are very dirty and large, it may be well to change occasionally and to prepare another clean ball of dough, as it is inexpensive and can be quickly prepared.

The market is full of patented wall paper cleaners, but none will do the work any better than the one indicated above.

Dirty wall paper can also be cleaned with the inside of fresh bread which has first been kneaded into a ball in the same manner as described for the flour dough, leaving out the plaster paris. This is employed by many cleaners and there is but little difference between the two.

QUESTIONS ON PAPER HANGING.

217. What is said of paper hanging in general?

218. What condition should the walls be in for paper hanging?

219. How are walls prepared for hanging wall paper?

220. How are wooden partitions prepared?

221. How is paper trimmed?

222. How is paste prepared?

223. How should the paste be applied?

224. How are the ceilings hung?

225. How are the side walls hung?

226. How are the borders hung?

227. How is burlap applied to walls?

228. How is smoked and dirty wall paper cleaned?

PAINTER'S TOOLS AND APPLIANCES.

229. Painter's tools may be divided into two classes: First, those which are required for the application of the paint, and, secondly, the tools and appliances necesary for the painter to get at his work with with ease and safety.

Many of the tools belonging to the first class were reviewed under the heading of "Brushes," for which see Paragraphs 15 to 30, and those are the most important of that class; the rest, which will be noticed below, are merely adjuncts of these—to take care of them, etc. Some few are indispensible but several could be dispensed with by the use of others equally as well fitted as they are to do the part wanted of them. So that a proper substitute may replace any of them, without the painting being made to suffer for it.

230. Brush keepers are of this character. Brushes are expensive and must be taken care of as otherwise they will not last long nor work as well as they should.

Really any empty vessel wherein a brush can be *hung*, but not *laid*, suspended so that the hair will be surrounded by water, linseed oid or varnish, according to the character of the brush—but in which the brush will not touch the bottom, will make a brush keeper for ordinary brushes used in house painting. A wooden pail can have wires driven into its sides, forming an extended projection on the inside and upon them may be hung the brushes after having had a hole bored into their handles at a proper height, which will keep them from touching the bottom. Or a stout wire may be put through the center to which can be fastened a spiral spring coil of wire of sufficient strength to hold up the brushes where they are placed into it. The last is still better, as no hole need be bored into the brush handles.

Under Fig. 66, following, is shown a brush keeper made somewhat upon the above described plan but a galvanized iron pail is used instead.

Fig. 66—Brush Keeper.

Under the heading "Carriage Painting," a cheap and efficient varnish brush keeper is described which is used as an individual keeper, as all good varnish brushes should be, and under the following Fig. 67 is shown one where several can be hung together and kept free from

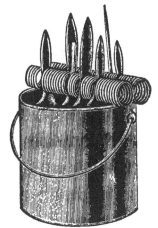

Fig. 67 —Paint Brush Holder.

dirt and dust. ‚It has a false bottom, where all dirt can settle.

231. Under Fig. 68 is shown what is known as painter's tinware, consisting of a calcimine strainer, calcimine pail and a paint strainer, with a pot to use paint

PAINTERS' TIN WARE.

Kalsomine
Strainers.

Paint Pails.

Paint Strainers.

from—this last holds one gallon and has no ears sticking up at its sides to catch brush and paint.

A wire should be soldered on about one-third of the way across the top, to wipe any surplus paint off the brush and to keep its sides clean; or a handy contrivance can be bought ready made which can be put on or

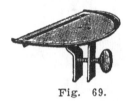

Fig. 69.

taken off at will—in a moment—which is still better, as it permits the cleaning of the pots without any interference with the wire.   This handy affair is shown in Fig. 69.

232.   Under Fig. 70 is shown a sanding bellows

Fig. 70.

which will be found a time saver over the crude and primitive way of throwing it on either by hand or with the old fashioned sandthrower.   Besides it will soon pay for itself in the cost of material saved by its use.

233. Scraping knives in various sizes and shapes to suit any reasonable desire are shown in Fig. 71. and

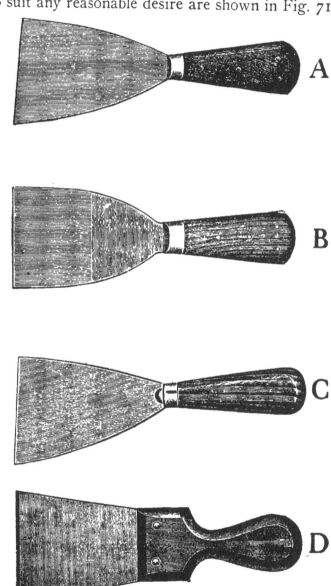

Fig. 71—Painter's Scrapers.

Fig. 72 which show an equal variety of stiff and elastic putty knives.

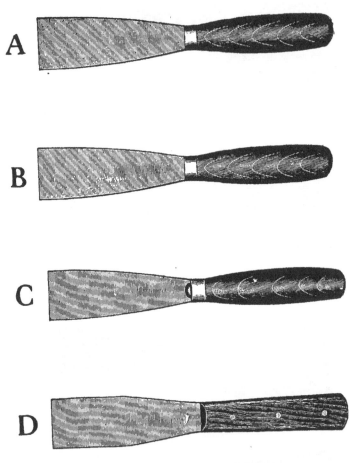

Fig. 72—Painter's Putty Knives.

Some triangular putty knives are made but one can grind them better to suit such bevels as are desired.

234. Fig. 73 shows a gasoline torch to burn off paint with. It is an indispensible tool to have and should have a place in every well regulated paint shop, as it will save money over any other method that can be used in removing old paint over large surfaces.

Fig. 73.

235. There are, no doubt, a number of other time saving and helpful devices which are being used in many paint shops besides the ones enumerated above, still be incomplete. Those reviewed cover about the most essential and the list of such could be increased indefinitely and whole field of the ones that are necessary to do good work with.

236. The next class of tools are in reality more appliances useful to get at the painting; but are as essential to the painting trade as those of the former class.

237. Ladders stand first in the list as they are the most important and are required by all painters to get at their work. These come in many forms and varieties suitable to certain situations or to do a certain

kind of work. The ordinary short length single ladders are too well known to require illustrating. They run from 10 feet upward in 2 feet graduations to 20 feet.

All ladders should be made of light but strong Norway pine sides with hickory rungs screwed into them.

Fig. 74.

241. Fig. 74 illustrates the better grades of extension ladders and the way they fasten together. They are made in two lengths from 26 to 38 feet, and usually in three lengths, from 40 feet upward.

Choose them with rollers as these assist in pushing them upward.

242. Fig. 75 shows the block and falls. Like the ladder, it can scarcely be dispensed with even in two or three-story buildings, as they save so much time in moving ladders besides being so much more convenient to do work from than ladders. They are indispensable for all buildings over three stories high. The rigging consists of two double blocks for the top and of two single blocks for the bottoms. The ropes should be of the very best manilla not less than ¾ inch thick, but

Fig. 75.

⅞ or even one inch is better and certainly safer, especially for long falls. A platform 18 to 22 feet long and two supports for same, which also serve to hook on the single blocks, and which have a wheel fitted in one end to roll down against the building sides without injuring them. Two large Swedish iron roof hooks into which the double blocks are fastened complete the "swing scaffold," as it is best known in many localities. It seems superfluous to say that nothing but the best of material should enter into their construction, as life and limb are in constant jeopardy while they are being used.

243.   Fig. 76 shows the ladder jacks of which there are a number of various shapes and forms, differing

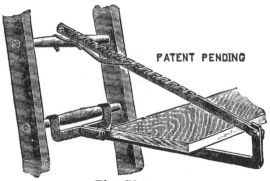

PATENT PENDING

Fig. 76,

but little, however, as to efficiency if well made from good, soft charcoal iron.   Two of these make one set. They are placed on two ladders and a walking plank put between them, resting on the jacks, making a bridge

Fig. 77.

between the ladders from which the painting can be done.

244.   Fig 77 shows a roof ladder.   This is attached to the end rungs of a ladder and then it can be thrown over the roof ridge which holds it firmly in place.

245. For inside painting, good strong, well braced step ladders are needed of various sizes from three feet upward. A poor step ladder is dear at any price and none should be too good if life and limb is worth anything to the men who have to use them. Some of the flimsy traps for eternity sold in many stores because

Fig. 78.

they are cheap may do for some ruralist to go up to glory with, but the painter has no use for them. Fig. 78 shows one that is well braced and which will not wiggle.

246. Painter's trestles are double ladders joined together at the top and which when spread out brace each other, making a solid support for walking planks

to be set upon two of these, which make one set.   Fig.
79 shows a pair supporting an extension walking board,
an ingenious contrivance enabling the workman to
lengthen or shorten it to suit the situation and side of

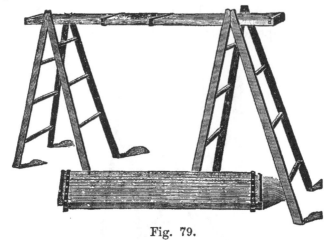

Fig. 79.

the room where they are used.   When done with, the
board can be compactly drawn together.

Fig. 80.

247.   Fig. 80 illustrates a plank supporter which is
very useful in interior work as it can be placed where
ladders cannot be set up or anywhere a board can
be set up. It fastens itself to any sized board that will

go through its jaws and at any height desired upon it and gives a firmer support to the walking board which may rest upon it and a step ladder.

243. Under Fig. 81 is shown an adjustable scaffold

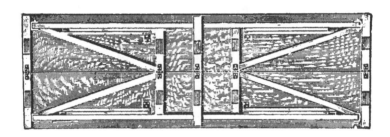

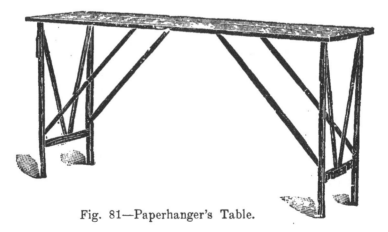

Fig. 81—Paperhanger's Table.

ing jack which should be extensively used, as they will save much time and money by doing with a few sets what would require a large number of old fashioned "horses" needed to support walking planks for the painting and decorating of interiors of buildings. They are made in three sizes, ranging from the lowest—3 feet—to a possible extension of 11 feet for the highest.

249.   Fig. 82 illustrates a shop paint mill which is an excellent piece of machinery for every paint shop to be equipped with. While it may not be considered as ab-

Fig. 82.

solutely necessary as now all pigments can be bought ground in oil cheaper and better ground than one can do it for himself. When the mill is handy it would pay to run it through many a mixture, which would be the better for having been put through the mill.

The above comprises all that is required to get at any work to be painted either upon the exterior or interior of buildings.

QUESTIONS ON PAINTER'S TOOLS AND APPLIANCES.

229. How many classes of painter's tool are there?

230. What are brush keepers?

231 to 249. Should be used to refer to.

PIGMENTS.

250. Pigment is a synonym of color. As under that heading every pigment of any value and its peculiarities, antipathies, etc., are treated upon fully, the reader is referred to Paragraphs 61 to 84 for the information required concerning them.

SCENE PAINTING.

251. Scene painting is an attractive branch of the trade and calls for considerable artistic ability, requiring special study and which if an individual once makes it a success, generally becomes a lifetime calling.

The painting of theatrical scenery, drop curtains, wings, etc., is usually done in water colors as it looks much better in that medium than when executed in flatted oil colors. Distemper dries perfectly flat and dead, which is hard to get from oil work as so much of the work has to be brushed over and over again, which would make it shiny in places. Were it even posible to make the oil painting look as good in the flat as the water color does, it would not have any advantage over it. To make the oil painting look as flat as the water colors would require them to be thinned altogether with turpentine; then it would not be as well bound as the water colors are, for these have a strong glue binding which will hold it on well, while the all-turpentine colors would dust off after a thorough drying from the rolling up and down of the scenes.

252. A scene painter should know many things more than is required in most branches of the painting trade in order to be able to represent whatever is required truly and naturally.

He must possess an ultimate knowledge of colors, not only such as all decorative painters should have, but also of their effects upon the vision at great distances from the object painted, and also of the effect that gas and other artificial lights have upon them. He must know beforehand what effects the blending of the colors will be when seen from the audience; for this blending will appear very much different to the man in the back part of the balcony than it will to the man on the stage even in daylight when there is no artificial light to change the color of the pigments, so he must be able to arrange his coloring schemes entirely different from what they look to be from the spot where the painting is done. This study of distant effects must be acquired beforehand or the finished work will be a failure from the artistic standpoint at least.

He should also make a study of the effect of gas and other artificial lights, as has been already intimated. For if he does not possess an intimate knowledge of these effects upon the various colors, some of them he will find so much changed as to be hardly recognizable at night.

It goes without the saying it that he must be a good off-hand designer or he will be apt to put out caricatures where such are not in demand. It is, of course, ex pected that every decorator should have a good knowl edge of drawing, but the scenic painter's must be of a higher character than that of any of the others. The eyes of the whole audience is focused, as it were, upon his work during most of the play and every portion of it will be examined and any fault in the details or incongruous coloring wil be noted and commented upon. Much of which would pass unnoticed in ordinary pictorial work, which one examines at a close range, and where the observation is not constant, as it is apt to be from the audience to the stage.

253. The material needed for scenic painting comprises nearly everything in the line of pigments that can be used in water colors besides glues to bind them on, metallic leaves such as Dutch metal, aluminum, silver leaf, and, sometimes even gold leaf, the metallic foils, tinsels, bronzes, flitters, brocades, with the various liquid sizings required for their application.

Whiting is the principal color used for either painting white or as a base upon which to build up light tints of any colors or by mixing in small quantities with these to render them more opaque. The mixing of tints also requires a greater knowledge of effects of colors than is necessary for decorators whose work is examined at close range. So the scenic artist in preparing his tints is forced to make them much stronger than is required for nearby work. At first he will be very likely to err in making his contrasts too weak, although they may appear unusually strong to him from the painting floor. As in the course of time the scenic artist will make use of nearly every pigment known, the reader is referred to paragraphs 61 to 84 regarding any information he may require concerning these. In subsequent paragraphs will be given a list of colors best suited to produce certain effects and for certain purposes.

To lay out the design of a scene nothing better than good French charcoal crayons will be found as the lines can be whipped out with a flogger while chalk lines will not always be easily effaced, retaining a faint outline, which is anything but desirable and which are mortifying when appearing upon otherwise well done work.

254. Glue is the material used as the binding material for the water colors. It is a matter of the first importance than that it should be of the best quality and of light color, at least for all light tints or colors with clear tones, otherwise the darker glues would change it or muddy it. The best glues to use are the thin-flaked ones known as calcimine glue. The ones of an ivory tone, nearly clear but not quite so, which are tough and do not break off short with an easy fracture, are the best. Avoid the opaque-looking white flaked glues; they might possibly be all right, but the chances are that they have been weighted down with some adulterating make-weight stuff. This can easily be ascertained by soaking the glue, melting it, diluting

it with water and letting it stand awhile as this white stuff will be precipitated down to the bottom of he vessel.

Glue should be of the consistency of a trembling jelly to mix with the colors, but should be melted and mixed hot or at least warm enough so as not to jell; so, when trying a new kind it will be well to weigh it, soak it in cold water over night, and melt it with the usual quantity of hot water and set it aside to jell; if it is about as thick as usual, it shows that the glue is about of the same strength—if it jells any weaker, then it shows lack of strength. It is well to weigh out any quantity of the glue needed as then the average quantity of water used ordinarily, proportionate to the weight can be added to it and the glue water kept up to a uniform strength.

Good glue will take up seventeen to eighteen times its own weight of water while soaking up over night and will swell to many times its former bulk, so the package should be much larger than needed to hold the dry glue. The amount of water absorbed is of itself a very good indication of the value of a glue, as poor glue has not as great absorbing power as the better kinds have.

The glue water should not be much stronger than that of a trembling jelly, for there is danger that if it be made much stronger of the colors showing up shiny when they dry. Again, one should guard against the opposite danger of having it too weak to bind the colors sufficiently to hold them on well.

255. The tools used in scenic painting do not differ materially from those used by other decorators.

For the sizing of canvas and the layin in of ground colors a good calcimine brush 6 or 7 inches wide make an excellent tool.

For the laying in of large bodies of color 2, 3 and 4 inches flat, double varnish bristle brushes with a few assorted sizes of oval chisel pointed sash tools will suffice.

A few dozens of round, flat, triangular, long and short fresco bristle lining brushes will be needed as nearly all the details of the decorative work as well as the lining up will be done with these. No finer brushes will be needed, such as artists' or decorators' camel's hair pencils, as the work must be coarsely done and the bristle fresco liners are good and small enough for any purpose. Some of the leaves, grass, etc., can and must be done with the sash tools and even larger brushes.

Pallet knives and a marble slab and stone muller to grind down coarse colors with which cannot be obtained ready ground in distemper as is sometimes the case in the smaller towns. The above will not apply in the larger cities, where usually all colors can be bought ground up in distemper. It is true that many colors can be procured ground fine dry; such should be bought in that way as they are cheaper and answer as as well as those ground in distemper, but many are too coarse in their dry state and must be ground with the muller where it is impossible to buy them properly ground.

Straight edges with beveled edges of various sizes such as fresco painters use in lining are needed, some longer ones for laying out a level and plumb bob, T squares and triangles, large wooden leg dividers, chalk and chalk lines; also some charcoal for chalk line. Floggers to whip out charcoal marks and a palette board to hold colors. This palette board naturally must be made upon an entirely different plan than the common flat form of the ordinary one. It must be made with an edge on three sides to retain the cups into which the colors are put. Some advise a complicated affair with compartments in it to hold the colors in, but they give much trouble to clean. If a compartment becomes dirty the rest may need no cleaning; it is next to impossible to do it properly. The better way is to have tin vessels of proper size which can be lifted out singly as needed and the raised edge will keep them from slipping off the board when the palette is tilted up, as it sometimes requires to be. The vessel holding the glue water should be of different shape so as to be easily recognized and it will be well to have three or four of them so that the brushes used in different groups of color may not muddy it up and render it unfit for use for colors of a different tone.

The above are the principal tools needed for doing the work; no doubt that many more might be added to the list but it is possible to do the best of work with the ones mentioned. In the following paragraph will be described a few appliances necessary for the proper equipment of a scenic studio.

256. The location of a studio is very important to the professional scenic painter. The amateur who only has an occasional job to do will have to necessarily content himself with such accomodations as he may find in an ordinary paint shop, but the latter are unhandy for such work and they will be much hampered in getting at their work as they will have to do the painting from cramped and uncomfortable positions, which usually tell more or less upon the quality of the work done. Few ordinary paint shops have ceilings of sufficient height to accomodate the frame of a large scene or of a drop curtain. Even in many of the theatres and opera houses there are no special arrangements made for the painting or repairing of scenery, although the majority of the newer built ones have arrangements made for this at the back part of the building.

The studio, however, which is built with a special view of being used as a workshop where scenic painting is to be the exclusive business carried on should be built according to the requirements needed for the speediest and easiest methods of executing the work. The building should be three ordinary stories in height and should be well lighted on the top floor where all the painting is done. The lighting should all come from above, from skylights in the roof, as only untrammeled, direct light will do and no side light should be allowed, so that the third story will be windowless.

The floor itself should be so built that it will not touch the walls around the room by about twelve inches, leaving an empty space of that width all around it. The same arrangement should be carried out upon the second floor, too. This will permit of the largest sized scenery and drop curtains to be raised and lowered at will from the top to the bottom on the first floor. It is needless to say that the second and first floors may have as many windows as may be desirable for them to have, as no painting will need to be done on those floors.

The top floor must be equipped with machinery to raise or lower scenes quickly and there are several patented capstan-like rolling machines which do the work handily and quickly. But any handy carpenter can readily make up a homemade affair that will do the work nearly as well as the others and at much less cost. The above arrangements will enable the scene painter to stand erect at his work in executing the painting. Being secure and feeling so on a solid floor, this assurance will enable him to do twice as much work or more with greater ease to himself than he could possibly do in any other manner.

257. The amateur will be under many disadvantages in doing his work, but frequently special scenery is wanted in the smaller towns where there are no facilities provided other than such makeshifts as may be

found. The painter should secure a place high and wide enough to accommodate the frame upon which the canvas or muslin upon which the scenery is to be painted, will be stretched. , This canvas should be a few inches wider and longer each way than the size of the finished scene is to be. It should be evenly stretched upon the frame and all wrinkles removed, then securely tacked on, when it will be ready for the sizing.

The sizing should be rather stout. Soak glue of a good quality until it has absorbed all the water it is capable of, then melt it over a slow fire and in the proportion of about one gallon of water to eight ounces of dry glue so that one pound will make about an ordinary 12-quart pail full of sizing when melted; then proceed to apply this size to the cloth on the frame but do not touch the size to within one inch of where it is tacked on to the frame, leaving one inch of it unsized all the way around the frame (top, sides and bottom being left unsized for one inch). This is very important as other wise the cloth would not dry evenly but wrinkled and it would be very difficult to take them up even after re-tacking it over; in fact it could hardly be done while the unsized cloth on the frame and the inch of it left unsized will take up the strain and the cloth will dry evenly and tight.

When dry, proceed to fill the cloth or canvas with a good, solid coat of whiting, which has been strongly sized with glue water. This coat should be well worked in,. cross brushed and laid off, so as to insure a perfectly well covered ground to work upon. If this ground coat has not been properly done there will be trouble afterwards in doing it over, besides loading the canvas with the unnecessary weight of another which will make further trouble in causing suction so that the painting of the details of the scene will be more difficult than over one coat ground well done.

258. The painting proper of the scene is very much the same as that of any other similar kind of decorative work either in perspective, lineal or free hand painting and will present no great difficulty, especially to one who is used to free hand decoration in distemper, that is, at least, in so far as putting on the colors goes, as that is about the same; in fact it is less difficult in that there is no great preciseness required—but the very seeming freedom and carelessness in the execution of daubing on the painting is all calculated upon and the results of it are as well known in the mind of the scenic artist as the most precise is to the decorator who paints for near-by effects. This very coarseness is discounted beforehand with a full knowledge of certain effects it will produce at a distance and the seeming carelessness is all in the eye of the onlooker.

Scene painting has to be made bold and the colors must be put on strong without regard as to their looks in the immediate vicinity. Colors at a distance blend together so that if they are gradually shaded as for work which is to be closely seen, they would appear very tame either not shaded at all or as a solid shade or tone of one color all blended into one. For the same reason the details too must be put on much stronger colors than for near-by painting. This requires quite a study of distant effects and all amateurs are timid and afraid of going too far—they have to catch on to it gradually when experience will teach them to become more bold in the use of strong coloring and every mistake made becomes an instruction which will eventually make the amateur's work better on the next job he undertakes after he has noted the tameness of the combination used.

There is another phase in the painting of scenery which will give beginners trouble at first and that is the changed appearance of some colors under artificial light such as gas, kerosene or gasoline illumination and in a lesser degree under electric lighting. In a subsequent paragraph is given a list of colors to use to produce the best effects for the painting of various shades and for special purposes which will look well under artificial light. The combinations can be made from such as are named to suit the ideas of the painter.

259. Colors can be used either opaque or transparent when they are naturally so. Some of the transparent ones can be made more opaque by the addition of whiting, but it will somewhat change the tone making them a little lighter, so it must not be over done. If a full deep opaque tone is wanted of a naturally transparent color, it will have to be made by mixing several pigments together that will produce a similar color to the one desired. To explain: If a solid burnt sienna brown

is desired, the natural burnt sienna being transparent and as whiting would reduce its depth, it should be made artificially from solid and opaque colors and a similar color made from Venetian red, ochre and black and this would be solidly opaque.

The blues seem to give the most trouble of any as most of them appear greenish under artificial light. Some of the ultramarines have a greenish tone even in daylight and when used should be very carefully selected as the true blue shades of it are after all the best blues to use in making up blue tints for scene painting.

The chrome yellows become much lighter under gas light so that the painting done with those yellows must be made much deeper if the scene is to be used where the lighting is done with gas.

259. *Purples* are readily made by mixing some of the blue and Indian red taken from the palette and mixed on the mixing board to which can be added whiting to produce the shade of it wanted.

Where considerable color of one tint is wanted as for skies, etc., it is better to prepare it ready for use in a separate can or pot.

For skies—they should be first put on with the solid color and then the brush can be dipped in this and that color and applied where wanted, and blended in while wet and as many variations produced as wanted.

Foliage greens should not be made from chrome green as these contain chrome yellow and under gas-light would appear much lighter toned; besides, that no good foliage green can be made from them as they are too positive. They are best made from ochres, raw sienna, Prussian blue and glazed with some green lake where a rich effect is desired. The chrome yellow may be used but they must be made deeper in order to produce the effect wanted and this would look unnatural by day light.

For clouds mix verditer and orange chrome. For cold gray clouds add a litle black. For lights in clouds mix yellow ochre and madder lake, or any other good crimson lake, or yellow ochre and orange chrome.

For sea water use Dutch pink alone or raw sienna and black Prussian blue. Water reflects the color of the skies and the image and coloring of near-by objects such as houses, trees, etc.

For moonlight skies a good tint is made from verditer or indigo or its equivalent in Prussian blue and black, lightened up with whiting. For clouds add black and more blue.

For rocks, stone, etc., raw and burnt sienna, Indian red, chrome greens and black, vandyke brown, ultramarine, rose pink and ochres. Black and Venetian red toned down with a little whiting makes a good stone color for many purposes.

For distant foliage, Dutch pink alone or raw sienna and black, or raw sienna and a trifle of Prussian blue.

Gold tones are best made from ochres and Dutch pink, raw sienna and Vandyke brown. For the lights use flake white and lemon chrome yellow or medium chrome yellow according to the shade of it wanted.

For trunks of trees and branches according to species and tones desired, Prussian blue, yellow ochre, raw and burnt sienna, ultramarine Dutch pink, raw and burnt umber and maroon lake for an overglaze.

For grass the chrome greens in all shades of it, using extra light chrome green for the high lights, mixed with pale chrome yellow or medium chrome yellow.

For dead leaves, raw and burnt sienna, raw and burnt umber.

For stone buildings, yellow ochre, raw sienna; raw and burnt umber; ultramarine blue, Venetian red and black.

For brick, Venetian red, and for shadows add ultramarine blue.

For fire reflection use orange mineral. In all the above it is understood that whiting is used to make proper shades of all the tints wanted.

In making out the above list all the colors useful in making the tints are given—not that all should be mixed together, but such should be selected from them to mix the shades wanted. Some of them, as Prussian blue, lampblacks, etc., are very strong and but little of such should be used as little is needed to produce much effect. It is better to add several times if needed in mixing a tint than to spoil the shade by adding too much at the start of making them. It is only by many trials that a beginner can expect to produce proper shades at once. All such should carefully try the shades by drying them as recommended before.

QUESTIONS ON SCENE PAINTING.

251. What material is chiefly used in scene painting and why?

252. What should a person know in order to become a scene painter?

253. What material is chiefly used in scene painting?

254. What is said about glues? .

255. What tools are needed for scene painting?

256. How should a scene painting studio be arranged?

257. How should the cloth or canvas be prepared for the painting?

258. How is the painting done?

259. Give colors required for making the various tints.

SIGN PAINTING.

260. Signs in some form or another have probably been in use as long as commerce has existed, or at least some equivalent for it to let people know that at such a place something was for sale or exchange. They certainly existed and were in use during the Roman empire, and traces of them have been handed down in an unbroken chain ever since.

During the middle ages before printing, and later when universal education had made everybody familiar with the form of letters and with the reading of them, most of the signs were of a pictorial character and as trades all had trade marks the business was represented by that plus some peculiar sign that denoted the individuality of the proprietor. Even as late as the middle of the nineteenth century, before the introduction of forced education, pictorial signs were still largely used. Novelists such as Dickens refer to such signs freely in their writings, and shops and inns were called after and known by the picture represented on their signs. Many of the older men living today can well remember the practice as it existed in the days of their youth. Some of those signs were certainly very crude in the drawing and in the painting of the subjects as there were botches in those days as well as at the present time. But, good or bad, they appealed to the unread as well as to the educated and a servant girl told to go for something to the sign of the "Lion Head" or to the "Three Black Crows" had no need of being told the rest in order to know what place was meant.

Some of the greatest painters in all countries have been guilty of painting such signs as favors shown to some friendly "hosts" at taverns and elsewhere and such, no doubt, must have shown considerable talent in the execution.

But at the present time since everybody can read, this fashion is obsolete at least in business houses, locations of shops of all kinds of trades, professions or manufactures. But there is still an enormous amount of pictorial sign work done in what is known as "advertising signs," much more in fact than at any other period of the world's existence.

The idea is as good now as in the older days, as people will read a well displayed advertisement to find out what the advertiser has to say about the picture on the sign which has riveted their attention, where, otherwise, without such aid on account of the multitude of such signs they would have passed it by unnoticed. So, it can readily be surmised that a general sign painter in order to make good in all branches of his business must be very versatile and artistic in his knowledge.

261. Sign painting can be divided into several branches:

1. The *commercial,* which includes the painting of signs upon sign boards to be hung up on buildings or on the buildings themselves. It may be in all kinds of oil work, plain or shaded, and includes gilded signs on wood, but as gilded signs are specially treated upon and that it really is a separate branch from oil painted signs which many otherwise good sign painters are not familiar with, it is entitled to a separate place in the describing of it.

2. Show card painting has become specialized into a separate branch and requires training of a different order. One stroke muslin sign work, while upon a much larger scale, properly belongs to this class of work, although much of it is being done by all regular sign painting shops. But for the sake of describing

under a proper classification it will be noticed under this division, which, after all, is and must be arbitrary.

3. Gilding on glass and gold lettering on wood with accessories such as ornamentation of the letter with pearl flakes, etc., bronzing, etc.

4. The advertising signs in all their forms, which include pictorial painting, etc.

Each one of these four artificial divisions of the sign painting trade will furnish sufficient variation in the use of special skill to keep one pretty busy usually, and as each also requires a different handling, the specialist who makes it his sole business acquires more skill and dispatch in doing his work.

462. The above classification of the trade is an artificial one made for the purpose of examination into its details. It is also made by the large shops in the selection of workmen who are kept within the limits described in the classes described in the former paragraph.

As a matter of fact no such distinctions exist in any of our large city shops. They take everything in the line of all of the four classes with possibly the exception of advertising bulletin work, which is made a special business by itself.

In the country towns, too, the sign painter must be able to do any and all kinds demanded as he seldom has enough work to employ specialists, and frequently no more than he can do himself. So, the general sign painter must be able to do a fairly good piece of work at the risk of being lowered in the estimation of his customers, if he does not in all branches of the business, from the painting of a dainty show card and gilding on glass to the painting of a big pictorial sign on the broadside of a large barn.

So it can readily be seen that a general sign painter must possess a high class of knowledge. To be successful and a good workman, the sign painter must be a good judge of distances and possess an accurate vision in order to save time in laying out a sign within a given number of feet and to balance it properly. He must be able to judge at a glance what sort of letters will work best for the various situations of a sign and right for any kind of business as all are not equally adapted for all alike. When his work is to be surrounded with dozens of others he must be able to give his own sufficient individuality, that passers-by will notice it and that it may not be confounded with the rest.

He must be able to draw accurately and to scale and also be well versed in perspective for a truthful representation of buildings and machinery upon wagon covers and advertising sign boards. He must be a good judge of color effects at a distance and for nearby ones, sign painter must be able to do a fairly good piece of work too, as the job is seen from both near and far. So he has to arrange a sort of compromise between the two extremes. As much of his work is done upon glass, he must be a good gilder not only on wood but glass and everything where he is required to work upon.

263. The material required for doing sign work comprises about all the colors known to the house painter or decorator not only ground in oil but all the water colors, and those ground in japan or varnish for wagon work. Besides all sorts and kinds of gold and other metal leaves, bronzes, flitters, metallics, etc., for show card work and for the latter to be able to squeeze out raised letters and ornaments from a plaster paris bulb and squeezers, pearl flakes, diamond dust, etc.; he will need nearly all the usual accessories listed in art store catalogues at some time or other in the prosecution of his business.

Much of this material will be used but seldom, and need not be carried in stock.

264. The tools required to do sign painting comprise those used by the house painter for the preparation of grounds, for the painting of the sign proper, and in addition thereto a good assortment of sizes and shapes of camel's hair, ox hair and sable lettering brushes, from No. 1 to 12. Some ¼, ½ and 1-inch camel and ox hair one-stroke flat brushes, which are great time savers not only for the making of letters at one stroke, as their name indicates, but which are useful in all regular sign work as well. He will also need striping brushes, gold tips, etc., putty and palette knives, charcoal and chalk crayons, ladders, swing stage blocks and falls, step ladders, easels and frames to stretch muslin signs upon, an air brush for show card work, tin pots and strainers, etc., etc.

Previous to describing the methods used in doing sign work it will be well to give a few general directions for the beginner, as these presuppose a knowledge of making the letters. It will be impossible to give a lengthy "expose" of all that a novice will have to go through to learn how to paint letters; time and experience is required to make a good workman in the sign painting business as well as in any other. But a person who is handy with the use of brushes can soon perfect himself so that he can do all the ordinary sorts of sign work, and gradually work himself up to a higher degree of excellence upon the more intricate parts of the trade.

The best practice the novice can have is to make straight perpendicular lines equidistant from each other —then horizontal ones and slanting ones at all angles and in both directions. When he can make them straight, equidistant and successively so any number of times, and when he has practised on curves and recurves so he can reproduce them consecutively at will, too—he has mastered the sign painting trade. A solid week or two, ten hours a day, at that kind of work will do it. It may be monotonous and may become disgusting, but there is nothing like it to learn fast. All letters resolve themselves into straight lines and curves so that the time which is seemingly wasted enables a beginner really to form any letter at sight when he is master of his straight line strokes and curves.

Letters are not all of the same width, nor will all letters look well separated from each other by an equal spacing as in print. The painter can usually arrange his spacing so as to balance up any deficiency, excepting where two open topped letters come following each other as an A following an L for instance; the wide space looking empty as it will at the top is very hard to balance just right. In such a case reducing the width of the L will help it some but it must not be to the extent of being strikingly so. When an open top letter is followed by one with a wider top than its foot as a V or Y or a T the top can be extended into the space which really belongs to the L if it was square with good effect. So can a V following an A trespass upon the top space of the A with good effect upon the balancing of the wording. Letters with straight line bodies like an H, N, M, E, R or U should be spaced as near equally apart as can be and any of these following an open top letter should be set as close to it as can be done. An I should have more space allowed between it and its neighbors than any other, or it may be confounded with another adjoining straight-bodied letter; the curved letters as O, Q or B, R, and P can be set a trifle closer to a straight-bodied letter than two straight bodied letters can. If the above directions are followed in spacing there will be little trouble in balancing the letters in a word properly—so that they will look at their best.

As the letters for all kinds of sign work are nearly the same in their formation it will be well to notice them here once for all, the proper allowance of size, etc., being made by the reader for the different kinds of work.

With all the innumerable styles of letters which one can see in a type foundry catalogue, aside of Old English or German text and Script, the whole of them are simply variations of two primary styles of letters.

The Roman with its make-up of fine and heavy bodied lines is the author of all such with or without extending spurs and the heavy bodied block is also the prototype of all such with or without extending spurs, thick or thin, shaded or unshaded.

There has been a number of off hand nondescript styles of letters which have had a season or two at the most of faddish popularity, which certainly cannot claim any relationship to the two standard styles described. They make diffcult reading and one might as well have a sign written in Egyptian hieroglyphics or Turkish as a mongrel type which has to be studied over before it can be made out. Life is too short for people to waste much of it in solving puzzles and then there is a general return to the standard styles and its numerous variations, which are certainly plentiful enough to suit almost any taste.

Below are shown a few of the leading styles and their modifications: Fig. 83 shows a pure style of Ro

MODES

Fig. 83.

man in a proportion where they show their elegant form to good advantage although the Roman type looks very well in an extended form even very much wider than it is high. On the reverse when Roman type is narrowed up, as in Fig. 84, it loses some of its beauty

MERCER

Fig. 84.

and at a distance becomes less distinct.

Roman lower case is shown in Fig. 85 and it, too,

repairing

Fig. 85.

possesses the same beauty of form as its capitals. While signs in several lines usually look best in various styles of letters for each line, or at least for every other one,

Roman capitals and lower case may be used alone and give a very neat result, as shown in Fig. 86.

This Desirable
RESIDENCE
to be Let.

For particulars
apply to

Fig. 86.

It was stated before that all other styles were simply variations of the Roman and block, so in Fig. 87 is

MAKER

Fig. 87.

given an illustration of such variation, and in Fig. 88 another shaded where the modification is still stronger, but where the original type can be plainly seen.

Fig. 88

In Fig. 89 is shown the other standard form from which all other thick-bodied letters sprang from. Fig.

MAKER

Fig. 89.

90 is probably a better sample of it as being less elongated, but its lines are proportionately much thinner than

MAPS

Fig. 90.

Fig. 89, and this will answer to show some of the many variations in the type. In Fig. 91 the above type some-

Fig. 91.

what mingled with a spray of Roman is shown with extended spurs, and in Fig. 92 and Fig. 93 is shown a

DENT

Fig. 92.

HOUSE

Fig. 93.

thicker bodied letter and an elongated one of the same order. Many styles of letters are compounds of the two main ones so that it is sometimes difficult to tell to which they belong the most, as Figs. 92 and 95.

DRAPER

Fig. 94.

CASE

Fig. 95.

Bookseller

Fig. 96.

Engraver

Fig. 97.

Old English is shown in Figs 96 and 97. It is elegant, too, in form with its succession of thin and heavy lines and is frequently used in church text on account of its gothic form with which form religion has cast a hallow of sacredness.

Script is extensively used in sign painting. It may be any style of letter desired, all of them look well. Some of the signatures of the proprietors for whom the

Good Stabling

Fig. 98.

signs are painted sometimes have them imitated upon them. All script signs look neat. Fig. 98 shows one style which is largely used, and Fig. 99 shows one which is continuous as in actual writing.

Rustic letters are very appropriate for many situa-

Fig. 99.

tions and trades, as for gardeners and florists, etc.; an illustration is given of such in Fig. 100.

267. Shading letters improves them very much if properly done and renders them more attractive if the coloring is in good taste. Where shading looks at its best, there must be no crowding in the spacing but a

Fig. 100.

liberal allowance made for the shade, and some over. Crowded letters do not look well, shaded.

In shading letters do not let the shading color come close to the letter itself but leave a margin wide enough that the ground may show between it and the letter itself. It should not be too large, but large enough to be visible.

The taste of the painter can be exercised in the selection of proper shading colors to suit the location, character of the business and the fitness of it for the purpose. An undertaker, for instance, should not have his sign shaded crimson, neither would it do for the doctor. Some sober tones, a compromise between the color of the ground and that of the letter always makes a neat appearance.

Double shading in two or more colors is often resorted to to produce showy signs.

Probably the neatest effect in shading is to use a darker shade of the same color for the underside or under parts of the lettering. This gives it a block effect which is absent from shading done in one solid color, and as shading is done to give an impression of thickness to the letters, the shading done in the above manner will show it much truer and better than a solid shade would.

Shadows are sometimes used to good advantage; unlike a shade it is not placed next to the lettering but at a distance from it, but connected with it at the bottom as the shadow of a man or tree or any standing object would appear from a given angle. Lettering may be outlined with some other color in either thick or thin lines all around them and variegated, or the bodies painted in two or more colors with or without ornaments upon the body. When properly done, this kind of work looks well for certain kinds of signs, but to be in taste, it must be suitable to the business or it will soon be an eyesore of which the owner will soon tire.

The above directions, it is hoped, will suffice to enable the novice who has been reading this to do a creditable piece of work if he has familiarized himself with the proper formation of letters, and as this advice is applicable to all kinds of sign painting from a show card to a mammoth bulletin sign no further reference as to how to do the work will be made in what follows except in so far as a different application of the rules given may necessitate further explanations.

268. The painting of signs on sign boards or on wooden, brick or stone buildings may well form a section by itself, and as this forms a branch of the trade which gives more employment in all its varieties than all the others put together—with the exception of advertising bulletin signs (which will be treated separately), it is well worth the closest attention.

If the sign is to be painted upon a board in the shop or upon a building, they should be primed as recommended for exterior house painting by using nearly clear linseed oil (raw) with just enough white lead in it to tint it so that it can be plainly seen when applied to the lumber. If upon a sign board, the back of it should be thoroughly primed, too, in the same manner as the front in order to keep the water from soaking up behind it. The next coat of paint should be given fairly stout, with ¼ turpentine mixed with ¾ raw linseed oil for a thinner, ith a very small quantity of good japan drier added to it. The back part of the sign should be coated with this too; these two coats will be enough for the back of the sign, but the front should have another rather flatter than the usual outdoor third coat, because a glare is very undesirable for a sign ground. For the better class of sign work it is better to give the third coat 2/3 raw linseed oil and 1/3 turpentine put on rather thick, but brushed out thin which will give the board a good, even gloss all over it. When still tacky, apply a coat of flat color to it, which will be held firmly by the partially dried third coat, and then there will be no danger of its giving away very soon as the building has in all probability been already painted; if the paint is in good condition the painting of the sign may have to be done upon it just as it is and this very often happens. If a ground coat is to be painted upon it for the lettering, give a coat of raw linseed oil tinted with the ground coat color and when dry it should be given a heavy, well brushed outcoat of the ground itself, thinned with half raw oil and half turpentine. If the buildings are new and have never been painted they should be treated as stated under the heading of "Exterior Painting," and the space to be occupied by the sign coated over with the proper ground for it. This ground space should be thinned flatter than the rest of the painting.

269.   Spacing and balancing a space for the sign is where the practiced eye of the professional save him much time.   Generally speaking, and upon the average, each letter is supposed to occupy a given space and for the purpose of filling up a line, it is safe to cut up the number of inches in the space, making due allowance for beginning and ending, also for space between the words by the number of inches each letter would occupy.   The painter will dot off the number of inches to be occupied by the separate letters on the sign, keeping track of the number of them as he goes.   Then he will roughly sketch out the space each letter will actually occupy, making all necessary corrections as to the variations already spoken off as existing between the various letters and it will be found that the calculation based on the supposition that each shall occupy a similar sized square will not be found much out of the way, and that if there is an exception to the rule it can very soon be adjusted by the next rough sketching of it over, and making the proper allowances.

The professional painter will not need to even count out the number of his letter spaces, but will sketch out his wording at once and will seldom have to efface it to make room for a second sketching as it will be sufficiently near right to enable him to proceed with the lettering and to correct anything wrong in the sketching as he paints it out.   The novice, however, should not attempt this, as it would be too risky for him, and until his vision is so well exercised that he can judge of the right sized letters to make to fill up a given space, he should not only roughly sketch the letters but mark them out in the exact spot which each is to occupy. In that way he will be sure to come out alright.

If there are several lines of work to be done it will be well, especially if the lettering is all done with capitals, to change the style of each line somewhat.

It is usual to paint the name of a firm or person owning a business in larger letters than the rest of the sign. Then the line of business itself should be very promiuently displayed, while the details can be painted in much smaller letters than either of the two principal ones.

The styles, shadings, etc., referring to the lettering were fully noticed in Paragraph 267.

270. Show cards and muslin sign painting has come to be specialized insomuch at least that men who are better skilled in the execution of this kind of work than others are usually kept at it in all the larger sign shops. As now it is quite the fad to have these made and shaded with an air brush, it requires a practical use of this tool to do good work with it. Much of it is done in tasty colors and dainty use of roman lower case, and some show considerable ingenuity in the display made. Muslin work, likewise, requires a peculiar kind of skill; not that it is more difficult than that of the regular sign board work, but that the handling is somewhat different, being usually done with one-stroke letter brushes and off hand, and requires a different application of the

knowledge equal to both—of the proper formation of letters.

Muslin is usually stretched tight upon frames and sized, although now muslin can be bought all ready sized, ready to go to work upon it. As time is money and the time required to size and stretch ordinary unsized muslin will much more than make up for the cost of that ready prepared, this is now practically the only kind used for all this kind of work.

Muslin sign work, being done at one stroke and off hand, is very rapidly done by the experienced ones. They are usually employed for hurried work and for a temporary purpose, for the announcement of some special sale and it is not of so much importance about the lasting quality of the work as the looks and speed in painting them. In the aggregate, they make up a big share of the sign work being done in all sign shops today in city or country towns.

271. Gold signs on wood and glass constitute a class of sign work requiring additional skill besides that of the ability to form letters properly, which is common to all the different branches of the trade. This additional skill is that of the proper handling of gold leaf. This is not to be acquired in a day, but is the result of considerable practice. Some learn it in a much shorter time than others, and some never learn it well. Gold is so fragile that the least breath will send it flying in all directions. But, after all, when its peculiarities are well

understood, and the proper care taken, it is not such a difficult thing to learn how to handle it.

For the purpose of examination gold sign work will be taken up under two headings:

1. Gold signs upon opaque surfaces, such as wood, metals or japanned tin, etc., and—

2. Gilding on glass, where gold instead of being applied over a surface as before, is applied under it and shows through, requiring a very different method of handling in each case.

272. Wood surfaces, tin (japanned) and painted window shade cloth are the surfaces upon which gold signs are usually painted; each requiring much the same manipulations in the application of the gold, but some variation in preparing the surfaces for the gilding.

Gold leaf sticks closely to anything that has the least greasiness and tackiness; therefore the surface over which it is to be applied must be free of the least bit of it or else the gold will surely attach itself where it is not wanted, and the work spoiled thereby, and it is in this respect that the preparation of the surface mainly differs between the various surfaces mentioned.

Signs gilded on wood are usually smalted and when that is the case, as the ground is cut in around the letters after they have been gilded, it does not make so much difference if some of the gold happens to stick to portions of the boards besides that of the sizing for the letters as the cutting in of the ground will cover it over; if, however, the surface is to be left in the ground color over which the gold is applied, and no smalt is used as is sometimes done when a gold sign or ornaments are painted upon a building of wood or stone, then great care must be taken that the surface will be in a condition that the gold shall not stick to it.

The only proper surfaces for all gilding which is not afterward to be cut in is a *dead flat,* not an egg shell gloss even will do, unless it is first deadened or all its stickiness killed.

The usual method of preparing sign boards to be gilded is to give them three coats of paint as noted in Paragraph 268. The last coat should be given in a dark lead or slate color, so that the black ground to be cut in afterward can be plainly seen, and no spots will then be missed. The last coat must be as nearly flat as it is possible to make it, so that it may be properly bound. It should have a full week, at least, for hard drying. After it has been sand papered as free of brush marks as possible (and this sandpapering should have been resorted to after each previous coat), it will be ready for the sizing.

Nothing but an old, fat, oil size is to be used for outside exposed work, as nothing else would be able to withstand the ravages of the elements. This fat oil can be prepared by any one by exposing linseed oil in shallow vessels exposed to air and light for a few months. It can be bottled up afterward and will always remain in a fatty condition. Linseed oil in that condition seems to have lost much of its power to absorb oxygen and should have some good japan dryer added to it to make it dry. Unlike other linseed oil, however, it remains in a tacky condition for some time, some days even before it will eventually dry hard. It is when in that partially dried, tacky condition only that it is fit to be gilded upon. If gilding is attempted while it is sticky and leaves an imprint upon the finger when touched, it will come through the gold and dull or tarnish it—when dry, but still tacky, is the proper time to apply the gold. If the surface is good and dry when the size for the lettering is applied, and one has been careful not to touch the ground with the fingers or with anything greasy the gold can be applied so that it will stick to the sizing only, but as said before, it does not matter so much if the sign is smalted.

In aplying the size it is well to mix with it a little medium chrome yellow as then there is less chance of leaving a part of a letter unsized as it would show the omission at a glance.

It is well to prepare the size and to test it beforehand so as to know how long it will take to dry it and how long it holds in good condition for the gilding, then to bottle it up and label it with its record of drying. Some need a quick size; others again who have large surfaces to gild need it to hold the tack a long time and a gilder should have a 24-hour, a 48-hour and a 66-hour size. The last would be seldom used except upon work where the operator could not get back to it for some days after applying it.

· These gold sizes in fat oil can be bought ready prepared in most of the supply stores. As they are more
carefully tested and great care taken of having them
just right, it is much better to buy them in that way
than to waste the time necessary to prepare them for
one's self.

The gilding is done in the same manner as stated in
Paragraph 146, to which the reader is referred for
further explanations.

273. For surfaces which are not to be cut-in and
for japanned tinware, etc., the surface should be rubbed
over with whiting after having first been washed over
with alcohol and a chamois skin to remove any greasiness. This rubbing over with chalk will deaden the
ground so that gold will not adhere to it, but care must
be taken not to touch it as there is sufficient tackiness in
the touch of the fingers rubbed over the ground to make
the gold adhere to it sometimes.

Some take a raw potato and rub over the japanned
surface with the freshly cut side of it, cutting slices out
of it and rubbing all over the surface with it before
sprinkling chalk or whiting over it. The gold size is
then applied and the gilding is done as upon wood described in the preceding paragraph. After the surplus
gold has been brushed off and dusted, clean the whiting
by washing it with a soft sheep's wool sponge and water.

274. Window shades are frequently used for sign
work and they are very appropriate to the purpose.
Usually it is the lower part only that is lettered as the

upper and central portion of it is ordinarily rolled up, leaving only the lower portion of it visible then— at least during business hours.

If the painting of the sign is to be in oil colors, the painting should be laid out and done in precisely the same manner as it would be upon a board sign.

If to be gilded, the surface being always a dead flat, hard and free from tack, it is an ideal surface to work upon. Unless one has been careless and greased portions of it the gold will not adhere to its surface and one can get a clean-cut edge if a rightly tempered size is used, which should be some quick fat oil size, or if quicker work is desired, some good gold size japan.

275. Gilding on glass has been fully explained under the heading entitled, "Gilding," in Paragraph 149, and the reader should carefully read that over for explanations of the proper way of applying the leaf and other details affecting gilding on glass.

Cleanliness cannot be too strongly insisted upon as the work will surely look lame somewhere if this has not been scrupulously attended to before the gilding is commenced. Rub the whole surface of the glass with alcohol that no grease or dirt of any kind may come between the gold and the glass as it will show through it. It is well to also clean the outside of the glass as sometimes specks which one sees and which it is thought are on the outside may possibly be on the inside instead —besides it is better to have it clear to see through.

The design of the lettering and- ornamentation should first be drawn upon manilla paper and pricked through with a tracing wheel or needle to make a pounce of it; then sandpapered on the reverse side to open up the holes better and so they will not clog up. Take the design and using it right side up proceed, to pounce it on with whiting upon the outside of the glass. As this whiting will show very faint, it is better to take some tailor's chalk or a piece of hard soap sharpened up to an edge and mark out the outlines of the designing, as otherwise the wind and other agencies might obliterate them.

Then proceed to apply the gold leaf on the inside so that every part of the outlined design on the outside shall have been covered over with the leaf and in an hour or two afterward follow up with another coat of gold leaf to make sure that no part has been overlooked and to cover up all cracks and defects in the leaf put on before. This double gilding is the only sure way of making a creditable job of gilding.

When dry the gilding is ready for the backing. Now take the design and pounce it on the inside, upon the *back side* of it so that it will correspond to what was outlined on the outside and in as nearly the same place as it occupied there. The pouncing should be done with some dark dry color as it will show plainer upon the gold. Some gilders use black asphaltum varnish to back up gold with, but a good coach black in japan thinned with carriage japan and turpentine or a black rubbing varnish will be found better, and will work better under the brush. Two coats should be given. Some gilders use a chrome yellow ground in japan and thinned as stated before instead of a black. It is certainly more sensible, as should an unseen defect be in the leaf the chrome yellow backing will render it unnoticeable while the black will show through it.

In a day or two wash the surplus gold off and the sign will be ready for the shading if any is to go on, or for outlining, etc. This will give a good plain, solid burnished gold sign.

276. Ornaments in matt gold for parts of letters, or for shading them are quite the fad now. It is being used in shaping letters into a bevelled appearance, and in scroll work on the inside of the letter, or for making the center all matt, and hundreds of variations. These effects of burnished gold and matt are fine if well made and in the beveled letters often would fool one who did not know how such effects are produced.

The process is very simple and easy. All the parts which are to show matt are first painted on the glass with linseed oil and turpentine mixed together so as to work freely under the brush; a very little lemon or medium chrome yellow should be added, but not sufficient to show opaque. The painting *must* be transparent to allow the gold to show through it, or the beautiful effect would be lost.

The introduction of other ornamenting material in the make-up of a glass gilt sign, especially in those that are framed and used for advertising purposes, is frequent. For such purposes circular and any other form of openings are left for the filling of pearl flakes, flitters, etc. These openings are surrounded with a gold line. Sometimes photographs are inserted in them. Such make variety and in these advertising framed glass signs license runs riot on trying to obtain new effects. As they are usually expensive and hung in offices where they can be closely examined, and at leisure, fancy styles of lettering may be indulged in to almost any extent one can wish for; so that would appear ridiculous in a staid and sober street business sign, will be all right for this class of work.

277. Advertising signs can be arranged under two heads: First, those done upon buildings, either on wood or brick, and, second, those done on bulletin boards specially erected for such a purpose.

It is not intended here to go into all the details of this great business, as it would need too much of the space of this manual. This business is usually made a separate one, and many are usually under the control of large concerns who have contracts for advertising all over the country, keeping many gangs of men at work during the open season.

While the general sign painter in the city will not be greatly interested in them, the sign painter in the smaller towns may derive quite a revenue from the erection of bulletin sign boards upon the leading entrance streets to his town and the yearly rent derived from these will make quite an item in his bank account. Few towns are so small that its merchants will not want to be represented upon its bulletin and it will be easy to get them into it, if a few of the leading ones can be induced to make a start at it. At any rate, the nearby big town clothiers, dry goods and other houses will all be eager for good spaces upon them. Besides general advertisers, if written to, and proper explanation is given, will gladly avail themselves of the opportunity which usually will cost them less than the big advertising firms could afford to take similar work for, away from the city, and under big expense in sending out gangs of men for the erection of bulletins and to do the painting.

These bulletins can be made uniform in size and the space let at so much per square foot, including the painting and taking care of it. Or they can be made to suit the ideas of the advertiser. They can be made of wood all through or with a wooden frame to which is nailed galvanized iron sheets.

The wood should have three coats of paint upon the face, and for protection to the boards and to keep them from warping, should have two coats on the back. The galvanized iron should be given one coat of red lead priming and two coats of lead paint over it and when done in that way will hold the paint without scaling, as well as wood.

There is more display for skill in bulletin advertising sign work than is needed in ordinary commercial sign lettering. There is a possibility in the use of colors here not afforded in regular sign work and one should be well versed in the proper harmonizing of these. As much pictorial work of nearly everything manufactured under the sun, the advertising sign painter should be able to draw and paint with accuracy anything and everything that may be demanded of him from a rocking chair to a threshing machine or a building, figures in the bust or full drawn, landscapes, etc. Of course, he will not be expected to produce artistic work in all that the word implies, but the nearer he can call his productions by that name, the better he will please his customers as well as himself.

Work upon the bulletin boards is usually done in the ordinary way as it would be in the shop upon the prepared ground, or it may be done as it is usually done upon the outside walls of brick or frame buildings by painting on the design and lettering first with a heavy color made short so it will cut to an edge without running, by using about one half kerosene oil with linseed oil and benzine in the thinning. This sets quickly upon unpainted surfaces especially, and can be immediately worked upon and cut in with the ground color which is usually black, and being prepared from lamp black covers solidly in one coat.

QUESTIONS ON SIGN PAINTING.

260.   What is said regarding sign painting?

261.   How many branches can sign painting be divided into?

262.   What should a sign painter know?

263.   What material is needed for sign painting?

264.   What are the principal tools required in a sign painting shop?

265.   How are letters made?

266.   How many kinds of primary forms of letters are there?

267.   How are letters shaded?

268.   How are signs painted on sign boards and upon buildings?

269.   How should the lettering be spaced upon each line?

270.   How are show cards and muslin signs prepared and painted?

271.   What is said of gold sign painting?

272.   How are gold signs on wood, etc., painted?

273.   How are japanned tin surfaces gilded?

274.   How are gold signs painted on window shades?

275.   How should the glass surface be prepared for the gilding?

276.   How is the matting of the gold surface produced upon glass gilding?

277.   Tell what is said concerning advertising signs and their painting?

STAINS AND STAINING.

278. Staining, as the name indicates, is the operation through which certain substances are changed from their natural color to another. Unlike painting, it does not cover, or at least should not cover up, any of the designs which may be upon the surface the staining is applied to; so woods which are the principal material upon which the painter usually applies stains, should show its veins, pores and other details as clearly after the staining as before its application. Therefore, it is easily to be seen where the difference lies between it and graining; as some people frequently confound the two terms. Staining does not pretend to make another wood out of the one it is applied over, or, at least, to change its veining into an entirely different wood, while graining does. It is true that the dividing line is rather difficult to see at times and that some graining is done sometimes by staining, but it is not the prime object of it, and the great bulk of it is done for a different object in view.

279. Many woods change their colors greatly by aging. Oak, for instance, will become almost a black in time, maple will become of a deep buff brown. Mahogany will take on a deep burnt sienna red brown tone and so on through the whole list of woods.

Now it is impossible to age wood much faster than nature does it and when the effect of age is desired upon new wood the only way open to obtain the results at once, without waiting, is by staining the woods to the tone they would have taken by waiting patiently several hundred years to elapse. Again, many people desire certain tones and colors in a room to harmonize carpets and wall hangings into a good combination, and such do not hesitate to order furniture or wood work to be stained in any color of the rainbow they have a fancy for. It certainly is not in good taste to stain woods in colors which do not belong to them, as blues, greens, etc., and while this is a free country, etc., as long as a person is not sent to the penitentiary for committing outrages against nature, nor to insane asylums, it is very probable that the practice will go on undis turbed. But it is vulgarity, to say the least of the praetice, and painters should not encourage it.

Stains are useful and fill a legitimate object in dec oration when properly used, and many an ugly-looking, cheaply finished up house inside woodwork can be made more cheery and less of an eyesore if colored up by staining. If graining is permissible—and it is—with as much good reason for it as the representation of objects and scenes upon canvas to look at and enjoy— then for the very same reason it, too, has its "raison d'etre," for it is enjoyable and agreeable to the owner or it would not be put there. Graining may, and would be, objectionable if done in any but the colors which naturally belong to the wood it imitates, and for the same reason that a painter's picture of a green horse would not be, nor should not be admired. It has been stated before that the line of demarcation between graining and staining was hard to distinguish at times, and it is as much of the staining of mahogany, mottled maple, etc., partakes more or less of that character.

280. So, to distinguish it from the ordinary staining of wood which is done all over without any special preparation, it will be called grained staining. This grained staining is done so as to change the character of the wood being stained over so that it may look more natural and resemble the wood which the stain is supposed to transform it in—in its veinings. Now, the cheap, soft maple has none of the marking of mottled maple, nor has birch any of the feathered markings of mahogany which it is made to imitate so much and so that ihe mahogany staining which is done over it may appear more natural and pleasing these mottlings are put on the bare wood before the staining proper is put on all over. Even veinings can be put in to good effect with a fan overgraining brush and some fine imitation of many woods can be made upon the bare wood in stain graining. The wood over which such is made, however, must not possess any marked character of their own as they would be brought out by the stain and a double appearance of different veinings would look ridiculous.

281. There are two ways of staining wood, or rather of preparing the coloring matter used in making the stains used over them. Both have their uses and are better adapted for certain purposes than the other.

One is to thin the color with linseed oil and the other is to dissolve it in water.

282. Oil stains have an advantage over water stains in that upon the bare wood it acts as a primer and partial filler and that they do not raise the grain or pores of the wood—which water stains certainly do. They protect the wood from humidity and mishaps of various kinds, and but that oil stains are not as penetrating as water stains are, and for that reason are easier marred and damaged, they would be superior for general use in hardwood staining. On this account mainly, notwithstanding their good traits otherwise, they are seldom used except for the staining of pine partitions and soft woods of little value, manufacturers of furniture and other hardwood finishers preferring the great drawback of the raised grain to cut down, to the danger of having their work spoiled by the shallowness of the staining. Another reason also is that as most of the oil stains are prepared from finely ground pigments, which all have more or less opacity, as siennas and umbers, although called transparent or semi-transparent, they do not give as clear a tone of stain as the water stains do, so that a portion of the details in the veining of the woods stained with them is lost or hid by the opacity of the pigment in the stain.

283. Water stains dissolve the substances used in the making of them and this solution must be entire, or when partial only, as when obtained by maceration or percolation, the stain should be run through a funnel

filled with percolating paper to free it from specks **of** undissolved foreign matter.

A good water stain should hold the dissolved coloring matter in solution without precipitation, or it will be of little value unless used with constant agitation and even then it will hardly make a satisfactory stain free from specking, so such should be avoided. For this reason the earth colors, such as the siennas, umber, etc., which are not soluble in water but would be only held in suspension in it, are not fitted for water stains, however good they may be for oil stains. Therefore, the substances required for the making of water stains must be entirely soluble in it, or at least the substance used must have a portion of it that is soluble and which can be extracted out of it by either maceration or percolation.

284. The stains which are made from soluble sub stances as some of the aniline dyes—alizarine, purpurine, nigrine, etc., which are entirely soluble are easily made by simply dissolving them with hot water, usually.

Those made by percolation are also easily made, the ingredients to be percolated being simply placed in **a** funnel which has been first covered inside with an unsized percolating paper through which the dissolved stain will pass but which will hold back any undissolved matter.

The stains made by maceration require considerable more time, some of them requiring fully two weeks to become entirely dissolved. When so dissolved, they should be filtered through filtering paper as stated for the percolation process.

Sometimes the process of maceration and of solution is hastened by boiling, but again in others it would ruin the stain, so that in subsequent paragraphs where recipes are given as to how to prepare them from various substances unless boiling is plainly stated to be the proper way of dissolving the coloring, cold or only moderately warm water should be used.

With the above instructions it is hoped that there will be no trouble in obtaining good results in the preparing of stains from the formulas given.

Many of the formulas given are of old time tested quality and are good—but too tedious to make in our twentieth century times, but there are some who still want them. The list of such has been abridged, however, giving only a few for each color of wood. Few persons can afford to spare the time necessary for their preparation, and upon the whole it is a question as to whether it will pay them to do so, when they can be made ready for use in a few minutes from the prepared dyes or stains, all ready made, and for sale at most of the supply stores.

285. There is a class of prepared goods which have been used in immense quantities of late—i. e., the *varnish stains*. Most of them are sold under fancy names, copyrighted by their manufacturers, but which is the same thing after all. They usually consist of cheap varnish, colored with some dye, soluble in volatile

oils. Why they are used to the extent they are is a conundrum, accountable for only because of the extensive advertising given them.

The work done with such can never be as good as that done with a previous stain covered over with varnish of good quality afterward. All varnish stains set quickly with the consequence that the laps of the brush show all over the job and make it look uneven, while, had the stain been applied first it would have a much better appearance—besides if finished over with a good coat of varnish the assurance that the job will remain good for sometime afterward, especially upon floors, etc., where good quality for wear counts for something.

RECIPES FOR MAKING OIL STAINS.

286. Any finely ground transparent or semi-transparent color ground in oil will make an oil stain. If a dark color is wanted it must not be thinned with as much oil; if a light colored stain of it is desired, then it must be thinned out with more.

All the aniline and alizarine colors made which are soluble in oil can also be used to make oil stains so that an immense range can be had. These are not quite as permanent as those made from oil colors—but those made from alizarine are dependable.

1. *Oil Oak Stain.*—(Light oak.) Raw sienna, raw umber; 2/3 of the former, 1/3 of the latter. Thin with raw linseed oil to suit. Add enough turpentine to make it set and a little liquid dryer.

2. *Oil Oak Stain.*—(Dark oak.) Raw sienna, raw umber, burnt umber; 1/3 of each. Thin with raw linseed oil as stated in No. 1.

3. *Oil Walnut Stain.*—Burnt umber or Vandvke brown, thinned as directed for No. 1. Add more drier if Vandyke brown is used.

4. *Ebony.*—Drop black, thinned with raw linseed oil, turpentine, and liquid dryer.

All colors of stains obtainable from either transparent oil colors or aniline soluble in oil in any shade desired can all be made in the manner stated above and those should suffice as an indication as to the "how to make them."

SPIRIT STAINS.

287. Alcoholic stains are but little used, not only on account of their expense but because they raise the grain of the wood as bad as water stains do. Some instrument manufacturers, however, want them as well as others for special uses, so a few of the more important ones are given.

5. *Yellow.*—Tumeric powder, 1 oz.; alcohol, 1 pint. Digest four days, shaking occasionally and strain. To be brushed over the wood until the color wanted is obtained.

6. *Yellowish Red, Orange.*—Add an alcoholic solution of dragon's blood to the degree of redness wanted to the above; apply it in the same way.

7. *Mahogany.*—Dragon's blood, 1½ ounces; carbonate of soda, ½ ounce; alcohol, 1 pint. Digest a few

days to make it dissolve, filter and brush it over after the application of the following wash: Wash over the surface with dilute nitric acid.

8. *Ebony.*—Dissolve extract of logwood in denatured or wood alcohol to any shade desired. Strain and apply. The color is afterward developed by washing over the surface with tincture of muriate of iron.

ANILINE DYES ON STAINS.

288. Many persons are afraid of the name aniline as it is the equivalent of "fugitiveness" in their thoughts, and the poorer kinds certainly are. But some are very useful and fairly permanent when properly put on and such as are made from alizarine are as permanent or even more so than similar ones made from any other substances known.

As each manufacturer makes these by processes somewhat different and requiring different treatment in fixing in the use of mordants, acids or alkalies, it will be well to ascertain exactly what is needed by asking the dealer about it, as what would be good for one would harm another.

Another great trouble in these dyes is that there is no nomenclature known among dealers—each manufacturer having adopted a name of his own for the colors he produces, so that there is an endless row of trouble ahead for those who are looking up a new line of these colors to work with. He has to learn over and to forget all about what he had learned before in order to adapt himself to the different handling required for those made by a different manufacturer.

Those soluble in linseed oil or turpentine require the liquids to be moderately warmed and some little time to perfect the solution. Those soluble in water usually are readily dissolved and below is given a typical recipe to indicate how they are all made and which will suffice for all the others.

9. *Mahogany.*—Bismarck brown, 1 ounce; water, 3 quarts. Let the water be boiled, pour upon the Bismark brown and dissolve. It is ready to use as soon as it has cooled.

WATER STAINS.

289. Really under the heading of water stains most of the aniline dye stains really belong, but it was thought best to treat of them separately and to place under this heading the old stand-by recipes which have been in use, some of them, from time immemorial. The list is a large one to pick from, but as these are now but seldom used, it has been cut down to one or two sample ones for each of the leading woods.

10. *Light oak.*—Quercitron bark, 2 oz.; water, 1 gallon; macerate for two weeks, filter and use.

11. *Dark oak.*—Quercitron bark, 4 oz.; water 1 gallon; macerate for two weeks, filter and use.

12. *Walnut No. 1.*—Permanganate of potash, 1 ounce; Epsom salt, 1 ounce; water, 1 quart; dissolve, strain and apply, repeating until sufficiently darkened.

13. *Walnut, No. 2.*—Nutgalls, crushed, 3 ounces;

concentrated lye, 4 ounces; Vandyke brown, (dry) 8 ounces; boil till the bulk is reduced one half. When cold apply to the wood with a cloth or pad.

14. *Mahogany, No. 1.*—Fustie chips, 8 ounces; madder root, 1 pound; water, two gallons. Boil for two or three hours; strain and apply boiling hot.

15. *Mahogany, No. 2.*—Make a decoction of logwood chips by boiling them in a closely covered vessel for two hours in twice their bulk of water; strain; add a small quantity of chloride of tin; this will give it redness. Be your own judge when to stop. Apply two coats.

16. *Cherry.*—Spanish anetto, 1 pound; concentrated lye, 1 ounce; boil for half an hour, boil more to concentrate it. Gamboge added to it will concentrate it.

17. *Ebony, No. 1.*—Extract of logwood, 3 pounds; concentrated lye, 1 pound; water, seven pounds; dissolve by boiling, strain and apply hot or cold. When dry go over the work with a strong solution of vinegar and iron.

18. *Ebony, No. 2.*—Sulphate of iron, ½ pound; Chinese blue, 2 ounces; nutgalls, 3 ounces; extract of logwood, 2 pounds; vinegar, 1 gallon; carbonate of iron, ¼ pound. Boil over a slow fire for two or three hours, strain and apply hot or cold.

19. *Rosewood.*—Any of the mahogany stains will make a rosewood stain if applied over and over until the proper depth has been attained and then stained over with an ebony stain, very lightly put on. Then after-

ward run over with a camel's hair brush loaded with the ebony dye in irregular veins all over the surface. The grain of the natural wood being straggling and occurring in a haphazard sort of way it should be imitated as close as possible.

20. *Crimson.*—Brazilwood, pulverized, 1 pound; water, 3 pounds; cochineal, ½ ounce; boil the Brazil wood with the water for half an hour. Strain and add the cochineal. Boil gently for another half hour; let it cool and it is fit for use.

21. *Violet.*—Make a solution of orchil and soluble indigo blue of such strength as required. Strain and apply when cold

22. *Blue.*—Indigo blue, 3 ounces; sulphuric acid, 1 pound. Put the two together in a porcelain dish and let the indigo dissolve, which will take twenty-four hours or more. Shake it up occasionally to hasten the process. Add a pint of boiling water and strain, applying the stain to the wood while hot. Before the indigo stain has completely dried, wash over the surface with a solution made of 3 ounces of cream of tartar in one quart of water.

The above will suffice to give an idea of the trouble and difficulty in making the easiest ones made of the old timers. It is much easier to use the ones ready prepared and cheaper in the end.

QUESTIONS AS TO STAINING AND STAINS.

278. What is said of staining?

279. Why is staining resorted to?

280.   What is grained staining?

281.   How many different methods of staining are there?

282.   Where are stains in oil most useful?

283.   What kinds of woods require water stains?

284.   How are water stains made?

285.   What are varnish stains?

286.   Oil stains.—Recipes, how to make them.

287.   Spirit stains.—Recipes, how to make them.

288.   Aniline stains.—Recipe, how to make them.

289.   Water stains.—Recipes, how to make them.

STENCILS AND STENCILLING.

290.   This is the stencil age.   This method of embellishment in ornamenting surfaces is becoming more and more popular and it has passed from the exclusive use of the decorator into common household use by every one having something in the home worthy of being made more beautiful by using them.   In other words it has become a fad and with the history of past fads in mind, the time will come when it will come to a stop from the very excesses to which it is put.   It will, of course be overdone, and that, as other fads before that are gone and been forgotten, will once more be left where it has a legitimate existence into the hands of professional decorators.

Stencils, in repeated and conventional decoration, will always be used.   One could almost assert that ever since decoration has been introduced into the world that in all probabilities stencils were used in repeating designs, and some of the remnants which have been preserved unto our day which are found in museums of antiquities, would indicate that the ancients were not ignorant of its use.

291. Stencils are used for many purposes which the subject matter of this book does not treat upon, such as decorating of textile fabrics, commercial stencils used in marking of boxes, barrels, etc. Stencils therefore will be treated from the standpoint of the decorator and the uses he can make of them in either water or oil colors. Stencils are also extensively used in making numerous duplicates of a given sign by sign painters, either for use upon muslin signs or boards in one or many colors.

MATERIAL USED IN CUTTING STENCILS.

292. The material used in the making of stencils differs according as to what use they are intended for.

Sheet brass is used for commercial purposes and would be the best for the decorator too, but for its cost and the difficulty of cutting them.

A specially prepared resined clear, or rather semi-transparent paper, is much used for the purpose by the decorators. This paper cuts a very smooth edge and being tough the ties do not break easily.

Good manilla drafting paper is also very useful and while not sized like the resin paper above, after it has been coated over with two good coats of orange shellac it will withstand the pouncing of the stencil brush about as well and as long as the specially prepared resin paper will.

Cartridge paper, not too thick, makes an excellent material upon which to cut stencils.

Printer's press bedding manilla paper is also much used and can be procured at any printing office when possibly some of the others might not. The above paper is tough and pliable and but that it stretches somewhat too readily, it is the equal of the others in all other respects. It is well to give it a coat of linseed oil on both sides before it is shellacked, as after such a coating it is not so likely to stretch.

To cut the stencils upon, a smooth level surface hard enough to not be dented by the knife must be procured.

Most decorators prefer a piece of plate glass. Some use sheet tin and for a short time no doubt that may be best, but tin soon gets scratched over when the knife will catch and a clean cut line is then out of the question.

A lignum vitæ block well smoothed is the best, but such are not readily obtained anywhere while plate glass can and for this reason if no other it is more used and with good success than any other.

A good stock of stencil brushes from ½ inch to 1½ inches (see Figs. 18 and 19) are indispensable in order to insure good clean work. The larger ones are used mainly upon duplicated muslin signs, some use as large as a 2 inch brush for this purpose as these will hold enough color to coat over the stencil without refilling. Punches for cutting round holes. The colors used in either water or oil are the whole list of pigments useful in either classes. Some charcoal and drawing crayons to design the ornaments to be cut out and of course, all the requisite thinners for the colors, as linseed oil, turpentine and orange shellac varnish.

Last, but not least, some good stencil knife. While it is possible to cut a stencil with an ordinary pocket knife, the blades in most of these are not formed just right to cut stencils quickly, nor will the cuts made be as clean as the ones which are specially prepared for this purpose and which are found for sale in any of the larger supply stores.

293. It is always best to draw the design upon the stencil paper which is about to be cut before the paper is oiled when this is necessary as in the printer's press bedding manilla paper. This is unnecessary for all the others mentioned, but all should have at least one if not two coats of orange shellac given them after the cutting. Where a stencil is to be used over and over a good many times in water colors, especially, it will be well to give them two coats at least. The constant wetting otherwise will make them flabby and it is impossible to make a good showing with such, and much valuable time will have to be wasted in waiting for them to dry before they can be safely used again.

294. The designing of a stencil will depend upon the use it is intended for. It may be a simple fillet or serpentine line or it may be the most intricate of designs in one or many colors

If in one color only, the whole of the design is cut out upon the one stencil—excepting that what are known as *ties,* which must be left here and there to hold the design together, and to stiffen it up. Those ties instead of detracting from the beauty of the finish, are really helpful in producing effects not otherwise obtainable and in the hands of the skillful designer instead of proving a hindrance as many suppose them to be, they will enhance the beauty of the design. Even the human face and form can be produced in one color stencils with fine effects by the judicious selection of the proper place for putting in the ties.

It is frequently necessary to leave ties in a stencil where color must be used in order to hold it together. In such a case the ties must be filled in by hand. As the texture of the paint put in with the pouncing of the stencil brush some little care will have to be exercised in order to put the color in with a brush that it does not differ too much from the rest of it to be noticed and it will be well to use the stencil brush itself as much as possible in pouncing them over in order that the coloring may look all alike.

295. Below are given a few illustrations of easy stencils to make. In Fig. 101 and Fig. 102 are shown

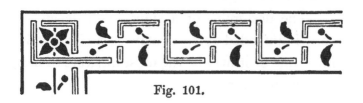

Fig. 101.

some simple one color stencils, supplemented by hand painted lines.

Fig. 102.

Stencils in one color can be made more attractive by the use of varied coloring of the ground coats over which they are placed, Figs. 103 and 104. The upper

Fig. 103.

Fig. 104.

part in both those designs being in a deeper tone than that of the lower half. These are also supplemented with hand painted lines.

In Fig. 105 the middle portion is painted of a deeper tone, also the rest of it, and the herring bone section of

Fig. 105.

it must have separate small hand painted lines painted on each side of it. In the figure the herring bone shows

Fig. 106.

in the white, but this would necessitate an extra stencil and is unnecessary as the black or whatever color is used will cover it up and it may as well be painted all over with the rest of it above. A broader hand painted line above between the upper broken line and at the bottom another finer hand painted line, finishes the stencil.

In Fig. 106 is shown a combination of a hand painted molding and of a one color stencil below it or the stencil may be placed below a plaster molding properly colored. This design has only two small hand painted lines.

One color stencils may be made more effective sometimes by using different colors or tones of one color in different parts of it. This requires but little more addi tional time in its execution. The different colors or tones must each be put on with different stencil brushes is all the difference.

296. In preparing stencils where more than one is used in the same color, all that will be required of the second one will be to draw and cut out the parts which show as ties in the first one. This gives the effect of solid hand painted work and lines can be worked out in stencils so as to resemble hand painted lines in the same manner.

297. If two or more colors are to be used in stencil work, a separate stencil must be made for each color used. Great care must be taken that each stencil regis- ters perfectly over each other and an allowance must be made of say 1/32 part of an inch so as to insure the cov- ering over and good joining of the two or more colors.

The ties in such a case are of no importance as the next stencil will cover them over. Some beautiful work is done in multi-color stencils which will sometimes puzzle the inexperienced and set them at guessing whether the work is not hand made. An experienced stencil cutter can obtain some very close imitations of hand work in that way and the sign painters obtain really better looking work by the use of several stencils than is usually done by hand in all but the highest priced work.

298.   The designs for the several stencils or for the single ones having been drawn out in full upon the face of the stencil paper, the sheet should be placed upon the plate glass or lignum vitæ block or whatever the cutter has decided to use to cut upon. Then with the set of 3 cutting knives provided of the specially made ones mentioned the cutter proceeds to cut out all of the design with the exception of the ties already mentioned. While the stencil cutting set of knives is not absolutely necessary, where one has considerable stencil cutting to do, he will find it very poor economy in trying to do his work with an ordinary knife, nor will his stencils look as well, as no matter how careful he may be there will be some ragged edges.

The round holes, especially the smaller ones, are much better and quicker made with a punch. The ordinary harness maker leather punches are the best for the purpose. The stencil should be placed over a level wooden block and the punch struck with a hammer. Being hollow the paper is forced up it and when done with it, a pencil will push it out of the punch. One should be used with it. The stencil bruch should be dip-various ones from ¼ upward to an inch. When a circle is larger than that they can be cut with a knife much easier than the smaller ones.

When the stencilling is done in several colors and re-quires several stencils to be cut, it has already been stated that they must register perfectly over each other or the work will be imperfect. This should be attended to. in the drawing out of the design, but registering guide marks should be cut in to enable the operator when shifting it to a new position to so place it that it will be just right otherwise no matter how well the design has been drawn nor how perfect each stencil may register with the others, a botchy effect will be produced by the unevenness of the lines.

299. The stencils having been cut should now re-ceive the coats of shellac varnish already mentioned. Orange shellac is the best to use as it is stronger than the white. It should be brushed over carefully over both sides of the stencils and these should be hung up to dry which will require 8 to 12 hours according to the sea-sons. If the first coat has been put on in the morning, a second coat can be put on in the evening when they will be fit for use the next morning.

The above is far the better way. Many who are in a hurry will give each coat one hour apart and will be using them perhaps within another hour, but they will not stand the hardship of those who have been done in the slower way and broken ties and limber stencils will hardly compensate for the waiting of a few hours longer.

300. Rooms may look square but may not be and belie their appearance. So to make sure of good results a chalk line should be used and a plumb bob to guide one in making perpendicular lines with it. If the ground is to be parti-colored this should of course have been done before the stencilling begins. All the lines for the various stencils to be used in a room having been struck, the work of painting them on may begin.

301. The colors used may be either water colors or colors in oil. If they are water colors they should be mixed somewhat thicker than is usual for ordinary application upon the walls, also a trifle more of the binder should be used with it. The stencil brush should be dipped in the color and then rubbed out upon a board or sheet of metal in order to work the color in well and to remove a superabundance of it on its surface which would blur and make a blotch upon the stencil. It is hard to describe exactly how much or how little should the brush hold and a few trials by the operator will soon teach him the proper quantity his brush should carry. The colors being ready he should place his stencil on the line at the proper part for the beginning. If the stencil is a large one he should first fasten it on to the wall with small thumb tacks made on purpose for this use. These tacks have a wide face somewhat similar to those used in fastening drawing paper to boards. The points are

short and will not hurt the plaster. This fastening insures the stencil against slipping and relieves the operator from having to hold it at arm's length, which is a tiresome job, on a ceiling especially. It gives him the use of both of his hands and enables him to press down the stencil close to the plaster ahead of the other which holds the brush with color. The color should not be brused over as in ordinary painting as that would surely cause some of the color to run under the edges of the stencil and make a blur, but should be pecked on in much the same way as a wall stippler is used. The left hand of the operator being free if he has fastened the stencil on the wall as directed above can slip along just ahead of the brush to smooth and hold down the paper very closely to the wall and much better work will result from it. Clean cut outline is the chief beauty of good stencilling and ragged edges are pretty sure indications of a second class workman.

302. All that was stated in the preceding paragraph excepting as to the preparation of the colors, applies for work done in oil colors. The same care must be exer cised all the way through the stencilling. The stencils in either case should be cleaned off of accumulations of colors near the edges as they would in time prevent the close contact required to make a clean cut edge.

The color should be mixed much thicker than for wall work and either flat or semi-flat to match the character of the rest of the walls. The brush should be very carefully rubbed over the board at each new filling to remove the surplus which would surely blur and with pecking strokes the color should be applied over the stencils. After the color has been mostly worked off the brush there is not so much danger of its running under the edge of the stencil and it may be used in a twirling way over it without much danger in the hands of a workman who is used to it; the novice, however, is not advised to undertake it till he is sure of himself and of the proper condition when it will be safe to do so.

If the above directions are followed out there is no reason why a painter of ordinary ability may not do a great deal of decorative work which he could easily do at a remunerative price for himself, yet cheap enough as to interest many property owners who have an idea that all such work, which is ordinarily classed as fresco painting is too costly for the pockets of ordinary people. Many fairly good decorators have become such by first commencing to do some very plain stencilling then gradually growing into more difficult phases of it until familiarity developed stencilling with a blending of free hand and pouncings. When a painter has once started on the road (no matter how low) to decoration, he is sure to become so interested and to so love the work that he will use every effort to learn more and more until he finally becomes truly worthy of the name of *Decorator*.

QUESTIONS ON STENCILS AND STENCILLINGS.

290.   What is said of stencils?

291.   What are stencils chiefly used upon?

292. What materials are used for the making of stencils?

293. How is stencil paper prepared for the cutting?

294. How are the stencils designed and tied?

295. Give examples of how one color stencils can be used in and over varied colored grounds?

296. What effect is produced by work done in two stencils in one color?

297. What effects are produced by work done in two or more stencils in various colors?

298. How are stencils cut?

299. How are stencils shellacked?

300. How are rooms prepared for the stencilling?

301. How are stencils painted on in water colors?

302. How are stencils painted on in oil colors?

VARNISHES.

303. Varnishes have the property of making a gloss or an enamel upon the surfaces over which they are applied.

Their uses in antiquity is far beyond the ken of men or history and in one instance at least more has been lost than has been learned since. In times so very remote that it is impossible to even guess a date within several hundred years, the Chinese produced a glass varnish which was used in coating over articles and which is indestructible. There are many specimens to be found of it and they are as perfect today as upon the day that the varnish was applied, so that one can truly say of it that it is indestructible. The Chinese themselves have lost the art of making this varnish and so far with all the knowledge modern chemistry has put into the hands of men for scientific researches our *savants* have been unable to unravel the mystery connected with it. This varnish dates back so far that even Chinese literature which dates back several thousand years before Christ, makes no mention of its discovery.

Aside of this, lacquers were and had been in use also from time immemorial by the Asiatics, both Chinese and Japanese and the East Indies knew its uses in very ancient times.

The varnish industry as we know it now is of comparatively recent origin and it is not so very long back when many of the painters were in the habit of preparing their own varnishes, as no factories such as produce it at this time had any existence then.

Formulas galore were in vogue then and many a painter paid a good bit of money for recipes known and handed down from father to son as an heirloom. Some of them have been handed down to us in both written formulas and in print, so that we can form as pretty good idea of what our forefathers had to do when they wanted a can of varnish for use, for they had it to make.

Most of these recipes are loaded down with quite a number of unnecessary ingredients but the recipes would have been just as good without seven hairs from the inside of the left ear of a white hare, and must have put the painters of the sixteenth, seventeenth and

eighteenth centuries to considerable trouble in catching
the hares and then pulling the hair out of the hares. And
such an array of names for gums as they had—enough
to confound all but a twentieth cenury skeptic who has
them all classed into very small groups with rosin at the
top, of which our forefathers knew little about and
cared less. ,

Up to the middle of the nineteenth century varnishes
were still made by many painters, although factories began to prepare them in a commercial way and for sale to
the trade some time before and in a very humble way
compared to the manner in which the large concerns engaged in its manufacture today do.

England and France have the honor of having the
oldest varnish factories in the world and compared to
many other industries they may be called recent. Their
preparations, however, did not extend down to the
needs of the house painters, as they catered mainly to
the wants of the carriage trade. Some of those old
English and French varnish manufacturers' names are
still in use and the lineal descendants of the families are
still connected with the concerns making the varnishes
today. Tradition having handed down the great value
of their output said tradition having started when few
knew what varnish was and when but few were engaged in its manufacture, it has enabled these old concerns to hold trade against all comers at prices for their
products in which the family names weigh more and for
which more is paid for by the consumer than it is really

worth to him. There is no doubt about the excellencies of their output but our laterday manufacturies are making just as good goods and at a price for which family name does not count in the making of it.

304.   Varnishes are made from various gums and gum-resins and with various solvents. As for certain specific purposes each are better adapted for use in the one that any of the others, all are useful then for certain kinds of work.

Some of the gums used are soluble only in alcohol and are known as spirit varnishes of such character is shellac varnish. Others again are soluble only in volatile oils, as turpentine, etc.

Others are soluble in linseed oil under certain conditions or in combination with volatile oils. For practical purposes, however, varnishes may be divided up in three principal classes with many subdivisions in the three groups:

1.   Varnishes with an alcoholic base solvent.

2.   Varnishes with a volatile oil base solvent

3.   Varnishes with a fixed oil base solvent, of which more will be said hereafter after the character of the gums used in preparing them has been looked into.

305.   The gums chiefly used in preparing varnishes are not many. The principal ones are *gum copal*—which is not a true gum insomuch that it is a fossil and will not dissolve in either water or volatile oil as all true gums do. It is chiefly imported from Africa and comes in many qualities. It ranges in color from a pale, nearly

transparent tone of yellow, to dark brown and opaque chunks and in all sorts of intermediate tones between the two. The lightest and clearest is the most valuable and the intermediate shades decrease in value according as they approach the darker brown shades. Varnishes made from this gum are the most desirable of all and the solvent under heat and special treatment of the manufacturer is mainly linseed oil, which gives the varnishes made from it its greater durability and elasticity.

Kauri gum—is a resin gum of a semi-fossilized sort. It is found where original forests of the kauri pine formerly existed and that is of better quality than that which is obtained from the trees by exudation.

Animac.—A gum-resin derived from a sort of leguminous tree and probably from several varieties of the same specie. In its exudation insects are caught in it and come to market with them imbedded in the chunks, hence the name. The gum is not as hard as the copal gums of good quality and varnishes made from it have not the wearing qualities of the one made from high grade copal. The varnish makers use many of the gums in a blend to obtain varnishes adapted for certain definite purposes by the judicious mixing of various gums.

Amber is used in making certain varnishes. It is a fossilized resin and is found in many countries. The chief source of supply, however, is from Germany, where it is found imbedded in the sand along the Baltic sea shore.

Damar is a soft whitish gum which exudes from coniferous species of trees in India and Ceylon. It is soluble in the volatile oils and yields a very white varnish of too soft a nature to be of much practical use except as a paper varnish for which on account of its pliability, it seems well adapted also on account of its colorless nature.

Sandarac is also the product of conifers, but is of little better quality although harder than our own resin derived from yellow pine

Gum mastic is derived from a nut bearing tree of the Grecian archipelago, and exudes from the trees where incisions are made, in the shape of small tear like pebbles. It is also too soft for other uses than that indi cated for damar gum varnish.

Resin of yellow pine extraction is used in many ways by varnish factories in connection with other harder gums and with China wood oil it yields some kinds of varnishes useful for many purposes. Since the introduction of wood oil in connection with varnish making, it has rendered its use possible where before it would not have been thought of. This wood oil seems to make it harder and more pliable at the same time and it is replacing many of the soft gums which are mentioned above as it is very much cheaper than any of the others.

Sticlac and Shellac may as well be reviewed together, as shellac is only sticlac refined for commercial use and immense quantities of it are used by the industries of the country besides the use of it made by the hardwood finishing trade. It is the product of vegetation and is soluble in alcohol mainly.

The solvents are alcohol, turpentine and linseed oil.

306. The manufacture of varnish is an intricate, complex business requiring a long apprenticeship and accumulated experience and while the ways of making varnishes are well known, each manufacturer has little tricks of his own in the making of certain grades and in the ripening or blending of various gums which are carefully guarded.

It requires a large capital besides for to properly conduct a varnish manufacturing business. The ripening of varnishes requires months and even years to fit them for certain uses.

It is much cheaper for the consumer to buy the varnishes he uses ready for application than it would be for him to make them, even if he had the know how which he has not, and a person now who would undertake the making of his own varnish as "in ye olden tymes" would be considered as a fit subject for a lunatic asylum. Such easily made ones as shellac varnish, however, do not come under the same heading, and any one can readily make them for himself; all that is required is to give the alcohol sufficient time to dissolve the shellac, but it will not pay one to make it as he cannot buy the shellac nearly as cheap as the manufacturer does and it will probably cost him as much as the ready prepared article besides the trouble thrown in.

307. The cheapest forms of varnish made are of course made entirely from resin dissolved in cheap mineral volatile oil with some paraffin oil put into it in order that the brittleness of the resin may be counteracted.

The so-called "surfacers" are but little better than the gloss oils and may be classed together. They are chiefly used in coating over plastered walls to stop the suctions previous to the applications of water colors.

308. Because a varnish may be cheap it need not necessarily be a poor one, nor will a high priced varnish necessarily be a good one, simply because high priced material enter into its composition. So there are a number of cheaply made varnishes which are as good and possibly better for the purposes for which they are used than others which would cost many times more per gallon. Since manufacturers have been able by the proper use of wood oil, paraffine oil and linseed oil, to use resin and the darker colored gum copals to prepare good wearing varnishes by blending at a low cost, immense quantities are used by the trade and with good results.

These cheaper varnishes of course all contain resin in greater of lesser quantities grading up in quality from something but little better than the surfacers on upward in quality and price up to extra No. 1 coach and light hard oil finish (so called) of this character are the *Furniture varnishes; coach varnishes*, including *No. 1 coach* and *extra No. 1 coach.* Some of them so good that they will rub and the whole grade in qualities of the so-called *hard oils* of which enormous quantities are used in finishing cheap interior wood work.

309. The house painter and hard wood finishers are chiefly interested in the following varnishes, which all varnish houses now make a sepcialty of under some fancy proprietary name, but which are probably all prepared in much the same manner by all of them ·

Interior varnish for inside wood finishing. The bet ter grades carry a fine lustre and all are rubbing varnishes, and polish well.

Outside varnish, usually an elastic varnish, but a slower dryer than the interior brands. Supposed to stand the weather, but they do not—at least not very long. Manufacturers should add to the label after the word Outside—*when well protected from sun and rain.* But then the varnish would not sell so well.

Floor varnish completes the trio which every painter and wood finisher is interested in. This is made from very hard gums so as to stand the hardships it is subjected to from being walked upon, cleaned and brushed over.

All the varnishes which have been mentioned so far are varnishes which are used in house construction by house painters and wood finishers even the so-called coach varnishes. These are never used by the carriage painter, however much the name would indicate that it **is.** They are chiefly used in the same way as hard oil finishes for the cheaper kinds of furniture and pine finishes in room work; in short they are all about on a par with furniture varnish.

310. The carriage trade uses a higher grade of varnishes than the average which is used in house work, so they cost more. Competition, however, has reduced the fancy prices asked and obtained by our English cousins across the water since American manufacturers have gained the experience enabling them to make as good carirage varnish as that which formerly was all imported.

While carriage varnishers as a class by itself is of a better quality than the first ones reviewed, they are by no means all equally good, nor is it necessary that they should be. A cheap wagon or vehicle will not and ought not to receive the same treatment as an expensive coach, for if it did—it would not be cheap. Nor need the varnish be as good in the repainting of old vehicles as for first class work. So there are grades and qualities in carriage varnishes as well as in house varnishes.

The *carriage rubbing varnishes* exemplified what is said in the preceding paragraph. They are made to rub in from 12 to 60 hours. The slower ones being the best and most expensive.

The *wearing body varnishes* are and should be made from the very finest material and all manufacturers try to excel in their output of it. It too is made in several qualities. The palest which is made from the costliest gums is the highest priced, while the darker gums used in the lower grades of it cheapens the cost, while aside of the color the quality remains nearly as good. Some of the wearing body varnishes are made to dry quicker than others for hurried work. Generally speaking the slower drying ones are the best for wear.

The *gear varnishes,* for the varnishing of running parts, are made to stand more hard knocks than any of the others and are to be found in many degrees of paleness and of quickness in drying. The slower driers are the more elastic.

Manufacturers all have a long list of carriage varnishes, describing each so that the person buying it may know just what to expect from it. All of them can be classed in the three kinds mentioned. The black rubbing is simply a rubbing varnish into which a black color has been ground and could be made in the shop, but that the mixture would not be as smooth and well ground together unless the shop is equipped for it. So all the numerous varnishes listed are simply varieties of those three—many being made in different qualities of paleness, elasticity, etc.

311. As everything that has a gloss is a varnish, *asphaltum varnish* is entitled to the name. It is classed by itself for the reason that there is only one place where it can be useful and that is upon ironwork. It is made from asphaltum, a mineral gum too well known to need any introduction. It is melted and at as low a heat as possible turpentine or benzine or naptha is mixed in with it to make it fluid enough to be brushed

out upon metals. That made from turpentine is the best to use, as the smell of the others is against them, especially in interior work. It dries quickly and the operator must not wait too long in joining up, or a lap will result. Where registers or iron work are to be coated over with it they can be warmed, then the varnish will flow level and free of brush marks.

Asphaltum varnish is useful also to the sign painter in show card writing and in the painting over of brass and copper plates for etching, and brass and metal signs.

The above comprises about all the varnishes useful to the painters.

QUESTIONS ON VARNISHES.

303. What is said of varnishes?

304. How many classes of varnishes are there?

305. Name the gum-resins chiefly used in the making of varnishes?

306. Will it pay to make one's own varnishes?

307. What are gloss oil and the so called surfacers?

308. What other cheap varnishes are there?

309. What grades of varnishes are chiefly useful in hardwood finishing?

310. Name the principal carriage varnishes?

311. What is asphaltum varnish and what are its uses?

VARNISHING.

312. The operation of varnishing, which is simple enough to look at, is, nevertheless, one which requires

a great deal more knowledge than appears from simple casual observation. Everybody may put on paint so that it will look well and it would seem that any one could do the same with a varnish brush, but such is not the case. Good varnishers are the exception, and some men have tried for years to acquire the knack, but failed to do so.

There are so many things to be taken into consideration in order to insure good varnishing that the wonder is, not that there are so few good varnishes, but that there is so much of it that is done that proves good as there is under such conditions as exist.

313. *a.* Varnish, unlike paint, is most sensitive to the atmospheric and barometrical state of the weather. It is so sensitive that a draught of air will cause trouble in the varnish room, so that carriage factories, which are the only places where perfect conditions for doing perfect varnishing can be established, all have taken the greatest of care to guard against every element entering into the possibility of making trouble in the varnish rooms.

As far as possible the varnish room is located farthest away from the blacksmith shop where sulphurous fumes are generated, and from which noxious gases arise. To guard against draughts double windows should be used and a ventilating air shaft should carry out all the bad air of a varnish room and all outer air entering should be filtered free of dust.

Steam coils and radiators are the only heat permissible, as the varnish room should be maintained at a uniform degree of temperature during both the application of the varnish and its drying. No varnishing can be done when the heat is below 70 degrees Fahrenheit, and the room should never be allowed to cool down below that. There is but little danger of trouble arising from overheating, but a great deal can be expected from sudden changes, and this is never allowed in a first class carriage factory. The greatest troubles arise from barometrical changes and these cannot be altogether guarded against. An exhaust fan and heat will help to reduce damage by humidity to the lowest degree, and where draughts of the outer air are prevented there is usually no damage done.

The above may cause dismay to the beginner and he may well think that if varnishing can only be done under such conditions he may as well give up any hopes of ever becoming a varnisher. In the above was given the description of a varnish room such as the better class of vehicle manufacturers actually do have, and where fine jobs are varnished.

b. As all carriage shops, and especially the repair shops, cannot have such a varnish room, they have to put up with what they have and make out the best they can out of it. As each shop will have, probably, its own peculiar conditions each will have to adapt them so as to come as near to the description given of a first class one as it is possible for it to do so. The proper amount of heat must be maintained during the varnishing and drying. Dust must be kept down and out, and outer air, too, or there will be blooming and the 1001 varnish deviltries to annoy and make one's life miserable.

c The furniture factories are all equipped so as to obtain good results in their varnishing departments. While the usual class of furniture varnishing does not require the same amount of care as that which is done in the carriage shop, high grade polished furniture requires nearly if not quite as much precautions. Even for the very cheapest grades of furniture, the least speck of dust will hurt the looks of the cheapest kind of finish and that must be guarded against. So the varnish rooms of such establishments should, and are usually equipped so as to prevent changes of temperature and dust nearly as thoroughly as first class carriage shops are.

d. The painters and hardwood finishers who have the interior of a new house to finish and complete are not so fortunately situated for doing their varnishing and they must make out the best they can. Yet they will be expected to turn out perfect work and as it is located where it will be under the constant vision of the occupants the least flaw in the work will be sure to be found out and to be brought home to them oftener than they like.

In the summer and early autumn they can manage fairly well; the rooms should be dusted over and over again until there is an assurance of every speck of it is out of the way, and the wood work as well as the floors and walls should be wiped with a damp chamois skin, which will collect all that has been left after the dustings and sweepings. The doors and windows must be closed and the former locked to keep intruders and the dust they would bring—out. This exclusion must last not only during the time required for the application of the varnish, but also during the whole of the time required for its drying safely out of the way of dust sticking to it.

It may seem puerile and harsh to keep out callers, but first class work cannot be done otherwise. After a room has been finished everything should be removed out of it into the next one to be varnished and the door locked so that not even the steps of the varnisher may cause a forgotten atom of dust to rise and fasten itself to the varnished surface.

e.   The above is plain sailing and very good varnishing can be done at that time of the year, but in cold weather the troubles begin.

In houses which have a steam heating apparatus or a hot water system the difficulty will not be so great, but where the heating is by hot air or where it must be done with stoves, it is very troublesome. The temperature must be maintained above 70 degrees, Fahr. It is difficult to establish an even heat, especially with stoves, and in the latter case dust galore will be sure to be raised. When the heating is done by stoves, it will be well to arrange it so that considerably more than 70 degrees may be present in the room before the varnishing begins, then to fill the stoves and regulate them to keep the heat going for several hours more without the having to touch them again after the varnishing. After filling them up proceed to wipe up all dust with a chamois skin, slightly dampened, and go on with the varnishing, keeping out intruders until the varnish is dry.

314. It is customary with a few varnishers to mix two kinds of varnishs together when they do their work.

This should never be resorted to. When a varnish does not work well, better give it up and procure one that is better suited to the work being done.

If the varnisher will bear in mind that the varnish he is using is probably the result of a blend made from several tanks of varnishes, which have been ripening for months and years at the factory, and that the manufacturer who knows all the particulars and the peculiarities of every one of his tanks should certainly be the proper one to make the mixing, and that if he has failed to make it good, certainly the man who knows nothing whatever about that varnish or the one he mixes with it, will certainly make a mess, and probably a botch of it.

Varnishes are tempered just right for their application at the factory, so they require no thinning with either turpentine or oil, especially the latter. Trouble in the shape of sweating and stickiness will surely follow such thinnings.

The cheaper varnishes, composed nearly all of turpentine thinner, when long exposed to the air, may become too thick for application; in such a case the addition of turpentine is allowable but the varnish should first be warmed and the turpentine added and well incorporated with it by shaking at intervals of fifteen minutes for an hour before using.

315. When pouring out varnish to be used on a job, never pour out much more than is needed to complete the job. It is better to go again for more, if not enough. *For varnish once taken out of the can and exposed to the air should never be poured back into the can.* How many painters have learned this lesson only after bitter experiences! They will argue that it is foolish and that no possible harm can follow—and they learn after it is too late that it ruins a *good varnish* to pour it back and that it queers all the rest of it in the can.

How and why it does so would be hard to explain, and it may remain one of the many other mysteries connected with varnish which no amount of reasoning can explain satisfactorarily to one seeking to understand it. Varnish is a touchy affair—worse than an old maid to handle. It will only be handled in its own good way and no other.

316. The tools required for varnishing will depend upon the kinds of varnishes used and also upon the surfaces to be gone over and the finish desired. The whole list of varnish brushes made from bristles, cam-

el's hair, badger, sable, ox hair, etc., are used. They are shown in their varied shapes under Figs. 12, 15, 16, 17, 31, 40 and 41. Varnish brushes should be well taken care of and each should be kept in an individual brush keeper, if possible, and hung in the kind of varnish that it is used in, nor should it ever be used for any other. At least all the finishing and flowing varnish brushes should be so kept. Where the above is impossible, or when the varnish brushes are used in the cheaper varnishes, they may be hung up in linseed oil in such a keeper as is shown in Fig. 57. The linseed oil must be carefully washed out of the brushes with benzine or naptha before using again.

317. The application proper of the varnish will now follow after all the precautions to guard against chances of the varnish going wrong have been taken.

It is a simple enough looking affair and words will hardly convey the intelligence sufficiently clear to warrant the reader in going ahead and undertaking to do a job of varnishing immediately upon his having read the "how to do it."

He will probably know as much about it if told to dip his brush in the varnish pot and rub it on the surface where it is wanted as he would in a long essay which he will get mixed up in, and which will puzzle him much more than it will enlighten him.

All there is in varnishing is the putting of it on surfaces with a brush. The beginner should not attempt **to put** on the more difficult flowing coats until he **has** acquired the knack and use of the brush upon the varnishing of cheap yellow pine interior partitions or wood work. He should put on his varnish crosswise first, and lay it off afterward the long way of the boards, using the tips of the brush to even it up nicely.

One of the greatest drawbacks to the beginner in his attempts at applying varnish is his fear that he is putting on too much and that it will sag on him, therefore, he works and works it out to the last limit; he does what is known as *"skinning it on"* in varnish slang.

Now, skinned on varnish never looks well and makes the job look like a man in a dress suit with plow shoes on. Varnish, to look well, must be put on full; if it be the right sort for the purpose it will not be any more likely to sag put on full than it will otherwise unless it is grossly overdone. The work, too, will be much freer of brush marks, as it will tend to flow together and to fill up the gaps left by the hair of the varnish brush. Skimpy varnishing will show every one of these and much more specks of dust, which a heavy coat will absorb and into which they will sink below the surface.

Many varnishers among the wood finishers and carriage shop operators when varnishing on the best work, lay on the varnish full, but evenly; vertically first, and then square it up horizontally. It will not prevent sagging of varnish that has not been put on evenly, but where it has been evenly and fully applied it will give the varnish coat the best chance of setting without sags.

It is hoped that the novice in varnish application will not be deterred from trying his skill by whatever may have been said regarding the difficulties that go along with it. - The causes of trouble being known, it is possible, with a little trouble, to circumvent them so that they become harmless.

Some men are born good varnishers and fall into the right way of it like a gosling to a pond of water, and no one knows till they try what they may be capable of. With care, the proper use of the brush can be acquired when it is not natural to a person. It is, of course, much more pleasant to have been born a varnisher, but some of the best varnishers commenced by aggravated cases of sagging in their first attempts at it. "Try, try again," is a good motto if it is old fashioned. The man who is observant will note where he has erred and the next job will be more perfect because the experience had on the former one will guard him against committing the same mistake again; such men will grow into good varnishers.

QUESTIONS ON VARNISHING.

312. What is said of varnishing in general?
313. *a.* What conditions are required for good varnishing?
    b. How should the varnish room be arranged in carriage shops?
    c. How should varnish rooms be arranged in furniture factories?

    d. How should the interior of houses be prepared for the varnishing in cold weather?

314. Should two kinds of varnish be mixed together before aplying?

315. When there is a surplus of varnish left over after a job is done, should it be poured back in the can?

316. What tools are needed in varnishing?

317. How is varnish applied?

VEHICLES.

318. The term "vehicle" has a double signification in the paint trade. To the carriage painter it means one thing and to all the others it means another. To the carriage painter it means anything made that will carry persons—coaches, carriages, buggies, phaetons, landaus, etc., etc.—and what the others know as vehicles he calls thinners.

There is a tendency towards a more uniform designation for the liquids used in the application of paint and thinners are becoming generally used by all kinds of painters.

Vehicle, which means a carrier of something, is still used widely, and is certainly most appropriate for the purpose that liquids are employed—the carrying of the pigment in the paint in which they enter.

319. Some vehicles contain within themselves the binding qualities which serve to hold the pigment firmly where it has been applied in the painting. Others do

not, and such must have had some substances dissolved through their agency which upon the evaporation or drying of the vehicle will remain and bind the pigment firmly.

320. The fixed oils are of the first character. They contain within themselves the drying and solidifying properties necessary to hold the paint, which in their liquid condition they served to convey to the surfaces painted. As all have been already reviewed, and their properties noted in the section headed, "Oils and Driers," the reader is referred to what is said concerning them in Paragraphs 194 to 202.

320. The volatile oils are used more as adjuncts to the fixed oils, japans and varnishes, than they are altogether alone—as they possess no binding qualities of their own whatever. These, too, have been fully described under the heading of oils and driers in Para graphs 203 to 208, to which the reader is referred for fuller information.

321. Japans, varnishes, etc., are used almost exclusively in the painting of carriages, car and vehicle painting of every sort. These, being compounds, owe their binding qualities aside of that of linseed oil, which they may carry in their composition to such gums or gum resins which enter into them. Drying hard, they pave the way for good varnishing over them, and will not sweat through as oil coats would.

322. Water is the vehicle used in all water color or distemper work. Water, having no binding proper-

ties of its own, must have some binding substances
added to it and which must be soluble in it in order
that the colors applied through its medium will stay
where they are placed.   Many substances soluble in
water will do this nicely.   Some of the vegetable gums
as gum arabic, for instance, make excellent binders for
water colors, and but for their cost and scarcity would
be used much more extensively than they are.   As it is,
their use is chiefly confined to artists who paint in water
colors.   Should it be used in the quantity required for
binding one-hundreth part of the water colors used in
wall coloring, there would be a howl about the price
jumping away up above the already very high cost of
it, as it is now.

Gum Tragacanth, and other gums, have been used
in a small way for certain specific purposes, but none
possess any value worth considering, except gum
arabic, which, it is seen, cannot be obtained in sufficient
quantity nor at such a price as to make its use possible
in general house work.

322. *Glues* are the only material which the calciminer and water color decorator can use.   While they
are not as clean as gum arabic and will deteriorate
much quicker in warm weather, upon the whole, they
have answered well the purposes for which they are
used—of binding the colors.

There is much variation in the qualities of glues.
They are made from the offals of animals derived from
skin clippings, hoofs, bones, etc.; those parts which

otherwise would have little value. Some of the strongest glues are made grom the bladders and intestines of fish.

Glues may be put into three general classes:

1. Derived from fish.

2. From clippings of hides, and cartilagenous parts of animals.

3. From the boiling of bones.

The first, when made exclusively from fish bladders and intestines, are the strongest and clearest. The second, made from animals' skins, is but little inferior to that made from fish and are very strong, too. The thin calcimine grades of light cream color are the best to use for color binding. The thin calcimine glue of an opaque white color is usually adulterated with some make-weight material, so that notwithstanding their good looks they are not so strong as the light buff-colored, semi-transparent kinds.

The third class of glues, made from bones, are not as strong as the others. They are cheaper in price, but dearer in the end.

323.   There is an easy way to determine the value of a glue. While it may be called "empirical," one can attain to something near its worth by a simple process of weighing, say, one ounce of glue, and putting it to soak for a day. It must then be drained of water and re-weighed. Glue should absorb about eighteen times its former weight of water. If it falls much below that it will not be as strong as it should be, and, conse-

quently, more of it must be used to accomplish the same amount of binding that a lesser quantity of stronger glue would do.

QUESTIONS ON VEHICLES OR THINNERS.

318.   What is understood by the word, "vehicle?"

319.   What are the fixed oils?

320.   What is said of volatile oils?

321.   In what way are japans and varnishes used as vehicles?

322.   How many classes of glue are there?

323.   How can good glue be determined?

WATER COLORS.

324.   As to all intents and purposes water color painting-distemper painting, fresco painting in water colors and calcimining are all one and the same thing, and as under each of those headings full directions are given for the treatment of walls and for the application of colors, and, under, "Mixing of Colors," as to their preparation for use—the reader is referred to those headings for any information he may desire about water colors, either for their application upon walls in plain tints, or as used in decorations as in "fresco," etc.

KEY TO PLATES

All plates shown have been photographed from actual work in graining and marbling done by students at the Chicago School of Painting, Decorating and Paper Hanging. ⎰

PLATE I

Door in oak heart growth done in water colors.

PLATE II

Door in quartered oak in oil—(wiped out).

PLATE III

Door in black walnut; stippled and veined in water colors.

PLATE IV

Door in walnut root or curled walnut, in water colors.

· PLATE V

Door in mahogany, in water colors.

PLATE VI

Dado panelled up in mahogany in water colors.

PLATE VII

Dado—in marbles—panels are various colored and formations of marble, stiles and upper slabs, white and black veined—base in black, white veined.

PLATE VIII

Two panelled cupboard doors—top one in conglomerate sienna, the bottom in veined fissured sienna marble, surrounding stiling in black veined white marble.

INDEX

A

Index

Index

C

Index

Index

Index

Index

H

Index

Index

I

J

K

L

Index

M

Index

Index

P

Index

Index

Index

S

Index

Index

T

V

W

Index

THE UP-TO-DATE
HARDWOOD FINISHER

A PANELED CEILING IN OAK

Frontispiece

PREFACE

Some twelve or fourteen years ago, I prepared a little manual on "Hardwood Finishing," which became quite popular, and to some extent remains so up to the present writing. The little work, however, was far from complete, and I have been asked by a large number of woodworkers to extend the limits of the work, or to reorganize and add more to the subject of wood preparation.

After considering the matter, I was impressed by the latter suggestion, as the title "Hardwood Finisher" seemed to be somewhat misleading, as the intention of the book was to give general instructions in finishing woods of all kinds—hard and soft—and not only making them ready for the varnisher and polisher, but also to instruct the workman in the latter process as well as the former. I have therefore embodied in this new work a number of directions for making and finishing the raw wood, making it ready for the finisher or varnisher and polisher; and have also given directions and formulæ for mixing the materials and applying them to the prepared wood.

It goes without saying, that to make a work of this kind useful, it must contain much that has been published before, and much that is taken from the workshop and from the experience of workmen, many of whom have given me their own methods of working. I am also indebted to a number of current journals, such as "Carpentry and Building," "The National Builder," "Scientific American " "The

Carpenter," "The Woodworker" "The English Mechanic," "The Painter's Gazette," and several others, to whom I offer thanks for such matter as I have made use of.

While the present work may not be as complete as it might be, I have some reason to think it very much superior to any work of the kind now in the market, as it covers more ground, and deals with the subject of wood-finishing in a more extended and complete manner than any other work devoted to the subject that I know of. However, be this as it may, every effort has been made to obtain the best and latest information on the subject and to put it in such a form that the regular every-day workman may understand what is intended to be conveyed. If I have failed to make everything clear to the reader it is because of the lack of ability on my part, not because of desire to do so.

FRED T. HODGSON.

The Up-to-Date Hardwood Finisher

PART ONE

INTRODUCTORY

Wood is, and always has been, one of the most important and useful materials that Dame Nature has vouchsafed to bless humanity with, and the latter's necessities and ingenuity have made the best of the circumstances.

It need hardly be said that Nature seemed to have well understood the wants of her children and provided for them in a most liberal manner, for it is said that nearly one-third of the earth's surface is covered by trees; all of which are, in some form or another, contributory to the wants and pleasures of man.

The introduction of machinery for the rapid working of nearly all kinds of intricate mouldings and shapes of woodwork has, in a great measure, had a tendency to elevate the taste of the whole community, though I must confess that artistic excellence of a high order, in the mechanical arts, is now scarcely found among our younger workmen, machinery having almost done away with the necessity for the fine kinds of hand and brain work. Fashion, which rules despotically in the wardrobe, influences, to a greater or lesser degree, the style and finish of woodwork and, to a certain extent, the kind of wood that must be used for certain purposes. Thirty or forty years ago no other wood than clean white pine would be permitted to do service in a building. All woodwork had to be pine; floors, doors, windows, even to the bath fittings. Then Dame Fashion sent forth her decree and a mixture of white and Southern pine was used, followed shortly afterward by the abominable mixture of ash, walnut and chestnut. Some architect, who deserves well of his country, introduced all walnut and all mahogany fitments; and at once people of taste who saw this manner of finish noticed its superiority over the medley; and the fashion then of finishing in one kind of wood became the rage. Wal nut was found too dark for general purposes and was soon abandoned for the lighter woods; chestnut, sycamore, ash, cherry, birch and oak were then tried, but I believe I voice the opinion of a majority of architects when I say that, with the exception of oak, the light-colored woods were not successful, from an æsthetic point of view, and it is on record that many buildings finished in these woods have since had their woodwork cleaned and stained to imitate darker woods or have been painted. One of the valuable qualities of white oak is, that it grows richer in color as it gets older, and no matter how it is finished, so long as the grain is visible, it mellows and improves with age. This is a quality that no other of our American woods possesses in the same degree. All the oaks have this quality to a certain extent, but the white oak (*Quercus alba*) possesses it more than any other. Mahogany, too, has this quality largely, if true Spanish mahogany is used, but little of this is in the market; though there are many woods that have the appearance of mahogany, and are called mahogany, such as cherry and black birch, and both buyer and user are oftentimes deceived, and pay for what they do not get.

Americans have often been reproached with willfully or ignorantly ignoring or destroying their own handsome woods, while importing from abroad at excessive cost, and the payment of heavy duties, foreign woods which are much inferior to many of native growth. This folly prevailed at a time when it was fashionable and even popular to believe there was no merit in domestic productions of any sort. This state of things, however, is now at an end, and in the neighborhood of all large towns, and in country places as well, a finish in hardwood is the rule, and a finish in pine the exception, if the building to be finished makes any pretension of being "up to the times."

With regard to the difference in cost between a finish in the best clear pine, and the best selected hardwood, there is really but little, if any, if we take into consideration durability and good taste. As between pine wood and good, well finished hardwood, the disparity in value and merit is so very little as to completely silence any comparison. Between poor pine and poor hardwood the preference should be by all means given to the former; because poor pine as it reveals its defects can be puttied and painted in a manner to disguise them; whereas the defects of poor hardwood are almost incurable. The rationale of the subject seems to resolve itself into the following statement:

Modern taste in expensive dwellings calls for the free use of hardwoods. It is immaterial which are used, but highly essential that the best seasoned woods should be selected; and, further, that they should be skillfully treated and finished.

The principal recommendation of hardwood is that it admits of a treatment which renders it impervious to the effects of atmospheric changes and, therefore, can be made more durable and ultimately less expensive than pine wood. A hardwood that is well seasoned before use, that is treated with proper fillers to close up its pores, and then finished with successive coats of suitable varnish, well rubbed in with pumice-stone, being finally brought to a higher flat finish, presents the most attractive, serviceable and reliable style of woodwork than can be introduced into a house. Well finished hardwood obviates the expense and annoyance of constant renewals, which pine work calls for in patching, puttying and painting. The most brilliant gloss of finished hardwood can be restored by a skilled person without disturbing the furniture or carpets of a house.

Pine work seems peculiarly and incomparably adapted for cheap work. A good article of common pine, suitable for ordinary work, can be procured and worked at considerably less expense than would be involved in using good hardwood. The use of poor hardwood in any work should not be tolerated or thought of under any circumstances, for the simple reason that it is certain to create annoyance and expense, which no house-owner, especially of moderate priced property, should be subjected to.

Pine, however, is not the only soft wood that may be used in house finishing, but it is the most popular, because the most plentiful and doubtless the most satisfactory to deal with. Basswood, poplar, elm, whitewood, spruce and hemlock all make fairly good finishing woods when properly selected and properly treated; but, with the exception of elm, perhaps, all of them require to be either painted or stained before a good finish can be obtained. Elm, black ash and chestnut have all coarse grain, and are unsuited for tasteful work, though all right for ordinary fitments; and indeed may be used for kitchen or bathroom finish in fairly good houses. Later on I will deal with each one of them, and some other of our native woods at length.

The present methods of hardwood finishing are comparatively new, so far as the manner of operation and materials are concerned; as I can find nothing dating farther back than 1850 in the vast amount of literature at my command that treats in any way intelligently on the subject; true, there are methods of varnishing, lacquering and French polishing given; also treatment on finishing in wax, notably a small pamphlet containing a treatise on "The Shining Up of Woodwork," dating as far back as 1809, and published in London. This little treatise is the first to make mention of a wood-filler being employed. The author says that "the pores of the wood ought to be sealed up with a mixture made of ground chalk or rotten stone coloured like the wood, and mixed with glue water. Cover the work to be shined up with the mixture, then wipe off and when hard and dry, smooth off finely with shark-skin and hair-clothe." He then goes on to show how to finish in wax or with shellac, as the case may be. He says nothing of French polishing, but gives directions for varnishing and rubbing down with rotten stone.

To-day there are quite a number of works published on wood-finishing, which shows how much interest is taken in the subject.

The introduction of the modern methods of polishing

finished woodwork has so reduced the cost of fine furniture and elaborately finished woodwork, that now the poor man may have in his house one or more pieces of finely wrought work, as well as the man of wealth. French polishing was a costly operation, and made more costly because of the secrecy surrounding the process. Experts were bound not to teach others the process unless they were well paid for it, and the pupil was compelled to take a solemn oath that he would not divulge the secret or convey to others the method, unless he was paid a large sum, often as high as $100. French polish when well done is certainly a fine finish, and while still costly, is often employed in finishing high-class furniture and woodwork in costly buildings, but its general use is rapidly falling off; yet no wood-finisher is completely rounded off unless he has thorough knowledge of the best French polishing, and in the present work I purpose giving a thorough description of this method, with illustrations of the appliances made use of in the process.

While it is not my intention to write a treatise on the useful woods of America, I do not think it will be out of place to describe a few of them, showing their manner of growth, their peculiarities, durability, and the uses they can be put to, with directions for working and finishing them.

In every description of wood the elementary composition of the organic tissue is the same, but the latter is found associated with very variable organic elements, according to the species of the tree.

Pine trees, for example, contain turpentine, and oak trees tannin. The combustible part of wood is this same organic tissue.

The exterior characteristics of woods are very different from one another. Thus certain wood is soft and tender and of a loose tissue, whilst another is hard and of a compact grain. Thence there is quite a natural division into two classes. The first includes all the soft and tender woods, amongst which may be mentioned the pines, white wood or plane tree, bass-wood, poplar, etc. The second includes all the heavy and hard wood, such as the oaks, maples, beech, birch, cherry, walnut, etc.

When wood is first cut down as timber, it contains from 40 to 45 per cent of water, but this quantity gradually lessens until it is said to be thoroughly seasoned, when it only contains from 5 to 7 per cent. Moisture, however, is always present in wood, and as it gets older, if exposed to the air, will take in from 10 to 15 per cent. It then becomes very hydrometrical, and loses or absorbs water according to the state of dryness or humidity of the surrounding air.

The density of wood, like that of all porous bodies, can be considered in two different ways, and can be looked for under its apparent volume. The only method which can then be employed consists in forming a block of the wood, the volume of which can be easily measured, and then taking the weight of it. The ratio of this weight to that of the same bulk of water would be the density sought for. This density for the same wood varies according to the degree of seasoning it has had, and to the form and position of the fibers in the sample. A block six inches square cut from a knot, or burl, or a cross-grained part of a tree, would be considerably more dense, and weigh more, than would a block of a similar size cut from the same tree, if it was straight-grained and uniform.

It is the density of the harder woods that makes them popular with wood-finishers. A hard, close-grained wood requires little or no filler, and offers better opportunities to the polisher than do the woods of lesser density.

The use of nearly all kinds of hardwood in the general finish of good houses, has completely taken the place of using pine or other soft woods in wainscoting, floors, doors and general fitments. The variety of the woods employed in these finishings has greatly increased within the last few years. How so many of these beautiful and suitable woods could have fallen into disuse within the present century is one of the decorative mysteries of this period. Walnut, which was the pioneer of the new departure, still remains in use, where cost is no object, although its dull color and unpolished surface are dingy and somber. It has had its use, however, in directing attention to the employment of solid woods, though it is now on the retired list. Mahogany is at present in high favor, the variety known as San Domingo mahogany being especially rare and desirable. When new it has a reddish yellow tone, which grows dark and rich with age. The old wood is much in demand for use in interior finishings and for furniture, and the genuine old pieces are highly prized by their possessors. Cherry is popular for common use, though at first falsified by the red stain, which destroyed its natural beauty and gave it no artificial excellence. Unstained cherry has a yellowish brown color, polishes well, and is excellent for interior woodwork, its moderate cost making it available for general use, though now getting very scarce. If any stain is required, it should be in the dark tones resembling mahogany color.

Black birch is one of the most beautiful native woods, having a grain resembling that of mahogany, and taking a fine satin-like polish. Unstained, it has a warm, rich yellow tone, and its darkened finish can hardly be distinguished from the more costly tropical wood. Yellow birch, though less beautiful and costly, is excellent in grain and color and is often used for fine floorings. The different varieties of oak are well adapted to interior uses, the wood being solid and durable, while each year of wear adds a depth and richess of color and a smoothess and polish to its dark surface. It has a beautiful grain, and is a popular wood for interior finishings and the floors of modern houses. After centuries of wear this useful wood is found in the houses of both humble and royal history as black and smooth as ebony. Butternut resembles oak in color, though not in grain, polishes finely and takes a carved decoration well, and ash and elm are often found as deceptive substitutes for oak, especially in its darker or so-called antique stains. Rosewood is one of the most beautiful woods in use, rich and deep in tone and capable of a mirror-like finish. It is costly enough to keep the merit of rarity.

Apple wood carves finely and polishes well, making excellent panels; so also does the wood of the pear tree. Maple is in high favor, bird's-eye maple being one of the choicest of the light-colored woods, and especially suited to dainty and sumptuous uses. Chestnut and ash are serviceable and inexpensive light woods.

As these woods come into more general use, their genuineness and elegance giving to the houses in which they are placed one of the strongest assurances of that permanency which is the best element of the new

Renaissance, they will be more and more enriched with ornament. And here it will be difficult to avoid the besetting sin of abundant means and inartistic taste, which unfortunately are so often found in company. The honesty of material and the uses which it serves should never be concealed under complex decoration. Most hardwoods are beautiful enough in grain and color to give lasting satisfaction, and for every-day use no decoration beyond a touch of good carving should be applied. Where something more sumptuous is sought, carving and inlaying will make them elegant enough to satisfy the most exacting taste, and when properly varnished or polished no other method of decoration can excel it in beauty or refinement.

I have deemed the foregoing introduction necessary, as it will enable the workman to have some idea of the development of the art of joinery, and the transition from the use of pine and the softer wood to that of the hard wood.

In the following, it is my intention to take each of the woods most in use; describe them, say what I think they are best adapted for, and the best way to finish them, as far as my knowledge extends. By this means the reader will have, under one head, all the book contains concerning the particular wood he is about to finish.

THE BETTER WOODS TO MAKE USE OF

The wood most made use of at the present writing for interior finish, is oak. It is made into doors, sashes, stairs, base, cabinet cases, and wainscot.

The working of oak, particularly in the framing up of panel-work, differs somewhat from ordinary pine or other soft wood panel work, inasmuch as the latter is generally painted and picked out in two or more colors; thus rendering it imperative to use sound stuff, and to have the work above suspicion. The material is generally so thin that the paneling should be stiffened with stout canvas glued to the back, which is often primed with red-lead paint to afford protection from

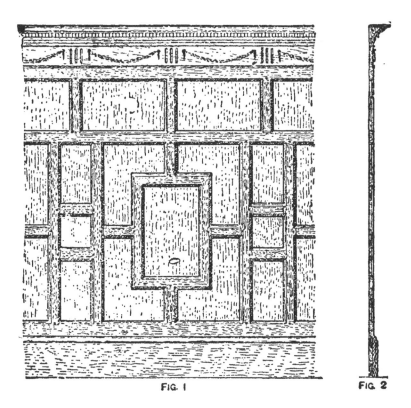

FIG. I   FIG. 2

damp when the work is to be placed in a new building. It is usual to frame up the work with stuff varying in thickness from seven-eighths of an inch to one and a quarter inches, finished sizes. In some workshops it is not considered necessary to clean up the back of the work, though I think it always best to dress down the joints on the back, and true it up with plane and straight-edge. All joints should be close and perfect, and tenons and mortises should be in the center of the

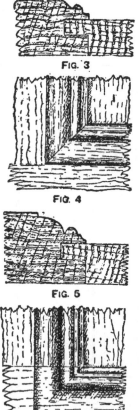

FIG. 3

FIG. 4

FIG. 5

FIG. 6

stuff, and all should be well glued together and left to dry before fixing.

The panel-work shown in Fig. 1 is framed with 1¼ in. stuff, got to thickness and widths as shown in Fig. 2. The center framing is mitered together at the corners, which are further strengthened by the insertion of a cross-tongue joint, while the side rails and top and bottom muntins are tenoned and pinned like all the other tenons in the framing. The moulding stuck on the edges (or in the solid) is not mitered in the same way as for ordinary work (see Figs. 3 and 4); but the mitered corners are worked as shown in Figs. 5 and 6, thus forming butt joints with mason-mitered corners to all moulded edges. These corners are worked on the bench after the paneling is glued up and cleaned off.

The bottom rail is tongued into the skirting as shown in Fig. 8, and the top rail meets the festooned frieze board under the small necking mould as shown, the frieze board being tongued to the dentiled cornice also. This cornice is double-dentiled, one row of dentils being cut farther back than the other, as shown in Figs. 7 and 8. As usual with built-up cornices, this section can be worked on the four-cutter moulder or on a spindle machine; the dentiling, however, being

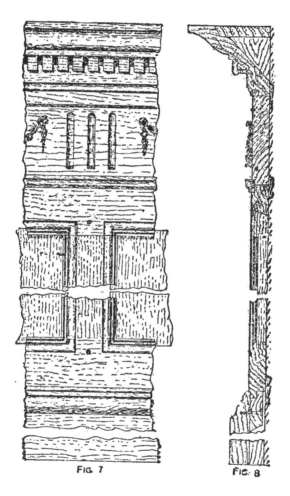

FIG. 7   FIG. 8

best cut by hand. A cover-board lies at the back of the cornice, which is back rebated to receive the front edge of the cover-board. The three flutes over the top muntins have rounded-out top ends, and finish at

the bottom on a splay; whilst the festoons are pref·
erably cut out of the solid, but are generally planted
on unless otherwise specified.

In fixing this class of work, which is, as a rule,
screwed up, all fixing screws should be hidden, or the
holes should be bored to take "corks" a little larger
than the screw head, and the "corks" should be cut
from wood closely matching that in which the hole is
bored.   The framing must be fixed as true and upright
as possible (especially at external corners where
mitered vertical joints occur), and be well scraped and
cleaned down after the fixing is done.

The illustrations are reproduced to the following
scales: Figs. 1 and 2 are three-eighths of an inch to
the foot; Figs. 3 to 6, half full size; Figs. 7 and 8, one
and a half inches to the foot.

While it is not the intention to enter into the subject of joinery in this work, it will not be out of place
to make a few remarks on the manner of doing some
odd jobs of work that are not generally discussed in
books of this kind, or if discussed, are not done so
with a view of showing how the wood should be prepared for the polisher.   The examples given in the
foregoing are only offered as an illustration of how
similar work should be prepared when made from
solid wood.   Where the work is composed of material
"built up" or veneered, the manner of preparing it for
the finisher may be very different, but this I will dis
cuss later on.

Suppose a column, or a pillar or spindle is required
having a spiral form· unless the workman is well
acquainted with the method of laying out spirals, he
will be up against a proposition which he will find
difficult to solve.   To meet a condition of this kind, I

show the following method of setting out such work. This example is intended to be prepared for the lathe, but, of course, it may be executed without the aid of a lathe, but in such case much patience and skill will be required.

The sketch Fig. 9 shows the method of setting out the twist or spiral. First turn the wood round; then divide the circumference into four with lines, as shown, marked all the way down. Then, having decided on the size of your twist—and the same details apply to any size and depth —mark the cross-lines, and then the diagonals, which you can easily do with a twist of the leg in the lathe, and both sides as shown by dotted lines. The gouge, held in this direction, will follow the required twist. It is supposed the operator is acquainted with lathe work to some extent, and is aware of the methods and appliances made use of in turning spirals, and the sketch is only intended to instruct him in the manner of laying out the spiral. This will be found useful even in work where the column, etc., is not turned in a lathe, but is wrought by hand.

FIG. 9.

Handwork of almost every kind in woodwork is rapidly going out of fashion —more the pity—but now and again, men are found who insist on having their work done by hand, and it is well that every joiner should know how to go about the work with intelligence when such work is required. With this idea in view, I give herewith a few instructions and illustrations to help the workman when he is confronted with problems such as I have indicated.

Often dovetailing—an almost lost art—has to be done by hand on some particular job or piece of work, and, in order to prepare the workman for this purpose, I offer the following instructions, and give the accompanying illustration, which I think will materially aid him in his efforts.

Dovetailing to a great many young workmen proves a pitfall, yet, when the method of laying out the work is once understood, it all seems easy enough. A dovetail joint, if made properly, requires no screws or nails, to hold it together or to bring the parts down to a proper joint; but in order to attain perfection there are one or two points which must be attended to when making this kind of joint. First, the stuff must be faced up properly, using the trying plane, on the flat surface. In passing, I will just mention that in dovetailing, whether boxes, drawers, or whatever is being made, the face *side* is always the *inside*, and the face *edge* is the bottom *edge*.

Another point which is often neglected is to put in plenty of "pins" or dovetails. A very good rule for ordinary work in soft wood is to space them not less than 1½ in., or more than 2¼ in., from center to center; for hard wood, or for small work in thin wood, they should be spaced closer still.

In setting out the pins, or rather the mortises in which the pins have to fit, a half dovetail should be placed at both top and bottom, as shown in Fig. 10, and the intermediate "tails" should be brought to an extreme point as shown at B in the drawings—that is, if neatness is an object; but if this has to give way to strength, then "tails" of the shape shown in Fig. 11, should be used.

The bevels of the "tails" should be as shown in the drawings, and in no case should they be shaped as at ,M, Fig. 14. If made like that, there would be great danger of the sides splitting off at E, and although this shape at first sight would appear to be stronger than the other, it is really not so in

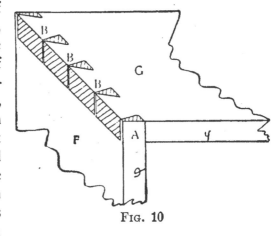

Fig. 10

practice. Also if one, two or three, or even more articles of the same size are being made, the dovetails need not be set out on one piece only. The whole could be placed together in pairs as shown in

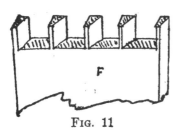

Fig. 11

Fig. 12, and the marks squared over as shown, then screwed in the vise together, and all cut at once with a fine tenon or back-saw, first of all sawing all the pieces off to exactly the same length

To mark the pins, screw one of the ends upright in the bench vise, with the top end about half an inch above the bench top, as at F, Fig. 13, taking care to keep the face side toward the bench. Then lay one of the sides on it, as at G, so that the squared-over marks

on the edges of G coincide with the inside of F, as at
H. With the front end of the same saw as was used to

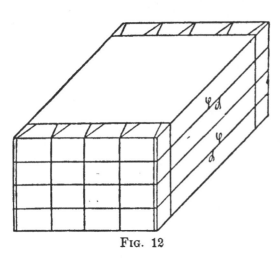

FIG. 12

cut the "tails,"
used as shown at
I, mark the po
sition of each
one on the end
grain, and, be-
f o r e removing
the side board,
n u m b,e r each
piece as shown
in the figure so
that it is known
which pieces go
together.

All four corners of each job in hand must be done in
the same way, unless perhaps the work is for drawers or

where the front
only is required
to be dove-
tailed, although
particular no-
t i c e must be
taken that the
face *side* of the
vertical p i e c e
must be towards
the bench, and
t h e horizontal
p i e c e under-
neath; and in

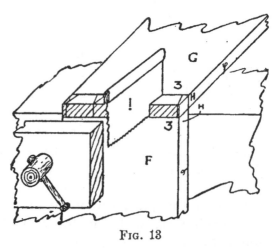

FIG. 13

addition remember that the face edges of both pieces
must always come together. These are the edges which

must be kept level while marking. Neglect of these points is the reason of failure to produce good work when making dovetailed joints.

In cutting the "pins" some regard must be paid to the kind of wood being used; soft pine requires more wood left outside the marks than oak or other hardwoods, but taking ordinary work in any of the softer woods, about a sixty-fourth of an inch clear on each side of the

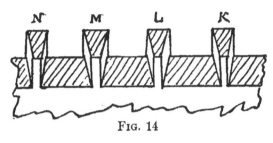

Fig. 14

mark will be ample, leaving rather less at the two half dovetails at the edges.

I should have stated before that in cutting off the stuff for the ends of the box (or whatever is in hand) about half an inch extra length should be allowed, and in squaring across, this extra length should be given to the pin at each end, to be cut when the job is put together.

Before the pins are sawed down, the marks on the outside (that is, where they come to a point) must be squared down as a guide

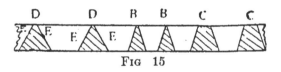

Fig. 15

for sawing parallel with the edges of the boards. This is a somewhat important part, and in Fig. 14 I have endeavored to show how they should and should not be cut. The "pin" K is parallel from point to heel, and this is correct, but not easy to manage. The "pin" at L is cut wedge-shaped, larger at the heel than at the point, which is bad, being liable to split the boards, and also to show a badly fitting joint outside. M is cut slightly smaller at the heel than at the point, which is a good fault—there is no fear of splitting, and, unless overdone, a good fitting joint will result.   N is cut out of parallel, which is the worst of all, and must on no account be done.

All the pins being cut, the spare wood must be cut out, using very thin, sharp chisels.   Some workers use a bow saw to remove the spare wood between the pins, but I do not consider it any advantage—the chisel has to be used after, and it is quicker to remove all the wood with the chisel at one time.

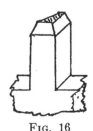

I must not forget to emphasize the fact that it is necessary, in setting out, to use knife or chisel for all cross lines, both on the sides and ends.   Pencil will not do at all, if good work is expected.

FIG. 16   Before putting together, each "pin" must be slightly pointed on all three sides, as shown in Fig. 15, so that they will enter freely, without bruising the wood.

When putting together, the "pins" should be well glued and the sides driven on at once, using a block which is large enough to reach quite across the whole work.   If this is omitted, splitting is apt to result.

I have not touched upon putting the work together, as I do not think it necessary, because when the dovetails and "pins" are properly cut, they will be found to go together without any paring or cutting. Indeed, dovetails of any kind requiring fitting before going together may be put down as a botch job and unfit to be further finished.

In this, I have dealt only with simple work, but

there are other kinds of dovetailing, and I present several of them below.

In the figure shown at 17, the end view of a "lap dovetail" is represented, a style which is well known to every joiner who is familiar with drawer making. The method is the same as described as regards the sides, but the ends of the front are gauged on a certain distance, which should, if possible, be the same as the thickness of the sides, and the dovetails are stopped at the gauge mark.

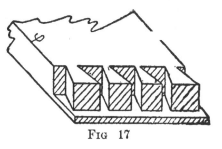

FIG 17

The method of marking is the same as before, and the only difference is in cutting the "pin," which has to be done largely with the chisel, as the saw can only be used to start them with.

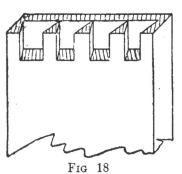

FIG 18

The appearance of the "pins" when cut is shown in Fig. 18, and those who can do the ordinary dovetailing will have no difficulty in making the "lap" dovetail.

In Fig. 19 is shown wnat is sometimes called "secret," but it is really double lap dovetailing. One part is done as shown in the figure, making the mortises the same size as the pins, and cutting them as shown. The corresponding member is worked as in Fig. 17, the necessary marking being done as in Fig. 13, and marking round point, then cutting them out with saw and chisel. The appearance of this when done is shown in Fig. 20, which is the one marked A, at the side, and Fig. 21, on the top edges; and as will be readily understood, very careful work is necessary in

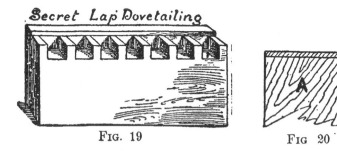

Secret Lap Dovetailing

FIG. 19

FIG 20

order to make a good job, and, presuming this, the joint is as strong as the ordinary dovetail.

By mitering the top edges, as in Fig. 22, the appearance of this part is as Fig. 23, and if done properly is an improvement. It does not add much to the difficulty of making the joint.

Secret dovetailing proper is a difficult job for any but an experienced man to undertake, but I will deal

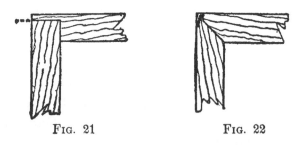

FIG. 21

FIG. 22

with it later on if space permits. It makes a good strong joint if done well, and the appearance is the same as a mitered joint.

Sometimes the end of the drawers, as shown in Fig.

23, is rounded off as shown in Fig. 22, and when such is the case, the drawer projects from the face of the framework as shown by the dotted lines.

⁻ In order to enable the workman to better understand the whole theory of dovetailing, I present herewith a couple of sketches which show how secret lap dovetailing may be executed in several ways. Figs. 19 and 24 show how the pins and mortises are laid out

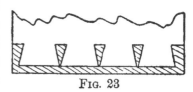

FIG. 23

when the pins are simply no more than a square tenon.

Secret lap dovetailing is used for a great variety of objects, such as sewing machine covers, instrument cases, etc. Where the dovetails require to be hidden it is not so important that the joint should be at an angle, as the corners can be rounded up to the joint. The difference between secret and plain lap dovetailing is that in the secret method the pins are shortened and the dovetails not cut through, as shown in Figs. 17 and 18, and when put together, in Fig. 22.

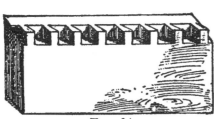

FIG. 24

Miter dovetailing, Figs. 25 and 26, is a much more intricate operation, and calls for greater care on the part of the workman. After carefully planing up the wood to a thickness, first gauge on the inside only the thickness of the lap on the end, remembering that the gauge for the lap will also be the gauge by which the ends of the pins and dovetails will be shortened, as shown in Fig. 27, where the dotted lines show the manner in which each piece must be rebated. After rebating, cut the pins, then mark the dovetails and chop them out, after which proceed to miter the laps on both pieces and cut the

Mitre Dovetailing

FIG. 25

FIG. 26

miter across the edge, and, if neatly done, the joint will go together at the first trial.

Bevel or splay dovetailing is much more difficult than any of the preceding, and is not so generally known. The required bevel being given, proceed as follows: First joint the ends to the required bevel, then, without changing the angle, joint the bottom edge to the same bevel as the ends, working from the inside. Now comes the most important part of the operation. The ends must be beveled on the thickness of the wood. This is obtained by laying the blade of the square on the beveled bottom edge, then shooting the ends to the square, working still from the inside of the wood.

FIG. 27

If this part is omitted, the result will be that when the job is put together it will be not only open on the inside but will not be level on the outside—more or less, according to the angle of the sides. Gauge on the thickness of the wood as for plain dovetailing. In cutting the pins, a center line through these should be parallel with the bevel of the bottom edge as shown in Fig. 28, and not cut square to the inside of the job as in plain dovetailing. If this be neglected, and the angle is much, the dovetails will be cut across the grain, and have no strength. After marking the pin with a marking point, before cutting the dovetails, mark them across the ends also, parallel to the bevel of the bottom edge as in Fig. 29,

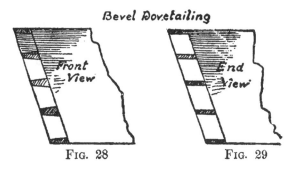

Bevel Dovetailing

Front View

End View

FIG. 28   FIG. 29

and cut accordingly. I would strongly advise the workman who has never made a bevel dovetail to try it upon two pieces of wood, as more will be learned from a little practice when the difficulties have to be surmounted than from any amount of study.

The illustrations shown in Figs. 30 and 31 will convey to the reader a better idea of lap and miter dovetail than the previous ones. Fig. 30 shows the finished corner, the face of the work being shown at F. This may be rounded off if it is so desired. Fig. 31 shows a corner all ready to be driven together, which will have a mitered lap. AA shows both front and side; the shaded laps show the miters.

Another style of bevel dovetailing is shown in Fig. 32, where the pins are at right angles with the line of

slope as shown at AA and BB. This style of dovetailing is well adapted for trays, hoppers and similar
work. All stuff intended to be used in bevel or
splayed work, that is to be dovetailed, must be prepared with butt joints before the dovetails are laid out.
Joints of this kind may be made common, lapped or

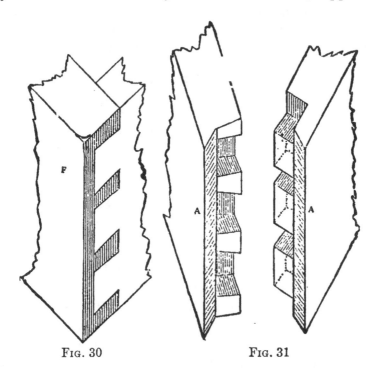

FIG. 30   FIG. 31

mitered. In making the latter, much skill and labor
will be required.

In making veneered doors there are a number of
different methods practiced by workmen, but it is not
in the province of this work to describe them all, or
indeed, any of them at great length, but when a
number of veneered doors are to be made at one time,
the following method, which is adopted in some large

factories, may offer some suggestions that may be found useful:

The first operation is to take common coarse white pine boards, with sound knots, and which have been well kiln-dried, the stock used being generally 16 feet long, 1x12 inches, and surface it on both sides by a Daniels planer without regard to thickness. Some boards are thinner than others, while others are warped in drying, and the thickness of the boards is

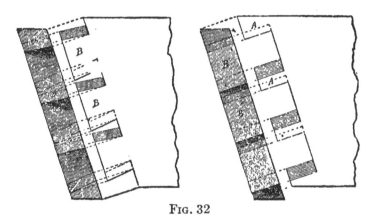

FIG. 32

immaterial, perfectly seamed surfaces only being necessary. After the stock is planed it is cut into such lengths as the bill of doors calls for. They are ready now to be glued up. The face board, of whatever hardwood is to be used, is planed generally to ¾ inch thick, and is also run through a Daniels planer. The stock is now ready to go to the gluing press, and as the Daniels planer makes the best gluing surface in the world, no scratch planing is needed. After properly heating in a box the stock is brought out and carefully glued, the hardwood face parts being marked for it. From three to five parts are put in the press at one time, and a pressure of 20 tons, brought down by screws, is put upon these parts. After remaining in the press the proper time they are taken out, and generally remain several days before being worked up, which gives the glue plenty of time to harden. When ready to work again these parts are taken to a Daniels planer and squared up, after which the parts are taken to a very nice cutting table or bench saw, and are cut up to sizes required, leaving them ⅛ inch large for future dressing. It is a positive necessity that the saw cuts free and clear, as heating has a tendency to warp the stock or spring it slightly, which would make it necessary to dress the stuff again. If the saw does not heat, the stiles come out perfectly straight, and these stiles can be laid on a Daniels planer bed and a light shaving taken off. They are now straight, and if the saw table is in good condition, square; the other side may be finished with pony planer or with a Daniels. A Daniels is preferred, because it makes a better gluing surface. The work is now ready for the veneering, the thickness of which is immaterial, as it may vary from the thickness of thin paper to ¼ inch. Heated cauls are now used for the veneer, and the stiles, if heated at all, are just warmed and the veneer glued on by piling up with a hot caul between each stile. The old-fashioned way of making veneered doors may do very well when only two or three doors are to be made, but in these days of sharp competition, manufacturers are obliged to adopt the quickest methods compatible with efficiency and good finish.

The doors or other work—for this method will apply to wainscot or any similar work—should be placed in a dry room for a day or two, when they may be finished up and made ready for the polisher or varnisher.

If first-class doors are required, it is always better to build up the stuff for the stiles and rails, and glue them together before they are veneered. A white pine door is about the only door that can be made successfully from solid wood. In a house with, say, a dozen doors, what other wood is there that will absolutely hold its place during a reasonable period? Certainly yellow pine will not do it. A solid oak door is a pest, and should not be put in a house except under written instructions. Sycamore cannot be used solid, and certainly neither gum nor maple. Possibly walnut or butternut might, but who would think of using them under present conditions?

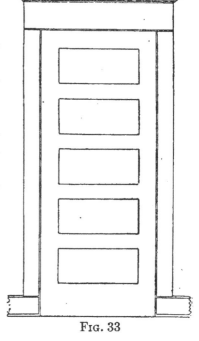

Fig. 33

The door shown in Fig. 33 is an illustration of one of the most serviceable doors made. The section of stile shown in Fig. 34 will give an idea of the manner in which the stiles and rails are built up; the veneer showing on the outside, also the panel.

Work of this kind may be used outside as well as for inside, and no one need fear unpainted white pine or oak for outside work. There is in Europe abundance of woodwork, exterior and interior, that has not been tickled by a brush in over five hundred years. All the native Swiss cottages are unpainted on the exterior.

All of the half-timber houses of France, no matter how richly decorated by the great artists of the chisel, are unpainted, and we have known of work in white pine and quartered white oak without the use of paint which has been in existence for centuries untouched by paint, and time justified the experiment. Nothing is more beautiful than the natural grain of the wood and its natural weathering under a proper transparent finish. It takes some courage to organize and push through an innovation of this kind, and one is beset by many warnings, but the beautiful result justifies the effort.

FIG. 34

The following method of making veneered doors was described by H. T. Gates in "The Woodworker" some time ago. It will doubtless be found of much benefit to workmen employed in factories where veneered doors are made in quantities. The hints and suggestions are to the point, and the instructions are clear and may be readily understood. The subject of veneered doors is one that has often been discussed of late and much light on it has been thrown, yet it will not suffer, if the subject is again brought forward, inasmuch as the various factories have particular ways of their own of producing this rapidly growing popularity in the door line. Instead of trying to lay down any fixed rule, saying thus and so shall they be made, let us consider some of the essential points which may be adapted to suit each condition as the manufacturer finds it.

I. **Equipment.**—Aside from the usual door-making machinery, this consists of larger facilities for preparing and applying glue, veneer press, resaw for veneers and panels (unless they are purchased from a dealer in veneers), a warm room where the glue may be applied and material gotten ready for the press. Unless the factory is already supplied with a large kettle for preparing glue, it will be found of advantage to make a large copper kettle that will fit the holes in the heater, but large enough to hold three or four ordinary-sized kettles of liquid glue. This can be done by making it higher and wider about the flange, as shown in Fig. 35. In this way sufficient glue may be made ready for a good-sized batch of doors without fear of running out.

Fig. 35

Of course, these remarks do not apply to the factory having modern glue-spreaders, hand or power-feed, which are very essential in strictly veneer establishments. Our remarks apply only to the shop where veneered doors are one of the many by-products, so to speak, which accompany the usual line of mill work.

For spreading the glue by hand, procure a 4-inch flat wall brush and prepare it by pouring alcohol gum-shellac into the roots of the bristles, and driving blind staples into the butt end, as close together as possible, thus preventing the bristles from coming out. Have a pair of "horses" about 3 feet high, strongly made, and having an angular piece on the top, to prevent waste of the glue, and squeezing it off the work at the bearing point—see Fig. 36.

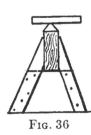

Fig. 36

Make the veneer press wide enough between the uprights to permit of veneering a table top or wide panel if needed, and have two rows of screws, so that two stacks of cores may be pressed at one time. A strong press can be made with 6x6-inch maple cross-pieces and ⅞-inch round iron rods, with jambnuts to hold the upper piece in place, having regular veneer press screws at least 1⅜ inches diameter. The bedpiece should be lagged up and trued, so that it will be straight and out of wind. To prevent the work from sticking to the bed, it should be covered on the top with zinc or tin—see Fig. 37.

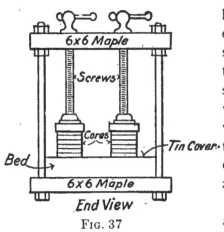

End View
Fig. 37

For resawing veneers and panels, where there is no band resaw, a gauge (Fig. 38) and pressure roller (Fig. 39) used on the band saw table, and 1½-inch saw in proper trim, with right management should turn three or four veneers out of inch stock, which may be applied direct to the coring without dressing, as described later on.

To do a good job of gluing to advantage it is necessary to have a warm room, so that a large batch of material may be worked at one time. There are various other purposes to which this room may be put, but

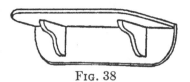

Fig. 38

to make a veneered door properly, without waste material or lost time, a warming room is very essential. First, the parts of wood to be glued must be thoroughly warm; also the temperature of the room where the work is to be done must be such as not to chill the glue and hinder its spreading and making good joints.

It is taken for granted that our factory has a hand jointer, pony planer, mortiser, tenoner, sticker, door clamp and drum sand-

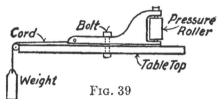

Fig. 39

er. It is a question whether veneered doors can be profitably made without the few essentials here enumerated, and where they are made in quantities, special machinery for spreading glue, cutting mouldings, presses, clamps, panel-raisers, etc., will be needed.

II. Materials.—Dry coring is the first thing that is required to make good doors. It is usual to cut up the material and put it in the dry (or warm) room referred to above, or in a dry-kiln, properly stacked, and leave it there as long as possible to drive out every particle of dampness. All waste material of suitable size and too poor to be used for any other purpose may be used for coring. It is preferable to have the strips wide enough so that when glued up they may be split through the center to make two stiles or rails—see Fig. 40—thereby saving much labor in gluing, which item cuts quite a figure in veneered door work. The stock sawyer

Fig. 40

can lay aside such material from time to time and have it stored as mentioned, so that there is a supply of dry stuff to draw on when a batch of doors is wanted.

The glue for coring need not be of high grade, and where quick preparation is desired, a ground or pulverized bone glue will answer the purpose admirably. The men soon become accustomed to handling the glue and it needs no soaking, as the flake or noodle glue does. For veneering a medium grade of hide-stock glue is to be preferred; one that is free from acid, clear in color, and not too quick-setting. It will pay to follow up the glue question more closely than we usually have done to obtain good results with economy. The glue for veneering does not want to be too thick. Practice in the work makes the workman proficient in its preparation. It should flow freely from the brush without being "tacky," as the painter would say.

The veneers and panels should be cut up and resawed before they are kiln-dried. The ends should be glue-sized, and they should be stacked straight and even in the kiln. Those who have tried resawing kiln-dried hardwoods, are aware of what a sorry job it makes; and how the veneers buckle, spring out of shape, pinch the saw or make it run crooked. When the saw has not too much set, the veneers may be glued onto the cores without planing, provided the sawing is a good, smooth job. Care must be taken in dressing veneers or panels, not to chip them out, as that is ruinous in this class of work.

III. Construction.—The man who is doing this work needs to be familiar with the work and its methods to do it well and economically. Filling the doors is the first work towards the desired end. A list of the size, style, thickness of doors and kinds of wood should be on each working bill, and follow the material in its progress out of chaos into stiles, rails, panels and finally the finished product. This bill should include the edge strips, the width, length and thickness of each bundle of cores, the finished size of the parts they are intended to make, and the number and both the sawing and finished size of veneers and panels.

After the sawyer has the material cut, and it is thoroughly dry, the one who does the gluing assembles the cores, puts them on the heating coil and prepares his core glue; the pieces are spread on the horses and given a coating of glue, assembled in batches, and put into the press, the surplus glue being squeezed out by this process, which includes putting the edge strips on each stile requiring one.

After they have been allowed to set sufficiently, they are taken to the jointer and the straightest side trued up. If they are built-up for making two pieces, they are resawed and again jointed and thickened to desired size on the pony planer.

They are now ready for veneering. They are again put in the warm room over the coils; when warm, they are put on the horses as before, and spread with glue on both sides; a bottom board is first laid and then the veneers and cores stacked in regular order. The veneers must previously be carefully looked over, poor ones culled out, and any pin holes, porous spots or checks covered by gluing a piece of paper over, to prevent two stiles from being stuck together by glue oozing through such spots. They are again pressed out, and when dry, trued and sized to width. They are now ready to be laid out, same as any blind-tenon door.

The framing must be done in a first-class manner, with true joints and tight tenons. In fact, all machine work on veneered doors must be carefully done to have true work and tight joints.

Instead of putting the panels in when the doors are

put in the clamps, the framework is glued together with open panels, the stiles and rails being grooved, and after the doors are polished and put on the finishing bench, a panel strip is put in all around the edge of each panel, to which the panel mould is glued and nailed. The moulding is put in one side first,

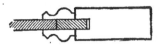

FIG. 41

panels laid in, and moulded the other side, as shown in Fig. 41. This arrangement prevents the moulding from pulling away from the stiles, should the panels shrink, and allows enough play for the panels to keep straight with the natural working of the wood in the changes of the atmosphere. There is advantage, too, in gluing up the framework without the panels. This cannot be done in the case of solid moulded doors.

The finish of a veneered door should be first-class; the panels, moulds and framework well sandpapered, and flat surfaces scraped smooth, as every defect seems magnified when the filler and varnish are applied.

Special care should be taken not to scrape, scratch or mar the face of the doors in shipping. Many a good door has been injured by careless packing or handling in shipping, after the cabinetmaker has finished his job. They should be crated, if shipped on a railroad or by boat, or they will not be worth much on arrival at their destination.

Wedged Doors.—The day of the wedged door has passed, and all modern-built houses contain what is known to the trade as "blind-tenon doors." The "dowel" door is practically a blind-tenon door. In plants where a set of dowel door machinery has not been installed, the problem of making these doors presents itself.

The advantages of this door are the saving of lumber on the rails, of time in laying out all stiles both sides and mortising them from both sides, the neat appearance of the stiles, especially on natural-finished work, and the ease with which they may be glued together.

Several points must be kept in mind in order to secure success. Let the stock sawyer cut all rails

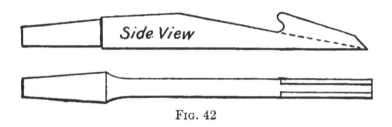

Side View

Fig. 42

exact, so the tenon will not touch the bottom of mortise before the shoulder is tight at the coping. The tenons should fit more snugly both sides and endways than in the old way, to hold well and make tight joints on the muntins. The glue should be applied to the mortise in such a way that it reaches the tenon, as well as the shoulders of rails and stiles, to make a strong job of the gluing.

The cleaning out of chips from the mortise has been a difficult problem, and it is not yet solved satisfactorily. Chain-saw mortises obviate this, but they have their faults, too. The "lip" chisels, Fig. 42, clear out the loose chips, but leave the fine chips that are pounded down by the action of the chisel, to be removed. In order to do this, a long S-shaped chisel with large wooden handle, Fig. 43, is used. The blade is ¼-inch wide, and tapers from 0 at the cutting edge to ¾ or ⅞-inch at the handle.

This is a slow, laborious job. An easier method is

to use a twist drill bit in a horizontal boring machine, leaving the arbor in a fixed position and moving the stiles back and forth, both lengthwise and sidewise, by hand. The bit should not be quite as large as the mortise, so as not to enlarge it and make the tenons fit

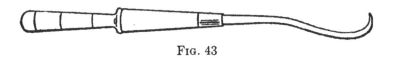

FIG. 43

too loosely. Straight-flute bits, double-pointed bits, flat pieces of steel sharpened on edges and points, and various other patterns of cutters have been tried, and drills give the best satisfaction; only, they are easily broken.

The doors should be framed and stood in a hot room for about a week, to dry out. When ready to glue together, they are warm and do not chill the glue as it is applied. The kind of glue has much to do with the rapidity with which doors may be glued up. Expensive glue is not required for this work, but a strong, *quick-setting* glue is needed, so that the doors do not have to remain too long in the clamp, thus retarding the work. A light-colored glue, having had a sufficient quantity of oxide of zinc mixed with it by the glue manufacturer, is the kind required. Using this, the man at the door clamp can take them out. of the clamps about as fast as he can properly apply the glue, without their springing apart at the joints so as to require small clamps to hold them.

Bear in mind, in making blind-tenon doors, you must have good machine work, dry lumber, snug fit to tenons, quick-setting glue, all applied in a good, sensible manner. The kinds of wood and styles of doors both affect the results obtained, and must be made the subject of study in order to succeed.

A good tool for rubbing out the surplus glue after the veneering has been put in place is shown in Fig. 44. The rubbing part may be made out of an old plane iron, or from a worn-out scraper.

THE CHOICE AND USE OF GLUE

Glue is an article which plays an important part in carpentry. It is therefore to the interest of all to know

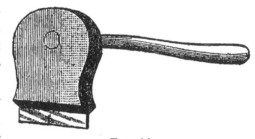

how to choose a good article, and also how to use it properly for various kinds of work.

First, as to how to recognize a good article. It is really useless to recommend

FIG. 44

mend Russian, Scotch, French, etc., as there are good and bad qualities of each, and we make as good glue in this country as anywhere in the world. Neither does the test of looking through the cakes at the light, and choosing those of only a bright color, apply in all cases, although it is a fairly good test with thin glue, that is, glue which is sold in thin cakes. The best test which the writer has found is to break a cake into two or three pieces, either by forcibly bending it, or by striking with the hammer. If the fractures present a smooth, even surface, the glue is poor in quality; but if, on the contrary, they present a ragged appearance, leaving any amount of sharp splinters, it is evidence of good quality, and may be depended upon. The latter is to be preferred, as being best able to stand the damp weather without going mouldy and perishing.

The best way to prepare glue for use is to break up sufficient to fill the inner vessel of the glue pot into small pieces, and fill the vessel with water. After soaking a few hours, the outer vessel can be filled with water, and allowed to boil. When this takes place, give the contents of the inner vessel a good stir occasionally until all is melted, when the glue should run off the brush freely, and be almost as thin to all appearances as good linseed oil.

In glueing up joints of any description, or in repairing furniture, the great object is to get the wood into as close contact as possible before the glue begins to set; and the best way to manage this is to put on plenty of glue, boiling hot, and by means of pressure or by rubbing the parts together, to rub out as much as possible. The general idea is that a certain amount of glue must be left in a joint, and that it will hold best if it is reasonably thick. Greater mistakes were never made. The thinner the better, and the less left in the stronger the joint will be; therefore it follows that unless the parts to be joined fit closely together, a strong joint is impossible.

The glue pot must be kept free from dust and damp, as glue which goes mouldy, or gets mixed with foreign matter, is useless; therefore, unless it is used fairly often, only a moderate quantity should be made at one time.

The outer or water vessel of the glue pot should be large, so as to be capable of holding enough water to keep the glue hot long enough for any reasonable job. A small water vessel is a continual nuisance, owing to its continually boiling dry when making glue, and failing to hold the heat when using it. Therefore, when purchasing, do not get one which holds less than a quart of water at the least. The extra cost will be saved in a very short time.

For large establishments where much glue is required, special appliances are provided, and may be obtained from most dealers in plumbers' goods.

For glue to be properly effective it requires to penetrate the pores of the wood, and the more a body of glue penetrates the wood, the more substantial the joint will remain. Glues that take the longest to dry are to be preferred to those that dry quickly, the slow-drying glues being always the strongest, other things being equal. For general use no method gives such good results as the following: Break the glue up small, put into an iron kettle, cover the glue with water and allow it to soak twelve hours; after soaking, boil until done. Then pour it into an airtight box, leave the cover off till cold, then cover up tight. As glue is required, cut out a portion and melt in the usual way. · Expose no more of the made glue to the atmosphere for any length of time than is necessary, as the atmosphere is very destructive to made glue. Never heat made glue in a pot that is subjected to the direct heat of the fire or a lamp. All such methods of heating glue cannot be condemned in terms too severe. Do not use thick glue for joints or veneering. In all cases work it well into the wood, in a similar manner to what painters do with paint. Glue both surfaces of your work, excepting in case of veneering. Never glue upon hot wood, as the hot wood will absorb all the water in the glue too suddenly, and leave only a very little residue, with no adhesive power in it.

REMARKS ON VENEERING

A wood suitable for veneering requires to be
thoroughly well seasoned, free from knots and shakes,
and should not contain turps. The best of woods for
the purpose are mahogany and American walnut,
although good pine answers well for ordinary purposes.
The surface, if flat, is carefully planed with the
trying plane. It is then well toothed over with the
toothing plane—first the lengthways of the wood and
afterward the crossways—care being taken to tooth
the work thoroughly. If you are working pine, use a
coarse toothing iron; if mahogany or other hardwood,
a finer iron is requisite. If the wood presents a
hollow or rounded surface, it is shaped with suitable
planes, rasps and files, and finally well prepared crossways with coarse glass paper such as strong No. 2 or
No. 2½.

The next preparation is sizing. To make the size,
take one part of good glue and boil it well with 50
parts of water; then brush over the ground-work while
hot; allow to dry, and, if there should be any defects
in the ground-work, fill in with stopping. Make your
stopping by mixing some finely ground plaster of Paris
with hot glue and water, enough to form a moderately
stiff paste. Then lay in where necessary with a chisel,
taking care to allow for shrinkage; let it dry, then
level off with a rasp.

Having sized the ground-work over, next proceed to
the preparation of the veneer while it is drying.
Look carefully to the wood before cutting it, and see
that it is done in such a manner as to get the grain of
it to the best advantage. Cut it rather larger than the
surface it is intended to veneer, to allow for leveling
at the ends and sides. Most veneers, such as mahog-

any, oak, chestnut, maple, sycamore, birch, satinwood and various other woods, are ready for cutting as received from the merchant; but some, like burr walnut, brown oak, Amboyna, etc., present an uneven surface, called "backly." When this is the case, damp one side with clear water, lay it down with its dry side upward, and put the wet side of the next veneer upon it, repeating the operation till all are done. Take particular care to keep each veneer, if there are more than three or four, in its proper order as you damp and turn over, and do not on any account get them mixed. Let the wood stand about four or five hours, then lay them out to allow to nearly dry and they will be ready for cutting out.

The next process is flatting. Get two pieces of wood (dry, straight pine will answer), rather longer than the veneer, and heat them on a stove or before a bright fire; then place the veneer together between the hand screw, and allow it to remain for about half an hour; repeat this operation until the veneer is perfectly dry and thoroughly flat.

Our wood is now ready for filling in. If it is perfectly sound this operation is, of course, unnecessary; but it frequently happens, especially with burr walnut, that it contains holes that require filling. To do this, take a piece of the veneer (off the edges of that already cut out), and flat it precisely as the other. Select the part of it which matches best with the grain of the wood around the hole to be filled in. Place this underneath the hole. If you have a stamp rather larger than the hole, you may now cut it square or circular and the piece for filling it at the same time. If not, take an ordinary pocket knife having a sharp point and cut your hole and veneer the required shape.

When you have filled in the wood, lay it on a flat board, then press the piece in with a hammer. If they are rather large use one or two finely pointed tacks to keep them in position. Now cover all the pieces with strips of paper, selecting a strong paper such as copy book or note paper for the purpose—one that is not too thick—and glue it on one side. Take care to use glue just thick enough to hold the wood in position. Pay particular attention to this, or it will cause a good deal of trouble. You will find it best to cut the paper in strips about 1¼ to 1½ inches wide. Lay it on a board to glue and smooth it over your veneer with a damp rag.

Jointing.—We now procee´ to jointing. Place the veneer in the position it will appear when laid. Observe that it matches. If you are to have one joint with two veneers or two joints with four veneers, see that the grain of the wood forms a figure having both sides alike. If the veneers have b en kept in their right or following order, this will not be difficult. If you are working a thick veneer (saw cut), make the joints with an iron plane or ordinary trying plane on the shooting board; if using thin veneer (knife cut), make them with a chisel and straight-edge. Take particular care to have the bevel edge of the chisel against the straight-edge when cutting or it will run, and you may come off with an ugly cut. Now put the jointed edges together on a deal board, and tack one edge down; put the tacks about ¾ inch from the jointed edges and about 2½ inches apart. Having tacked one piece down, put the other up to it and tack it in the same manner. Now cover all the joints with paper, glue together in the same manner as previously mentioned in the filling in; smooth it well down with a damp rag and allow to dry. If the weather is hot it is best to cover your joints to prevent them drying too quickly. A good and simple method is to lay your board with the veneer downward on the floor. Let the joints dry, then take out the tacks and knock the head holes in with a hammer from the underneath side. Put the veneer aside until you are ready for laying it. It is best to cover it up and keep the air from it by placing it under a board or wrapper.

There are two ways of laying veneer—by means of a caul or a veneering hammer. I shall describe both methods, although the first is of greater importance, and should, whenever practicable, be adopted, but in certain cases which I shall mention the second is extremely useful.

Veneering by Caul.—First make a caul, then take a piece of well-seasoned cedar or pine, rather larger than the surface intended to cover (about 1 inch to 1½ inches each way), and plane it up true on both sides, if the work is flat. If otherwise, make it to the requisite shape to fit the work, hollow, round, or whatever it may be. If it is necessary to shape the caul, use thicker stuff, and it is advisable to screw on two or three battens on the back. When making shaped cauls it is best at the same time to get out the pieces of wood necessary to form a flat surface when the wood is put in the caul. Thus, suppose we wanted to veneer a door having a rounded surface on one side and a hollow one on the other. We have made a hollow caul to correspond with the rounded surface having its under side flat. Now put the rounded side of the door in the caul and shape your piece of wood, rounding it to fit the hollow side. They should be 2 inches wide—the same width or a little larger than the

caul, and 5 inches or 6 inches apart.   If one side only
of tne wood is shaped these woods are unnecessary.
If the wood is not wide enough, make a good joint,
dowel it together, and take it to pieces for heating.
The caul, if likely to be much in use, should be
covered with zinc.   Cut the metal out large enough
to cover the face of it, with sufficient to turn over the
edges and ends, and fasten it on with flat-headed zinc
or copper nails.

Numerous failures in unaccustomed hands may be
ascribed to bad glue.   Nothing but the very best glue
should be used for veneering.   Get the very best
glue you can, break it up and boil thoroughly.   It
differs so much in strength that the proportion of
water cannot be given, but after breaking up in pieces
just cover with water and allow it to soak; then boil
off with frequent stirring.   It will, if good, now
require about half as much water as previously added
to bring it to the right consistence for veneering.   It
should be spread evenly with the brush and be free
from lumps.   Having made the caul and prepared the
glue, get the hand screws and cramps to commence
laying.   Heat the caul on a stove or before a bright
fire.   If it is to be doweled together, and if it is more
convenient, take it to pieces, taking care to mark your
joints first.   If you intend laying two similar pieces of
veneer on flat surfaces, heat both sides of it and do both
pieces together.   If not, get one side of it well heated,
as hot as you can without letting it burn.   While it is
heating, set the hand screws and cramps open as near
the distance as you will require them, and place handy
for the work.   Now glue the ground-work well, and
if the veneer shows any signs of being backly glue it
slightly on the underneath side, as this will help tc

soften it. Having finished gluing, put the veneer on the work and smooth it over gently with the hand. Then see that the caul is hot enough, and that its surface is free from any small cinders or dirt. Now rub it over with a greasy rag, and lay it gently on your veneer. Draw the work and caul a little over the edge of the bench, just enough to get the hand screw on; put it on very gently, then tighten as much as possible. You can then stand it upon the floor, and if you have nobody to hold it for you rest the hand screw against the bench while you put on the remainder. They should be placed about 6 inches apart, and mind that they bite fairly. Do not get any screws tighter than the other, or you will only get the pressure at the outside and inside of the cramps. If you have a piece of work so wide that the screws will not reach the center from either side or the ends, get two pieces of wood 2 inches or 2½ inches thick and about the same thickness, plane them up, slightly rounding on one side, put their rounding sides facing each other on the work, and hand screw them at each end; they will then tighten in the middle and give sufficient pressure. Let the caul remain on for nearly an hour (in very hot weather longer will not hurt), then undo the hand screws, and if the caul sticks, insert the edge of a thin metal square, the back of a hand saw, or anything of a similar nature, between it and the veneer, and work it carefully about until you get them apart. If the glue has been used thick enough and the caul well greased, there will not be very much trouble, and they will often come apart themselves, or by giving the end of the caul a tap with the hammer, or on the end of the bench. See that the veneer is down. Feel it all over with the hand. If it is up you will be able to tell by the hollow sound on tapping it with the tip of your finger, as well as by the raised appearance called blisters it will present when held to the light. If you heat your caul sufficiently, use the glue thick enough, and put the hand screws on properly, you will not be troubled with blisters. Should, however, there be any, let the work stand for one or two hours, and then put a smaller hot caul on when required until well down all over.

To level the veneer, first lay it (veneer downward) on a board and scrape off with a chisel as much of the glue that has come over the edges as you can. Now put it on the bench screw, and level toward you, with the paring chisel if thin veneers; if thick, use a smoothing plane. Put it aside to dry. If you have two pieces of the same size put them with their veneer sides together; if only one, place it so that the air does not get to the veneer; allow to stand for two or three days, then scrape off the paper for filling in pieces and jointing with a chisel, having previously damped it with hot water. The work is now ready for sizing. This operation may be dispensed with, but it is decidedly advantageous, especially if working wood which has an open grain. The size, which should be about the same strength as that used for the ground-work, is brushed or rubbed over the veneer with the hand, then wiped off as dry as possible with a cloth.

As has already been mentioned, this method is useful in certain cases. We sometimes want to veneer an edge, to put a narrow slip of veneer on some small surface where it would be very inconvenient to caul it down. If you are working a wood of a glossy or greasy description, like satinwood or rosewood, its nature will not admit of sufficient pressure by this process, nor should it ever be adopted for work where water will act injuriously. I believe the prevailing opinion is that veneer requires a good deal of water to make it lie. In the first process, you will remember that it is laid quite dry. In the second process water is used, and if we consider that a damp surface tends to cause the wood to cast as it dries, we can readily understand where it should be used.

Veneering Round and Tapering Columns.—Occasions often arise where it is desirable to veneer columns of varying size and shape, and just how to do the work to the best advantage is a question not always readily determined by the workman.

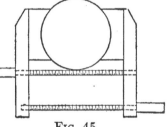

In commenting upon this matter a well-known authority offers the following suggestions concerning tapering columns:

"The success of this work depends entirely on the proper cauls. The spong-

Fig. 45

ing and gluing is the same as the work previously mentioned. Take a circular column 3 or 4 inches in diameter, the core to be made of any suitable material. Pass a piece of paper around the core and make a straight joint through the center and we have the exact size of the veneer. A caul of tin with a cleat on each end for the purchase of the hand screws is to be made as in Fig. 45, leaving the top open for an inch or more to give the glue a chance to escape. Apply the glue to the core and pass the veneer around it, not forgetting, however, to sponge the veneer before doing so. After screwing together, put the whole in the steam box to warm up the stiffened glue. After the work has become thoroughly warm, take it out and give the hand screws a few turns, then lay it aside until the glue is set. Take off the hand screws and dispense with the tin cauls. The ends may then be brought together, as shown in Fig. 46, only the caul on the joint is to be heated.

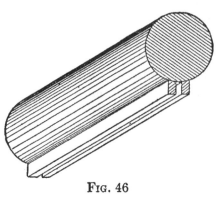

FIG. 46

"Fig. 47 is a tapering column. The work is the same as above described, only the shape of the veneer is different, which may be got either by passing paper around, trimming on both ends and making a straight joint in center of column, or by laying out the diagram, as in Fig. 48. In explanation thereof, let A, B, C, D represent the column in question. To find the shape of a veneer to pass around this column extend AB and CD to E. With the radius EC and ED, describe the arcs CF and OH, which will be the required shape, and the distance AF and IH will pass half-way around,

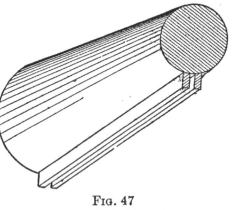

FIG. 47

and the veneer requires to be cut as large again to pass all around the column. Under no circumstances make more than one joint. By following the instruc-

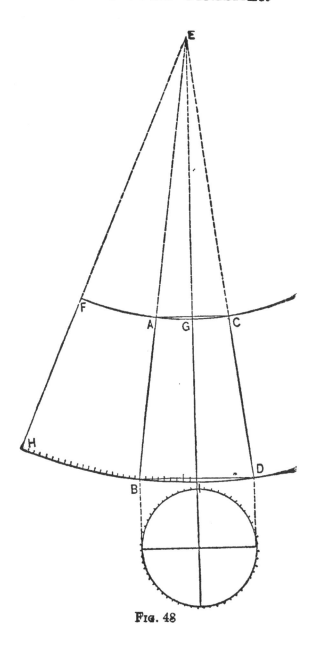

FIG. 48

tion herein given any fair mechanic will be enabled to
execute a creditable piece of work."

In veneering small work, such as picture frames,
clock stands or similar work, cauls should be reverse
of the moulding or face of the work to be veneered,
and the top of caul, when laid on the moulding, should
be parallel with the under side of the work, so that
caul and work can be gripped firmly with hand screws,
when the veneer is being glued in place.

The section shown in Fig. 49 is known in the trade
as a plain chamfer, and Fig. 50 shows a method by
which such a frame may be veneered
without taking it to pieces. Veneer
⅛ inch thick can only be laid with
cauls; and a suitable one is shown,
and also the method of fixing it.
The dotted outline of the caul is
shown in section in Fig. 49, with the
veneer between it and the base.   If
the frames are polished, remove
the polish carefully with a sharp scraper; avoid working the surface into holes, but leave it rough from the
scraper.   Cut the veneer to a width that will allow
sufficient margin for beveling, as shown in Fig. 49,
and tooth or scratch the under face with a saw.   Joint
the inside edge to a correct bevel, cut to a miter and
joint the ends in a miter joint, bedding the veneer
either on a piece of the moulding or on a waste piece
chamfered to the same angle; this is to obtain a vertical
face to the miter.   Next prepare the caul (as shown
in Fig. 49) out of a piece of deal.   The caul should be
¼ inch shorter than the veneer, and mitered at each
end; not cut square as shown in Fig. 50; which is
drawn thus for clearness.   Make the caul slightly

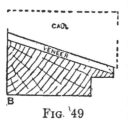

FIG. 49

round in length and beveled, so that the two surfaces marked AB (Fig. 49) are parallel. Well glue the veneer and the frame, lay the veneer in the proper position, place a strip of paper on the surface of the veneer, and lay the caul (preferably hot) upon this paper and fix with hand screws as shown, the more screws the better. Take care that the inside edge of

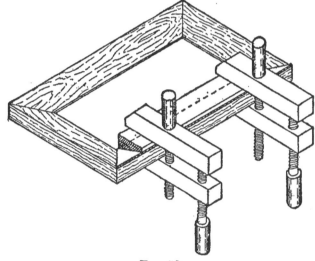

Fig. 50

the veneer is flush with the edges of the frame. Proceed to fix the opposite side in like manner; then wipe off the superfluous glue with a rag dipped in hot water, and wash the miters clean; then fit in the two end pieces, which can be fixed in the manner described for the sides. Allow twelve hours to dry, then clean off the back edges and scrape up the faces.

MAKING READY FOR POLISHING

If the workman who finally finishes woodwork had the selection of the materials out of which the work

is formed, and wrought the work himself, the following suggestions would scarcely be required, for he
would see to it that the material was free from shakes,
cracks, worm holes, doze, sap and fractures; and he
would so choose his material that the full beauty of
the grain would show, when the polish coat went on.
He would also see that the work was *clean;* that is,
that no plane marks were visible, no rough spots or
cross-grains noticeable, and that all angles were sharp
and definite, all mouldings smooth and not a nail head
or screw top to be seen, nor any point that could
suggest a nail head. As a rule, however, the workman who puts on the last finishing touches never
makes the work, though he is *always* expected to
cover and hide all the faults of bad workmanship, bad
selection of timber, and a thousand other objectionable things in connection with work over which he
has had no control. In order to aid the finisher as
much as possible, I give a few hints herewith, for the
use of the workman whose duty it may be to prepare
and put up the work to be finished. The suggestions
given are equally applicable for hard and soft woods,
and I trust they will not be out of place.

First, then, see that the material is dry, free from
imperfections, of the full sizes required, and of such
variety of grain as may be suitable for the purpose
intended. Next, make all joints close and as near
perfect as possible, as on this point rests, in a great
measure, the artistic appearance of the work. Make
all angles sharp and clean, and all mitered mouldings
true and with perfect intersections. Never use glass
paper where a scraper can be applied, and when a
large quantity of mouldings of similar contour and size
are to be employed; it is always better to make a

scraper their reverse shape, and use it in cleaning and preparing the mouldings for the varnisher, than to use glass paper for the purpose.

The scraper illustrated by Fig. 51, and shown handled by Fig. 52, is an aid in producing surfaces more flat and regular than can be produced with the plane alone. Its use does not dispense with the plane; on the contrary, any surface on which the scraper

FIG. 51

is to be used must previously be planed as level and smooth as plane can make it. But the plane, in doing its work—no matter how sharp it may be, or how closely the back-iron is set up to the edge of the cutting iron, or how straight across the edge the cutting iron is sharpened—is liable to leave marks and ridges on the face of the work, which, on hard woods, are not effectively removed by the use of sandpaper alone. The scraper is used after the plane has finished its work, and previous to the final operation of sandpapering. In addition to the removal of the ridges left by the plane, the scraper is used for dressing up all kinds of cross-grained surfaces that occur

FIG. 52

in curly and figured solid and veneer woods; but as far as possible this use of the scraper should be avoided. Excessive dressing up of a cross-grained patch on a panel, a stile, or a table-top will most certainly show, and spoil the flatness and general appearance of the article when it is polished. As a rule, such excessive scraping is resorted to in consequence of the plane having been sharpened and set badly, or of some other technical oversight or unskillful manipulation.

The scraper is a thin and very hard steel plate, about 5 in. by 3 in., or 4½ in. by 2½ in., and slightly less than $\frac{1}{16}$ in. in thickness. The long edges are sharpened in a peculiar manner. Both of the long edges may be straight, as in Fig. 51, and at AB, Fig. 53, or one edge may have round corners of differing radii, as at

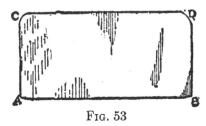

FIG. 53

CD. These corners are often useful in working up hollows and mouldings generally. The "straight" edge AB, it will be noticed, is not quite straight throughout its whole length. Near the ends the edge is gradually rounded off, to prevent the corners catching in the surface that is being operated on. In this respect, the commercial scraper (Fig. 51) is incorrectly shaped. The cutting power of a scraper depends upon, first, the quality and temper of the steel of which it is made; and, secondly, upon the proper formation of the burr or feather along its edges. Also, the faces of the steel plate must be perfectly bright and free from rust marks or indentations of any kind. It is by no means an uncommon thing to find any rusty piece of sheet steel—a piece of an old hand saw or try-square, for example—being used as a scraper. The smallest appreciation of why the scraper cuts would indicate how useless such material is for this particular purpose. On the other hand, scarcely anything better can be found for making a scraper than a piece of broken saw blade, provided the sides of it are still polished and bright. The fact that the saw was broken may easily be taken to indicate a higher temper than usual in the blade, thus fitting it exactly for the purpose of a scraper. The temper of an ordinary saw blade is not usually hard enough. Provided that there is enough elasticity to "give" in the operator's hands as it is being pushed along, the scraper should be nearly too hard for an ordinary file to touch. If it can be filed easily, then its edge will soon be gone. At the same time, if the steel is merely hard without the required amount of elasticity, the burr will strip off as it is applied to the work, leaving a coarse, jagged edge which is worse than useless.

The correctly sharpened scraper is a real cutting tool, and not, as its name suggests—and as in practice it often is—a mere abrader of the surface. When in good working trim, the scraper should, if desired, take off shaving after shaving perfectly uniform in thickness, and nearly as wide as the cutting edge is long. But such a performance is rarely required of it, and never when the plane has previously done its work properly. Too much emphasis cannot be laid on the fact that the proper duty of the scraper is not to make a surface, but to correct the irregularities on it. In explanation of the cutting action of the scraper, a diagrammatic figure is shown in Fig. 66. The figure correctly illustrates the cutting principle, though it does not represent a true section of the scraper. In use, the scraper is held firmly in both hands and tilted forwards, away from the operator, until the cutting edge grips the surface of the wood, exactly as shown in Fig. 54. It is then kept steadily at this angle, and made to cut a fine shaving at each stroke as it is being

pushed away from the operator in the direction from
E to F (Fig. 54).

The proper formation of the burr edge is of the
greatest importance.   Having procured a suitable

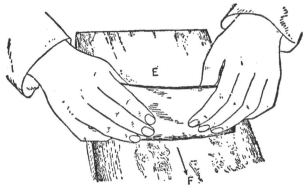

FIG. 54

steel plate, a usual but not recommended method is
as follows: The plate is laid down on the bench as
shown in Fig. 55.   A narrow chisel, brad-awl or gouge,

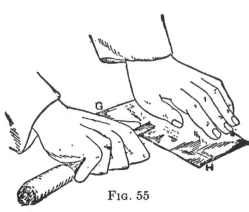

FIG. 55

as shown in Fig.
56, is then laid on
the scraper hori-
zontally, and with
considerable pres-
sure is stroked
backwards and
forwards from end
to end of the
plate, G to H,
Fig. 55.   After
about 10 or 12
strokes the scraper is turned over and the other side is
treated in the same manner.   This completes the first
part of the process of sharpening.   Next, the gouge

is placed vertically against the edge, as shown in Fig. 57, and stroked to and fro with about the same pressure and firmness as the sides of plate received,

FIG. 56

and about the same number of times. Or else, for this second part, the scraper may be placed on its corner on the bench, as shown in Fig. 58, and held firmly in the left hand, while the right hand deftly strokes the convex side of the gouge with a quick action and considerable pressure, once or twice in an upward direction, as from I to J in Fig. 58. The scraper is then tried on the work to determine its sharpness. If, after this process, the scraper fails to cut satisfactorily, it is laid down on

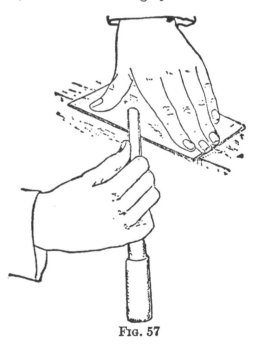

FIG. 57

the bench and the two processes are repeated. The following is a better method of sharpening a scraper: First, have the scraper ground so that its edge shall be straight and square, and slope up at the ends, as shown at A and B, Fig. 53. It should then be placed on its edge on a fine-cutting oilstone, as shown in Fig. 60, and rubbed backwards and forwards until all traces of the grinding have disappeared. Then it should be laid flat on its side, still on the oilstone, as in Fig. 61, and rubbed until the sides are bright and polished all along the edges. If any false burr or feather-edge has been

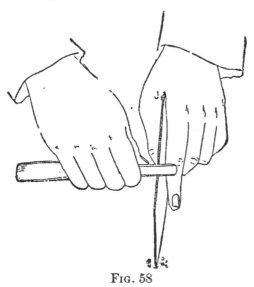

FIG. 58

created in this last process, the scraper must be set up on its edge again, as in Fig. 60, and rubbed a little more, until two perfectly square and sharp corners appear all along the scraper. Now, if due care has really been taken in making the corners perfect and square, the scraper in this condition would produce shavings tolerably well on any hardwood; but the shaving would be the result of abrasive and not of cutting action. It is purely a matter of choice if, at this stage, a smooth-backed gouge is passed to and fro over the side of the scraper, as in Fig. 55, with the object of imparting a still higher polish to the plate of steel at the places where the burr is to be formed. But the greatest care must be taken not to press too heavily, and also to maintain a perfectly level position with the gouge, while the polishing is being done. As stated, this polishing of the side is not really necessary, and the scraper would cut very well without

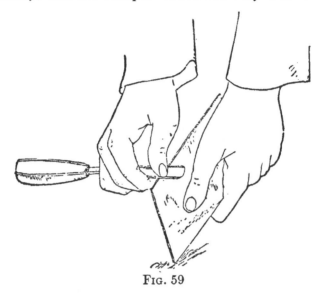

Fig. 59

its supposed assistance. Next, the scraper is placed on its corner on the bench, and a flat and smooth-backed gouge is passed once—or at most twice—along the edge. The scraper

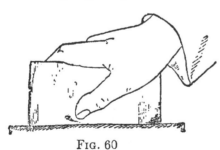

Fig. 60

during this operation may be held either as already shown in Fig. 57, or as is here recommended and shown in Fig. 61; or it may be fastened in the bench-vise. The aim in this particular action is the production of an exceedingly fine burr, scarcely enough to be called a burr at all, but a perfectly regular bending over of the corner; the gouge must be very lightly pressed, or it will cause the burr to curl up too much, and also it must be kept nearly, though not quite, horizontal. With regard to resharpening the scraper, when this becomes necessary, the scraper must be placed upon the oilstone and rubbed up again to perfectly square corners as previously described in connection with Figs. 60 and 61.

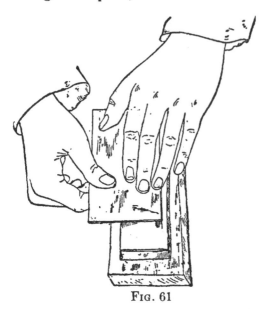

FIG. 61

There are other methods of sharpening scrapers which are made use of by some workmen; indeed, nearly every workman, after experience, will adopt such method as will seem to him to be the best for the purpose. There are workmen who seldom or never use an oilstone, but employ a fine file instead, and draw file the edge of the scraper as shown in Fig. 63. This is done by placing the scraper in a vise and with a smooth, flat file making the edge perfectly square and as straight as possible after the manner of jointing a hand saw. Next place the file squarely across the edge and pass it from end to end of the scraper two or three times. This operation is known as draw-filing, a plan view of the position and direction of the file being shown in Fig. 63. Treat all four edges

FIG. 62

the same way. The edge, as it will now appear, is shown enlarged and exaggerated in Fig. 64. Remove the scraper from the vise and lay it flat on the bench, then taking the gouge, Fig. 56, rub out straight all the wire edges, keeping the gouge on the scraper and passing it quickly back and forth after the manner of stropping

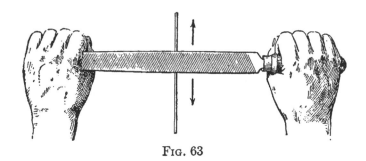

FIG. 63

a razor. The edge will then appear as in Fig. 65. Now, taking the scraper in the left hand and holding it firmly edgewise on the bench, place the gouge across the edge, making a small bevel with the side of the scraper, and draw it upward two or three times, using considerable pressure. This will turn the edge back as it was after filing, but it will now be straight instead of grooved, and smooth instead of ragged. All of the eight edges must be treated in the same manner, when they will appear as in Fig. 66, and the scraper should now take off a shaving like a smooth-plane, but much finer.

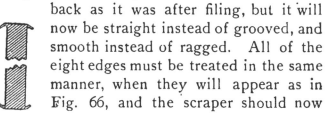

FIG. 64   FIG. 65

In order to resharpen the scraper it is not necessary to go through the filing operation again for some time— simply flatten out the edges and turn them again with a little more bevel than before. This can be done

very rapidly.   In order to avoid too many stops,
always keep three or four scrapers at hand and sharpen

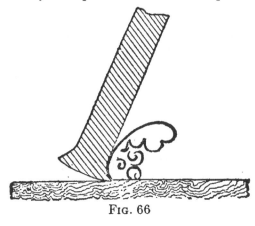

them all at once.
The best thing
with which to hold
the scraper is a
piece of sandpa-
per, with the
sanded side next
the scraper. This
gives a good grip
and prevents the
tool from burning
the fingers.

FIG. 66

Some people file the edge of the scraper rounding,
to prevent the corners from catching.   This is not at
all necessary, as the
action of pushing the
scraper bends it slight-
ly, which raises the cor-
ners somewhat   The
sharpening of a scraper,
however, like the sharp-
ening of a hand saw,
takes considerable prac-
tice and no little knack·
so if at first one does
not succeed it is only
necessary to keep peg-
ging away at it until
success crowns the
efforts, for it is well

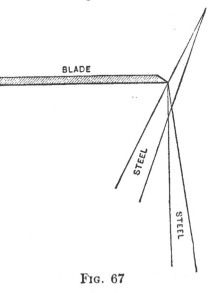

FIG. 67

worth all the trouble.   It may be mentioned incident-
ally that a good burnisher may be bought all ready at

any good hardware store. Leather curriers use them for turning the edges of their knives and they are better than a gouge because of their being tempered harder and more highly finished.

The true theory of a scraper, for some purposes, may be described as follows: Where there is a lot of superfluous wood to remove, as in hardwood floors or other similar work, where it is not desirable to use a smooth plane, it is well to file or grind the scraper to a bevel, the same as a plane iron, and bring it to a keen edge on the oilstone; then proceed to burnish it. Hold the burnisher slightly at an angle with the bevel as indicated in Fig. 67, and draw it lightly across the blade. Then increase the angle and the pressure, repeating the process until the burnisher is at nearly right angles with the blade, after which run

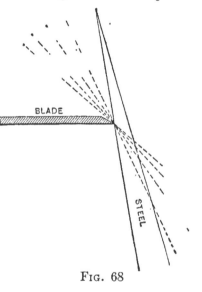

FIG. 68

the burnisher back and forward a few times, first one side and then the other, as indicated in Fig. 68, when it is ready for use. When it becomes a little dull, do not turn the edge back, as many do, but use the burnisher as shown in Fig. 68. A good blade will stand for two or three hours without filing or grinding.

For fine work file or grind the blade perfectly square on the edge and get it perfectly smooth on the oilstone. Then hold the burnisher as shown in Fig. 69, the dotted lines indicating how to start and the full lines how to finish. In all cases finish the operation as shown in Fig. 69. If unsuccessful the first time, do not give up the job, for the scraper is a tool that requires a great deal of practice in order to become expert in sharpening.

Defective Sharpening of Scrapers.—A frequent mistake is to put too great pressure on the gouge, and to stroke too much. One or two strokes should be quite

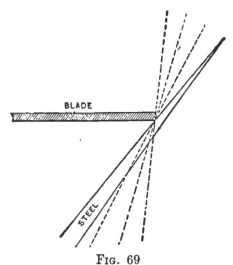

BLADE

STEEL

Fig. 69

sufficient to give the scraper the proper edge. At all events after the scraper has had a couple of strokes of the burnisher or gouge, it should be tried, and if it does not grip the work properly, give it a few strokes more. Scrapers with a high temper require more burnishing than if soft or medium temper, but if overdone, the edge will crumble and it will not do clean work. Soft scrapers are easier handled than hard ones, but require a great deal more sharpening, and this sometimes leads to rough work, as the workman will not take time to repeatedly put his scraper in order. As before stated, the workman should have at least three or four scrapers on hand, and they should always be kept in good order. It is a good plan to have a little box or case in the tool chest purposely to hold scrapers, for two reasons: The workman will always know where to find them when wanted and, secondly, it will save the edges from being broken or damaged by being jolted or rubbed against other tools.

Varieties of Scrapers.—There is a new scraper in the market which is said to be superior to anything made in the scraper line. A representa-

FIG. 70

tion of it is shown in Fig. 70, which is taken from an advertisement. I do not know of my own knowledge how the scraper works, but, judging from its shape and setting, I should think it theoretically correct.

FIG. 71

Other shapes of scrapers are shown in Figs. 71 and 72. The first of these is intended for smoothing up hollows and rounds. A number of these should be kept on hand, with curves of various radii. Fig. 72 shows a scraper made purposely for cleaning out hollows of various curvatures, and will be found very useful on work

FIG. 72

where there are a number of curves or other hollow mouldings. Often the workman may have to make scrapers to suit certain kinds of work, and when such is the case, he should make it a fixed rule never to change them, but to keep them in his tool chest, and make others, when necessary, from new material. An old hand saw blade generally answers quite well for scrapers, and one saw will make a couple of dozen scrapers of different sizes and shapes.

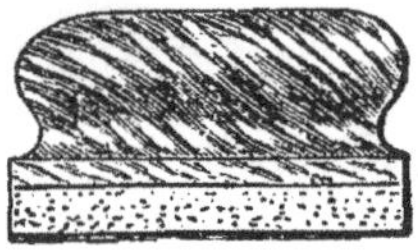

FIG. 73

How to Use Sandpaper.—For properly using sandpaper a rubber is needed. A piece of mahogany or clean pine, 5¾ in. by 3 in. by 1 in., shaped as in Fig. 73, answers well if a piece of sheet cork is glued on the face as shown. Fold a piece of sandpaper, 6 in. wide and about 10 in. long, into three, place it sand side downwards, and put the face of the rubber on the middle division. Grasp the rubber so that the ends of the sandpaper are held firmly on its back and sides (see Fig. 74), and work then can be commenced.

A solid rubber about one inch thick makes an excellent block for the purpose. A piece of rubber belting glued to a piece of basswood also makes a good rubber block.

FIG. 74

Rasps and Files.—The woodworker occasionally uses rasps, and these generally are half-round, though sometimes flat. The cabinet rasp shown in Fig. 75 is not a very coarse one. Cabinet and wood rasps range from 4 in. to 14 in. in length, and at 12 in. and less the price is about 4 cents per inch. The extra 2 in. in a 14-inch rasp adds nearly 50 per cent to the price. Files also are used, for smoothing up hardwood. When a file is used, it should be pushed and drawn in the direction of the grain. The file usually employed by carriage makers for smoothing up spokes and other work is generally a half-round bastard file, and when properly used makes exceedingly smooth work. A finer file than the bastard is shown in Fig. 76. This is sometimes used for finishing narrow flat work.

SAWS FOR WORKING HARDWOOD

Saw-filing is an art unto itself, and few men ever attain the art to perfection. To file a saw in such manner that the working of it is a pleasure requires an amount of skill and a high order of technical knowledge that can only be acquired by thought and experience; yet a properly set and filed saw is a real necessity in the making of good joiners' work, and, while every workman cannot become an expert saw-filer, he ought at least to possess such knowledge of the art as will enable him to set and file his own saws in such a manner as will enable him to execute such work as he may be called upon to make; and to this end, I propose to offer

FIG. 75   FIG. 76

a few instructions and remarks that will assist him in managing his own saws without the employment of expert aid.   It is not my intention to go into the matter of saw-filing to any great extent, as that subject will probably be discussed at length in another volume, but what I do offer will, I trust, be up to the mark.

All workmen in wood require two saws, namely, a cross-cut saw, and a rip-saw.   The shape of the teeth in these saws differs, also the size, and each requires a special form of tooth and a different style of filing.

Many workmen think that so long as the tooth of a saw has a sharp edge the shape of the tooth is a matter

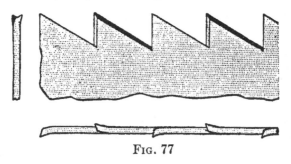

Fig. 77

of small importance, and as a result of this ignorance or indifference they are always in trouble with their saws, and their work becomes much more laborious than if proper attention had been paid to the shape of the teeth.   Substances of different texture cannot be cut advantageously with the same tool; in fact, the tool must be adapted to the work if the best all-round results are to be produced.   Fig. 77 illustrates a form of tooth suitable for an ordinary hand rip-saw. The tooth points number about four to the inch, and the front of the tooth is upright, that is, at an angle of 90°.   The face of the tooth should be filed to an angle of 85° to 87°, or 3° to 5° from the square.   Some experts contend that the teeth of a rip-saw should be filed dead square. The object in filing them a little on the bevel is that the teeth may cut more freely and easily when they have become a bit dull, there being then what is termed a little clearance cut in the teeth. In nearly all timber there is, it is well known, a certain

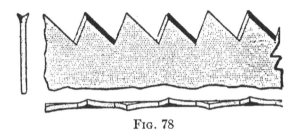

FIG. 78

amount of fiber to be cut either directly or obliquely across, and teeth that are filed square will not, whether they are sharp or dull, divide this fiber so easily as teeth that have a slight bevel.

The illustration, Fig. 77, shows a saw tooth that works quite well in the softer woods, but for the harder

FIG. 79

woods a little more plane or angle on the cutting edge would cause the saw to cut with less labor; and if the were about five teeth to the inch, it would cut with ea any kind of hardwood.

The teeth shown in Fig. 78 are well suited to a hand saw used for cross-cutting soft wood. The tooth

points in this saw may number five or six to the inch.
The front of the tooth slopes at an angle of about 105°
The face of the tooth in sharpening should be filed to
an angle of from 55° to 60°. The softer the timber
that is to be cross-cut, the more acute should be the
angle of the teeth, as the keener edge separates the
fibers more easily. Fig. 79 shows a form of hand saw

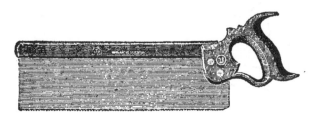

FIG. 80

tooth suitable for cross-cutting hardwood. The number
of tooth points may be from six to eight to the inch,
and the front of the tooth should slope at an angle of
110° to 115°, according to the hardness of the timber
to be sawed. The face of this tooth should be filed to
an angle of 70° to 75°, because the cutting edge must

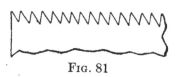

FIG. 81

be less acute owing to hardwood fibers being more compact than those of soft wood.
The whole number of saws
made use of by the wood-
worker amounts to some six or eight, comprising the
rip, cross-cut, hand, panel, tenon, dovetail, bow or
turning, and keyhole. The hand saw type includes
the hand saw proper, the ripping, half-ripping, and
panel saws, all of similar outline, but differing in
dimensions, and in form and size of teeth. There is
no sharp distinction between these tools, as they merge

one into the other; yet at the extremes it would be impossible to substitute the ripping and panel saws one for the other. The hand saw, however, which is a kind of compromise between extremes, is used indiscriminately for all purposes.

A tenon, or back-saw, is shown in Fig. 80. It is made in different lengths, and the blades are not all made the same width. The dovetail saw is a back-saw with a very thin blade; it is not much used in this country, only by Euro-

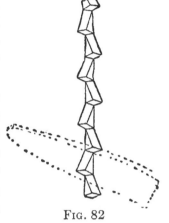

Fig. 82

peans. It is intended especially for very fine work. The other saws named are for special purposes, and

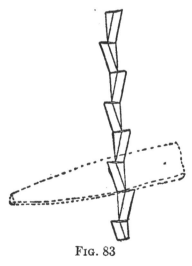

Fig. 83

need not be described here. The methods of filing, however, are about the same as described for the saws first named, with the exception of the bow or scroll saw. This saw, which is intended to cut with and across the grain, or obliquely to it, should have its teeth filed with a sharper plane than a rip-saw, but not quite so sharp as a cross-cut saw; in other words, it wants a hybrid tooth, "between and betwixt" a cross-cut and a rip-saw tooth. (See Fig. 81.)

The set of a saw is important, and this is shown in

Figs. 77, 78, 82 and 83.   The teeth at both point and
butt of a hand saw should be very slightly smaller than
those in the middle, as it is at the last-named point
where the greatest force is exerted in every down
stroke.   But it is absolutely necessary that the set is
the. same from point to butt of every saw, whether rip
or cross-cut.   The middle of the cutting edge of a
cross-cut saw should be slightly rounded, being
highest at about the middle. . The saw being still in

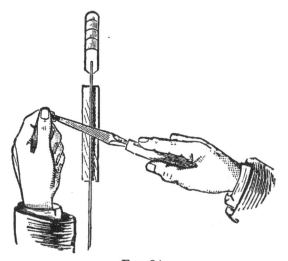

FIG. 84

the saw vise, insert the file in a handle, and grasp it
with the right hand, taking the point of file in the left,
as shown in Fig. 84.   Place the file against the face of
that tooth nearest the handle that inclines away from
the worker, holding the file at an angle with the blade
or saw as shown in Fig. 84.   Then lower the right
hand to about the angle shown in Fig. 85 (which shows
the left hand removed).   The file should be held
obliquely across the saw blade, as in Figs. 83 and 84,

the point end of the file being inclined towards the saw handle as illustrated by Fig. 84. Gently push the file forwards, lifting it at the end of stroke, returning it, and again pushing it, until the point of the tooth has a keen edge. Repeat this upon each alternate tooth until all upon one side are sharpened. Serve the other side in the same manner. Be careful not to press the file against the back of the tooth, as unevenness will surely result.

Keep all saws slightly rounding on the edge. The rip-saw and the hand saw may have a full quarter of an inch rounding with advantage. All saws, except circulars, have a constant tendency to get hollow, and this must be prevented; and the only way to prevent it is to file the teeth down by passing a partly-worn file along the edges till it touches every tooth. Then, in filing the teeth take care only just to take out this bright mark—not one touch more or that tooth will be shorter than its neighbors. A saw properly sharpened, and in good order, has each tooth do its proper share of cutting and no more.

FIG. 85

Sharpening Tenon Saws.—Sharpening tenon saws is practically the same as sharpening hand saws. It may happen, however, that some of the teeth will be much larger than others, this being due to the file not having been held at the same angle in sharpening each tooth. Fig. 81 shows the saw teeth improperly sharpened, the front of the large teeth inclining much

more than the front of the small teeth.   If the teeth
in one range are found to be filed smaller than those
in the other, file the back of the smaller teeth to a
more acute angle, keeping the file at the same time
well against the front of the other tooth at the bottom, and see before the filing is finished, that the front
of the next tooth has been filed up to its point, as it
is the front, not the back, of the tooth that does the
cutting.   To regulate the teeth of the saw, file every
tooth in succession, shooting the file straight across
the teeth.   After filing all the teeth from one side,
turn the saw, and file as before from the other side.
When the teeth are fairly regular, the flat file may be
run over them lightly.   This will bring the teeth
uniform in length.   Now file every alternate tooth,
first on one side and then on the other side of the saw,
as shown in Fig. 84.   Hold the file as nearly as
possible to the same angle in each case, as it is on
this filing that the regularity of the teeth depends.
When all the flat places caused by the file when
topping the teeth disappear, cease filing, as any further
filing may cause low teeth, which tend to make the
saw cut irregularly.   When the saw is so filed that all
the teeth get their equal share of cutting, the saw may
be said to be well filed.   When the teeth are filed as
shown in Fig. 83, there is a larger and better cutting
edge than with the one more obtuse.   If the points
only of the teeth are allowed to do the work, the action
is a scratching and not a cutting one.

One of the great difficulties in hand sharpening is to
get the bevels of the teeth exactly alike.   A number
of mechanical arrangements to guide the saw and
effect this object have been tried with more or less
success.   In one of the best of these devices a circular

casting is divided and indexed from its center each way, giving bevels for each side of the saw, or square across. The file is fitted into a guide, and is held by a set-screw. The index shows the pitch at which the file is set, and a rod passes through holes in a graduating ring and guides the file. The frame upon which the ring is held slides in grooves cut on each side of the vise in which the saw is fixed; a table connected with the guide is arranged and indexed so as to give the required bevel and pitch for the kind of saw to be filed, and it is only necessary to set the ring for the bevel, and the indicator for the pitch, and the apparatus is ready for use. As the filing is proceeded with from tooth to tooth, the frame follows, giving to each tooth on one side of the saw the same bevel, pitch, and size as on the other, thus leaving the saw, when filing is finished, with the teeth all uniform in size, pitch, and bevel, so that each tooth will do its share of cutting equally with the others, thus turning out more and better quality of work with less expenditure of energy. An old-fashioned way of getting the right angle of a tooth of a hand saw in filing is shown by Fig. 86. A hand saw blade is narrowest in width at the point, and broadest at the butt; and the slope of the back, compared with the line of teeth, is almost always uniform for all saws; and if a square be placed against this back, a tooth may be filed whose cutting edge is perfectly in line with the edge of the square. All the teeth being thus filed and afterwards set, a saw which will answer

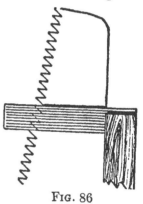

FIG. 86

general purposes is produced, and one which will suit the worker who has but one hand saw. It will cross-cut soft woods and rip hard woods, thus being a kind of half-rip. Moreover, this square may be used as a gauge, the teeth not necessarily being filed as shown; and if the rake or lead be very much, an adjustable bevel may be used.

PLANES GENERALLY

In workshop practice, planes are the tools chiefly used for smoothing the surface of wood after it has been sawed to approximate size. In its simplest form,

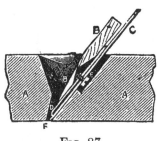

FIG. 87

a plane is a chisel firmly fixed into a block of wood by which it is guided in its cut, and the amount of wood taken off in the form of a shaving is reg-ulated to a nicety. In fact, such a simple tool actually is used sometimes, when a proper plane of the requisite shape and of a suitable size cannot be procured. To make the construction of an ordinary plane quite clear, a section of one is illustrated by Fig. 87, in which A shows the section of stock; B, the wedge; C, cutting iron; D, back iron; E, the screw for fastening irons together; and F is the mouth through which the shavings pass upwards. A plane is simply a copying tool, and a notch in the plane-iron at once proves that the pattern produced corresponds with the edge of the plane-iron, and all the imperfections of this edge will be copied on to the stuff. In all planing oper-ations the edge of the tool is the pattern, which is copied in reverse on the wood. If a hollow is required to be produced on the wood, a tool is used with a round edge of exactly similar form to the hollow we wish produced. In machine planing the pattern is the edge of the tool, which produces a similar surface upon the wood.

Direction of Grain in Planes.—For flat planes such as jack, try, and smoothing planes, the grain must be straight and, of course, run lengthways of the tool. The wood is selected from a center plank of beech as near to the bark as possible; in all planes, the wood nearest the bark, that being the hardest part of the wood, becomes the sole or working surface. The wood is seasoned thoroughly, and never is used until at least three years after cutting. Moulding planes mostly work on the spring, and need not have the grain so straight as flat planes. Hollows, rounds, and rebate planes are exceptional, however, and should have the grain as straight as possible, because the rebate plane is cut right through, and is liable to cast or warp if not quite straight-grained; and most of the hollows and rounds, being thin, are liable to cast also if not of straight, mild, and well-seasoned wood. Wood for plane making should be as free from knots as possible.

Jack and Trying Planes.—The jack plane, Fig. 88, is the first applied to the wood after it has been sawed This plane is always employed to remove the roughness of the work before finishing up with trying and smoothing planes. It is made up of five parts— namely, the stock (which should be 17 in. in length), the toat or handle, the wedge, the cutting iron or cutter (2⅛ in. broad), and back iron. Immediately behind the iron is a handle, which, in use, is grasped only by the right hand in planing fir; but in heavy planing, and especially in hardwood, it is necessary to place the left hand across the front of the plane to press it down, to cause the iron to take hold of the wood. When using both hands to the plane, the left is placed with the four fingers lying across the top near the fore end, the thumb passing down the near side. Well-seasoned beech is a suitable wood for the stock. The construction of the trying or truing plane is almost exactly the same as that of the jack

Fig. 88

plane, but it is much longer, so as to produce truer surfaces.

Using the Plane.—When using the plane, always keep the plane well oiled in front of the iron; be sure and work with the grain as shown in Fig. 89, whenever possible. A far thicker shaving can be taken off smoothly in this way than if worked as shown in Fig. 90, which is working against the grain and requires more careful work with a more finely set plane. Do not use the plane at an uncomfortable height. When the board to be planed is in position, and the worker takes hold of the plane ready to begin work, a line drawn through his elbow and wrist should be rather lower than higher at the wrist, though if the forearm is

level it will do fairly well.   Do not attempt to take off
thick shavings at the outset, and do not be disappointed if a shaving is not taken off from end to
end at the first trial.   If the wood has any hollow in
it, it will be impossible to do this, and even if it is
perfectly straight it is sometimes difficult to do it.

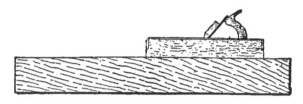

Fig. 89

There is always a tendency to plane off too much near
the bench stop, as the arm is apt to be raised at this
point.   Errors of this kind can be avoided by careful
practice and attention.   It is a good idea to try to
plane the center of the material rather than the margin,
for if a good plane is in proper order it is impossible
to make the work too hollow or concave; whereas

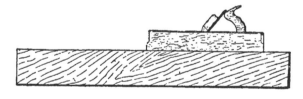

Fig. 90

however good the plane, careless use of it can and will
make the work convex in every direction.
   In making use of the smoothing plane for finishing
up stuff, it should be held as shown in Fig. 91, the
right hand grasping it firmly at the back, whilst the
left hand steadies it in front.   In starting, the tool is

applied to the fore-end of the board, and gradually worked backwards, thus taking out any marks previously used tools may have made.   It should be held firmly, and lifted sharply at the end of stroke, or a mark will be left where the plane finished.   The work is continued until the board presents a perfectly smooth surface, without marks of any kind.   The left hand should frequently be passed across the face of the board, as any marks made by the plane can be readily detected in this manner.   It may also with advantage be held so that the light passes across its surface from the side, thus showing up imperfect planing.   Should there be too much iron out, a few blows with the hammer at the back of the plane will draw it back.   Take care to tighten up the wedge again.   A few drops of linseed oil applied to the face of the plane will facilitate the planing.

Fig. 91

The proper method of setting an iron in a plane so that it will not show lines or marks on the work, is sometimes quite a difficult operation, as the iron is

Fig. 92

expected to be perfectly square and straight on the face.   It is always well to either round off the corners of the iron slightly, or grind them with a slight bevel, which will keep the corners from "digging in."

The smaller, or break-iron, whose office is to bend up the shaving somewhat sharply so as to ensure the cutting of the other iron, and to prevent its splitting off the surface of the work, should be placed so as to come within one-eighth of an inch of the extreme edge of the cutter for rough work, and within one-twentieth for finer or finishing work. The two should then be placed in position so that the edge projects the smallest possible degree below the sole. The position can only be determined by looking carefully along the

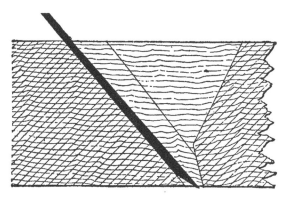

Fig. 93

bottom of the plane, with the front of the same next to the eye, as in Fig. 92. The edge will, if correctly formed and placed, appear quite parallel with the sole. It is then ready for use. The same rule applies to the small as to the large planes, except that in the jack-plane the iron projects rather more, as it is used for roughing down a surface. The trying-plane, which is longer, as before stated, and intended for edging boards which are to be joined lengthwise, is always very finely set, and the mouth is narrow. The break-

iron is also set very close down to the cutting edge.
The longer the plane the more accurately level and
true will be the work done by it.

New planes are often a source of trouble owing to
the shavings getting fast in the mouth, the plane
refusing to take any more until the wedge and iron
have been removed, and all cleaned out.   The cause
of this difficulty is that the mouth of the plane is too
narrow, as shown in Fig. 93.   Sometimes workmen cut

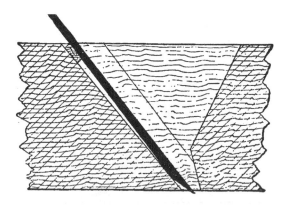

Fig. 94

a little out with a chisel, but in many instances this
results in spoiling the tool, because in a short time
the bottom of the plane wears away, and the mouth
gets larger, subsequently getting so large as to require
a piece to be set in to lessen the opening.   The mouth
of the plane can be kept open as long as needed by
gluing a strip of soft leather, about three-fourths of
an inch wide, in the mouth of the plane under the top
end of the iron as shown in Fig. 94.   When the plane
bottom is sufficiently worn the leather can be removed

and the iron put back into its original position. The leather causes the iron to be more upright, and consequently there is a larger opening in the mouth (two thicknesses can be put under if necessary).

Pitch of Plane Cutting Iron.—To assist the reader to understand correctly the principles of plane-iron sharpening, the following information is given. The seat of the plane-iron is made at different angles, to give the pitch to suit different kinds of work. The four angles most in use are as follows: Common pitch, in which the seat for the back of the iron is at an angle of 45° from the sole (this inclination is usually employed for all planes for soft wood); New York pitch, which has an angle of 50°, and is adapted for use with mahogany and other hard, stringy woods; middle pitch or 55°, and half pitch or 60°, which are employed with m o u l d i n g planes, the former being for

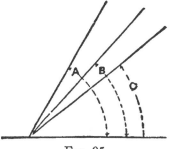

Fig. 95

soft wood and the latter for the harder kinds. Fig. 95 affords an idea of three angles, A giving the set of a half-pitched plane, B that of an ordinary plane, while C shows the inclination of an extra-pitched plane. The pitch or angle at which the cutter is set is of importance. There are three angles involved in this case: (1) The angle between the cutter and the surface of the work; this should be as small an angle as possible. It is obvious that if the surfaces of the cutter and the work were perfectly parallel, the cutter would glide over the surface without cutting, except under great pressure. By making the cutter edge rather than its whole surface touch the work, the tendency to cut and to continue the contact is secured. The angle, which may be called the clearance angle, or the back angle, should only be enough to secure this condition of contact. (2) The angle of the cutter itself. The more acute this angle the better, if only

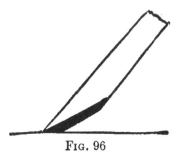

FIG. 96

the material will stand the strain and face the work without losing its edge. (3) The front or remaining angle may be found by subtracting both (1) and (2) from 180°, if dealing with plane surfaces, and is available for the passing away of the waste material; in the case of the plane, however, this is limited, in order to provide means to prevent the shaving being torn up in advance of the cutting action. This provision is made by the front portion of the plane, and to be efficacious must be in contact with the work and as near the edge of the cutter as possible to allow waste to escape. A few experiments with a knife will show that for soft materials a slight angle is best. This involves a thin knife, and its side almost in contact with the mate rial to be cut; but as harder things are tried the stiff-

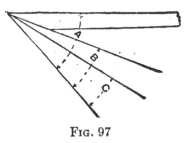

FIG. 97

ness of the cutter, and the consequent angle, must be increased, not because it is merely desirable, but because it is absolutely necessary to have a stronger cutter. The more upright an iron is set, the less liable is it to tear up the wood in planing; but in the same degree the iron loses its edge more quickly, is more likely. to jump and chatter, and is more laborious to work. In toothing planes the irons are set upright, and in "old woman's tooth," planes or routers nearly upright. In working with an upright iron, the action of the tool is a scraping one, while the more the iron is inclined the nearer it approaches the action of splitting the wood. For this reason an ordinary or extra-pitched plane is more liable to splinter up the surface of a piece of work; but this accident may be in great measure prevented by using a properly adjusted back iron. Moulding planes, rounds and hollows, bead planes, and others that work without a back iron, are usually preferred set to the half-pitch angle; while for

FIG. 98

working on end-grained stuff, extra-pitched tools, such as shoulder and bull-nosed planes, give the best results. In examining the side of a plane-iron, it is found to be made up of an iron back faced with steel. The steel, welded on to the iron and distinguished by its brighter color and finer grain, acts as a cutting edge, the iron being required to give sufficient stiffness to prevent chattering. When newly ground and sharpened, a plane-iron has three angles, one due to the pitch, A, Fig. 97, one made by the grindstone, B, and one made by the oilstone, C. The angles A and B do not alter, but C gradually becomes more acute with sharpening on the oilstone, until it lines with the face of the plane, as in Fig. 98, when the iron refuses to cut properly, and requires grinding. The pitch angle A (Fig. 96) varies in planes by different makers, as described above.

Oilstones for Sharpening Plane Irons.—A good oilstone, capable of putting a keen edge on the plane irons, is a necessity to all woodworkers, but more particularly to the hardwood finisher. The Washita stone, manufactured by the Pike Mfg. Co., or other fast cutting stones are useful for removing the waste or superfluous metal from the iron when it is too thick; but it is seldom that one of these stones can be trusted to leave a keen edge on the tool. Turkey and Washita stones are the only ones that have the two good qualities combined of cutting quickly and leaving a good edge.

FIG. 99

Most other oilstones are slow cutters, but they are to be relied on for leaving a good, keen edge. It is necessary that the oilstone should be kept perfectly level, or it will not be possible to get a true edge. The stone should also be free from grit, or the iron will be gapped in sharpening, and will leave ridges on the planed work. In sharpening the iron after it has been newly ground, the hands should be kept low to make the bevel correspond nearly with that made by the grindstone. As time goes on, when the iron is resharpened the hands are kept a little higher upon each occasion (see Fig. 97), until it becomes thick, as in Fig. 98; then it must be again put upon the grindstone. Some workers find it convenient to use two oilstones—one as a quick cutter, to some extent superseding the grindstone, the other for finishing the edge.

In using the oilstone, first put a few drops of good oil upon the stone, and grasp the iron as in Fig. 99; the right hand is at the top, and the thumb and fourth finger pass under. Place the whole of the fingers of the left hand upon the iron, with the thumb at the back, as seen. Now put the cutting edge (previously ground to a bevel) upon the stone in an oblique direction, as shown in

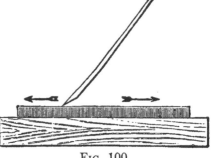

Fig. 100

Fig. 99, bearing in mind the previous remarks on the necessary inclination. The iron should now be rubbed up and down the stone, pressing it down with both hands. If the edge had been examined before placing it upon the stone, it would have been found to show a fine white line. The object of sharpening is to remove this, which must be done by rubbing on an oilstone. Having accomplished this, turn the iron face down upon the stone, and rub it lightly a few times (see Fig. 100). The iron should now have the appearances

Fig. 101

Fig. 102

indicated by Fig. 101. If the face of the iron has not been kept perfectly flat, it would appear as Fig. 98, and would be of no use as a cutting iron. If the iron has been rubbed too long, a wire edge will appear and utterly spoil the cutting properties of the iron unless removed. This may readily be done by rubbing the iron alternately upon each side until the wire edge falls off.

When the iron is judged to be sufficiently sharp, it should be cleaned, whetted on the left hand, and its edge tried for keenness. Some try the edge by passing the thumb gently across it, but its sharpness may be judged by looking directly at it. In a sharp tool the edge is not visible to the naked eye, while if the iron should be blunt, the edge will be seen as a bright line.

SECRET OR BLIND NAILING

Secret nailing is sometimes called "blind nailing," also "chip nailing" and "sliver nailing," and is the art of finishing work in a manner which leaves no mark of nail holes or screw heads exposed to view, which, under the ordinary method of doing work, would require puttying before the painter could apply the finish.

The process of secret nailing is only used on occasional jobs of hardwood finish where an extra fine job is required. The process is very simple and can be followed by any mechanic of ordinary skill and ability. Take a very thin and sharp paring chisel, ⅜ to ½ inch wide, to raise the "chip." A sharp knife should be used to make two cuts with the grain of the wood, the width of the chisel apart, to keep the sides of the chip from splitting. The chisel should be set at a steep angle at first, till the proper depth is reached, and then made to turn out a piece of wood of even thickness, about a sixteenth of an inch or near it, and of sufficient length to admit of driving the nail or screw. Care should be taken in raising the "chip" not to give it too sharp a curve or too great a thickness, as it is liable to break off while being straightened out again.

Some mechanics prefer a gouge for raising the "chip"; the gouge should be $\frac{5}{8}$ to $\frac{3}{4}$ of an inch wide and of a quick curve. In this case no knife is needed, as the corners of the gouge will cut the wood as it advances. The cut being made and the "chip" properly raised, a nail or screw may be driven in.

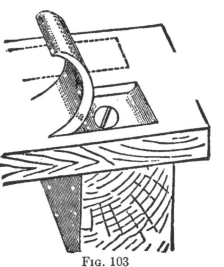

See that the nail or screw head is sunk below the surface of the recess, so that the "chip" will fit back in again without any obstruction. Now take properly prepared glue

FIG. 103

and apply to the "chip" and recess, and press the "chip" firmly in place, rubbing the face with a smooth block till the glue holds, and finish by using a little sandpaper.

If there is any difficulty about the "chip" breaking off, moisten the wood with a little water applied with a sponge to the part where the "chip" is to be raised. This will be found to be a great advantage if working on brittle wood.

As stated previously, when putting up hardwood

finish, where it is desired that no nail or screw heads should be in sight, it is always better to make use of glue whenever possible; this will be found to be much more satisfactory than blind nailing.

The methods of secret nailing, as described in the foregoing, are shown in the diagrams, Figs. 103 and 104. The first shows how a square chip is raised so that a screw or nail can be put in place, after which the raised chip *a* can be glued down in place, covering the head of nail or screw.

FIG. 104

Fig. 104 shows how the work is done by using a gouge instead of a chisel.

Sometimes blind nailing is done by driving headless nails in the edge of the work, "toe-nailing" them in the work just as matched flooring is laid. This is not a satisfactory way to do work and is not recommended, though there are cases where it will answer quite well.

PART TWO

WOOD FILLERS AND HOW TO APPLY THEM

There is no part of the art of wood-finishing that is more important than that of the filling, and the greatest of care should be exercised both in the choice of filler and the manner in which it is applied. The stain given to it must also be considered, in order that the color and texture of the wood being finished may not be disfigured or spoiled.

Fillers are used by all expert polishers for much the same reason that size is used before varnishing—viz., to prevent immoderate absorption of the polish by the wood. Polish, or even thick varnish, when applied to wood, sinks in or is absorbed in places, instead of remaining on the surface in a uniform coat. Here and there it will be observed that the polish or varnish has given more gloss than elsewhere. Where the gloss is brightest the varnish has sunk least.

The grain may be filled up by going over the wood with polish till the pores are closed, and some beginners may want to know why anything else in the nature of a filler should be used. The reason is that comparatively valuable French polish need not be used when a cheaper material serves the purpose, the use of which also saves time. Woods that are open in the grain and porous specially need a filler, while fine, close-grained woods do not, and may be polished without. Still, a suitable filler can do no harm to any kind of wood, however fine the grain may be, so there can be no disadvantage in going over it with one preparatory to polishing. Though it may be a slight waste of time, a preliminary rub over with polish suffices when working on a fine wood, such as olive or rosewood, which are both close and hard. To attain the desired thin, glossy film of shellac, which shall not be liable to grow dull unreasonably soon, the woods ordinarily used in furniture—ash, oak, mahogany, walnut, cherry, etc.—should have the grain filled, for they are all of comparatively open grain; ash and oak, being especially coarse, are called by polishers "hungry woods " Polishers usually give such woods one or more coats of spirit varnish as an aid to filling up the grain.

Before commencing the process of filling-in, thoroughly brush all dust out of the grain of the wood, for this is wood-dust, sand from the sandpaper, and dirt—all inimical to grain luster if mixed up with the grain stopper.

Amongst the best "fillers" is a preparation manufactured in Bridgeport, Conn., and known as "Wheeler's Wood-filler," and though it may cost a little more than home-made or other fillers, it is certain to give satisfaction. This filler has for its base a form of mineral silica in an atomic shape, which permits it to be ground or pulverized into a very fine, dust-like condition, in which each particle assumes a needle-pointed form, which enables them to enter into the pores of the wood and give to the work a gloss-like surface.

For filling a cheap class of work, many polishers content themselves with giving the work one or two coats of glue or patent size, heavily stained by the addition of some dry pigment. For mahogany finish add Venetian red till it gives quite a red tinge; for walnut add brown umber; for pine, add yellow ocher.

Apply the size hot with a brush, and rub it in lightly with a piece of rag, finishing the way of the grain, and taking care in the case of turned or moulded work to get the filler well in the recessed parts. Of course, work that has been sized will not need filling-in.

As many different kinds of fillers are used, and each has its advocates, it will be advisable to name the principal fillers used in the trade, and to make a few remarks about each, so that learners can experiment with them, and perhaps finally fix on that which may seem to suit best. All will be found reliable, for good work is turned out by polishers with any of them, and even an extremely prejudiced individual would hesitate to say that any one is really bad, though he uses only that which suits him best. Sometimes, owing to the price, he uses the easiest and quickest, irrespective of its quality.

Wood-fillers ready for use are made for most kinds of wood, and, as a rule, they require only thinning with a little turpentine. When it is desired to make a filler instead of purchasing one ready made, proceed as follows: Take a portion of either china clay or corn-flour; add boiling linseed oil, and stir until the mixture is of the consistency of putty. Then add patent dryers and thin with turpentine. If the wood on which the filler is to be used is to be kept light in color, use raw oil and the lightest variety of dryer. Further remarks on home-made fillers will be found later on.

In woods employed for house and cabinet work there are two distinct natures; therefore different treatment is required in finishing. First, there is the coarse or open-grained wood, having its surface perforated with innumerable pores or cells. In order to obtain a smooth and even finish, these pores should be filled up to a level with the hard grain, or, as the grainer would term them, the "lights" of the wood. Next we have the fine or close-grained wood, which, like the preceding, also contains these pores, but they are of a very fine character, and simply sealing them up with a liquid filler will enable one to produce a fine, smooth finish, which we shall consider farther on.

I will now return to the open or wide-grained wood, which requires more attention and care than the closer-grained wood, if the same results are expected. There are many things that will serve the purpose of fillers and make pretty fair work; among these may be mentioned china clay, silver white and corn-starch; the best of which is probably the last named. This is well adapted to the work, being equally useful with light, or when colored with dark wood; one fault with it is that it never hardens. China clay—the English is the best—makes an exceedingly good filler; it is light in color, very fine and dries as hard as cement.

There are a hundred ways of preparing fillers for use, and nearly as many different materials for making them; we would recommend, however, that wherever it is possible, Wheeler's patent wood filler be used; though we are aware that in many cases it may not be advisable to use it, and to meet these rare conditions the following mixtures may be substituted.

A filler should be so mixed that the greater portion of the vehicle will penetrate into the wood, leaving the pigment on the surface to be rubbed into the pores, and still retain enough combining property to form a hard and impenetrable surface. This depends entirely upon the proportions of the vehicles employed, and different pigments require different quantities of vehicle. Proceed with the mixing by filling the pot two-thirds full of the dry pigment, then add boiled linseed oil, producing the consistency of putty, then dilute with about one part japan and two parts turpentine. Should it be required to keep the wood as light as possible, replace the boiled oil with raw, using a smaller quantity, but a little more japan. For all light wood the light japan should be preferred, although there are many who never use anything but the common brown. Naphtha can also be employed in place of the turpentine, somewhat reducing the expense; but, as naphtha evaporates much faster, it prevents the operator from covering an extended surface without running the risk of having it dry hard. This causes difficulty at "rubbing it in" and wiping off the surplus, although "wiping off" should not proceed until the filler has flatted—or, at least, "set." This to a certain extent the operator can accelerate or retard by omitting or adding a small quantity of oil, keeping in view the fact that the smaller the quantity of oil used, the lighter colored, but the less durable, will be the finish.

Oil is sometimes used as a filler, but its use is not recommended; applied directly to the wood, its effect is to swell the fibers, or "raise the grain," which remains in that condition until the oil becomes entirely dry or disappears. During this time the fibers are gradually shrinking, and consequently moving or checking the varnish. The qualities essential to a good filler are that it shall readily enter the porous portion of the wood, and shall very soon harden and render the wood impervious to the varnish, which should lie smoothly upon the surface, giving brilliancy and effect to the natural beauty of the wood; and that

it shall not raise the grain of the wood; and that it
shall not change the color of the wood.   These conditions are satisfactorily fulfilled by few of the home-
made fillers ordinarily used in shops, and while I give
a number of recipes, my readers are advised that they
will obtain better satisfaction, at less cost, by purchasing some of the patent fillers now coming into general
use.   In these fillers very little oil is used and a large
amount of dryers, so that the wood becomes perfectly
dry and hard in a few hours, preventing any swelling
or shrinking of the fibers of the wood after the varn·sh
is applied.   The following fillers should be allowed to
dry until quite hard.   A period of about eight hours is
usually sufficient, but it is better to let the work stand
for twenty-four hours before touching it with sandpaper.   In applying a filler it should always be borne
in mind that the substance of wood consists of a
multitude of small tubes lying side by side.   These
tubes or cells are not continuous from top to bottom
of the tree, but are comparatively short and taper out
to points so that they are thickest in the middle.   Most
of the common woods have the walls of these tubes so
thin that liquid is readily absorbed by them and carried
into the substance for some distance.   Different kinds
of wood differ much in the shape and arrangement of
these cells.   In filling the pores the first step is taken
in providing an absolutely smooth surface.   We trust
mainly to mechanical force in rubbing in, aided by the
absorptive powers of the wood.   Formerly successive
varnishings and rubbings and scrapings took much
time, and when they were done, the final finish had
still to be applied, but the whole process has now been
simplified, by using fillers.

The careful workman will not leave "great daubs"

of superfluous filler here and there on the work, but will see that all corners and heads and quirks of mouldings are well cleaned off before it gets too hard to remove easily, and should there be any nail holes— which there ought not to be—he will have them filled with properly colored putty or cement and nicely smoothed down before he makes any attempt to put on his finishing coats.

Among the many home-made fillers I have endeavored to select the best.

Walnut Filler.—For Medium and Cheap Work. Ten lb. bolted English whiting, 3 lb. dry burnt umber, 4 lb. Vandyke brown, 3 lb. calcined plaster, ½ lb. Venetian red, 1 gal. boiled linseed oil, ½ gal. spirits turpentine, 1 quart black japan. Mix well and apply with brush; rub well with excelsior or tow, clean off with rags.

Walnut Filler.—For Imitation Wax-Finish. Five lb. bolted whiting, 1 lb. calcined plaster, 6 oz. calcined magnesia, 1 oz. dry burnt umber, 1 oz. French yellow, 1 quart raw linseed oil, 1 quart benzine spirits, ½ pint very thin white shellac. Mix well and apply with a brush. Rub well in and clean off with rags. Before using the above filling, give the work one coat of white shellac. When dry, sandpaper down and apply the filler.

Walnut Filler.—For First-Class Work. Three lb. burnt umber ground in oil, 1 lb. burnt sienna ground in oil, 1 quart spirits of turpentine, 1 pint brown japan. Mix well and apply with a brush; sandpaper well; clean off with tow and rags. This gives a beautiful chocolate color to the wood.

Filler for Light Woods.—Five lb. bolted English whiting, 3 lb. calcined plaster, 1 lb. corn-starch, 3 oz.

calcined magnesia, ½ gallon raw linseed oil, 1 quart spirits of turpentine, 1 quart brown japan, and sufficient French yellow to tinge the white. Mix well and apply with a brush, rub in with excelsior or tow, and clean off with rags.

Filler for Cherry.—Five lb. bolted English whiting, 2 lb. calcined plaster, 1½ oz. dry burnt sienna, 1 oz. Venetian red, 1 quart boiled linseed oil, 1 pint spirits of turpentine, 1 pint brown japan. Mix well, rub in with excelsior or tow and clean off with rags.

Filler for Oak.—Five lb. bolted English whiting, 2 lb. calcined plaster, 1 oz. dry burnt sienna, ½ oz. dry French yellow, 1 quart raw linseed oil, 1 pint benzine spirits, ½ pint white shellac. Mix well, apply with brush, rub in with excelsior or tow, and clean off with rag.

Filler for Rosewood.—Six lb. bolted English whiting, 2 lb. calcined plaster, 1 lb. rose pink, 2 oz. Venetian red, ½ lb. Vandyke brown, ½ lb. brandon red, 1 gallon boiled linseed oil, ½ gallon spirits of turpentine, 1 quart black japan. Mix well, apply with brush, rub in with excelsior or tow, and clean off with rags.

Another.—Stir boiled oil and corn-starch into a very thick paste; add a little japan, and reduce with turpentine, but add no color for light ash. For dark ash and chestnut use a little raw sienna; for walnut, burnt umber, add a small quantity of Venetian red; for bay wood, burnt sienna. In no case use more color than is required to overcome the white appearance of the starch, unless it is wished to stain the wood. The filler is worked with brush and rags in the usual manner. Let it dry forty-eight hours, or until it is in condition to rub down with No. 0 sandpaper without much gumming up, and if an extra fine finish is desired, fill again with the same materials, using less oil, but more of japan and turpentine.

Another.—Take three papers corn-starch, one quart boiled linseed oil, two quarts turpentine, one-quarter pint japan; cut in half the turpentine before mixing; it will not cut perfectly otherwise. For dark woods add burnt umber to color. When nearly dry, rub off with cloths. The above mixture must be used fresh, as it is of no value after it is four or five days old. The cloths used in rubbing as above mentioned should be destroyed immediately after use, as spontaneous combustion is likely to ensue from the ingredients employed. As a filler of wood to be stained, apply French plaster of Paris, mixed as a creamy paste with water, and after rubbing in, clean any surplus off; or use whiting finely powdered, or white lead slacked with painters' drying oil, and used as a filler. Another process is that of oiling, then rubbing crosswise to the grain with a sponge dipped in thin polish composed of melted beeswax, resin, and shellac, and smoothing the surface, when dry, with pumice-stone, or fine glass paper. Embody the work a second time with thicker polish, or a mixture of polish and varnish. The rubbers will work easily with half the quantity of oil which is ordinarily used. This second body should be rubbed very smooth with moist putty.

In the use of any filler, care must be taken in the selection of color, for the employment of a light colored filler on dark wood or *vice versa* would result in gross defacement, as the lighter color would show at the pores of the wood in the one case, and the darker in the other. Therefore, to avoid this, the filler should be as near as possible the color of the wood to be filled.

As a general thing, paint manufacturers who do not make fillers a specialty use opaque colors to stain their filler, as it requires a less quantity. This will do sometimes, but not always. But those which give to the wood a clear and bright appearance, and therefore produce the best results, are stained with transparent colors; those chiefly employed are burnt umber and sienna, Venetian red, Vandyke brown and charcoal black, the charcoal being ground fine in oil, while the others can be used dry and according to the following recipes with good results:

In mixing any or all dark fillers the same pigments used for the light (previously described) should be kept for a basis, with sufficient coloring to stain it to the desired depth of shade.

Filler for walnut is very often stained with burnt umber; this is reddish in hue and gives to the wood a pleasing effect. Others use Venetian red, darkened somewhat with lampblack; this is rather opaque, and tends to deaden the color of the wood. There is another article—namely, Vandyke brown—which gives fair results. In order to obtain a rich effect, the filler should be made considerably darker than the wood when new.

Fillers for mahogany, cherry, California redwood, and other woods of similar shade, should be stained with bunrt sienna, as they should be finished very clear. It is well to know that charcoal black and Venetian red will give the desired shade for any dark-colored wood in common use or for all colors in antique, but it does not show up quite as clear as some other combinations.

For rosewood, charcoal as a stain will suffice, and for vanilla or Brazil-wood the use of rose-pink will give good results.

The methods of mixing these fillers are quite numerous. It is impossible to give the proportions definitely, owing to the strength of the colors or the transparency of the chief ingredient, but one cannot go astray by following the preceding rules.

Mix the light pigment to a paste with boiled oil, which must be well stirred up. Then in another pot mix a quantity of the colored pigment with turpentine or naphtha; and when thoroughly "cut," or dissolved, add sufficient of it to the light to give the shade required. After this is obtained, dilute with turpentine or naphtha and japan, as directed in mixing light filler. This applies to all colors except black, which is seldom obtained finely ground unless in oil, and properly thinned down.

There are many finishers and firms who exclusively use manufactured fillers, and in consequence meet with many difficulties as to the shade they require, as different manufacturers use different colors to stain their filler. But this difficulty can be overcome by a few experiments with the above-named stains.

As the foregoing gives pretty nearly all the fillers in general use, with the exception of some of the manufactured mineral preparations of which I will have more to say further on, I will now proceed to describe the method of application. The secret of this is to do the work well, quickly and economically. These points are dealt with in the following:

Have your filler mixed to the consistency of ordinary lead paint; then apply to the prepared surface of the wood with a pound brush, or, what is still better, a 3-0 or 4-0 oval chisel varnish brush. In applying the filler it is not necessary to cover all the small beads and carvings; and if the filler be light, better avoid coating them at all; and if dark or antique, stain them with a little of the filler, much reduced with spirits of turpentine. For this purpose have at hand a small pot with a small fitch or sash tool.

By not filling the beads and carvings, the varnish is not so liable to run down in them, although sufficient remains to produce a finish equal to the balance of the surface.

After enough surface has been covered with the filler, so that what has been first applied begins to flatten, the process of wiping should immediately begin, using for that purpose either a rag or a handful of waste or excelsior. If the wood is very open grained, waste is preferable. With a piece of this that has previously been used and is pretty well supplied with filler, rub crosswise of the grain, rather rubbing it into the grain than wiping it off. After the whole surface has been gone over in this way, take a clean piece of waste or rag (never use excelsior for wiping clean) and wipe the surface perfectly clean and free from filler, using a wooden pick (Fig. 105), the point of which has been covered with a rag or waste, to clean out the corners, beads, etc. It is well to give these picks some attention, as a person once accustomed to certain tools can accomplish more and better work than with tools that feel strange in his hands; therefore, each finisher should furnish his own pick. As to their construction, these are best made from second-growth hickory, which can be procured at any carriage repair shop, such as old spokes, broken

FIG. 105

felloes, etc. They are made eight inches in length, half inch oval at one end and tapering down to the point at the other. Sharpen the oval end like a cold chisel, then smooth with sandpaper, which should also be used to sharpen the tool when the same becomes worn dull.

This picking out of the filler from beads, etc., can be accelerated by the use of picking brushes, several of which I show in Fig. 106, and which are manu. factured especially for that purpose, but it is not

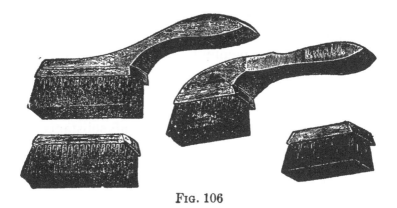

Fig. 106

advisable to use them on very coarsely grained wood, as they scrub the filler out of the pores.

There are several fillers used which do not require this picking and scrubbing. One is a liquid filler used chiefly for carriage finishing; but it can be used successfully on butternut, bird's-eye maple, curly maple, satinwood, hickory, etc. It is made from gum and oil. Another is a filler made from finely ground pumice-stone, mixed as other fillers. It is applied with a brush, and must be left to dry at least twenty-four hours; it is then sandpapered smooth, when an oil varnish is applied, rendering it completely transparent. This last can be used only upon light wood.

The workman, as a matter of course, will understand that different woods require slightly different treatment, and the finer-grained woods, among which are the pines, maples, cedars and poplars, of different varieties, and birch, cherry, beech, sycamore, white box, satinwood, etc., require no filling, not that a filling would prove detrimental to the finish—except upon stained work or white holly, which in order to maintain a clear color should never be filled—but, from the condition of all fine wood, it is superfluous, and only causes unnecessary labor and expense. At this point it will be convenient to pause to consider the subject of mineral or prepared wood-fillers.

A great deal of time and money have been wasted in attempting to make good fillers, to no purpose, and a great variety—as I have shown—of substances, as chalk, plaster of Paris, corn-starch, etc., etc., have been mixed with various vehicles and rubbed into the wood with but indifferent success. Most of these compounds labor under the disadvantages of forming chemical compounds with the oil and consequently they shrink very much on drying, so that though the surface may appear smooth when they are first put on, waves and hollows make their appearance as they dry. These waves, having round edges, are difficult to fill, the second coat building up as much or more upon the level spaces as in the hollows. It sometimes seems almost impossible with these fillers in the latter coats to make the hollows hold any substance, the filler clinging chiefly to the surfaces.

I have thought it necessary to show how the ordinary or home-made fillers act, and fail, in order to show by contrast how much easier it is to work efficiently with the mineral fillers. The mineral quartz, when mixed with oil, probably shrinks less in drying than any other similar known mixture. If a surface of wood be covered with this and then rubbed, the sharp and angular particles of the silica imbed themselves in the pores of the wood, closing them up, while the oil cements them fast. This is the foundation of Wheeler's wood filler, which we recommend for use by all wood finishers. When the pores have been filled with silica, and are cemented fast by the proper mixture of gums and oils, the difficult part of the work is done.

After a good surface has been made upon the article it is ready for the filler, which is to be selected according to the color desired. In putting the filler on, it is thinned with turpentine until about like flowing varnish, and is applied with a brush. Only so much of the surface is covered as can be cleaned off before it hardens. When it has set so that the gloss has left the surface, it is at once rubbed off with excelsior or shavings, going across the grain with the strokes. If the filler dries too fast or too light, a little raw linseed oil may be used in it.

Perhaps a better material for rubbing off than excelsior is hemp, or "flax tow." At any rate, the work should be finished with some finer material than excelsior.

For a nicer job the filler is rubbed in with a rubber, made by gluing a piece of sole or belt leather on the face of a block of wood and trimming the edges flush with the block. The rubbing is done after the filler has set and before it is cleaned off. If it dries off too light, a little white japan may be added on nice work.

The light-colored filler should be used on all work where light and dark woods are used together. The filling, it must be understood, is done by the silica, which will often be found in the shape of a sediment in the bottom of the mixture. Eight hours is generally considered a sufficient time for the filler to dry.

When the work with the filler is done, the surface of the wood ought to be like so much ground glass. Such portions of the wood as show a solid grain need very little filler. On Georgia pine, after the filler is dry, a little rubbing in the direction of the grain with very fine sandpaper is an advantage. If the filler has been properly used the desired results will be obtained with little labor.

The wood is now in a condition to receive the final coatings. Whether the work is to be polished or "dead finished," do not employ shellac or "French polish." If a "dead" surface is wanted, wax finish is easily put on, and as easily rubbed to a good surface. Several manufacturers in this country prepare a wax finish, which is a convenient preparation of wax and gums, and can be applied with a brush and then rubbed down with a woolen cloth, tied up to make a hard rubber, until a fine, lusterless surface is obtained. With mahogany and similar woods this greatly improves the color of the wood. When this has dried, which will be in the course of a few hours, the work is ready for use. The wax finish, like many of the furniture creams, has the advantage that it can be put on in a few minutes at any time to brighten up work when it has become dull. A piece of work prepared in this way, after four operations, will present as fine an appearance as the best cabinet work found in the furniture stores.

The materials which have been described, it will be noticed, are both manufactured articles. The prepared filler is indispensable; the wax finish can be made by mixing together, by the aid of heat, white wax and spirits of turpentine until they are of the consistency of thick paste. Another wax finish is made of beeswax, spirits of turpentine and linseed oil in equal parts. The addition of two drams of alkanet root to every twenty ounces of turpentine darkens and enriches the color. The root is to be put into a little bag and allowed to stand in the turpentine until it is sufficiently colored.

An altogether more durable surface can be made by a little change in the treatment. When the wood is filled, instead of applying the wax, take some hard oil finish, "Luxeberry," a preparation manufactured in Detroit, Mich., and put it on with a brush precisely like varnish. The coat should not be too heavy, especially on vertical surfaces, and the brush used ought to be a good one. This material gives a most brilliant polish. By rubbing it down with a woolen cloth and pumice-stone powder it can also be made dull. Hard-oil finish does not spot with hot or cold water, is slightly elastic and is not injured by pretty severe soaking in water. It gets hard in twelve hours or less in warm weather, and overnight in winter time. It is one of the best surfaces which can be used, and has the advantage of working very well in the hands of one who is not an expert in the art of finishing wood or handling varnish. It will make a very fair surface applied direct to the unfilled wood, in which case it is a good substitute for shellac.

Wax finish has the advantage that scratches can be easily repaired without sending to the cabinetmaker or the painter. Here a word of advice to the carpenter who does any work of this character may save him some trouble and make way for the further use of the same kind of finish. When the woodwork of a house is treated in this way, be sure to leave a little bottle of the wax polish with the housekeeper, with directions as to the method of using it. In sending out a "what-not," bookcase, or any other article of similar kind, put up a little bottle of the polish and show the owner, or, preferably the lady of the house, how to repair any little scratch and make the work look "as good as new." The fresh appearance of the work will be a good advertisement, while it will prevent complaints and dissatisfaction that often follow the use of work which, when injured, cannot be restored.

It may be said that either of the methods of finishing involves a great deal of labor. This is true; but the amount is not much greater than is needed for three coats of paint, and the cost of the paint would probably be more than the cost of the finish. The labor in one case can be of a cheap character, and in the other an experienced painter must be employed. The profit upon the "dead finish" can go into the pocket of the carpenter, while that of the painting must in any event be divided between the carpenter and painter, or belong to the latter altogether, who is, after all, the proper person to do the work.

I have now said about all that is necessary in the matter of "fillers" and "filling," but, as it sometimes happens that the old system of "sizing" has to be resorted to for certain kinds of work, I give herewith a formula for its construction and use:

Size of different kinds is sometimes applied to the

surface of wood to prevent absorption of the varnish. The kind of material used for the size is not important, the object being only to prevent absorption by a very thin coat of some substance not soluble in the varnish. For dark-colored wood, thin size, made by reducing ordinary glue with water, is generally used; but for lighter-colored surfaces a white size is used, which is prepared by boiling white kid or other leather or parchment-cuttings in water for a few hours, or until it forms a thin, jelly-like substance, which is reduced with water to a thin consistency, and used in a tepid state. Sometimes solutions of isinglass or tragacanth are employed in like manner. Unlike the best fillers, sizes of any kind do not improve the finish, and are sometimes a positive detriment to it. They are used solely as an economy to reduce the quantity of the varnish needed; their use is not recommended for the best work.

WOOD-STAINING GENERALLY

There are many cases where an article constructed of wood may be more conveniently and suitably finished by staining and polishing than by painting. The practice of staining woods is much less common in America and England than on the Continent, where workmen, familiar with the different washes, produce the most delicate tones of color and shade. Wood is often stained to imitate darker and dearer varieties, but more legitimately to improve the natural appearance by heightening and bringing out the original markings, or by giving a definite color without covering the surface and hiding the nature of the material by coats of paint. The best woods for staining are those of close, even texture, as pear and cherry, birch, beech, and maple, though softer and coarser kinds may be treated with good effect. The wood should be dried, and if an even tint is desired, its surface planed and sandpapered. All the stains should, if possible, be applied hot, as they thus pene trate more deeply into the pores. If the wood is to be varnished, and not subjected to much handling, almost any of the brilliant mordants used in wool and cotton dyeing may be employed in an alcoholic solution; but when thus colored it has an unnatural appearance, and is best used on small surfaces only, for inlaying, etc. The ebonized wood, of late years so much in vogue, is in many respects the most unsatisfactory of the stains, as the natural character and markings are completely blotted out, and it shows the least scratch or rubbing. Sometimes, in consequence of the quality of the wood under treatment, it must be freed from its natural colors by a preliminary bleaching process. To this end it is saturated as completely as possible with a clear solution of 17¼ oz. chloride of lime and 2 oz. soda crystals, in 10½ pints water. In this liquid the wood is steeped for ½ hour, if it does not appear to injure its texture. After this bleaching, it is immersed in a solution of sulphurous acid to remove all traces of chlorine, and then washed in pure water. The sulphurous acid, which may cling to the wood in spite of washing, does not appear to injure it, nor alter the colors which are applied.

Black.—(1) Obtained by boiling together blue Brazil-wood, powdered gall-apples, and alum, in rain or river water, until it becomes black. This liquid is then filtered through a fine organdie, and the objects painted with a new brush before the decoction has cooled, and this repeated until the wood appears of a fine black color. It is then coated with the following liquid: A mixture of iron filings, vitriol, and vinegar is heated (without boiling), and left a few days to settle. Even if the wood is black enough, yet, for the sake of durability, it must be coated with a solution of alum and nitric acid, mixed with a little verdigris; then a decoction of gall-apples and logwood dyes is used to give it a deep black. A decoction may be made of brown Brazil-wood with alum in rainwater, without gall-apples; the wood is left standing in it for some days in a moderately warm place, and to it merely iron filings in strong vinegar are added, and both are boiled with the wood over a gentle fire. For this purpose soft pear-wood is chosen, which is preferable to all others for black staining.

(2) 1 oz. nut-gall broken into small pieces, put into barely ½ pint vinegar, which must be contained in an open vessel; let stand for about ½ hour; add 1 oz. steel filings; the vinegar will then commence effervescing; cover up, but not sufficient to exclude all air. The solution must then stand for about 2½ hours, when it will be ready for use. Apply the solution with a brush or piece of rag to the article, then let it remain until dry; if not black enough, coat it until it is—each time, of course, letting it remain sufficiently long to dry thoroughly. After the solution is made, keep it in a closely corked bottle.

(3) One gal. water, 1 lb. logwood chips, ½ lb. black copperas, ½ lb. extract of logwood, ½ lb. indigo blue, 2 oz. lampblack. Put these into an iron pot and boil them over a slow fire. When the mixture is cool, strain it through a cloth, add ¼ oz. nut-gall. It is then ready for use. This is a good black for all kinds of cheap work.

(4) Two hundred fifty parts of Campeachy wood, 2000 water, and 30 copper sulphate; the wood is allowed to stand 24 hours in this liquor, dried in the air, and finally immersed in iron nitrate liquor at 4° B.

(5) Boil 8¾ oz. logwood in 70 oz. water and 1 oz. blue stone, and steep the wood for 24 hours. Take out, expose to the air for a long time, and then steep for 12 hours in a solution of iron nitrate at 4° B. If the black is not fine, steep again in the logwood liquor.

(6) It is customary to employ the clear liquid obtained by treating 2 parts powdered galls with 15 parts wine, and mixing the filtered liquid with a solution of iron protosulphate. Reimann recommends the use of water in the place of wine.

(7) Almost any wood can be dyed black by the following means: Take logwood extract such as is found in commerce, powder 1 oz., and boil it in 3¼ pints of water; when the extract is dissolved, add 1 dr. potash yellow chromate (not the bichromate), and agitate the whole. The operation is now finished, and the liquid will serve equally well to write with or to stain wood. Its color is a very fine dark purple, which becomes a pure black when applied to the wood.

(8) For black and gold furniture, procure 1 lb. logwood chips, add 2 qt. water, boil 1 hour, brush the liquor in hot, when dry give another coat. Now procure 1 oz. green copperas, dissolve it in warm water, well mix, and brush the solution over the wood; it will bring out a fine black; but the wood should be dried outdoors, as the black sets better. A common stove brush is best. If polish cannot be used, proceed as follows: Fill up the grain with black glue—i.e., thin glue and lampblack—brushed over the parts accessible (not in the carvings); when dry, paper down

with fine paper. Now procure, say, a gill of French polish, in which mix 1 oz. best ivory black, or gasblack is best, well shake it until quite a thick pasty mass, procure ½ pint brown hard varnish, pour a portion into a cup, add enough black polish to make it quite dark, then varnish the work; two thin coats are better than one thick coat. The first coat may be sandpapered down where accessible, as it will look better. A coat of glaze over the whole gives a piano finish. N.B.—Enough varnish should be mixed at once for the job to make it all one color—i.e., good black.

(9) For table. Wash the surface of table with liquid ammonia, applied with a piece of rag; the varnish will then peel off like a skin; afterwards smooth down with fine sandpaper. Mix ¼ lb. lampblack with 1 qt. hot water, adding a little glue size; rub this stain well in; let it dry before sandpapering it; smooth again. Mind you do not work through the stain. Afterwards apply the following black varnish with a broad, fine camel-hair brush: Mix a small quantity of gas-black with the varnish. If one coat of varnish is not sufficient, apply a second one after the first is dry. Gas-black can be obtained by boiling a pot over the gas, letting the pot nearly touch the burner, when a fine jet black will form on the bottom, which remove, and mix with the varnish. Copper vessels give the best black; it may be collected from barbers' warming pots.

(10) Black-board wash, or "liquid slating."—(a) Four pints 95 per cent alcohol, 8 oz. shellac, 12 dr. lampblack, 20 dr. ultramarine blue, 4 oz. powdered rotten stone, 6 oz. powdered pumice. (b) 1 gal. 95 per cent alcohol, 1 lb. shellac, 8 oz. best ivory black, 5 oz.

finest flour emery, 4 oz. ultramarine blue. Make a perfect solution of the shellac in the alcohol before adding the other articles. To apply the slating, have the surface smooth and perfectly free from grease; well shake the bottle containing the preparation, and pour out a small quantity only into a dish, and apply it with a new flat varnish brush as rapidly as possible. Keep the bottle well corked, and shake it up each time before pouring out the liquid. (c) Lampblack and flour of emery mixed with spirit varnish. No more lampblack and flour of emery should be used than are sufficient to give the required black abrading surface. The thinner the mixture the better. Lampblack should first be ground with a small quantity of spirit varnish or alcohol to free it from lumps. The composition should be applied to the smoothly planed surface of a board with a common paint brush. Let it become thoroughly dry and hard before it is used. Rub it down with pumice if too rough. (d) ½ gal. shellac varnish, 5 oz. lampblack, 3 oz. powdered iron ore or emery; if too thick, thin with alcohol. Give 3 coats of the composition, allowing each to dry before putting on the next; the first may be of shellac and lampblack alone. (e) To make 1 gal. of the paint for a blackboard, take 10 oz. pulverized and sifted pumice, 6 oz. powdered rotten stone (infusorial silica), ¾ lb. good lampblack, and alcohol enough to form with these a thick paste, which must be well rubbed and ·round together. Then dissolve 14 oz. shellac in the ·emainder of the gallon of alcohol by digestion and ιgitation, and finally mix this varnish and the paste together. It is applied to the board with a brush, care being taken to keep the paint well stirred, so that the pumice will not settle. Two coats are usually necessary.

The first should be allowed to dry thoroughly before the second is put on, the latter being applied so as not to disturb or rub off any portion of the first. One gallon of this paint will ordinarily furnish 2 coats for 60 sq. yd. of blackboard. When the paint is to be put on plastered walls, the wall should be previously coated with glue size—1 lb. glue, 1 gal. water, enough lampblack to color; put on hot. (*f*) Instead of the alcohol mentioned in *b*, take a solution of borax in water; dissolve the shellac in this and color with lampblack. (*g*) Dilute soda silicate (water-glass) with an equal bulk of water, and add sufficient lampblack to color it. The lampblack should be ground with water and a little of the silicate before being added to the rest of the liquid

(11) 17.5 oz. Brazil-wood and 0.525 oz. alum are boiled for 1 hour in 2.75 lb. water. The colored liquor is then filtered from the boiled Brazil-wood, and applied several times boiling hot to the wood to be stained. This will assume a violet color. This violet color can be easily changed into black by preparing a solution of 2.1 oz. iron filings, and 1.05 oz. common salt in 17.5 oz. vinegar. The solution is filtered, and applied to the wood, which will then acquire a beautiful black color.

(12) 8.75 oz. gall-nuts and 2.2 lb. logwood are boiled in 2.2 lb. rain-water for 1 hour in a copper boiler. The decoction is then filtered through a cloth, and applied several times while it is still warm to the article of wood to be stained. In this manner a beautiful black will be obtained.

(13) This is prepared by dissolving 0.525 oz. logwood extract in 2.2 lb. hot rain-water, and by adding to the logwood solution 0.035 oz. potash chromate.

When this is applied several times to the article to be stained, a dark brown color will first be obtained. To change this into a deep chrome-black, the solution of iron filings, common salt, and vinegar, given under (11) is applied to the wood, and the desired color will be produced.

(14) Several coats of alizarine ink are applied to the wood, but every coat must be thoroughly dry before the other is put on. When the articles are dry, the solution of iron filings, common salt, and vinegar, as given in (11), is applied to the wood, and a very durable black will be obtained.

(15) According to Herzog, a black stain for wood, giving to it a color resembling ebony, is obtained by treating the wood with two fluids, one after the other. The first fluid to be used consists of a very concentrated solution of logwood, and to 0.35 oz. of this fluid are added 0.017 oz. alum. The other fluid is obtained by digesting iron filings in vinegar. After the wood has been dipped in the first hot fluid, it is allowed to dry, and is then treated with the second fluid, several times if necessary.

(16) Sponge the wood with a solution of aniline chlorhydrate in water, to which a small quantity of copper chloride is added. Allow it to dry, and go over it with a solution of potassium bichromate. Repeat the process two or three times, and the wood will take a fine black color.

Blue.—(1) Powder a little Prussian blue, and mix to the consistency of paint with beer; brush it on the wood, and when dry size it with glue dissolved in boiling water; apply lukewarm, and let this dry also; then varnish or French polish.

(2) Indigo solution, or a concentrated hot solution

of blue vitriol, followed by a dip in a solution of washing soda.

(3) Prepare as for violet, and dye with aniline blue.

(4) A beautiful blue stain is obtained by graduallv stirring 0.52 oz. finely powdered indigo into 4.2 oz. sulphuric acid of 60 per cent, and by exposing this mixture for 12 hours to a temperature of 77° F. (25° C.). The mass is then poured into 11-13.2 lb. rain-water, and filtered through felt. This filtered water is applied several times to the wood, until the desired color has been obtained. The more the solution is diluted with water, the lighter will be the color.

(5) 1.05 oz. finest indigo carmine, dissolved in 8.75 oz. water, applied several times to the articles to be stained. A very fine blue is in this manner obtained.

(6) 3.5 oz. French verdigris are dissolved in 3.5 oz. urine and 8.75 oz. wine vinegar. The solution is filtered and applied to the article to be stained. Then a solution of 2.1 oz. potash carbonate in 8.75 oz. rain-water is prepared, and the article colored with the verdigris is brushed over with this solution until the desired blue color makes its appearance.

(7) The newest processes of staining wood blue are those with aniline colors. The following colors may be chosen for the staining liquor: Bleu de Lyon (reddish blue), bleu de lumiere (pure blue), light blue (greenish blue). These colors are dissolved in the proportion of 1 part coloring substance to 30 of spirit of wine, and the wood is treated with the solution.

Brown.—(1) Various tones may be produced by mordanting with potash chromate, and applying a decoction of fustic, of logwood, or of peachwood.

(2) Sulphuric acid, more or less diluted according to the intensity of the color to be produced, is applied

with a brush to the wood, previously cleaned and dried. A lighter or darker brown stain is obtained, according to the strength of the acid. When the acid has acted sufficiently, its further action is arrested by the application of ammonia.

(3) Tincture of iodine yields a fine brown coloration, which, however, is not permanent unless the air is excluded by a thick coating of polish.

(4) A simple brown wash is ½ oz. alkanet root, 1 oz. aloes, 1 oz. dragons' blood, digested in 1 lb. alcohol. This is applied after the wood has been washed with aqua regia, but is, like all the alcoholic washes, not very durable.

Ebonizing.—(1) Boil 1 lb. logwood chips 1 hour in 2 qt. water; brush the hot liquor over the work to be stained, lay aside to dry; when dry give another coat, still using it hot. When the second coat is dry, brush the following liquor over the work: 1 oz. green copperas to 1 qt. hot water, to be used when the copperas is all dissolved. It will bring out an intense black when dry. For staining, the work must not be dried by fire, but in the sunshine, if possible; if not, in a warm room, away from the fire. To polish this work, first give a coating of very thin glue size, and when quite dry paper off very lightly with No. 0 paper, only just enough to render smooth, but not to remove the black stain. Then make a rubber of wadding about the size of a walnut, moisten the rubber with French polish, cover the whole tightly with a double linen rag, put one drop of oil on the surface, and rub the work with a circular motion. Should the rubber stick it requires more polish. Previous to putting the French polish on the wadding pledget, it ought to be mixed with the best drop black, in the proportion of

¼ oz. drop black to a gill of French polish. When the work has received one coat, set it aside to dry for about an hour. After the first coat is laid on and thoroughly dry, it should be partly papered off with No. 0 paper. This brings the surface even, and at the same time fills up the grain. Now give a second coat as before. Allow 24 hours to elapse, again paper off, and give a final coat as before. Now comes "spiriting off." Great care must be used here, or the work will be dull instead of bright. A clean rubber must be made, as previously described, but instead of being moistened with polish it must be wetted with spirits of wine placed in a linen rag screwed into a tight, even-surfaced ball, just touched on the face with a drop of oil, and then rubbed lightly and quickly in circular sweeps all over the work from top to bottom. One application of spirits is usually enough if sufficient has been placed on the rubber at the outset, but it is better to use rather too little than too much at a time, as an excess will entirely remove the polish, when the work will have to be polished again. Should this be the case, paper off at once, and commence as at first. It is the best way in the end. (*Smither.*)

(2) Lauber dissolves extract of logwood in boiling water until the solution indicates 0° Beaumé. Five pints of the solution is then mixed with 2½ pints pyroligneous iron mordant of 10°, and ½ pint acetic acid of 2°. The mixture is heated for ¼ hour, and is then ready for use.

(3) To imitate black ebony, first wet the wood with a solution of logwood and copperas, boiled together and laid on hot. For this purpose, 2 oz. logwood chips with 1½ oz. copperas, to 1 qt. water, will be required. When the work has become dry, wet the

surface again with a mixture of vinegar and steel
filings.   This mixture may be made by dissolving 2 oz.
steel filings in ½ pint vinegar.   When the work has
become dry again, sandpaper down until quite smooth.
Then oil and fill in with powdered drop black mixed in
the filler.   Work to be ebonized should be smooth and
free from holes, etc.   The work may receive a light
coat of quick-drying varnish, and then be rubbed with
finely pulverized pumice and linseed oil until very
smooth.

(4) One gal. strong vinegar, 2 lb. extract of logwood,
½ lb. green copperas, ¼ lb. China blue, and 2 oz.
nut-gall.   Put these in an iron pot, and boil them over
a slow fire till they are well dissolved.   When cool,
the mixture is ready for use.   Add to the above ½ pint
iron rust, which may be obtained by scraping rusty
hoops, or preferably by steeping iron filings in a
solution of acetic acid or strong vinegar.

(5) Common ebony stain is obtained by preparing
two baths; the first, applied warm, consists of a logwood decoction, to every quart of which 1 dr. alum is
added; the second is a solution of iron filings in
vinegar.   After the wood has dried from the first, the
second is applied as often as is required.   For the
first-named bath, some substitute 16 oz. gall-nut, 4
oz. logwood dust, and 2 oz. verdigris, boiled in a
sufficient quantity of water.   A peculiar method of
blackening walnut is in use in Nürnberg.   On one of
the Pegnitz Islands there is a large grinding-mill, turned
·by the stream, where iron tools are sharpened and
polished.   The wood is buried for a week or more in
the slime formed by the wheels; when dug out it is
jet black, and so permeated by silica as to be in effect
petrified.   Another way to ebonize flat surfaces of soft

work is to rub very fine charcoal dust into the pores with oil. This works beautifully with basswood and American whitewood. A brown mahogany-like stain is best used on elm and walnut. Take a pint decoction of 2 oz. logwood in which ½ oz. barium chloride has been dissolved. This gives also, when diluted with soft water, a good oak stain to ash and chestnut. But the most beautiful and lasting of the browns is a concentrated solution of potash permanganate (mineral chameleon). This is decomposed by the woody fiber and forms hydrated manganese oxide, which is permanently fixed by the alkali.

(6) For the fine black ebony stain, apple, pear, and hazel wood are the best woods to use; when stained black, they are most complete imitations of the natural ebony. For the stain take: gall-apple, 14 oz.; rasped logwood, 3½ oz ; vitriol, 1¾ oz.; verdigris, 1¾ oz. For the second coating a mixture of iron filings (pure), 3½ oz., dissolved in strong wine vinegar; 1½ pint is warmed, and when cool the wood already blackened is coated 2 or 3 times with it, allowing it to dry after each coat. For articles which are to be thoroughly saturated, a mixture of 1¾ oz. sal-ammoniac, with a sufficient quantity of steel filings, is to be placed in a suitable vessel, strong vinegar poured upon it, and left for 14 days in a gently heated oven. A strong lye is now put into a suitable pot, to which is added coarsely bruised gall-apples and blue Brazil shavings, and exposed for the same time as the former to the gentle heat of an oven, which will then yield a good liquid. The woods are now laid in the. first-named stain, boiled for a few hours, and left in it for 3 days longer; they are then placed in the second stain and treated as in the first. If the articles are not then

thoroughly saturated, they may be once more placed in the first bath, and then in the second. The polish used for wood that is stained black should be "white" (colorless) polish, to which a very little finely ground Prussian blue should be added.

(7) Wash with a concentrated aqueous solution of logwood extract several times; then with a solution of iron acetate of 14° B., which is repeated until a deep black is produced.

(8) Beech, pear-tree, or nolly steeped in a strong liquor of logwood or galls. Let the wood dry, and wash over with solution of iron sulphate. Wash with clean water, and repeat if color is not dark enough. Polish either with black or common French polish.

(9) Oak is immersed for 48 hours in a hot saturated solution of alum, and then brushed over several times with a logwood decoction prepared as follows: Boil 1 part best logwood with 10 of water, filter through linen, and evaporate at a gentle heat until the volume is reduced one-half. To every quart of this add 10 to 15 drops of a saturated solution of indigo, completely neutral. After applying this dye to the wood, rub the latter with a saturated and filtered solution of verdigris in hot concentrated acetic acid, and repeat the operation until a black of the desired intensity is obtained. Oak thus stained is said to be a close as well as handsome imitation of ebony.

(10) One lb. logwood chips, 3 pints water; boil to 1 pint; apply hot to wood; let dry; then give another coat; let dry slowly; sandpaper smooth; mix 1 gill vinegar with 3 tablespoonfuls iron or steel filings; let stand 5 hours, then brush on wood; let dry; then give another coat of the first. This sends the vinegar deeper into the wood and makes a denser black; after

which paper smooth. Then polish with white French polish, as the white brings out the black purer than common French polish. The woods observed to take on the stain best are pear-tree, plane-tree, and straight-reeded birch; mahogany does not stain nearly so well as the former woods.

(11) Get 1 lb. logwood chips and boil them down in enough water to make a good dark color; give the furniture 3 or 4 coats with a sponge; then put some rusty nails or old iron into a bottle with some vinegar, and when it begins to work give the furniture a coat of the vinegar. This, if you have well darkened it with the first, will give you a good black. Oil and polish in the usual way, rubbing down first with fine paper if required. A quicker way is to give the wood a coat of size and lampblack, and then use gas-black in your polish rubber

(12) Make a strong decoction of logwood by boiling 1 lb. in 1 qt. water for about 1 hour; add thereto a piece of washing soda as large as a hazel-nut. Apply hot to the wood with a soft brush. Allow to dry, then paint over the wood with a solution of iron sulphate (1 oz. to the pint of water). Allow this to dry, and repeat the logwood and iron sulphate for at least 3 times, finishing off with logwood. Once more allow to dry thoroughly, then sandpaper off very lightly (so as not to remove the dye) with No. o paper. Now make a very thin glue size, boil in it a few chips of logwood and a crystal or two of iron sulphate, just sufficient to make it inky black. Paint this lightly over the work, allow to dry once more, again sandpaper lightly, and finally either varnish with good hard white varnish, or polish with French polish and drop black.

Floors.—(1) Get the wood clean, have some Vandyke brown and burnt sienna ground in water, mix it in strong size, put on with a whitewash or new paint brush as evenly as you can. When dry, give 2 coats of copal or oak varnish.

(2) If the floor is a new one, have the border well washed. Polish with sandpaper, rubbing always with the grain of the wood. Varnish with good oak varnish, put coloring matter into the varnish to suit your taste, but umber is best; if the floor is old and blackened, paint it.

(3) If old floors, you will not make much of staining anything but black. The floor is to be well washed (lime and soda is best—no soap), the dye painted on, and, when dry, sized over and varnished with elastic oak varnish.

(4) Take ½ lb. logwood chips, boil them briskly for ½ hour in about 5 qt. rain-water, and strain through muslin. To this liquor add 6 oz. annatto (in the form of cake—not the roll); add also 1 lb. of yellow wax cut up in very small pieces. Place these over the fire, and let the wax melt, gently stirring it all the while. When melted, take the mixture off the fire; do not let it boil. Then with a paint brush lay it on the floor as hot as possible, brushing it always the way of the grain. Next day polish with a hard, flat brush made of hair, which may have a strap nailed to the back of it in which to insert the foot. The floor is afterwards kept bright with beeswax alone, a little of which is melted and put on the brush. Take care that the floor is thoroughly dry before commencing operations.

(5) Melt some glue size in a bottle; next get a piece of rag, roll it into a ball so that it will fit the hand

nicely, cover this with a bit of old calico to make a smooth face; dip this into the size, and rub in a bit of brown umber; then go ahead with your floors, working the stuff light or dark as required. Keep the motion with the grain of wood; when dry, stiffen with polishers' glaze.

(6) Take Judson's dyes of the color required, mix according to the instructions given with each bottle, and apply with a piece of rag, previously trying it on a piece of wood to see if color would suit; rub with sandpaper to get off any roughness that may be raised with the damp, and varnish with fine, pale hard varnish, then slightly sandpaper and varnish again. Another method is to boil 1 lb. logwood in an *old* boiler, then apply with a piece of rag where the stain is required; when thoroughly dry, sandpaper as before, and well rub with beeswax to polish. This last process looks best when finished, but it requires a lot of elbow grease for a few months, and is extremely durable. To prevent the stain running where you do not want it, paste some stout paper.

(7) As a general rule, 1 qt. of the staining liquid will be found sufficient to cover about 16 sq. yd. of flooring; but different kinds of woods absorb in different proportions, soft woods requiring more for the same space than hard woods. The colors of the stains are various, so that one may either choose ebony, walnut, mahogany, rosewood, satinwood, oak, medium oak, or maple, according to the paleness or depth of color desired. Besides this, 4 lb. of size and 2½ pints of the best varnish are required to finish the 16 yd. above mentioned. The necessary purchases are completed by a good-sized painters' brush and a smaller one. The work can then be commenced. If

the wood is uneven, it must be planed, and rubbed down to a smooth surface; whilst the cracks and spaces between the boards, if very wide, may be disposed of by a process called "slipping," by which pieces of wood are fitted in. The floor must next be carefully washed, and allowed to dry thoroughly. The actual staining may now be proceeded with. The liquid is poured out into a basin, and spread all over the floor with the aid of the large brush, the small one being used to do the corners and along the wainscoting, so that it may not be smeared. It is always best to begin staining at the farthest corner from the doorway, and work round so that one's exit may not be impeded. It is also a good plan to work with the window open, if there is no danger of much dust flying in, as the staining dries so much quicker. After the floor is quite covered, the stainer may rest for about an hour whilst the drying is going on, during which there is only one thing relative to the work in hand which need be attended to. This is the size, which should be put in a large basin with ½ pint of cold water to each pound, and then stood in a warm place to dissolve. Before recommencing work, also, the brushes must be washed, and this is no great trouble, as a little lukewarm water will take out all trace of the stain and clean them quite sufficiently. The sizing is then laid on in exactly the same manner as the staining, always being careful to pass the brush lengthwise down the boards. If the size froths or sticks unpleasantly, it must be a little more diluted with warm water, and sometimes, if the sediment from it is very thick, it is all the better for being strained through a coarse muslin. The sizing takes rather longer than the varnish to dry, 2 or more hours being necessary, even on a warm, dry day.

Not until it is quite dry, however, can the last finish be put to the work with the varnish. For this it is always safest to get the very best, and to lay it on rather literally, though very evenly, and over every single inch, as the staining will soon rub off when not protected by it. The best way to ascertain whether it is varnished all over is to kneel down and look at the floor sideways, with one's eyes almost on a level with it.

Green.—(1) Mordant the wood with red liquor at 1° B. This is prepared by dissolving separately in water 1 part sugar of lead and 4 of alum free from iron; mix the solutions, and then add $\frac{1}{32}$ part of soda crystals, and let settle overnight. The clear liquor is decanted off from the sediment of lead sulphate, and is then diluted with water till it marks 1° B. The wood when mordanted is dyed green with berry liquor and indigo extract, the relative proportions of which determine the tone of the green.

(2) Verdigris dissolved in 4 parts water.

(3) 4.2 oz. copper, cut up finely, are gradually dissolved in 13 oz. nitric acid (aqua fortis), and the articles to be stained are boiled in this solution until they have assumed a fine green color.

Gray.—(1) Grays may be produced by boiling 17 oz. orchil paste for ½ hour in 7 pints water. The wood is first treated with this solution, and then, before it is dry, steeped in a beck of iron nitrate at 1° B. An excess of iron gives a yellowish tone; otherwise a blue gray is produced, which may be completely converted into blue by means of a little potash.

(2) One part silver nitrate dissolved in 50 of distilled water; wash over twice; then with hydrochloric acid, and afterwards with water of ammonia.

The wood is allowed to dry in the dark, and then finished in oil and polished.

Mahogany.—(1) Boil ½ lb. madder and 2 oz. log-wood chips in 1 gal. water, and brush well over while hot. When dry, go over with pearlash solution, 2 dr. to the quart. By using it strong or weak, the color can be varied at pleasure.

(2) Soak 1 lb. stick varnish in 2 qt. water until all the color is dissolved out; strain off the water, and add to the residue 25 dr. powdered madder. Set the mixture over the fire until it is reduced to ¾ of its original volume. Then mix together 25 dr. cochineal, 25 dr. kermes berries, 1 pint spirits of wine, and ½ oz. pearlash, out of which the color has been washed by soaking in a gill of soft water. Add this mixture to· the decoction of madder and varnish, stirring well together, and adding so much aqua fortis as will bring the red to the desired shade.

(3) DARK MAHOGANY.—Introduce into a bottle 15 gr. alkanet root, 30 gr. aloes, 30 gr. powdered dragons' blood, and 500 gr. 95 per cent alcohol, closing the mouth of the bottle with a piece of bladder, keeping it in a warm place for 3 or 4 days, with occasional shaking, then filtering the liquid. The wood is first mordanted with nitric acid, and when dry washed with the stain once or oftener, according to the desired shade; then, the wood being dried, it is oiled and polished.

(4) LIGHT MAHOGANY.—Same as dark mahogany, but the stain being only applied once. The veins of true mahogany may be imitated by the use of iron acetate skillfully applied.

(5) The following process is recommended in "Wiederhold's Trade Circular:" The coarse wood is

first coated with a colored size, which is prepared by thoroughly mixing up, in a warm solution, 1 part commercial glue in 6 of water, a sufficient quantity of the commercial mahogany brown, which is in reality an iron oxide, and in color stands between so-called Indian red and iron oxide. This is best effected by adding in excess a sufficient quantity of the dry color with the warm solution of glue, and thoroughly mixing the mass by means of a brush until a uniform paste is obtained, in which no more dry red particles are seen. A trial coat is then laid upon a piece of wood. If it is desired to give a light mahogany color to the object, it is only necessary to add less, and, for a darker color, more, of the brown body-color. When the coat is dry, it may be tested, by rubbing with the fingers, whether the color easily separates or not. In the former case, more glue must be added until the dry trial coat no longer perceptibly rubs off with the hands. Having ascertained in this way the right condition of the size color with respect to tint and strength, it is then warmed slightly, and worked through a hair sieve by means of a brush. After this, it is rubbed upon the wood surface with the brush, which has been carefully washed. It is not necessary to keep the color warm during the painting. Should it become thick by gelatinizing, it may be laid on the wood with the brush, and dries more rapidly than when the color is too thin. If the wood is porous and absorbs much color, a second coat may be laid on the first when dry, which will be sufficient in all cases. On drying, the size color appears dull and unsightly, but the following coat changes immediately the appearance of the surface. This coat is spirit varnish. For its production 3 parts spirits of wine of 90° are added in excess to 1 part of red acaroid resin in one vessel, and in another 10 parts shellac with 40 of spirits of wine of 80%. By repeated agitation for 3 or 4 days, the spirit dissolves the resin completely. The shellac solution is then poured carefully from the sediment, or, better still, filtered through a fine cloth, when it may be observed that a slight milky turbidity is no detriment to its use. The resin solution is best filtered into the shellac solution by pouring through a funnel loosely packed with wadding. When filtered, the solutions of both resins are mixed by agitating the vessel and letting the varnish stand a few days. The acaroid resin colors the shellac, and imparts to it at the same time the degree of suppleness usually obtained by the addition of Venetian turpentine or linseed oil. If the varnish is to be employed as a coat, the upper layers are poured off at once from the vessel. One or two coats suffice, as a rule, to give the object an exceedingly pleasing effect. The coats dry very quickly, and care must be taken not to apply the second coat until the first is completely dry.

(6) 7.5 oz. madder, 8.75 oz. rasped yellow wood, are boiled for 1 hour in 5.5 lb. water, and the boiling liquor is applied to the articles until the desired color has been produced.

(7) 1.05 oz. powdered turmeric, 1.05 oz. powdered dragons' blood, are digested in 8.75 oz. of 80 per cent strong alcohol, and when the latter seems to be thoroughly colored it is filtered through a cloth. The filtrate is heated and applied warm to the article.

(8) 17.5 oz. madder, 8.75 oz. ground logwood, are boiled for 1 hour in 5.5 lb. water. This is filtered while still warm, and the warm liquor is applied to the wood. When this has become dry, and it is

desired to produce a darker mahogany color, a solution of 0.525 oz. potash carbonate in 4.4 lb. water is applied to the wood. This solution is prepared cold, and filtered through blotting-paper.

(9) 0.35 oz. aniline is dissolved in 8.75 oz. spirits of wine 90 per cent strong. Then another solution of 0.35 oz. aniline yellow in 17.5 oz. spirits of wine 90 per cent strong is made, and this is added to the aniline solution until the required reddish-yellow color is obtained. By adding a little of a solution of aniline brown (0.35 oz. aniline brown in 10.5 oz. spirits of wine 90 per cent strong), the color is still more completely harmonized, and a tint very closely resembling mahogany can be given to elm and cherry wood with this mixture.

(10) 0.7 oz. logwood is boiled in 3.5 oz. water down to about ½. This is then filtered, and 0.12 oz. baryta chloride is dissolved in it.

Oak.—(1) Mix powdered ocher, Venetian red, and umber, in size, in proportions to suit; or a richer stain may be made with raw sienna, burnt sienna, and Vandyke. A light yellow stain of raw sienna alone is very effective.

(2) Darkening Oak.—Lay on liquid ammonia with a rag or brush. The color deepens immediately, and does not fade; this being an artificial production of the process which is induced naturally by age. Potash bichromate, dissolved in cold water and applied in a like manner, will produce a very similar result.

(3) In Germany, the cabinetmakers use very strong coffee for darkening oak. To make it very dark: iron filings with a little sulphuric acid and water, put on with a sponge, and allowed to dry between each application until the right hue is reached.

(4) Whitewash with fresh lime, and when dry brush off the lime with a hard brush, and dress well with linseed oil. It should be done after the wood has been worked, and it will make not only the wood, but the carving or moulding, look old also.

(5) Use a strong solution of common washing-soda, say one or two coats, until the proper color is obtained. Or you may try potash carbonate. Paper and finish off with linseed oil.

(6) A decoction of green walnut-shells will bring new oak to any shade, or nearly black.

(7) A good method of producing the peculiar olive brown of old oak is by fumigation with liquid ammonia; the method has many advantages beyond the expense of making a case or room airtight and the price of the ammonia. It does not raise the grain, the work keeping as smooth as at first. Any tint, or rather, depth of the color can be given with certainty; and the darker shade of color will be found to have penetrated to the depth of a veneer, and much farther where the end grain is exposed, thus doing away with the chance of an accidental knock showing the white wood. The coloring is very even and pure, not destroying the transparency of the wood. It is advisable to make the furniture from one kind of stuff, not to mix white oak with red, and so on. They both take the color well, but there is a kind of American live oak that does not answer well. In all cases care must be taken to have no glue or grease on the work, which would cause white spots to be left. The deal portions of the work are not affected in the least, neither does it affect the sap of oak. The best kind of polish for furniture treated in this manner is wax polish, or the kind known as egg-shell polish. The

process of fumigation is very simple. Get a large packing case, or better still, make a room in a corner of the polishing shop about 9 ft. long, 6 ft. high, and 3 ft. 6 in. wide; pass paper over the joints; let the door close on to a strip of india-rubber tubing; put a pane of glass in the side of box or house to enable you to examine the progress of coloring. In putting in your work see that it does not touch anything to hinder the free course of the fumes. Put 2 or 3 dishes on the floor to hold the ammonia; about ½ pint is sufficient for a case this size. The ammonia differs in purity, some leaving more residue than others. Small articles can be done by simply covering them with a cloth, having a little spirits in a pot underneath. A good useful color can be given by leaving the things exposed to the fumes overnight. The color lightens on being polished, owing to the transparency thus given to the wood.

Purple.—(1) Take 1 lb. logwood chips, ¾ gal. water, 4 oz. pearlash, 2 oz. powdered indigo. Boil the logwood in the water till the full strength is obtained, then add the pearlash and indigo, and when the ingredients are dissolved the mixture is ready for use, either warm or cold. This gives a beautiful purple.

(2) To stain wood a rich purple or chocolate color, boil ½ lb. madder and ¼ lb. fustic in 1 gal. water, and when boiling brush over the work until stained. If the surface of the work should be perfectly smooth, brush over the work with a weak solution of nitric acid; then finish with the following: put 4½ oz. dragons' blood and 1 oz. soda, both well bruised, into 3 pints spirits of wine. Let it stand in a warm place, shake frequently, strain and lay on with a soft brush,

repeating until a proper color is gained.   Polish with linseed oil or varnish.

(3) 2.2 lb. rasped logwood, 5.5 lb. rasped Lima red dyewood are boiled for 1 hour in 5.5 lb. water.   It is then filtered through a cloth and applied to the article to be stained until the desired color has been obtained. In the meanwhile a solution of 0.175 oz. potash carbonate in 17.5 oz. water has been prepared, and a thin coat of this is applied to the article stained red. But strict attention must be paid not to apply too thick a coat of this solution, or else a dark blue color would be the result.

Red.—(1) The wood is plunged first in a solution of 1 oz. of curd soap in 35 fl. oz. water, or else is rubbed with the solution; then magenta is applied in a state of sufficient dilution to bring out the tone required. All the aniline colors behave very well on wood.

(2) For a red stain, a decoction of ¼ lb. logwood and ½ oz. potash in 1 lb. water is used as the bath, being fixed by a wash of alum water.   For scarlet, use 1 oz. cochineal, 6 oz. powdered argol, 4 oz. cream tartar, in 12 oz. tin chloride (scarlet spirits).

(3) Take 1 qt. alcohol, 3 oz. Brazil-wood, ½ oz. dragons' blood, ½ oz. cochineal, 1 oz. saffron.   Steep to full strength and strain.   It is a beautiful crimson stain for violins, work-boxes, and fancy articles.

(4) Beside the aniline colors, which are, however, much affected by sunlight, cochineal gives a very good scarlet red upon wood.   Boil 2 oz. cochineal, previously reduced to a fine powder, in 35 oz. of water for 3 hours, and apply it to the wood.   When dry, give it a coating of dilute tin chloride to which is added a little tartaric acid—1 oz. tin chloride and ½ oz. tartaric acid in 35 fl. oz. water.   If, instead of water,

the cochineal is boiled in a decoction of bark (2 oz. bark to 35 oz. water), and the tin chloride is used as above, an intense scarlet and all shades of orange may be produced according to the proportions.

(5) Take 1 gal. alcohol, 1½ lb. camwood, ½ lb. red sanders, 1 lb. logwood extract, 2 oz. aqua fortis. When dissolved, it is ready for use. It should be applied in 3 coats over the whole surface. When dry, rub down to a smooth surface, using for the purpose a very fine paper. The graining is done with iron rust, and the shading with asphaltum thinned with spirits of turpentine. When the shading is dry, apply a thin coat of shellac; and when that is dry, rub down with fine paper. The work is then ready for varnishing—a fine rose tint.

(6) Monnier recommends steeping the wood for several hours in a bath of 1200 gr. potassium iodide to the quart of water, and then immersing it in a bath of 375 gr. corrosive sublimate, when it will assume a beautiful rose-red color by chemical precipitation. It should subsequently be covered with a glossy varnish. The baths will not need renewal for a long time.

(7) 2.2 lb. finely powdered Lima red dyewood and 2.1 oz. potash carbonate are put in a glass bottle and digested in 5.5 lb. water for 8 days in a warm place; the bottle should be frequently shaken. It is then filtered through a cloth; the fluid is heated, and applied to the article to be stained until the latter acquires a beautiful color. If it is desired to brighten the color, a solution of 2.1 oz. alum, free from iron, in 2.2 lb. water is applied to the article while it is still wet. The last solution can be prepared by heat; when it has been accomplished, it is filtered. As soon as the stains have become dry, they should be rubbed

with a rag moistened with linseed oil, after which the
varnish may be applied.

Satinwood.—Take 1 qt. alcohol, 3 oz. ground
turmeric, 1½ oz. powdered gamboge. When steeped
to its full strength, strain through fine muslin. It is
then ready for use. Apply with a piece of fine sponge,
giving the work 2 coats. When dry, sandpaper down
very fine. It is then ready for polish or varnish, and
is a good imitation of satinwood.

Violet.—The wood is treated in a bath made up with
4¼ oz. olive oil, the same weight of soda-ash, and
2½ pints boiling water, and it is then dyed with
magenta to which a corresponding quantity of tin
crystals has been added.

Walnut.—Deal and other common woods are stained
to imitate polished walnut in various ways. (1) One
method is, after careful rubbing with glass-paper, to go
over the surface with a preparation of Cassel brown
boiled in a lye of soft-soap and soda. After drying,
the surface is rubbed over with pumice and oil, and
polished with shellac. The Cassel brown will not take
equally well on all kinds of wood, so that if not laid
on thick it sometimes comes off under the subsequent
pumicing; whilst on the other hand this same thickness
conceals, more or less, the grain on the wood beneath,
giving it the appearance of having been painted.

(2) Others use instead a decoction of green walnut-
shells, dried and boiled in the same lye, or in soft
water to which soda has been added. The decoction
of walnut-shells is apt to come off on the clothes as a
yellowish, adhesive substance.

(3) Others, again, employ catechu and potash
chromate in equal parts, boiled separately and afterwards mixed. The mixture of catechu and potash

chromate leaves a reddish-brown deposit on the surface of the wood, very unlike real walnut.

(4) The following is said to be a very superior method for staining any kind of wood in imitation of walnut, while it is also cheap and simple in its manipulation. The wood, previously thoroughly dried and warmed, is coated once or twice with a stain composed of 1 oz. extract of walnut peel dissolved in 6 oz. soft water by heating it to boiling, and stirring. The wood thus treated, when half dry, is brushed with a solution of 1 oz. potash bichromate in 5 oz. boiling water, and is then allowed to dry thoroughly, and is to be rubbed and polished as usual. Red beech and alder, under this treatment, assume a most deceptive resemblance to American walnut. The color is fixed in the wood to a depth of one or two lines.

(5) Mix dragons' blood and lampblack in methylated spirits till you get the color required, and rub it well into the grain of the wood

(6) LIGHT WALNUT.—Dissolve 1 part potassium permanganate in 30 of pure water, and apply twice in succession; after an interval of 5 minutes, wash with clean water, and when dry, oil and polish.

(7) DARK WALNUT.—Same as for light walnut, but after the washing with water the dark veins are made more prominent with a solution of iron acetate.

(8) In the winter season get some privet berries (black), which grow in most gardens, and put 2 oz. in ½ pint solution of liquid ammonia. This, applied to pine, varnished or polished, cannot be detected from real walnut itself.

(9) Take 1 gal. very thin sized shellac; add 1 lb. dry burnt umber, 1 lb. dry burnt sienna, and ¼ lb. lampblack. Put these articles into a jug and shake

frequently until they are mixed. Apply one coat with a brush. When the work is dry, rub down with fine paper, and apply one coat of shellac or cheap varnish. It will then be a good imitation of solid walnut, and will be adapted for the back boards of mirror-frames, for the back and inside of casework, and for similar work.

(10) Take 1 gal. strong vinegar, 1 lb. dry burnt umber, ½ lb. fine rose pink, ½ lb. dry burnt Vandyke brown. Put into a jug and mix well; let the mixture stand one day, and it will then be ready for use. Apply this stain to the sap with a piece of fine sponge; it will dry in ½ hour. The whole piece is then ready for the filling process. When the work is completed, the stained part cannot be detected even by those who have performed the job. By means of this recipe, wood of poor quality and mostly of sap can be used with good effect.

(11) DARKENING WALNUT.—Slaked lime, 1 to 4 of water, will do for some kinds of walnut; a weak solution of iron sulphate for others; and yet again for other kinds a weak solution of pearlash. Try each on the wood, and choose the one you like best.

(12) To give to walnut a dark color resembling rosewood, Hirschberg uses a solution of 0.17 oz. potash bichromate in 1.05 oz. water. This solution is applied to the walnut with a sponge, and the wood is then pumiced and polished.

(13) By a simple staining, furniture of pine or birch wood can be easily made to appear as if it had been veneered with walnut veneer. For this a solution of 3.15 oz. potash manganate, and 3.15 oz. manganese sulphate in 5.25 qt. hot water, is made. This solution is applied to the wood with a brush, and must be

repeated several times. The potash manganate is decomposed when it comes in contact with the woody fiber, and thus a beautiful and very durable walnut color is obtained. If small wooden articles are to be stained in this manner, a very diluted bath is prepared; the articles are dipped into it, and kept there 1 to 9 minutes, according as the color is desired lighter or darker.

Yellow.—(1) Mordant with red liquor, and dye with bark liquor and turmeric.

(2) Turmeric dissolved in wood naphtha.

(3) Aqua regia (nitro-muriatic acid), diluted in 3 parts water, is a much-used though rather destructive yellow stain.

(4) Nitric acid gives a fine permanent yellow, which is converted into dark brown by subsequent application of tincture of iodine.

(5) Wash over with a hot concentrated solution of picric acid, and when dry, polish the wood.

(6) ORANGE-YELLOW TONE TO OAK WOOD.—According to Niedling, a beautiful orange-yellow tone, much admired in a chest at the Vienna Exhibition, may be imparted to oak wood by rubbing it in a warm room with a certain mixture until it acquires a dull polish, and then coating it after an hour with thin polish, and repeating the coating of polish to improve the depth and brilliancy of the tone. The ingredients for the rubbing mixture are about 3 oz. tallow, ¾ oz. wax, and 1 pint oil of turpentine, mixed by heating together and stirring.

(7) 0.5 oz. nitric acid (aqua fortis) is compounded with 1.57 oz. rain-water, and the article to be stained is brushed over with this. Undiluted nitric acid gives a brownish-yellow color.

(8) 2.1 oz. finely powdered turmeric are digested for several days in 17.5 oz. alcohol 80 per cent strong, and then strained through a cloth. This solution is applied to the articles to be stained. When they have become entirely dry, they are burnished and varnished.

(9) 1.57 oz. potash carbonate are dissolved in 4.2 oz. rain-water. This solution is poured over 0.52 oz. annotto, and this mixture is allowed to stand for 3 days in a warm place, being frequently shaken in the meanwhile. It is then filtered, and 0.175 oz. spirit of sal-ammoniac is added to it. The stain is now ready, and the articles to be stained will acquire a very beautiful bright yellow color by placing them in it.

(10) BRIGHT GOLDEN YELLOW. — 0.52 oz. finely powdered madder is digested for 12 hours with 2.1 oz. diluted sulphuric acid, and then filtered through a cloth. The articles to be stained are allowed to remain in this fluid 3 to 4 days, when they will be stained through.

Most of the foregoing is taken from English, French, and German sources, but the following are methods usually adopted in American practice; but it is just as well that the finisher should be conversant, to some extent, with the practice of other nationalities as well as that of his own.

Stains may be classified as follows: Those made with oil and color, those made with spirits and color, those made with water and coloring matter other than anilines, and those made with water and anilines. Generally, spirit stains are made with anilines.

Water stains are those in which the coloring matter is mixed with water. A good mahogany water stain is made as follows: Fustic chips, 4 oz.; madder root, ½ lb.; water about 4 qt. This should boil for several hours and should be applied boiling hot, after being well strained.

For walnut: Vandyke brown, 1 lb.; strong lye, ½ pt.; water, 3 qt. This should boil down to about three pints, and should be applied to the wood when cold with a sponge or pad.

A good cherry stain can be made by mixing a pound of Spanish annotto, an ounce of strong lye, and water. Boil forty minutes. If not deep enough in color, boil more, and add a little gamboge to darken it.

There is very little difference between cherry and mahogany stains; the latter are somewhat darker, but may be reduced to answer.

Aniline stains are easily made, and are usually very even and free from cloudy spots when properly laid on. All or any of anilines will dissolve in water, oil, or alcohol, but will dissolve much quicker in warm liquid than in cold. Time will therefore be saved by having the medium hot.

One example of making a water stain from anilines will answer for the whole group. If for mahogany, use Bismarck brown, 1 oz.; add 3 qt. water boiling hot; stir until the brown is all dissolved. When cool it is ready to apply.

Many excellent stains for pine may be obtained by using the ordinary graining colors, Vandyke brown, raw and burnt sienna, ultramarine blue, etc., applied with a brush, without previous preparation, and then wiped off with a cloth—a method that brings out clearly the grain or marks of the wood, which in pitch pine, now being extensively used for fittings, are often extremely beautiful. A better method for general work, French polish being ordinarily too expensive, is where dark oak or mahogany stains are not wanted,

light varnishes, of which two coats are to be applied. The glue size with which the work is first coated, in order to fill up the pores of the wood, should not be too thick, as in that case it is liable to crack.

Logwood, lime, brown soft soap, dyed oil, sulphate of iron, nitrate of silver exposed to the sun's rays, carbonate of soda, bichromate and permanganate of potash, and other alkaline preparations, are used for darkening the wood; the last three are specially recommended. The solution is applied by dissolving one ounce of the alkali in two gills of boiling water, diluted to the required tone. The surface is saturated with a sponge or flannel, and immediately dried with soft rags. The carbonate is used for dark woods. Oil tinged with rose madder may be applied to hardwoods like birch, and a red oil is prepared from soaked alkanet root in linseed oil. The grain of yellow pine can be brought out by two or three coats of japan, much diluted with turpentine, and afterwards oiled and rubbed. To give mahogany the appearance of age, lime water used before oiling is a good plan. In staining wood, the best and most transparent effect is obtained by repeated light coats of the same. For oak stain a strong solution of oxalic acid is employed; for mahogany, dilute nitric acid. A primary coat or a coat of wood fillers is advantageous. For mahogany stains, the following are given: two ounces of dragons' blood dissolved in one quart of rectified spirits of wine, well shaken, or raw sienna in beer, with burnt sienna to give the required tone; for darker stains boil half-pound of madder and two ounces of logwood chips in one gallon of water, and brush the decoction while hot over the wood; when dry, paint with a solution of two ounces of potash in one quart of water.

A solution of permanganate of potash forms a rapid and excellent brown stain.

Oak or ash may be stained brown by using linseed oil and benzine half and half, and burnt umber or Vandyke brown incorporated with this. Maple can be stained green-gray by using copperas in water; oak will also be changed to a dark green blue through the same agency, the effect on ash being various shades of olive green. Ammonia applied to oak produces the bronze olive tint now used so much by architects.

Wash any compact wood with a boiling decoction of logwood three or four times, allowing it to dry between each application. Then wash it with a solution of acetate of iron, which is made by dissolving iron filings in vinegar. This stain is very black, and penetrates to a considerable depth into the wood, so that ordinary scratching or chipping does not show the original color.

A wash of one part of nitric acid in ten parts of water will, if well done, impart a stain resembling mahogany to pine wood which does not contain much resin. When the wood is thoroughly dry, shellac varnish will impart a fine finish to the surface. A glaze of carmine or lake will produce a rosewood finish. A turpentine extract of alkanet root produces a beautiful stain which admits of French polishing. Asphaltum, thinned with turpentine, makes an excellent mahogany color on new wood.

When describing the treatment of different kinds of wood, which will follow, I will have more to say regarding the method of staining.

VARNISHING AND POLISHING

French polishing was at one time the only method of polishing permitted to be employed on work of the first class, because of its permanency and uniform appearance, and the man who understood the process, and could mix the materials used, could always demand good pay and steady employment. Now, however, there are a number of methods and varnishes that are almost as good as the method and materials used in French polishing, and which can be applied at one-eighth the cost, and which when done look just about as well, though perhaps they will not be permanent. So, while French polishing still survives to some extent, and is likely to be practiced for many years to come, a description of the method and materials is quite necessary in a book of this kind; therefore no excuse is necessary to account for its appearance in these pages.

Varnishing, on which depends to a certain extent the beauty of the work, to be of a durable character should be done in a temperature of 65° F. or more, from the beginning of the work to the finishing of the same, day and night included. A higher temperature, if not over 125° F., will not harm fine varnishes; in fact, will turn out nicer work than in a lower temperature, and will enable a manufacturer to turn out work in a much shorter time. In a temperature of but 65° to 75° F. from four to six days between coatings is advisable, as this will give good and unfailing results. In 125° F. the same good results can be obtained in one-half the time. Varnishing departments, outside the filling and rubbing rooms, should be kept absolutely clean. The filling and rubbing rooms should be kept as clean as possible.

After cabinet-work has received one-half the varnish coatings and the varnish is perfectly dry, rub the surface with pumice-stone and water—use a piece of felt—to a smooth, even surface. Allow the work to stand 24 hours, and then begin the application of the last half of varnish coatings, giving the same time between coatings. After all the coatings are perfectly dry, go through the same rubbing process. A perfect, smooth surface for polishing will be the result. Let the work stand for 24 hours after this rubbing, then start polishing by moistening a fine piece of cloth with water, dipped in powdered rotten stone, thus moistening the same also, and begin to rub the surface of the work with a steady hand and evenly, in order to remove with this fine rotten stone the fine scratches, if any, which are generally caused by the rubbing of the pumice-stone. This accomplished, continue the rubbing with the palm of the hand instead of the cloth, using moist rotten stone, and rub the work until the fine polish required is obtained. The rotten stone then generally falls off the hand and you work in a dry dust. Wash the surface clean with water, using a fine sponge and chamois. Allow the polished work to stand 24 hours, then oil the same off with a light oil and a very soft rag or cotton bat. Take another fine rag or cotton bat and remove all the oil by rubbing or wiping the same gently, but absolutely clean, off the polished surface. To be sure this is accomplished, moisten the cloth or cotton bat with alcohol. The polish, if everything is done correctly, will then be finished.

Care should be taken that too much varnish is not put on the work. For good finishing only a minimum of material should be used if the grain of the wood is wished to be seen, for the less varnish used, providing a good polish is obtained, will bring out the details of the wood better than a dozen coats would. If one coat of varnish is not enough, two will be, and it is not good practice to employ more, nor is it good workmanship.

A room that is dark or damp will spoil the varnish, and a room that is excessively warm will keep the varnish.soft.   Barrels of varnish should not be stored in a very warm room, as the heat will open the joints in the barrels, and the varnish, which will be quite thin owing to the heat, will leak out.   In summer, varnish should be stored in a basement where it is cool.

Turning white is caused by the action of water or dampness.   The better the grade of varnish and the more elastic it is, the less liable it is to be affected by moisture.   In applying two coats of varnish, neither should be heavy, more especially the first coat.   If it is, it will not generally get thoroughly dry at the bottom before the second one is applied, and the result will be disastrous, as it will cause the last coat to crack, wrinkle, or sag, as it is called.   Another bad result of not giving varnish time to dry will be noticed by the last coat deadening or sinking away.   This is caused by the undercoat not having been allowed sufficient time to dry, resulting in the finishing coat becoming absorbed while in the course of hardening.

The varnisher must be careful that there is no oil on the surface to be varnished, as it will cause pitting, or little hollows in the varnish.   When varnish is so thick it does not spread well, it may be thinned by adding a little turpentine, but care must be taken that it is thoroughly incorporated in the varnish, as, if it is not, this will also cause pitting.   A long-haired, pliant brush is best with which to apply varnish.   It should be spread with long, steady strokes, drawn in a perfectly straight line lengthwise the grain of the wood. Oil japan or liquid dryer should never be added to good varnish.   Each coat of varnish should be given three or four days to harden before another coat is added or before the last coat is rubbed, if a rubbed surface is required.

One thing should always be considered before varnishing begins, and that is, that a good coat of colorless shellac should be laid on the work just as soon as the filler is dry and properly rubbed down. This will hermetically seal up all the pores and prevent the varnish from sinking or showing hollow spots on the work.

I show the style of brush which is generally used for applying shellac, in Fig. 107; it is taken from a dealer's catalogue, and is oval in section and metal-bound.

An excellent shellac varnish is made by dissolving 3½ lb. of orange shellac in 1 gal. of grain or wood alcohol. Let stand in a warm place until the shellac is thoroughly dissolved. If shaken once in a while, the shellac will dissolve quicker.

For making white shellac varnish, take 3¼ lb. of white shellac and mix with alcohol, grain or wood, the same as before. These proportions are offered only as a sort of guide, but they may be varied a little as experience will show.

FIG. 107

All varnish should be laid on with the grain if possible, or there will likely be sagging along the brush marks.

Where varnish is flowed the operator should not be "stingy" with his material or his work will not be

good.   There is a tendency always with the beginnei
to "lay off" his varnish too thin, or to "skin" it. as it
is termed.   It is always better to err on the side of
using too much, than too little varnish, if good work is
desired.   Too much varnish, however, should be
avoided, as the work will be apt to crack and become
disfigured in time.   The brushes shown
in Figs. 108 and 109 are among the best
for flowing purposes.

Generally, unless on the very hardest of woods, two coats of varnish are
necessary before the process of rubbing
can be commenced, as a good surface
cannot be obtained unless there is a
good ground to work on.

A few hints as to "rubbing" may not
be out of place.   First, see that the
varnish is dry and hard.   If an impression can be made on it with a finger
nail, it is too soft to rub; let it stand
awhile.

Never rub across the grain if it can
be avoided.

Always rub with the grain, lightening
the stroke at the ends.

Rub lightly at first and avoid making
bare spots.

Fig. 108

Use fine pumice-stone at first, and
all the time, until you get accustomed to the work.

Use a pad of felt about 3½x4½ inches for a rubber.

Rub with either water or with rubbing oil—the latter
preferred—or use linseed oil.

Sprinkle the pumice-stone powder on the work,
dip the rubber in the oil, then rub lightly.

Clean off the work with damp, clean sawdust and a brush, or with soft cotton wadding.

For mouldings, make reverse shapes, cover with felt, and proceed as with the flat surfaces.

After rubbing, the work is ready for polishing. This is done by making a mixture of half sweet oil and half alcohol. Then make a large wad of nice clean cotton and rub the work with a circular motion until the proper polish is attained. This requires some practice, but is easily acquired.

Another and a better method is to put on an extra coat of flowing varnish, then rub down with fine pumice-stone and clean carefully. After this, rub down with a lump of faced-up pumice, or with chamois leather and powdered rotten stone. Let the rotten stone become dry on the surface, then wipe off with the palm of the hand, which rubs up the work, with a rotary motion. A piece of fine linen or silk should be handy, on which the hand should be cleaned from time to time.

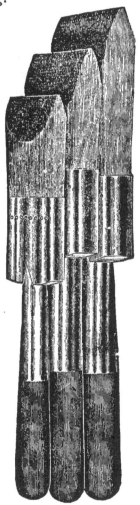

Fig. 109

If a dead finish is required, do not polish after rubbing over with powdered pumice stone and oil.

Of course, the operator must always bear in mind. during the several operations, that care and cleanliness

are two necessary factors, and without them, there
can be no such thing as satisfactory results.   A
slovenly workman should never attempt to polish, for
no good can come from it.   In all my experience,
which covers many years, I have never known of a
careless or slovenly man making good work in this
particular department.

French Polishing.—Much has been said and written
on this subject, and many comparisons have been made
between this and other methods of polishing, but the
writer, from his architectural experience and general
observation, does not hesitate for a moment in saying
that "French polished" work is much superior to any
or all other polished work, so far as durability and
effect is concerned.   True, other methods are—many
of them—much more economical and easier acquired,
but they do not have the staying powers that the good
old-fashioned French polishing has.

Although, as before stated, much has been written
on the subject, there is a certain sameness in the
descriptions, and I confess I do not see how it could
be otherwise, as the subject is one that can have only
one side to it; hence the sameness of description.

I will not attempt to write a description, as it would
be no improvement on former ones; so I offer the
following, which is taken from an English source,
that has been Americanized to some extent.

In French polishing, the wood has to be prepared
and various minor details attended to before this can
be done.   For example, the pores of open-grained
wood must be stopped or, as the process is generally
called, filled, to get a smooth surface and to prevent
excessive absorption of the liquid polish.   Then the
appearance of some woods is improved and enriched

by oiling them before applying the polish. This oiling, to a certain extent, darkens and mellows them, and brings up the figure.

The temperature and atmosphere of the place in which French polishing is done are of considerable importance. Work cannot be done properly in a cold or damp room, as then the polish will get chilled, and, as it sets on the wood, becomes opaque and cloudy. To avoid this the polisher should work in a warm room. The temperature for a living room, about 70°, is about that suited for polishing. In warm summer weather a fire is not necessary, but in winter it is. If the polisher notices that his polish chills, he must increase the heat of his room. If a moderate amount of warmth be brought near the surface as soon as any chill is observed, it will probably disappear. A small article may be taken to the fire, but with large work this course would hardly be convenient. In such cases a good plan is to hold something warm a short distance from the chilled surface, but on no account must it touch, nor must the heat be great enough to scorch the polish. A common plan, but not altogether a good one, is to hold a piece of burning paper near the chill. An ordinary flatiron is very useful for small chilled patches. When the article is cold or damp, chill is more likely to occur. It is, therefore, always necessary to make sure after a stain has been used that the wood has become thoroughly dry.

Not less important is the employment of suitable materials, both in the polish and in the tools of the polisher's art. These latter consist almost entirely of wadding or cotton wool and soft linen or cotton rags, from which the rubbers to apply the polish are made;

and a few bottles are wanted to hold the various polishes, stains, and their components.

The pad with which French polish is applied is called the rubber. Without it the French polisher can do little in actual polishing, although he may not require it in the preliminary operations of oiling and staining. However simple in itself the rubber may be, it should be properly and carefully made of suitable materials; otherwise good work cannot be done with it. Those who have seen polishers at work may be inclined to infer that no great care is necessary, for a dirty rag covering an equally uninviting lump of wadding is usually seen. Examination will show the rubber to be more carefully made than might have been expected, and the expert polisher would probably prefer it to a nice clean-looking rubber such as a novice

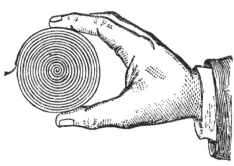

FIG. 110

would choose. Nevertheless, a dirty rubber is not wanted, for dirt is fatal to first-class work; hence the polisher should keep his rubbers scrupulously clean. They will naturally get stained and discolored with the polish, but that is a very different matter from being dirty. Old rubbers are preferable to new ones, provided they have been properly taken care of and not allowed to get hard.

For flat surfaces or fretwork a wad may be prepared by using a strip of torn woolen cloth from 1 in. to 2 in. wide. Cloth with a cut edge is not recommended for this purpose, as it is too harsh. Roll the strip very tightly into a wad about 1 in., 2 in., or 3 in. diameter, according to the size of the work, and tie tightly round with fine twine (Fig. 110). This will give as nearly as possible a rubber resembling Fig. 111. This wad is put into a double thickness of linen cloth, and the ends are gathered up like the ends of a pudding-cloth; they are not tied, but are grasped as a hand-piece while being used. This form of rubber would, however, be use-

Fig. 111

less for bodying up mouldings, beads, quirks, moulded handrails, newel posts, etc., and when polishing large mahogany doors or other framed furniture it would be impossible to get well into the corners of sunk panels, as in Fig. 112.

A well-shaped, soft, pliable rubber, with its rag

RUBBER

Fig. 112

covering free from creases, is to a practical French polisher equivalent to a sharp, finely set smoothing plane in the hands of a cabinet-maker. With such a rubber, made of wadding, one is enabled to get into corners, round turned work, and up to the edges of mouldings in a manner impossible with a hard, round rubber. To make it, take a sheet of wadding—this is 9 in. wide—and tear off a piece 6 in. long; this will form a conveniently-sized rubber, suitable for most work; but for small work use one of smaller size. Double the wadding, making it 6 in. by 4½ in

Squeeze this in the hand, keeping the skin unbroken, till in shape it nearly resembles half a bear. The rubber should then be charged with polish, and covered with a piece of soft, clean rag. In folding the rag, twist it on the upper side of the rubber. Each additional twist will bring it to a sharper point and cause the polish to ooze through its surface. It is not necessary to put a rag covering on the rubbers first used. The rubber must be kept free from creases, otherwise it will cause the surface to which it is applied to be stringy or full of ridges.

Though rags have been mentioned as suitable for the outer covering· or casing of the pad, some care in their selection is necessary. A piece with a seam across it would never do for a rubber, and anything which would tend to scratch the film of polish as it is being laid or worked on in the final operation of spiriting off must be carefully avoided. They must be either cotton or linen, and ought to be perfectly soft and fine or, at any rate, free from knots or lumps. Some polishers advise the exclusive use of linen, but this is a needless restriction. It may be mentioned that new material may be used as well as rags. To render this suitable, all traces of the sizing and stiffening with which it may have been finished must be removed by a thorough washing.

Any material to be used for a polishing rubber must be thoroughly well dried. Indeed, the necessity of avoiding damp cannot be too much insisted on. With regard to the substance of the rubber, white wadding is the best to use, and this is readily obtainable from any upholsterer or chemist. It may be purer if got from the latter, but it is certainly much dearer than any reasonable upholsterer would charge for something equally suitable. Wadding bought from an upholsterer has a thin skin on one or both sides, according to whether it has been split or not. This skin must be removed, leaving nothing but the soft cotton. For a few cents enough ought to be obtainable to last a considerable time. It may be useful to know that, if it is clean, the raw material used in cotton manufacturing districts will do as well as the finest wadding. Cotton flock, used by upholsterers as a stuffing for mattresses, chairs, etc., is not suitable for polishing, except perhaps for the coarsest work. Even for this it should not be used if anything better is available. Rubbers composed entirely of flannel are occasionally recommended for special kinds of work. It is doubtful if there is any advantage in using flannel, except for large, flat surfaces, which can be got over more quickly with a large rubber than with a small one. The novice is advised to use the wadding rubber, and to become an expert polisher with it before experimenting with anything else.

The size of the rubber will, to some extent, depend on the nature of the work, but that above given may be regarded as generally suitable. A very large rubber is not advisable at first, and the polisher, as he gains experience, must be guided by circumstances. In handling it, moreover, the polisher will be equally guided; a rubber of moderate dimensions is usually held by the tips of the thumb and fingers, but the polisher will probably find a large rubber can be more conveniently used by holding it in the palm of the hand.

The rubber must be charged with polish for use, and some care will have to be exercised in doing this. The covering of the rubber is opened so that a little polish can be dropped on the wadding. A convenient way of doing this is to have the polish in a bottle, the cork of which has a channel or notch cut in it to allow only a few drops to escape at a time. Some polishers dip a portion of the rubber into the polish, but the other method is more generally adopted. It must not be saturated; only enough polish to moisten the wadding must be used, or what will appear through the rag covering when pressed. The rubber having been thus charged, gather up the edges of rag as before directed. Then, to distribute the polish equally, press the rubber moderately firmly into the palm of the other hand. The rubber ought now to be ready for application to the wood, which may be assumed to have been properly prepared to receive its first coating of polish.

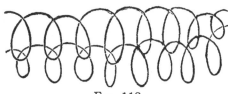

FIG. 113

At this stage the principal thing is to get a good body of polish evenly spread on the wood. How this may best be done depends on circumstances; but if the desired result is obtained, the precise method is of secondary consequence. Let it be assumed that the work to be done is a small, flat surface. With moderate pressure on the rubber, quickly wipe over the entire surface, first with the grain of the wood, then across it. Then, without delay, go over it more minutely, the motion generally adopted for the rubber being shown in the illustrations (Figs. 113 and 114). At first the pressure should be gentle, but it should be increased as the polish gets worked in and the rubber drier, though at no time must the rubbing decline to scrubbing.

While the rubber is in contact with the wood it must be kept constantly in motion. An important point is not to allow the rubber to remain stationary on the woodwork during temporary absence or at the end of the day's work. As the rubber gets dry it must be recharged with polish, but let the novice beware of using this in excess.

Old rubbers are better than new, so when done with they should be kept in an airtight receptacle, such as a tin canister or a biscuit box. When any job is finished, do not throw the rubber away under the impression that a rubber once laid aside becomes useless. This occurs only when it is left exposed to the air, because then it hardens throughout. If, as stated, the rubbers are kept from the air, only the outside covering will get dry and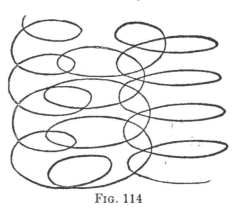

FIG. 114

hard, and this can be readily softened by rubbing it in raw alcohol.

Every time the rubber is wetted with polish it should be pressed in the palm of the left hand, which will equalize the polish. After the cover is put over, which should be some clean old cotton or print rags, the tip of the finger should be dipped in linseed oil and applied to rubber cover—just enough to keep it from sticking. As soon as the cover has a shiny appearance, it should be removed to a fresh place. As soon as the work has got a good body of polish on, it should be set away for at least ten hours, to allow for the polish to sink, which always takes place.

Before commencing to polish again, the work should be very carefully rubbed over with the finest glass-paper obtainable, taking care not to cut through the skin; then proceed as before. Be sure never to let the rubber stop in one place for an instant, as it will surely jake off the polish to the bare wood and spoil the job. After the work has sufficient polish on, it should be allowed to stand three or four hours before spiriting off.

The same rubber will do; only use spirits. Just damp the rubber, and cover three or four times double with cover, and rub very lightly over the work; but care must be taken not to make the rubber too wet, or the work will be spoiled. The same process will answer for pine or deal, only no filling is required, but a coat of clean patent size, before applying the polish.

The ingredients for the above kind of work are quite numerous, but shellac, dissolved in alcohol, is the basis of all French polishes, and some finishers use thin shellac varnish without other admixture, slightly moistening the rubber with linseed oil to prevent stickiness and make it work smoothly. There is a great variety of admixtures and diversity in the proportion of ingredients, but the differences are not material. I subjoin a number of recipes.

First and Best.—To one pint of spirits of wine add a quarter of an ounce of gum-copal, a quarter of an ounce of gum arabic, and one ounce of shellac.

Let the gums be well bruised, and sifted through a piece of muslin. Put the spirits and the gums together in a vessel that can be closely corked; place them near a warm stove, and frequently shake them. In two or three days they will be dissolved. Strain the mixture through a piece of muslin, and keep it tight corked for use.

Next.—Take one ounce each of mastic, sandarac, seed lac, shellac, gum lac, and gum arabic; reduce them to powder; and add a quarter of an ounce of virgin wax; put the whole into a bottle, with one quart of rectified spirits of wine; let it stand twelve hours, and it will be fit for use.

Another.—Put into a glass bottle one ounce of gum lac, two drachms of mastic in drops, four drachms of sandarac, three ounces of shellac, and half an ounce of gum dragon; reduce the whole to powder; add to it a piece of camphor the size of a nut, and pour on it eight ounces of rectified spirits of wine. Stop the bottle close, but take care, when the gums are dissolving, that it is not more than half full. Place near a warm stove until dissolved.

Other French Polish Recipes.—One pint naphtha, 3½ oz. orange shellac, ½ oz. elima. Darken with red sanders wood.

To one pint of spirits of wine, add half an ounce of gum shellac, half an ounce of seed lac, and a quarter of an ounce of gum sandarac; submit the whole to a gentle heat, frequently shaking it, till the various gums are dissolved, when it is fit for use.

Shellac, 6 oz.; naphtha, 1 qt.; sandarac, 1 oz.; benzoin, ¾ oz.

Three oz. shellac, ½ oz. gum mastic pulverized, and 1 pt. methylated spirits of wine added. Let it stand till dissolved.

Twelve oz. shellac, 2 oz. gum elima, 3 oz. gum copal, 1 gal. spirits of wine; dissolve.

The following must be well mixed and dissolved:

pale shellac, 2¼ lb.; 3 oz. mastic, 3 oz. sandarac, 1 gal spirits of wine. After the above is dissolved, add 1 pt. copal varnish, 1¼ oz. shellac, ½ oz. gum juniper, ½ oz. benzoin, ½ pt. methylated alcohol.

A Good Polish.—To 1 pt. spirits of wine add, in fine powder, 1 oz. seed lac, 2 dr. gum guaiacum, 2 dr. dragons' blood, and 2 dr. gum mastic; expose them, in a vessel stopped close, to a moderate heat for three hours, until you find the gum dissolved; strain the whole into a bottle for use, with a quarter of a gill of the best linseed oil, to be shaken up well with it.

This polish is more particularly intended for dark colored woods—for it is apt to give a tinge to light ones, as satinwood or airwood, etc.—owing to the admixture of the dragons' blood, which gives it a red appearance.

A Polish That Will Stand Water.—Take 1 pt. spirits of wine, 2 oz. gum benzoin, ¼ oz. gum sandarac, and ¼ oz. gum animé; these must be put into a stopped bottle, and placed either in a sand-bath or in hot water till dissolved; then strain the mixture, and, after adding about a quarter of a gill of the best clear poppy oil, shake it well up, and put it by for use.

Prepared Spirits.—This preparation is useful for finishing after any of the foregoing recipes, as it adds to the luster and durability, as well as removes every defect, of the other polishes and it gives the surface a most brilliant appearance.

Half a pint of the very best rectified spirits of wine, 2 dr. shellac, and 2 dr. gum benzoin. Put these ingredients into a bottle, and keep it in a warm place till the gum is all dissolved, shaking it frequently; when cold, add two teaspoonfuls of the best clear white poppy oil; shake them well together, and it is fit for use.

This preparation is used in the same manner as the foregoing polishes; but, in order to remove all dull places, you may increase the pressure in rubbing.

Polish for Turner's Work.—Dissolve 1 oz. sandarac in ½ pt. spirits of wine; shave 1 oz. beeswax, and dissolve it in a sufficient quantity of spirits of turpentine to make it into a paste, add the former mixture to it by degrees; then, with a woolen cloth, apply it to the work while it is in motion in the lathe, and polish it with a soft linen rag; it will appear as if highly varnished.

A French Polish Reviver.—Beat gum acacia and white of two eggs in a mortar until they amalgamate; then add ½ pt. raw linseed oil and best vinegar, 8 oz. methylated spirits of wine, 1 oz. hydrochloric acid and 2 oz. muriate of antimony. They are to be rubbed on the surface of the furniture until dry, and will give a brilliant and lasting polish.

It now remains to explain the several varieties of finishing in use; these are largely derived from the peculiar qualities of the different varnishes used. Polishing varnishes, which are very hard and durable, are so called because their surface can be brought to a high luster by rubbing with the proper materials. Flowing or finishing varnishes contain more oil than polishing varnishes, dry more slowly, and are softer, but their peculiar qualities are brilliancy and durability, fitting them for work requiring a brilliant gloss, such as veneered panels. Rubbing varnishes are those that dry sufficiently hard to admit of being rubbed to a smooth surface. Turpentine varnishes, being the cheapest variety, are employed for cheap work, such as common chairs, bedsteads, etc.

DEAD FINISH is a term applied to the finish produced by the reduction of any of the rubbing varnishes with powdered pumice-stone and raw linseed oil, the surface thus produced being left in the semi-lustrous state by omitting the polishing process. It is now more used than any other for body work, shellac varnish being generally employed because of its adaptation to the requirements of fine cabinet-work, and its properties of quick and hard drying. Copal, animé, and amber varnishes are also used, but are slower drying. The number of coats required depends somewhat upon the quality of the filler, but usually three coats, and sometimes less, are amply suffi-cient.

Bodying In and Spiriting Off.—The term bodying, applied to the polisher's art, means coating the wood with a thin, evenly distributed layer of the polish. The way in which this is done greatly affects the appearance and the durability of the gloss. When the body is too thin, the gloss subsequently given to it may at first be beautiful, but as the polish sinks or perishes the gloss fades. When the body is too thick the gloss may appear all right, but the work is apt to look treacly, as though varnish had been used; besides, a thick body impairs the pure tone of some woods. The high degree of excellence to which polishing is capable of being brought is seen only on the best cabinet-work. Polish on second-rate furniture or finish is generally in keeping with the inferior quality of the woodwork. The cheap, gaudy furniture which is often seen in shops must not be taken as models of polishing. The price paid for polishing is reduced, with the result that inferior polish is used and less time is spent on the work. Although the best materials and the expenditure of time and labor will not insure good work by unpracticed hands, they are important factors, and it will be wise to use materials of good quality.

To make a good average polish, neither too thick nor too thin, about six ounces of shellac to each pint of methylated or alcohol spirit will be required, but great exactitude in the proportions is not necessary. The proportions may vary according to the fancy of the polisher, and, to some extent, according to the nature of the work he is engaged on. If the polish turns out too thick, it can be thinned by adding more spirit; if too thin, the deficiency can be made up by adding more shellac. A rough-and-ready way of measuring the proportions is to half fill a bottle with the roughly broken shellac, and then fill up with ordinary methylated spirit.

The shellac dissolves gradually, and the process is hastened by an occasional shaking or stirring with a stick. Heat is not necessary; indeed, the preparation of polish by heat is dangerous.

Two kinds of polish are used. One, known as "white polish," is nearly colorless; the other is known as "brown polish," or simply "polish." The latter is always understood if unqualified by the word "white." White polish is made with white or bleached shellac; the other with ordinary orange or reddish-brown shellac.

Either polish may be used on any kind of wood, except where great purity of tint is required. The white is to be preferred for all light woods, such as light oak, ash, sycamore, satin, etc., while the brown may be used on darker; but even on these, white polish is good, with the exception of mahogany, the only ordinary fine wood for which a decided preference might be given to brown polish. Under ordinary circumstances, however, either polish may be used indiscriminately. The point as to brown or white polish for dark wood belongs to the higher branches of the polisher's art.

It will be seen that white polish is the more generally useful of the two, so those who do not care to keep both kinds may confine themselves to it. Through the slightly higher price of the bleached shellac, it costs a little more, but the extra cost is so small that it is hardly worth considering by those who use small quantities. Those who use polish in large quantities can have both kinds.

Polish bought ready-made may be equal to that made at home from the recipe given, for there is nothing to prevent manufacturers using the same ingredients, and many of them do. Still, from the impossibility of knowing the ingredients in ready-made polish, there is some risk attending its use. From the price at which some polish is sold, it is fair to suppose that something cheaper than spirit or shellac has been used; and though good polish may be bought, it is better for the user to prepare his own, which can be depended on. Bought polish may be thoroughly good in every way—brilliant, clear, and durable—but those who are best able to judge generally prefer to make their own polish to do the best class of work. Prejudice may account for this preference.

Manufacturers of polish assert that, in addition to shellac, certain gums or resins improve the quality of the polish, when used with knowledge and discretion. For instance, one gum may give increased elasticity, while another may harden the film; but for a good all-round polish, which can be relied on, many polishers assert that there is nothing to surpass a simple solution of shellac and alcohol. A few approved formulæ for polishes have been given, so that those who feel inclined to do so may experiment for themselves. Shellac is the principal ingredient in nearly all. Those persons who cannot polish with shellac and spirit alone will not be able to do any better with the more complicated mixtures; therefore, no one should remain under the impression that he will do better if he works with another kind of polish.

Enough having now been said about the material, we may proceed to the using of it for bodying. In the first place, the wood must be prepared by filling of one kind or another, and rubbed down smoothly with fine or worn glass-paper, in order to make it fit to receive the polish, for a high degree of finish cannot be got on a rough surface. The rubber, which consists of cotton wadding with a soft rag cover, with which the polish is applied, has been sufficiently treated on, so that nothing more need be said about it. Work, rubber, polish, and a little raw linseed oil being ready, bodying in may be proceeded with in the following way:

Moisten the wadding with polish; put the rag cover on carefully, so that it is without folds or wrinkles. Dab the rubber into the palm of the left hand to distribute the polish evenly, and cause it to moisten the rag at the bottom properly. Supposing the work is a panel or flat surface, the following will be found a good method of treating it, and it is one that is followed more or less closely by experienced polishers.

Rub briskly across the grain to get the surface covered with polish; then by a series of circular movements, as shown by the lines in Figs. 113 and

114, go over the whole of the work. A moderate pressure should be applied, which should be increased gradually as the rubber dries, but the movement should at no time degenerate into mere scrubbing. In order that the rubber may work smoothly without sticking, a little raw linseed oil should be applied on the face of the rubber. The less of this used the better, and if it can be dispensed with altogether no harm will be done. To make the rubber work smoothly a very little will suffice; the tip of a finger, moistened with oil, and touched on the face of the rubber, is all that is required. The rubber must not be dipped in the oil, nor must the oil be dropped on it from a bottle, for by these means more oil would be applied than is necessary, and this would be fatal to good work.

The only recognized oil used in French polishing is raw linseed. This may be worked over the natural woods in the first place, to give them that peculiar tone that cannot be gained by other means; otherwise the less oil used the better for the durability of the work. Bear in mind that it forms no part of polish in itself, being used only to enable us to work the gums easily; thus, without its aid the polish rubber would be apt to stick or drag, thus breaking up the surface instead of leveling it. On any surface in which spirit varnish forms a part this will be particularly noticeable; and in any case, it is next to impossible to get that beautiful level surface gained by spiriting out unless a little oil is used.

As the rubber dries, more polish must be applied to it, as was done in the first instance, with more oil as required. A small quantity of polish goes a long way, and the novice must carefully avoid making the rubber wet. It should be no more than fairly moist.

Many a beginner, noticing how tedious the work is with a dry rubber, may think that if he used more polish the desired result would be more quickly attained. If the object were merely to get the wood coated, this might be the case; but the result of using too much polish would be that the shellac left by the quick evaporation of the spirit would be ridgy and irregular, instead of in a fine, even coating or body. Anything approaching a flow of polish from the rubber must be avoided. When the rubber is not sufficiently charged with polish, the labor of bodying up will be unduly protracted, or may be rendered impossible if no polish can be rubbed onto the wood.

The first bodying-in process should be continued till it seems that the wood absorbs no more of the polish. There will be a perceptible gloss on its surface, but it will be streaky, and the rubber-marks will show very distinctly. All these marks will be removed later on. It may be thought that, if the polish is too thick or too thin, the result will be very much the same as if the rubber were too wet or too dry. The principal objection to having the polish too thin is that it will take more time in working a good body on the wood. It will, however, be better to risk this rather than to have the polish too thick. An experienced polisher would soon detect fault in either direction by the way in which the polish works, but the novice must be on the look-out for irregularities in the shape of lumps or ridges, and, with a little attention, he will have no difficulty in avoiding serious mishaps.

Let the work stand for at least a day, carefully covered up from dust; on examining it the body will be found to have altered in appearance to an extent which will depend upon how much the polish has sunk into the wood. The work must be again bodied up as before, always remembering to use as little oil as possible. Then it will be again laid aside, and the bodying process repeated till the polish no longer seems to sink in, even after the work has lain aside for a few days. When this stage is reached, the bodying may be considered complete, and the work ready for the first polishing operations. Before proceeding to consider these, however, the novice will do well to note the following hints:

The number of times the work will require to be bodied depends on circumstances. Fine, close-grained woods will not require so many as the more open kinds, such as oak, ash, mahogany, etc.; but for the best work, which is intended to be as durable as can be, it need rarely exceed four. An interval of one or more days may elapse between the successive bodies, the chief object of waiting being to let them sink as much as they will. If, after the work has been laid aside for a few days, the polish has not sunk at all, no advantage would be gained by giving it another body It is very seldom that the first body is enough, but often only one body is applied, where either low price or limited time will not allow of more; so those who wish to do polishing need not think the process cannot be hurried.

Still, imperfect bodying is not advisable, as such work will soon want touching up. When work is made merely to sell, one body, and that of the slightest, is sufficient—from the seller's point of view. if not from the buyer's. Between the bodyings, especially after the first and second, the surface of the work should be rubbed down with fine glass-paper—not to rub the body off, but just enough to smooth the surface. It may here be remarked that pumice powder, used in moderation, is useful for working down inequalities of surface. Sandpapering has been recommended as necessary after the first and second bodies, but the process may be done after any others, though it should not be required if the work has been skillfully done. In fact, the final bodying up may be regarded almost as the beginning of the spiriting off.

Before beginning to work a fresh body on a previous one, it is as well to wash the surface gently with lukewarm water, not using too much of it, in order to remove the grease and allow the rubber to work freely. The water must be thoroughly dried up before applying the rubber. In moderation the washing can never do harm, and is, generally, an advantage, though not absolutely necessary. When a long interval has elapsed, the washing should never be omitted, as dust will settle on the work; and it need scarcely be said that dust should not be rubbed into the polish.

When bodying up, polishers should see that their hands are clean and free from old polish, which is so often seen on them. If they are soiled with old polish or shellac, bits are apt to flake off and destroy the surface of new work. This may be an appropriate place to say that any polish which sticks to the hands may be washed away with hot water and soda, or with alcohol.

The body should be thin, as it is not so much the quantity of body on the wood as its quality that is important; it is also essential that it should be applied with sufficient intervals between the successive bodies to allow of sinkage.

Another important matter is to dry the rubbers well by working them on each body till dry, and not to moisten them frequently. By this means the film of shellac is kept thin. Neither a wet nor a dry rubber should on any account be allowed to stand on a surface being polished. The rubber must be kept moving, and should glide gradually on to the work, not be dabbed down on it. In the initial stages of bodying. care in this respect is not so important as later on, when it is absolutely necessary. The same precaution should be used when lifting the rubber from the work.

For the guidance of beginners, it may be stated that if they take care of the edges of the work the rest of the surface will look after itself. The reason is that the edges are apt to be somewhat neglected, and the polish to be less there than elsewhere. The secret of a good, durable polish depends primarily on a good body, and this, in its turn, on sufficient time having been allowed for sinkage.

The final operation in French polishing, by which the gloss is put on the body previously applied, is. known as spiriting off. In this operation rubber marks and smears of all kinds are removed, and the beautiful surface, known as French polish, is the result. Bodying is important so far as durability is concerned, but spiriting is more so with regard to finish. If the worker fails in spiriting, his previous efforts will, to a great extent, have been in vain. Disregarding staining, darkening, and other processes, with which a good polisher should be acquainted, the spiriting is perhaps the most severe test of skill in the whole process of polishing; and a man who can manage this part of the work really well may be considered a competent polisher.

The first operation to be described in the process of spiriting off partakes very much of the nature of body-ing in. At the beginning it is bodying, and at the end spiriting. The two processes merge one into the other. There is no abrupt break, as between filling and bodying, except for the intermediate stage, although the processes are well defined, both in character and purpose. This intermediate stage is not always practiced, but it is rec-ommended when good work is wanted. Briefly, spiriting off consists in washing the bodied surface with methyl-ated spirit. This being understood, the final bodying up, or first spiriting off, whichever this process may be called, consists in gradually reducing the quantity of polish in the rubber, and supplying its place with spirit. The polish is gradually reduced by the addition of spirit. till all the polish has been worked out of the rubber. The rubber may be charged, first with three parts polish and one part spirit; next time equal quantities; the third time three parts spirit and one part polish; and the fourth charging will be with spirit only. It does not follow that these proportions need be strictly observed, nor are they so in practice, but this example illustrates the process. The last rubber will be almost free from polish, and it should be worked till it is dry, or nearly so.

At this stage spiriting proper may begin, and a fresh rubber should be used. It need not be a new one, but it should be one which has been used only for spiriting, and which has no polish on it. It will be better if it has three or four coverings of rag on its face, which can be removed as they dry. If only one cover is used the spirit is apt to evaporate too quickly. The spirit in the rubber has a tendency to partially dissolve the shellac or body on the wood. This it does to a very limited extent, unless the rubber is made too wet, when there is danger of not only spiriting and smoothing the surface, but of actually washing away the body. This mishap must be carefully guarded against. There should be enough spirit to allow the surface of the body to be softened and smoothed, but no more, and the rubbing should be uniform, and not more in one place than in another. There is hardly any likelihood of the novice erring by using too little spirit, so he may be reminded that the less of it there is in the rubber at a time the better. The rubbing should be gentle at first, becoming harder as the spirit dries off, and oil must not be used on the rubber face, for when there is oil either on the rubber or on the work, the polish cannot be brought up.

The chief cause of failure lies in getting the spirit rubber too wet, and so softening and tearing up the gums. Many meet with success by dispensing with it, using instead a swab of clean, soft rag, fairly damp (not wet) with alcohol.

If the spiriting-off process is being done correctly the gloss will soon begin to appear, and when it seems approaching a finished condition, the rubber ought to be moved only in the direction of the grain, and not across it nor with circular motion. The final touches should be given with the soft rubber rag alone, care being taken not to scratch the surface, which is now softened by the action of the spirit. The surface will gradually harden, but for a time it should be handled with care, and nothing be allowed to come in contact with it, or it is very likely to be marked. It should also be protected from dust, for any settling on it may be retained by the polish, the luster of which would certainly suffer.

Hardwood finishers, and perhaps dealers in furniture who do not keep an experienced polisher, or who may not be able to get their work done out, may b reminded that, circumstancĕs permitting, polished work should be wiped over with a spirit-rubber an houɪ or two before it is finished, to freshen it up. If the surface is at all soft, neither packing mats, nor anyͺ thing else likely to injure it, should be allowed to come in contact with it. The polishing on many things sent long journeys is often greatly disfigured from mat and other markings, but they are easily touched up on arrival at their destination.

Some polishers make use of a glaze in order to kill ͺͺe oil, just before spiriting off, which is made as follows:

Gum-benzoin, 6 oz., dissolved in alcohol spirit 1 pt. Gums other than that mentioned may be substituted in order to cheapen the glaze for commercial purposes, or to suit the fancy of polishers who make up their own solutions. The glaze is used chiefly when leveling down spirit varnish, and for the purpose of imparting a bright finish to mouldings. As practical workers have always at hand rubbers that are specially charged with white polish, brown or red polish, and another rubber for glaze, a clear, bright finish on some kinds of work may be easily gained by passing the glaze rubber along the edges, sunk portions, or even over the whole of a flat surface just before clearing out with the spirit pad. The workman must not, however, suppose that such treatment will entirely kill the oil, if an excessive quantity of oil has been used. Any excess of oɪ̈ should be cleared off beforehand; or, better still, entirely avoided, if a good, lasting quality of work ıɞ desired.

Glazing, though an imitation, has a recognized acceptance among polishers. It is remarkably convenient occasionally, and in some cases possesses an advantage over spiriting, so that it may fairly be classed among the ordinary processes of polishing. When done in moderation, glazing is as useful on furniture carving as the application of spirit varnish. Such work is commonly said, and justly, to be French polished. The real objection to glaze finish is that, though at first the appearance is equal, it is not so durable as the other. Glaze may be said to be even superior to badly spirited finish, and here is the chief claim it has for notice. It is seldom that a casual polisher can manage to do spiriting thoroughly, for the reason that he has not sufficient opportunity of acquiring practice.

Nevertheless, finishing by means of glaze is not so good as the method by spiriting, when the latter is well done, and should be considered as a means of getting the same effect easily and quickly—an imitation, in fact, of the real thing; the difference between the spirit and glaze finishes is that in the one case the effect is produced by friction, in the other by the addition of a thin, fine varnish to the surface of the body of polish. In the former case the polish itself is polished; in the latter it is varnished with a mixture known commonly as glaze, but to which other names are sometimes given.

Among polishers who command a fair price for their work, glaze is of comparatively limited application, and is confined to those parts where the spirit-rubber cannot be conveniently used, or where its use is not necessary. Instances of such may be found in chair-rails and various parts of the frame. These are usually polished, more or less, before the chair is upholstered, or, at any rate, before the outer covering is put on, the finishing being almost necessarily done last of all. The less the chair is handled by the polisher the better, especially if the covering is a delicate one, for there is less risk of injury with one or two wipes over with the glaze rubber than with the more prolonged spiriting.

Glaze may be used with advantage in inlaid work, where the inlay is slightly, though perhaps not intentionally, higher than the surrounding wood. In such a case it is better to resort to glaze than to finish with the spirit rubber. On fretwork, also, glaze may often be used with advantage, and, generally, it is unobjectionable on parts which are not subject to wear and tear. It will stand a moderate amount of handling, but not so much as good, hard spirited-off polish, and the luster is not so durable.

Glaze, under one or other of its different names, may be bought ready-made, but, for reasons similar to those given in connection with French polish, the home-made article is to be recommended. The preparation of glaze is simple, the ingredients being gum-benzoin and methylated spirit. After the benzoin is dissolved, the solution should be strained through muslin to free it from foreign matter. The proportions may vary, but those given for polish do very well, and with the substitution of crushed benzoin for shellac the process of making is exactly the same.

Gum-benzoin differs greatly in quality, but the best should be used by the polisher. Compared with lac it is expensive, so that the saving which is attributed to its use is mainly in time, which is money, at least from a trade point of view. Cheap benzoin is not to be relied on, and in a strange place an experienced polisher would look with suspicion on any offered at a very low price, however satisfactory its appearance. Where material is liable to adulteration, the best way to avoid imposition is to go to a reliable dealer and to pay a fair price.

Glaze, as used by French polishers, can be bought ready-made at most color stores, as patent glaze; it improves with age. To make the genuine article, dissolve 6 or 8 ounces of best gum-benzoin in 1 pint of alcohol spirit. Keep it in a closely stoppered bottle, otherwise the spirit will evaporate quickly.

Glaze may be applied with either rubber, sponge, or brush; in most cases the rubber is most suitable and is most commonly used. It is made in the ordinary way as used for polish, but it must not be applied with pressure. The glaze is painted on rather than rubbed into the work, which must have been previously bodied in. There seems to be an idea that glaze or something put on bare wood will cause a gloss right off; but nothing will do this. A polish can only be got on wood by varnish, or by bodying-in and polish.

When using glaze, the rubber should be made wetter than for polish or spirit; but still there should not be sufficient to drip from it. It should glaze or wet the wood when the rubber is very lightly pressed on it. One or two wipes in the direction of the grain of the wood, with a somewhat quick motion, will put the glaze on. Always let the glaze dry before applying the rubber again to the same place. The coats may be repeated till the gloss is satisfactory, but the film of glaze should never be made a thick one.

If preferred, a sponge may be used exactly as a rubber would be, but it is questionable if there is **any** advantage gained; it is rather a matter of fancy. When a brush is used, the glaze may be applied as a varnish pure and simple. With a brush a mixture of glaze and French polish, either white or brown, according to the work, in equal quantities, may be used with advantage.

Glaze that is not so satisfactory in appearance as it should be, may sometimes be improved by passing a spirit-rubber lightly over it, though this should be done with great caution, to avoid washing it off. When carefully and skillfully done, there can be little doubt that a glazed surface may be often, if not always, improved by slightly spiriting it.

To glaze a wide surface, see that it is free from dull streaks and ridges and oil, and the rubber soft and free from fluff. Apply the glaze as evenly as possible, going over the surface several times, until the rubber is nearly dry; then, with the smallest quantity of oil and a little spirits, go over the glaze, very lightly at first, varying the direction of the rubber to avoid ridges. A *dull*, even surface may be obtained by adding one-third to one-half of sandarac to the solution of benzoin, and using the rubber only damp—not saturated.

Old French polished work may often be revived by being lightly gone over with glaze after the surface has been washed and cleaned with warm water. This treatment is often considerably better than that commonly adopted with furniture pastes, polishes, creams, and revivers of various kinds.

Wax Polishing.—Although the beauty of most furniture woods is enhanced to the highest degree by French polishing when well done, there are other processes which, though not capable of being brought to such perfection, are much simpler. Among these is wax polishing. This mode of finishing is remarkably easy, both as regards materials and manipulation, and the unskilled novice can manage to wax-polish almost as well as an expert. It is, therefore, a suitable process for the beginner.

Though any wood may be treated by waxing, it is generally confined to oak, especially after this has been darkened by fumigation with ammonia. The appearance of oak so finished is comparatively dull, but it has an attractiveness which French polish does not possess for all eyes.

For antique oak furniture—whether genuine or imitation—wax is the best finish, though varnish is often used. Wax polish, though it may not give the same amount of gloss, is clearer and finer. Varnish clogs the wood, and is apt to give a treacly look to any piece of furniture finished with it.

Mahogany may very appropriately be finished by wax polish, and for many purposes it may be superior to the dulled French polish so often seen. The top of a dining-table is apt to be rendered unsightly from hot plates or dishes injuring the polished surfaces. The heat burns or blisters the hardened shellac of the French polish, and a finish which is not so liable to disfigurement is preferable; this is found in wax polish. Usually, dining-table tops (unless French polished) are simply oil polished. Waxing is, however, less tedious, and at least as suitable for the purpose, and the readiness with which an accidental marking can be obliterated renders it particularly useful.

Wood stained black, to produce so-called ebony, may be wax polished. The result is certainly a closer approximation to the appearance of real ebony than when the work is French polished in the usual way. By polishing fretwork articles with wax they may easily be made to look better than many of them do when unskillfully French polished.

Though it has been said that any wood may be wax polished, there can be no question that this process answers best on the more coarsely-grained woods, such as oak and ash; for pine and other light woods of close texture it is not so well suited, unless they have been previously stained.

The ingredients for wax polish are, in the simplest mixture, beeswax and turpentine. Resin and Venice turpentine are occasionally added. Resin is added with the intention of hardening the surface; but provided the wax be of good quality, these additions are quite unnecessary, if not injurious, and a good result should be got from wax and turps.

Wax and turpentine alone are all the materials necessary to make a good wax polish, and when anything else enters into the composition the mixture is one of a fancy character. It is not proposed to discuss the qualities of beeswax offered for sale, and the polisher must decide what kind he gets. Some advocate the use of fine white wax, and possibly a better finish may sometimes be got with it than with the ordinary yellow wax, which, however, is the kind generally used; the only occasions when it might not be so good as the white are when extreme purity of tone is required for a light wood. Wood perfectly white is, however, seldom wax polished.

The way in which wax polish is prepared depends a good deal on the proportions of the materials. For a liquid polish, shred the wax finely, and pour the turpentine over it, leaving the two till they are incorporated. Cold turpentine will dissolve wax slowly, but a more expeditious method is to melt the wax by heat, and before it has time to solidify pour the turpentine into it. Caution is necessary when melting wax, and on no account should the turpentine be poured into the wax while it is still on the fire With ordinary care there is no danger, and the possibility of a mishap is suggested merely for the benefit of those who might otherwise overlook the inflammable character of turpentine vapor. Should the mixture be either too thick or too thin, there will be no trouble in altering its consistency afterwards.

To thin a mass which is too stiff, a very moderate warming, by placing the bottle in hot water, will reduce it to a more liquid form, as the turpentine already in it facilitates the change, and more turpentine is added. To stiffen the mixture, wax should be melted separately, and the original mixture added to it. The heat of the freshly melted wax will probably be sufficient to cause all the materials to mix. In any case, the wax should be thoroughly melted before the turpentine is added, as a lumpy mixture is neither pleasant to work with nor conducive to good finish. The natural tendency of a wax polishing mixture, exposed to the air, is to stiffen, on account of the evaporation of the turpentine. A considerable time must elapse before there is an appreciable alteration, and the fact that a change does go on, slowly, is mentioned to remind polishers that if they have a considerable quantity of the mixture standing over, they must not expect it to retain its original consistency unless kept in a closed vessel, such as a tightly-corked bottle.

A hint for those who think that the more ingredients a mixture contains the better it must be, and who are not satisfied unless there is a certain amount of resin in their wax polishing paste: Always melt the resin first, and add the wax gradually, and constantly stir. Whether resin be used or not, the mixture should be allowed to get quite cold before it is applied to the work.

Although the consistency of wax polish varies considerably, the comparative merits of different degrees of stiffness or fluidity must be considered, so that an intelligent conception of the polisher's aim may be arrived at. Suppose a piece of beeswax, without any admixture of turpentine, is rubbed on a piece of smooth, flat wood. Some of the wax adheres to the surface, which, when friction is applied, becomes glossy or polished. The labor, however, is considerable, and though dry wax may do on a flat surface, when mouldings or carvings are to be treated, the difficulties in the way of satisfactory application are considerable. The remedy is to soften the wax so that it may be got into all parts of the work. Melted wax might do, but in putting it on to the wood it becomes cold, and consequently reverts to its original stiffness. We have then to get the wax to a fair working consistency by means of some suitable solvent, which turpentine has proved to be. It is cleanly, inexpensive, and evaporates sufficiently quickly, besides mixing well with the wax. Some polishers prefer what others might think an excess of turpentine. When a stiff paste is used, the wax is apt to be deposited in excessive quantity, necessitating a considerable amount of rubbing, in places, to remove it. A fluid polish spreads the wax much more evenly, but no gloss can be obtained till the turpentine has disappeared, either evaporated or been absorbed by the wood. When the polish has been laid evenly over the work, this does not take long; so a thin mixture may be considered preferable to a very stiff one. A paste of about the consistency of butter in hot weather, might be regarded as a medium. Those who use a wax polish which could be poured would consider this stiff, while others who add very little turpentine, or who believe in resin, would consider it thin. A thick mixture or a thin one may be used, the result depending more on the manipulation of the material than on the material itself; and this manipulation may next be considered.

In the application of wax polish there is almost as great a variety in practice as in proportion of ingredients. The great thing is to have the wax—the turpentine is merely the vehicle for conveying this—evenly and thinly distributed, and so long as this is done it is of small consequence how it is managed. To spread the wax with, some use a piece of rag, while others prefer a stiff brush specially made for the purpose, and both get equally good results. After the wax has been spread the polish is obtained by friction, and the more you rub the brighter the polish will be. The brush or cloth used to rub the wax into the wood should not be employed to give the finishing touches. In this final friction it is essential that the cloth or brush used be perfectly dry, as if it is at all damp no polished surface can be produced. The final polish is best done with a perfectly clean rubber, and three sets of cloths or rubbers may be used. With the first the mixture is to be rubbed on the wood, with the second it is to be rubbed off till a fair amount of polish is got, while with the third the rubbing should be continued till the surface is as bright as it can be got.

The directions which have been given should enable

any one to wax-polish wood successfully. Hard dry
rubbing, with energetic application, is at least as important as the wax and turpentine; for, though more simple than the French polishing process, it is more
laborious.

Oil Finishing and Dry Shining.—The following description of the methods of oil polishing and dry shining
is taken largely from an English work on the subject,
and may be depended upon as being fairly correct and
up to date:

The simple process of oil polishing must now receive
attention; and there is still something to admire in a
comparatively dull oiled surface. The process simply
consists of rubbing in linseed oil and polishing with a
soft rag. The oiling and polishing must be continued
at intervals till the requisite shine is obtained. To get
the best results takes time and friction. Oil polishing
is not difficult, but it is decidedly fatiguing and
tedious. The more the surface is rubbed the better,
and the process may be extended over some weeks.
Patience and energetic application are still more essential than with wax polishing, for to get even the semblance of a polish or gloss within a week or two with
the aid of oil must not be expected. How long does it
take to finish a thing properly with oil? It may be
said the work is never finished. An oiled surface will
always bear more rubbing than it has had, and will not
be deteriorated by friction; still from one to two
months should suffice to get a good polish, which will
be durable according to the amount of labor bestowed
upon it during that time. This is more time than can
be devoted to the finishing touches of a piece of furniture generally nowadays, so it may almost be considered that oil polishing is an obsolete process.

Still, it does not follow that because the process is too long to be remunerative in ordinary work it should not be worthy of attention, especially as it has merits which recommen 1 it where speed is not a primary consideration.   One great advantage of it is that it is much more durable than either French or wax polish; it does not blister by heat like the former, nor spoil with water to such an extent as the latter, with which in general appearance it may be compared.   It is because it does not blister by heat that it is especially useful.   An ordinary French polished dining-table top shows the damage caused by hot dishes laid on it, unless great care has been taken.   On an oil polished dining-table top the same hot dishes might be placed almost with impunity; and it is chiefly dining-table tops that have prevented oil polishing becoming quite extinct.   Though the whole of a table, or anything else, may be polished with oil, it is usual, even when the top is oiled, to polish the legs and frame otherwise.

Linseed oil is the only material used in pure oil fin ish, but other ingredients have been used, till it is difficult to recognize the distinction between oil polishing and French polishing.   The two processes may overlap to an almost indefinite extent, but with these we have, at present at any rate, nothing to do, and to discuss them might only tend to confuse the novice. Authorities differ on the state in which the linseed oil should be used, some recommending boiled, others raw, and others various proportions of the two.   For ordinary work boiled linseed oil is perhaps the better, but this is not intended to imply that those who prefer raw oil are wrong; therefore any oil polisher who has an inclination for some fancy mixture of boiled and raw oils can use it.

The treatment is very much the same as in wax polishing. It consists in rubbing the oil well into the wood, not saturating or flooding, but scrubbing it, and then rubbing long and hard. The process may be repeated almost indefinitely, daily or at longer intervals, till a polish which is deemed sufficient appears. For example, take a table top, rub some oil well into it, and then polish with a rubber formed by wrapping some baize, felt, or similar material round a brick or other suitable block, the purpose of which is, by its weight, to some extent to relieve the polisher from using his muscles in applying pressure. The rubbing should be continued till the surface of the wood is dry. The only perceptible difference in the top will be the darkened appearance caused by the oil, as little or no gloss will appear at first. By repeating the operation, however, a polish will come up gradually, and a surface which in the opinion of many is superior to that of French polish will be the ultimate result. Should the polish sweat, some methylated spirit may be rubbed in. This will dry the surface without spoiling the polish.

Oil polishing is hardly suitable for anything but plain work, on account of the labor required; but any piece of work can be so polished if the necessary time and labor be given to it. Even when it is not deemed practicable to bring up a polish with oil, a very pleasing finish may be given to a piece of work by merely rubbing it with oil. The color is enriched to an extent which perhaps would hardly be credited by those who have not had frequent opportunities of seeing wood in the white and again after being oiled. In choice mahogany especially the improvement is very marked. Light oak is also greatly improved in tone.

Fretworkers who are not proficient in French polishing would be more satisfied with the appearance of anything they make if they simply oiled it instead of coating it with shellac, which has to serve for French polish.

Dry shining will be found a simple process after the ordinary methods of French polishing have been mastered. Finishing work by dry shining is the crudest and simplest way in which a gloss can be got on the surface of wood by means of a thin varnish of shellac and methylated spirit. It must not be mistaken for varnishing, as this process is ordinarily understood, for it is distinctly a process of French polishing. Even those who have managed to do bodying-up and spiriting-off, or even glazing, will find the operation of dry shining simple in comparison. It is the nearest approach to varnishing by means of a rubber, instead of a brush, that polishers practice. The wood is varnished with ordinary French polish, applied by means of the polisher's special appliance—the rubber.

Dry shining, unlike glazing, is not in any degree a substitute for the difficult process of spiriting-off, and those who think to get a high degree of finish on their work by means of dry shining may give up the illusion. When a really good finish is wanted, French polishing, as it is ordinarily understood, should be chosen, for there is no efficient substitute by which a like result can be got.

Dry shining can be used in any position where a high degree of finish is not necessary or customary. It is useful for finishing inside work—such as the insides of boxes, drawers, cabinets, and interior parts generally—and is often seen on the fronts of drawers and trays enclosed in a wardrobe. The chief advantages in connection with it are that it can be done expeditiously, and therefore cheaply; that it sufficiently closes the grain of the wood to prevent dust getting in and clogging it; and that it gives a certain degree of finish which wood, left in the white or altogether unpolished does not possess.

The wood is bodied-in without any preparatory filling, but otherwise precisely in the manner as already directed. It is not customary to take such precautions to get up a good body as there recommended. A better description of the process is to say that the wood is wiped over with the polish rubber; not much trouble is usually taken to do more than get the preliminary body worked on. There is no reason why the first body should not be allowed to sink, and the article then be rebodied if necessary. Much bodying-in would make the work almost as hard as that involved in ordinary French polishing, so that ordinarily the bodying-in dry shining is done more quickly.

When the bodying-in has been done to the satisfaction of the polisher, the rubber is charged with French polish, rather more fully than was recommended for bodying. Instead of being rubbed all over the wood in any direction, it is wiped over in the direction of the grain from end to end of the piece, very much in the manner mentioned in connection with glazing. The rubber may be moved backwards and forwards till dry, but a better way under ordinary circumstances is to let the polish deposited by each rub dry before going over the same place again. When using the rubber in finishing, it should have no oil; and if the former of these two methods is adopted it will be difficult to prevent the polish dragging, so the easier course should be adopted.

Repolishing and Reviving.—Having once mastered the fundamental principle of polishing, it is a comparatively easy task to give to a plain piece of wood a level and lustrous surface; and, by the use of stains that can be bought ready prepared, a fair imitation of any given wood can be obtained with but little labor. But the polisher who wishes to hold his own against all comers, must be able to do more than merely to stain and polish a plain piece of new wood.

When dealing with old work that requires repolishing, all dirt, grease, and furniture paste must be removed by careful washing with soda and warm water and powdered pumice-stone or bath-brick. It can then be French polished, or a fresher and more satisfactory appearance may be given by applying one or two coats of brown hard spirit varnish—such as can be bought at an oil and color merchant's—carefully with a camel-hair brush.

When varnished work has to be dealt with, first clean off all the varnish and then repolish in the way described in previous chapters, except that filling will probably be dispensed with. The varnish can generally be more easily removed by scraping than by papering. With care the varnish can be washed off with soda or potash and water, but on account of the liability to injure the wood it is scarcely advisable to adopt this method.

For removing polish from flat surfaces, the steel scrapers as used by cabinetmakers are the best tools to use. In turned and other work which has an uneven surface the old coating can nearly all be got off by application of strong hot soda water, to which may be added some oxalic acid in difficult cases. When a large quantity of work has to be treated, use the following mixture: ½ lb. potash, ½ lb. soft soap, ½ lb. rock ammonia, 1 lb. washing soda, 3 ounces of nitric acid, 1 gallon of water. Apply with a fiber or scrubbing brush, taking care of the hands. Swill off with plenty of clean water. When the work is dry, oil and fill in; then repolish.

Spirit varnish can be removed by washing with methylated spirit, which redissolves the lac. This is both a tedious and somewhat expensive method, which need be resorted to only for delicate mouldings and other work which cannot well be cleaned by scraping or by scouring with some liquid which, though it would remove the varnish, might stain and so spoil the wood. Alcohol, being neutral, may be used on any wood, as it will not affect the color.

When dealing with cabinets or other built-up work, the process of repolishing will be simplified somewhat by taking apart as much as convenient. It is a good plan to unhinge all doors, to remove all carvings that may be screwed on from the back, and to remove all knobs, brass fittings, etc.—not forgetting to put some tallying mark on each piece which might be liable to misplacement. Thus the doors can be better handled on the bench, the corners of panels can be worked up better, and the carvings can be varnished better. When the carvings are planted on, as is often done, a much cleaner job is made if these are first removed; for it is a difficult task to polish the open carvings equal to the flat surface.

Sometimes polished work is disfigured by fine little lines which are caused by cracks, resulting from sweating. These lines become visible through the dust settling on the exuding oil. This disfigurement can be averted almost entirely by occasionally carefully wiping

with a soft, damp cloth.   Sweating is not entirely pre-
ventible, but when the oil has ceased to exude, which
may not be for some months, the work may be
repolished with advantage.

The perfectly level, brilliant polish found on new
German pianos fills many an American French-polisher
with envy.   Unfortunately, this brilliant polish does
not last long, and the majority of the pianos soon have
a greasy, cracked appearance.   Indeed, there are but
few of these pianos with a polish gained by the legitimate process of French polishing.   This brilliant,
level polish is gained by a very liberal use of gum
sandarac, and when the polishing is completed the
pianos are set aside in a clean, hot room, which has
the effect of causing the polish or gums to flow to one
dead level.   Some makers use varnish very freely,
and, before passing to the hot room, level this by
means of pumice powder, tripoli, putty powder, and
sometimes flour.

When the requisite number of coats of varnish have
been laid, the surface is leveled with fine glass-paper
and linseed oil, or by the slower process of felt rubber
and pumice powder.   After being wiped perfectly
clean, a rubber made of soft flannel, or, better still, of
old silk, is used to rub carefully and lightly in a
circular direction with tripoli powder and oil, till the
surface is perfectly level and inclined to be bright; it
is then rubbed with dry putty powder and silk, and
finally brightened with flour.

The surface should be left perfectly free from any
trace of the polishing powders; neglect of this
accounts for the white patches sometimes seen on the
German pianos.   These patches are not so deep as
they appear at first sight, and may often be removed

with flour emery and linseed oil or turps without disturbing the polish.

To renovate the polish on these pianos is difficult, but when it is not very bad, a reviver made of equal parts of linseed oil, lime water, and turps is generally effective. The lime water and oil are first thoroughly mixed; then the turps is added, and the mixture is applied by means of wadding. The surface is wiped off with a rag, and finished with a clean, soft rag-swab, made fairly moist with methylated spirit. Should any trace of grease still remain, change to a clean place of the already moist rag, and sprinkle a few spots of glaze on its face, or, better still, wipe the face of the glaze rubber over the face of the clean swab.

Should this method prove ineffective it will be necessary to repolish, first removing the sweat or roughness by fine sandpaper and oil, or by washing with weak soda water and pumice powder. The polish used should be made with spirit instead of naphtha, and, to ensure its lasting qualities, it should be bodied up one day and finished the next.

To darken the birch frame of a chair, wipe it over with asphaltum dissolved in turpentine (one cent's worth in half a pint of turps). This stains without giving a painted appearance; should there be any difficulty in obtaining asphaltum, Vandyke brown may be used, mixed to a thin paste with liquid ammonia— or with a strong solution of common washing soda. This is thinned with water, till of the required tone, which will readily be found by trying its effect on any odd piece of wood. If French polish cannot be applied, the most suitable thing to use is brown hard spirit varnish.

For restoring polish that has faded from damp or

exposure to the sun, those stains which are used to stain the common woods will not be suitable. It may be convenient to remove only the upper surface of the polish, to color the faded portion so as to match its surroundings, and to repolish the whole. When the polish is not very bad, it is generally sufficient to smooth it well with a piece of worn glass-paper. When it is much scratched or faded, methylated spirit should be sprinkled upon it, and the surface well rubbed with No. 1 sandpaper, applied with a circular motion; it will then be found that only the upper surface of the polish will be removed. Before repolishing, it is advisable first to wash the article with water to which a little common washing soda has been added. This will remove any dirt, furniture paste, etc.; a little pumice powder or powdered bath-brick may be used to assist.

After the necessary cleaning off of dirt, etc., has been accomplished, any bruises must be removed, either by scraping out or by bringing up level, by means of a hot iron and moisture, or by filling up with hard stopping, or by the still better method previously given. When this has been done, and all defective parts made good, the surface must be wiped over with an oily rag; it assists the new polish to take kindly to the old. In scraping out the bruises, in cleaning off level any new piece, and in cleaning off the polish, it is probable that light patches may be made. More especially will these be made apparent if the damaged portion has been previously colored up by stains, dry colors, or dyed polish.

For coloring up or matching, it is generally sufficient, if the wood in hand is mahogany, to wipe over the damaged portion with red oil, which consists of ¼ lb. of alkanet root steeped in 1 pint of linseed oil, working up with red polish. Should the wood be walnut, many a little blemish and scratch in soft resinous varnish may be matched by wiping over with a solution of one cent's worth of asphaltum dissolved in ½ pint turps. Should the defect be a piece of sap or other light portion, go over the light portion several times with the polish rubber to prevent the grain from rising, and then saturate a small tuft of wadding with 3 parts of methylated spirits to 1 part of polish; on this wadding place a small quantity of Vandyke brown or brown umber, mix well, and carefully wipe over the light portions, thinning out with spirits if too dark, picking up a little more color if not dark enough, adding a little black if required.

Matching stains are used in French polishing because light and dark places often occur in the best selected woods, and in stained work, owing to the difference in the direction of the grain. To tone or harmonize the entire surface to one uniform shade, is technically called matching or coloring up, and requires a little tact and a good eye for color. On large flat surfaces colored polish may be used with advantage, but for small work it would be better to take a small tuft of wadding and wet it with 1 part polish to 3 parts spirits. With this take up a little yellow ocher and just a trace of umber or Vandyke brown. Press the wadding well on the back of a piece of worn-out glass-paper to equalize, and mix well. Try the effect on an odd corner of the work; if too dark, thin out with spirits; if not dark enough, pick up more color, or wipe over twice. Having gained the right shade, apply lightly with a straight or wavy motion as required. This would enable one to match the oak, but any wood can be matched by using suitable pigments, a red tinge being usually given by the addition of a few drops of Bismarck brown stain. Though it is possible to proceed to polish direct, yet it would be safer to set the stain by giving a coat of thin spirit varnish, and allow this to get quite dry before polishing. In matching up satin walnut, the polisher must use judgment, for the work can hardly be regarded as mechanical. The stain must depend on the color or tint of the lighter parts, and of the darker parts to which they are to be matched. Generally a little weak brown stain will do what is required. When necessary, it can be altered slightly in color by the addition of other pigments, according to the tints desired.

In matching, the wavy appearance of some woods may be given by a tremulous movement of the hand, and the mottled appearance of others by dabbing with a badger softener or clean, soft dusting brush while the color is still wet. Veins either black or red may be given by picking up a little dry black or red stain on the corner of the tuft of wadding and applying it carefully, taking some adjacent portion as a guide for pattern. For rosewood, red stain and dry black may be used in combination; for birch or oak, use yellow ocher. When the work in hand is large, and requires staining all over, and it is not possible to gain the desired result by means of dyed polish applied with the rubber, the colors should be mixed in a pot with 3 parts of spirit to 1 of polish, and applied with a camel-hair brush. The work is not so liable to get patchy with two or more coats of weak stain as with one strong one.

After laying on the stain, allow a few minutes to elapse for it to set, then smooth down with a piece of worn, fine glass-paper, and give a coat of thin brush polish or spirit varnish. This will set the colors previous to polishing, which can be proceeded with in about ten minutes. Mahogany, rosewood, and walnut, if not inlaid, are generally improved by the use of a polish tinged by the addition of a little red stain. Other colors may also be mixed with polish to be applied with the rubber. When using these dyed polishes, cease when just the right tinge is attained; another rubber may be used to finish off with clear polish.

In repolishing work, the foundation having been already laid, the polish is not required quite so thick as in polishing the bare wood. In the final stage, when finishing off, any trace of greasiness may be effectually removed by well rubbing with a swab of the clean, soft rag, fairly damp (not wet) with spirits, on face of which has been sprinkled a few drops of glaze.

Colors in a dry state known as pigments, such as Venetian red, yellow ocher, vegetable black or lamp-black, umbers, Vandyke brown, chromes, orange and lemon, greens, blues, flake white, etc., are useful. By the aid of these, the polisher is enabled to match woods and restore faded polish, far more expeditiously than can be done by staining or using dyed polish or varnish. Work that might puzzle the inexperienced for hours can be done in a few minutes by a knowledge of the use of dry colors. They are used in some stains by mixing with ammonia, glue size, pearlash, soda, and they are used to color the "filling-in" of whiting and turps to make it match the various woods. Venetian red is used for mahogany, umber for walnut, black for ebony, and sometimes to give an appearance of age to oak by making the grain appear dirty.

Sometimes the polisher has a job passed to him that, properly speaking, ought to be done by the painter. The quick-drying nature of the solutions of shellac, with which the polisher is the better acquainted, obtains for him the preference. For example, shields, etc., for the decorative purposes that may require five different colors and a coat of varnish, can be colored ready for fixing within twenty-four hours. To do this, lime blue, chrome yellow, vegetable black, flake white, and vermilionette or any other colors should be mixed with ordinary French polish to the consistency of thin paint, thinning out when necessary with alcohol spirits. Three coats of color can be laid on, stencil patterns cut and painted, borders and edges lined, and the whole finished with a coat of white hard varnish within twelve hours. To prevent the white getting a yellowish tinge, it is well to mix it with transparent polish made from white shellac.

To make imitation marble which wears well, give several coats of flake white mixed in polish; then put in the veins of blue or black with feathers, afterwards giving a coat of white thinned out with spirits. This has the effect of making the veining appear beneath the surface. When dry it is finished by giving a coat of good quality copal varnish.

THE FINISHING OF VARIOUS WOODS

It will be in order now to describe how to finish some of the more popular woods, in detail, though enough has been said in a general way to enable any workman to finish work in any wood made use of for building or decorative purposes, but a few lines devoted to some of our special woods may perhaps be of timely service to some owner of this volume. Oak, being the most popular and at the same time the most durable and the most used of our woods, is deserving of the first place.

Finishing Oak

We have in this country over forty kinds of oak nearly every one of which may be used for some special purpose; those most used for building finish and for furniture, however, are only few, among which are the white oak (*Quercus rulia*), rock oak (*Quercus primas murticola*) and black oak (*Quercus tindoris*). All of the above-named oaks are capable of being handsomely finished, the white and black oaks being the best and the red being next.

What is known as quarter oak is made by first sawing the log from end to end through the middle. Then each half is sawed from end to end through the middle, thus leaving four quarters. Each quarter has only three sides, one side the bulge part of the log, and the other two sides flat and coming to an edge. The boards are sawed off the sharp edge, and each sawing, therefore, throws off a board wider than the one before it. Sawing the quarters of the log in this manner, lumber possesses that beautiful cross-grained figure so much in fashion now that it has become somewhat of a craze. This cross-grained material finds favor in the finest furniture and interior work. The wood is susceptible of the very finest polish, and the cross-grain produces an effect made by both nature and the saw, that is quite superior to the art of the most skillful grainer. To effect a good imitation of antique oak, lampblack or Vandyke brown in oil is applied to the surface of the wood, darkening its natural hue; but this is not by any means best or the only way, but answers very well where other processes or methods are not available. With regard to giving oak an antique appearance, many opinions exist. Formerly—and probably the first—imitations of antique oak were produced by exposing the bare dressed surface to the steam of boiling ammonia. This process, however, it was impossible to apply to casings of house interiors, thus leading to the application of the aqua ammonia with a brush, but it is by repeated application that the desired results are produced. It stains the wood gray. There are finishers who claim this to be the only process by which to imitate Nature, but another, much faster and one which gives the same results, is to use strong vinegar with iron filings or shavings added; by a little experimenting this can be made to suffice with one coat, depending upon the amount of iron added.

A very clever imitation of the general antique can be obtained by staining the filler with Vandyke brown and charcoal, equal parts, using about 1 part of the colored to 4 parts of the light. Then there is another antique which imitates certain oak from the sixteenth century; the peculiarity of it consists in dark cloud streaks permeating the wood in every direction, some of them crossing the panels in a V-shape, others straight near top and bottom. To give them an odd appearance, a pair of panels can be clouded by streaking one three or four times and the other once or twice. These stripes vary in width from three to five inches. The wider streaks look well across the top of a table three or four times, or even partly across, while the narrow ones would do well around the legs and across the styles and rails of paneled work. In putting these on, they should be dark in the center and blend out at the edges.   This is done with an automatic paint burner, allowing the flames to scorch the wood nearly black; but care must be taken not to char it. After the work is all streaked, the wood is filled with filler stained with burnt umber mixed as for black walnut.

Care must be taken to have the filler stained to the proper tint, and in applying correctly.   By following the rules given under the head "Filling" the operator should have no trouble in making good work, and we here repeat the instruction.

After enough surface has been covered with the filler, so that what has been first applied begins to flatten, the process of wiping should immediately begin, using for that purpose either a rag or a handful of waste or excelsior.   If the oak is very open-grained, waste is preferable.   With a piece of this that has previously been used and is pretty well supplied with filler, rub crosswise of the grain, rather rubbing it into the grain than wiping it off.   After the whole surface has been gone over in this way, take a clean piece of waste or rag (never use excelsior for wiping clean) and wipe the surface perfectly clean and free from filler, using a wooden pick, the point of which has been covered with a rag or waste, to clean out the corners, beads, etc.   It is well to give these picks some atten-tion, as a person once accustomed to certain tools can accomplish more and better work than with tools that feel strange in his hands; therefore, each finisher should furnish his own pick.   As to their construction, those are best made from second-growth hickory, which can be procured from any carriage repair shop, such as old spokes, broken felloes, etc.   They are made eight inches in length, half inch oval at one end

and tapering down to the point at the other. Sharpen
the oval end like a coal chisel, then smooth with
sandpaper, which should also be used to sharpen the
tool when the same becomes worn dull.

This picking out of the filler from beads, etc., can
be accelerated by the use of a picking brush manufactured especially for that purpose, but it is not
advisable to use this on very coarse-grained oak, as it
scrubs the filler out of the pores.

Oak may be fumigated by liquid ammonia, strength
880°, which may be bought at any wholesale chemist's
at $1.50 a gallon. The wood should be placed in a *dark*
and *airtight* room (in a big packing case, if you like!),
and half a pint or so of ammonia poured into a soup
plate, and placed upon the *ground* in the center of the
compartment. This done, shut the entrance, and
secure any cracks, if any, by pasted slips of paper.
Remember that the ammonia does not touch the oak,
but the gas that comes from it acts in a wondrous
manner upon the tannic acid in that wood, and browns
it so deeply that a shaving or two may actually be
taken off without removing the color. The depth of
shade will entirely depend upon the quantity of
ammonia used and the time the wood is exposed. Try
an odd bit first experimentally, and then use your own
judgment.

Short pieces of stuff may be so treated by using an
airtight box. The box ready, a flat dish or plate of
strong ammonia should be placed in the bottom, so
that the fumes will *rise* and surround the object. All
that is now necessary is to place the article in the
box, nailing up as close as possible, and await results
Ten hours' exposure, using strong ammonia, should give
a good color; if not dark enough let it remain longer

bearing in mind, however, that the wood will present no noticeable change until oiled or brought in contact with a wet substance such as shellac. It is well, therefore, to note the progress by touching the wood with the wet finger, when it will show at once the stage it has reached.

There could be no better method devised to stain oak than this, when practicable, and in adopting it we simply anticipate nature, which, in time, through the action of the ammonia of the atmosphere, would present the same result. Mahogany may also be treated similarly with success.

Here is another method of making antique oak, and it might be added that white, and black ash, and chestnut, similarly treated, will give a fair imitation of antique oak. The job should be made of hardwood, with as full an open grain as possible to secure a fine effect. Sandpaper this and clean off. Then prepare a priming made of 1 part japan, 1 part raw linseed oil and 1 part rubbing varnish. Drop into ½ gal. of the liquid 1 lb. of commercial corn starch, such as is used for culinary purposes. Next take some good, dry, burnt Turkish umber, and add about ¼ lb. of this to the starch. Apply to the job a good flowing coat of this priming. Let stand until it is set and has soaked well into the grain, and then take a broad putty knife and stick it into the grain, working the knife crosswise of the grain. Again let stand a little while, and then wipe with rags; especially clean out all the corners, and get the job into as good condition as possible as regards having the grain well filled.

Upon the completion of the operation above described it will be found that the open grain has absorbed the starch and umber, and that these portions now show the dark shade suggestive of age, while all tne rest of the surface is also slightly darkened.

When again perfectly dry, give one coat of rubbing varnish, prepared by adding to it ½ lb. of starch to each gallon of varnish. This coat should be flowed on freely as a medium coat of rubbing varnish, but be careful not to have runs of sags. This ought to completely fill the wood, after which proceed to varnish, rub and finish the job in the usual manner. To produce a natural oak finish, follow precisely the same course as above described, with the single exception of omitting the umber. This will leave the wood in its natural color.

Some of the most attractive work in this line, however, is effected by simply spreading on the surface of the material a concentrated solution of permanganate of potash, this being allowed to act until the desired shade is obtained. Five minutes suffice ordinarily to give a good color, a few trials indicating the proper proportions. The substance named is decomposed by the vegetable fiber, with the precipitation of brown peroxide of manganese, which the influence of the potash, at the same time set free, fixes in a durable manner on the fibers. When the action is terminated, the wood is carefully washed with water, dried, then oiled and polished in the usual manner. The effect produced by this process in several woods is really remarkable. On the cherry especially it develops a beautiful red color which well resists the action of air and light, and on the other woods it has a very pleasing and natural effect.

Along with the foregoing may be added the following stains for oak: add to a quart of water 2 ounces each of potash and pearlash. This is a very good stain, but it should be used carefully, as it blisters the hands and softens brushes. The stain may be made lighter by adding more water.

To Darken Oak.—To darken the color of oak, any of the following may be used:

Liquid ammonia laid on evenly with a rag or brush will deepen the color immediately, and it will not fade, this being an artificial production of result produced naturally by age.

Bichromate of potash, dissolved in cold water, and applied with a brush, will produce a similar result.

A decoction of green walnut-shell will bring new oak to any shade or nearly black.

Another.—Two quarts of boiled oil; ½ lb. of ground umber, mixed in oil by colorman; 1 pint of liquid driers, stirred in; 1 pint of turpentine; mix. After cleaning and planing your boards, lay this on with the grain of the wood. If required lighter, add naphtha till the required shade is attained; it darkens with age. Give it twelve hours to dry; then varnish with wood varnish, or use only beeswax and turpentine The result is good in time, but slower than varnish.

Oak can be fumigated. by making a tent of some cheap oil cloth, which may be rigged up over a rough wooden frame. Of course, the tent must be made pretty tight. Don't let the frame touch the work, and when complete, cut a small piece that you can lift up and use as a peep hole. Then get a saucer full of liquid ammonia and place inside the tent—anywhere on the floor will do. Close the tent and await results. The more ammonia used the darker it gets, so you must use your peep hole and suit yourself. If you wish to polish it, give it a coat of beeswax and turpentine, let dry, and then brush or rub it well. For a dull polish, give it a coat of raw linseed oil, dry well, and then brush up. By "fumigation" you always get a good even tone; but, failing this, you can stain the work, and by simple means. Buy a little permanganate of potash at the chemist's, dissolve in water, and put on with a brush; when dry, give another coat if not dark enough. Another method is to get ½ lb. of black japan and dissolve in ½ pint of turpentine, and apply as before, or you can buy the stain ready-made; and the walnut *water* stain—not varnish stain—is a good one to make a dark brown oak color. If you find the stain brings up the grain—i.e., makes the wood rough—rub it down with fine sandpaper and stain again, but rub off fairly dry. All these are simple methods, which you could easily acquire.

Styles of Oak Finish.—As oak in its many and varied finishes is so very fashionable just now, an explanation of the effects of the several stains may be of interest, as so many of them are so closely allied as to confuse the uninitiated. Bog oak is a thin stain of medium color, giving quarter-sawed oak a slight tinge of green. It is about the same density as weathered oak, but of a green tone instead of brown, like weathered oak. Weathered oak is of a brown tone in close imitation of the rich old hue taken on by oak through time or from exposure to the weather. Antwerp oak is also brown, but of a deeper shade, producing an attractive antique effect. Black Flemish is a much-admired finish, especially when it is desired to produce an effect of great weight. It gives a piece of furniture a substantial appearance. Its black tone combines admirably with red wall covering and hangings. Brown Flemish is not unlike Antwerp, but of a much stronger brown tone. This is one of the most popular stains of the hour. It is quite permanent and produces a very artistic effect. The so-called gun-metal finish for oak is not unlike black Flemish, but gives a tinge of blue instead of deep black. Malachite, although light green, is not too intrusive. This is affected by many people of good taste and is quite popular, especially for staining ash. Tyrolean oak is as dark as black Flemish or bog oak, and is of a green tinge, instead of the blue of the gun-metal finish.

Golden Oak is very fashionable, being a brownish color with a sort of golden glow tint; it may be obtained as follows: Golden oak finish is not produced by the filler alone; in fact, the filler has very little to do with the result. The wood must be stained before it is filled, and, of course, the filler must be so colored or stained as not to mar or dull the effect. A mixture of gold size japan and genuine asphaltum varnish in about equal parts, thinned with turpentine, makes a good stain that will not raise the grain of the wood, dries quickly and hard, and, if wiped out properly, gives under varnish a rich effect, termed "golden," for want of another appropriate name.

To make a filler, mix one-third each of raw linseed oil, japan gold size and turpentine, and put into this mixture enough finely powdered silica or silex to make a stiff paste, and color this with burnt umber in oil, Vandyke brown in oil and a trifle of drop black to suit, being mindful that in golden oak only the high lights are yellowish brown, while the filled grain is decidedly dark. The mixture should be run through a bandmill. The best plan for you is to buy your golden oak paste filler, or at least buy the light paste filler and color it to suit your taste; for you cannot buy the raw material as cheap as the manufacturer, and making it in a small way will cost you more in the long run.

Another method, if the work is new, is as follows: Fuming is only possible when the articles are new and free from varnish, polish, glue, or marks of handling. The process consists of enclosing the articles—from which the glass and all brass fittings are removed—in an airtight room or box, on the floor or bottom of which are placed a number of shallow dishes containing strong liquid ammonia. The depth of color depends on the length of exposure, which may vary from twelve to thirty-six hours. Where this process is not practicable, the next best method is staining. The stain must be weak, the exact color required being afterwards obtained by the use of a polish made from orange shellac and a trace of color in the varnish. A suitable stain may be made by dissolving ½ oz. of bichromate of potash in 1½ pt. of water. To prevent the work coming up rough on the application of the water stain, the work should be first wiped over with raw linseed oil. The stain must be liberally applied, and rubbed well in with a rag, finishing off always in the direction of the grain. Before starting on the work, experiment on odd pieces of similar wood.

Flemish Oak.—To make a stain for Flemish oak, ½ lb. of bichromate of potash, dissolved in 1 gal. of water. Coat woodwork. When dry, sandpaper down smooth; then coat with best drop black, ground in japan, thinned with turpentine. Let stand five minutes and wipe off clean, then coat with pure grain shellac and sandpaper with No. o sandpaper; then coat with beeswax, 1 lb. to a gallon of turpentine, ¼ lb. of drop black mixed in the wax, then wipe off clean with cheese cloth.

Weathered Oak.—Give woodwork one coat of strong ammonia. When dry, sandpaper down smooth and stain it from the following colors: lampblack, ocher and 2 lbs. of silica to a gallon of stain. Wipe off with cheese cloth, then give one coat of pure grain shellac, then sandpaper and give one coat of wax and wipe off clean. If you should desire a brownish shade, put 1 oz. of bichromate of potash and ammonia, or if a greenish shade, put some green and stain.

Verde, or Green Finish.—One ounce of nigrocene dissolved in ½ gal. of water. Give woodwork one coat; when dry, sandpaper, care to be taken not to rub off edges; then fill with a bright green filler, with some white lead in the filler. When thoroughly dry, give one coat of pure grain shellac and then wax, or it could be finished with three coats of varnish and rubbed. This finish leaves the pores of bright green color, while the rest of the wood is almost black.

Black Oak.—One ounce of nigrocene to ½ gal. of water. Give woodwork one coat, then fill with a black filler, then one coat of shellac and three coats of varnish rubbed with pumice-stone and water, then oil and wipe off clean.

Austrian Oak.— Fill with a light antique filler, colored with raw umber. Give two very thin coats of shellac, colored with nigrocene and yellow to the desired shade, then sandpaper down and wax and wipe off clean.

Red Oak is a difficult wood to stain or fumigate, but it may be done as follows: Make a stain by mixing ground dry Dutch pink (this color is yellow) and a little dry drop black, with beer, and apply with a hog's hair brush. Try the stain on a piece of red oak, and get the exact shade if possible, taking care that you do not stain quite as dark as the fumigated parts. When dry, oil with linseed oil, and make a weak stain, using the same colors, mixed with alcohol, with enough button polish to bind the color. Lay on carefully with a camel-hair brush. It is better to giv two coats of weak stain, as the result will be a more even color. When dry, wax polished this will make a good job.

Oak Staining Generally.—There is no wood which may be treated in so many different ways as oak. It may be left in its natural state, or it may be oiled, or wax polished, or French polished in its natural color. It can be stained and waxed, stained and French polished in a variety of colors or tints, with the grain opened or filled, and it can also be fumigated. For bedroom furniture, if the wood is carefully selected, a very pleasing effect is obtained by waxing or French polishing it in its natural color, or slightly stained and polished with the grain open or filled, according to taste. Dining-room or library finish is generally stained a medium color or fumigated. All furniture is frequently stained very dark, and polished with the grain open.

If it is desired that the work should be finished in its natural color, fill in with Russian tallow and plaster of Paris, and polish with white polish. If it is required to be slightly tinted, stain the filler with yellow ocher and polish with button polish. For staining, the best stains to use are the powdered water stains, and some very effective tints may be obtained by carefully mixing green and brown stains together; apply the stain with a hog's hair brush, and if the grain should rise quickly, rub down with 1½ glass-paper before laying off the stain. When the stain is dry, oil with linseed oil, then give a coat of polish to fix the stain. It may then be polished with the grain open, and finished with a wet rubber, using no spirits. If a level surface is required, it must be carefully filled in, and not unduly hurried in the polishing. The latter applies to oak generally, as the wood is coarse, and consequently sinks a great deal.

A good dark oak stain may be made as follows: Dissolve 1 oz. of bichromate of potash in ½ pint of water, and 1 oz. of potash in ½ pint of water. When each are separately dissolved, mix together, and add dry powdered Vandyke brown. If a very dark color is required, add also a little powdered drop black; apply with a hog's hair brush, and polish as before stated. As sometimes the American potash varies in strength, the hair of the brush will curl up if it is too strong. If this occurs, add a little more water. Oak carvings give a much nicer appearance always if the grain is left open, even when the other parts are filled up. If they are stained, oil and afterwards give a coat of polish to fix the stain. When this is dry, brush well with a stiff-haired brush and rub with a dry cloth. It is sometimes advisable to oil oak before it is stained, as it often prevents the grain rising. The only disadvantage is that a little extra labor is required to make the stain bite.

Fumigated Oak.—The best kinds of oak for fumigating are the English wainscot, or Baltic. The red American oak does not fumigate well. The advantages of fumigating are that a more natural color is obtained than by staining. The wood is not made rough by the operation, and there is also a great saving in labor. The best method of fumigating is to construct an airtight chamber, lined with wood, and the joints

of the wood made airtight by pasting paper over them.
If the chamber is of the following dimensions it will
be found large enough for most purposes: length, 9 ft.;
width, 4 ft.; height, 6 ft. Portable inner frames may
be made with shutters, so that the size of the chamber
may be made smaller if necessary. The door should
have glass panels; this will permit of the work being
watched, and when the wood has become dark enough,
the door should be opened. Articles to be fumigated
should have all brass work removed; then place in the
chamber in such a position as to allow a free passage
for the fumes to get at all parts of the wood. Then
place half a dozen saucers (flower-pot saucers will
answer for this purpose) on the floor at equal distances,
and pour into each saucer $\frac{1}{4}$ lb. of spirits of ammonia,
strength of the ammonia to be 880°, then paper over
the joints round the door. The wood will darken
much quicker in hot weather. If a very dark color is
required, it may be necessary to recharge the chamber
after twenty-four hours, but a good color is generally
obtained in about five hours. It should be noted that
the work always becomes lighter after it is taken out
of the fumigating chamber. Consequently, the work
must be proceeded with directly it is taken out. If
any parts are too dark, do not oil them; all other
parts should be at once oiled, and given a coat of
polish. When dry, paper well with No. 1 glass-paper,
and wax polish or French polish with the grain open,
as in the case of stained dark oak. Small articles
may be fumigated by making a box airtight, and
placing a piece of felt upon a level floor; stand the
articles to be fumigated on the felt, and fill one
saucer with $\frac{1}{4}$ lb. spirits of ammonia. Then cover
the whole with the box, and place a weight on the top

of the box; this will prevent the fumes from escaping. It may be raised occasionally to see how the work is proceeding. This plan will answer better than if there is a lid to the box, as the fumes will not escape so much in this way.

Great care must be taken when using the ammonia, and the operator must particularly avoid inhaling the fumes. A good rule when charging a large chamber for fumigating is to have some one at hand in case of any accident, such as the breakage of the vessel containing the ammonia. Before the work is taken out of the chamber the fumes must be allowed to pass off by opening the door for a few minutes before entering. If this rule is carried out, no possible harm can happen.

Pollard oak is best treated by first oiling it, and then applying a coat of button polish. When the polish is dry, it must be rubbed down with No. 1 glass-paper and waxed or French polished. As sometimes pollard oak has very large cracks on the surface, these must be well stopped with wax stopping, which must be stained to match the wood. Before proceeding to wax or French polish, if the joints do not match in color, a little polish stain may be applied with a camel-hair pencil before it is polished.

For Removing Polish and Restaining Oak.—Saturate table with alcohol, keep it wet with it, and whilst wet scrape off polish which will have become softened. If legs are turned, or on shaped edges, etc., where scraper cannot be used, coarse sandpaper (Middle 2) will remove polish. Use plenty of spirit and sandpaper all over, and take care all polish is removed. It can be done in same way with potash—a slower process, and the potash will also burn anything it touches, but will stain the wood at the. same time. When all polish is removed, the table can be stained dark with *walnut water* stain. When wood is well stained in pores, wipe off with cloth and let dry; if not dark enough, give another coat. Another stain is made with turps and black japan, well mixed. A little Prussian blue powder will make either stain a greeny brown. For polishing, rub in raw linseed oil; let dry, and rub again; or for wax polish, melt beeswax on slow heat in a galley pot; add turpentine, about a third part; let cool. Wax should be soft as paste; if sticky, add turps; rub well into wood. Let dry and rub again for polish. Stain must be quite dry before oil or wax is put on.

To Finish Cherry

Cherry (*Prunus cerasus*).—This is a fine-grained wood, tough and light; is capable of taking the very finest finish. Is harder than baywood, and is a nearer approach in color, grain and texture, to mahogany than any other native wood.

One of the best methods for making cherry look like mahogany is to have the wood rubbed with diluted nitric acid, which prepares it for the materials subsequently applied. Afterwards to a filtered mixture of 1½ oz. of dragons' blood dissolved in a pint of spirits of wine is aded one-third that quantity of carbonate of soda. The whole, constituting a very thin liquid, is brushed with a soft brush over the wood. This process is repeated with very little alteration, and in a short interval of time the wood assumes the external appearance of mahogany. If the composition has been properly made the surface will resemble an artificial mirror, and should this brilliancy ever decline it may be restored by rubbing the surface with a little cold drawn linseed oil.

When cherry is nicely filled and rubbed well down and not varnished, it has a soft glow not possessed by any other, and has none of those distortions ot grain that are so unpleasant in mahogany. The timber is chosen from the wild cherry, which in New England and the North generally does not usually grow to a girth of more than 20 inches, but in some of the Western States and in the South frequently attains a diameter of 24 inches. The domestic fruit cherry gives some good specimens of small timber, but as the tree is rarely sacrificed until it is past bearing and is decayed, this source of supply is precarious. The facility with which cherry can be worked makes it a favorite with the cabinetmaker and the house-joiner; and it also possesses the quality of "staying where it is put," and that is more than can be said of many of the hardwoods.

I give below several stains for making pine and other suitable woods to have an appearance of cherry.

1. To prepare this color in water stain, boil in a gallon of water 1 lb. of Spanish annotto and 1 oz. of concentrated lye (potash). Should this not be deep enough, allow the water to evaporate by a gentle heat. The stain can also be darkened by adding gamboge previously dissolved in a weak potash solution.

2. Gamboge in oil, diluted with turpentine, and a little japan added as a siccative. This produces the same color in oil as the former in water stain, and can be deepened with dragons' blood in oil or finely ground burnt sienna in oil.

3. Mix together, by stirring, 1 qt. of spirits of

turpentine, 1 pt. of varnish, and 1 lb. of dry burnt
sienna; apply with a brush and after it has been on
about five minutes wipe it off with rags. This stain
takes about twelve hours to dry.

4. Take 1 qt. alcohol, 2 oz. of dragons' blood;
pulverize the latter along with ¼ oz. of alkanet root;
mix and let stand in a warm place a couple of days.
Shake frequently in the meantime. Apply with a
sponge or brush. Two or three coats may be required.
This makes a fine stain.

To finish cherry, the first and a very important
thing to do is to give the wood a thorough sandpapering, to remove finger and other marks, and make a
perfect surface to receive the stain. Next comes the
dusting off of the work, which also should be carefully
done, as specks of dust or dirt will cause bad work.
Stain should be put on with a four-inch oval brush, one
set with cement. Apply the stain freely, but do not
work it too much, as this would cause it to froth,
forming specks. Have the stain in a wooden, earthen
or enameled vessel, as metal will often alter the color
of the stain. Avoid laps when staining; do a section
at a time. But should a lap be unavoidable, then take
a sponge, wet with clear water, and wet that part of
the work already done and adjoining that which is to
be done, and then at once apply the stain. Have a
bucket of water and a sponge ready at hand. Any
part of the work taking too dark may be toned down
by means of the wet or damp sponge, causing it to
match the other and lighter work. Allow the stain to
dry thoroughly, after which it is ready for sandpapering with 000 paper. Next give a coat of shellac.
Finish with two coats of varnish, or with three coats
for extra fine finish. Rub with pumice-stone and

water, polish with rotten stone and water, and clean up with furniture polish.

Oil stains were formerly used, but aniline stains give much better color effects. Aniline stains may be bought ready prepared.

When sandpapering cherry be sure that you do not cut through, as it would show up white. Cutting through is liable to occur about mouldings, edges, etc. Use old, worn sandpaper there; for the more sunken parts redampen and rub the layers of paper from the back of old sandpaper, which will make it very pliable and soft.

Finishing Black Birch

Birch.—*Betula Nigra* or Canadian birch is superior to all other birches for constructive purposes, and when properly finished has a fine, quiet, refined look that commends itself to all lovers of domestic woods.

Black birch is a close-grained, handsome wood, and can be easily stained to resemble walnut exactly. It is just as easy to work, and is suitable for nearly, if not all, the purposes to which walnut is applied. Birch is much the same color as cherry, but the latter wood is now scarce, and consequently dear. When properly stained it is almost impossible to distinguish the difference between it and walnut, or cherry, as it is susceptible of a beautiful polish, equal to any wood now used in the manufacture of furniture and inside finishings.

To finish to represent mahogany, coat with a weak solution of bichromate of potash, then stain with rose pink, Vandyke brown and burnt sienna; then shellac, with a little Bismarck brown dissolved in the shellac. This makes a better stain and more lasting than a water stain.

There is a species of bird's-eye birch, but it is very scarce. An evidence of the weight and solidity of the wood is the fact that it will sink after being a few days on the water. It also possesses the quality of durability in a preëminent degree.

Birch is generally finished the same as cherry, and directions given under that head will apply here also.

Finishing Mahogany

Mahogany, cherry and black birch require about the same treatment, though there are some features in mahogany that differ a trifle from the other two woods. There is little or no grain markings in cherry or birch, while Spanish mahogany may be marked and penciled over its whole face; and the texture of the woods is very different to the touch.

Mahogany (*Svietened*).—The tree has a darkish-brown bark and a reddish-brown, coarsely fibered, streaky, hard wood. The tree grows to the height of 35 meters, and is pretty strong. Among the chief varieties is the common mahogany, with a very hard, very durable wood, which is never attacked by worms, and is excellent for ship-building; but its capability for taking a fine polish is its chief recommendation. *Mahagoni Haiti, Mahagoni Jamaika, Mahagoni Havanna* are the other chief kinds.

With perhaps the exception of our oaks, no wood possesses like advantages of combined soundness, large size, durability, beauty of color and richness of figure. So, when compared with other woods, mahogany costs no more to work and stands better than any other—the only point to weigh against this last great feature is the slight difference in the first cost of the wood in the rough; but if mahogany stands better and longer, and needs no attention afterwards, surely the sole advantage of less cost at first which any other wood may possess is overcome.

But another merit, equal to any thus far mentioned, is the warmth in its color and the glory in the figure of this beautiful wood. The air of elegance, artistic effect and gentle breeding it imparts to all its surroundings, its joy and life—all these cannot be measured by a few cents a square foot. Its growing splendor with age that gives increasing satisfaction may safely be contrasted with the tameness of other woods, which, though pleasing at first, deteriorate rather than improve.

When the real wood is used, but little more is necessary than to fill and varnish or polish, as it cannot be much improved upon. Sometimes, however, it may be deemed proper to darken it somewhat to take away the reddish hue that newly wrought mahogany presents, and this can best be done by darkening the filler, to suit the taste, trying the mixture first on a piece of the dressed stuff, until the desired shade is obtained. Staining the varnish or polish with dragons' blood or other suitable dyes, will also accomplish the desired end.

Staining by the fumes of ammonia will probably give the best results, as almost any tinge can be given the work, from the newness of youth to the mellowness of extreme age. This method is considered the best for imparting to mahogany the appearance of age, and for those wishing to avail themselves of an easy, clean and certain means of gaining the result, fumigating offers no serious obstacle to its accomplishment, the articles necessary being easy of acquirement, and at small expense.

To darken mahogany, wash it with very weak lime water, which allow to dry thoroughly. This gives a rich red color, more closely matching old mahogany than any other stain that can be used.

Antique mahogany may be obtained as follows: Take one-third linseed oil, two-thirds turpentine; coat woodwork and wipe off clean. When thoroughly dry, coat with bichromate of potash; then fill with a dark, rich filler; then shellac and give three coats of varnish and rub with pumice-stone and water, then oil and wipe off clean. If an extra good job is required, give woodwork one heavy coat of polishing varnish after being rubbed in water; then rub again in water and polish. In finishing mahogany, some put on the bichromate of potash without oiling, but they do not get as good a color. All mahogany should be oiled first, unless you want a very light color; then it should have a thin coat of shellac first.

In repolishing and reviving old work, first clean off all dust from the corners and rebates, then wipe all the polished portions with warm water and soda, and allow them to dry. Mahogany treated with spirit varnish is seldom satisfactory, but it is one of the best woods known for showing the fine effects of French polishing. Couch legs and chair turnings are generally bodied up with the brush, and finished with the rubber. If the surface is in fair condition after washing, no filling will be required; a rubber of good French polish worked out dry with spirit, and afterwards spirited out, or glazed, will give the desired result, if properly done. The polish will require staining with a little Bismarck brown or brown aniline dye, to brighten up the color. It would be a great advantage, and well worth the outlay, to put fresh gimp or leather banding round the borders; but this should not be done until the show-wood portions are repolished.

Walnut Finishing

Walnut (*Juglans Nigra*).—As this wood is seldom or never stained, it is unnecessary to say more about it other than it may be treated like oak, cherry or birch. It looks well filled and finished in shellac. Birch stained and properly finished looks very much like walnut, and with a little care in getting a proper tint in the stain, can scarcely be known from the real thing. "Filling," in walnut finishing, is one of the most important processes; if the richness of the wood is desired to be shown, as much depends on the "tint" as on the filling material.

Ordinary whitewood can be given the appearance of black walnut by first thoroughly drying tne wood and then washing two or three times with a strong aqueous solution of extract of walnut peel. When nearly dry, the wood thus treated is washed over with a solution made of one part (by weight) of bichromate of potash in five parts of boiling water. After drying thoroughly, rub and polish.

A number of recipes for making and applying stains to imitate walnut are given elsewhere in this volume, which see.

Regarding Cypress

Cypress (*Cupressus sempervierens*).—The light, the dark and the bald are good woods and are coming more and more into favor every day.

This wood contains a very small amount of resin, and a very high polish can be given it; in fact, because of its not being affected by moisture, it is being used for cisterns, hogsheads, and sugar, molasses and honey barrels. The red cypress is the favorite, and some of it is so heavy that it will sink upon being placed in water. The white variety is much lighter, and will float after being deadened a short while before being cut, but it has not the firm grain of the red. The red cypress has a straight trunk with a small top, and the bark when cut has a reddish tint. These woods may be treated like cherry or birch with good results. They look well when left their natural color and finished "dead finish."

Concerning the use of cypress for inside finish, it is all right if properly dried, prepared and put in place, but dry it must be, and there will be no trouble with its staying in place or shrinking any more than any other kind of wood. It may be remarked, however, that cypress is an exceedingly hard wood to thoroughly dry, but for a low-cost material there is nothing to equal it in appearance. Get good, even-colored cypress, finish it well and some people could not tell it from red birch. If one cares to have it stained, it takes first rate. In finishing up cypress, the painters' work is the most difficult, for if the proper materials are not put on the grain is very liable to rise, which will spoil the good effect and will show even after being rubbed down. It is susceptible of a very high polish, and when finished in the natural color of the wood is very handsome. It is used by architects as a basis for the ivory white finish many people fancy, but in any event the wood when used for interiors possesses too much natural beauty to cover it with paint.

As cypress costs less than any other suitable wood for exterior work, it is not only more durable, but it will take paint better than other woods, and the paint will not peel off. We have seen buildings shingled with cypress upon both roof and walls upon which no stain or paint had been used. In time such buildings take on the beautiful gray color which is so greatly admired by many people, especially for a country or suburban residence. The natural qualities of the wood make it possible to use either shingles or clapboards in this way without paint, and there is probably no other wood upon which vines can be grown with so much safety from injurious effects.

Cypress, viewed from the standpoint of the finisher, is no less remarkable thah when viewed from almost every standpoint. There is no wood which can be finished more economically, or which is more susceptible to the finer handiwork of the finisher and polisher. If the work is properly done, the result will be satisfactory in either case. It is true, notwithstanding, that the fine natural appearance of cypress is often greatly marred or even ruined by faulty methods of treatment, and for that reason care should be exercised in finishing it. The best results are obtained through the use of pure grain alcohol white shellac, which should be purchased of a thoroughly responsible dealer. Better results can be obtained from this quality of shellac than from the more expensive "refined shellac," so called.

Cypress requires no filling or sealing, and, if it is desired to permanently preserve the natural color of the wood, no oil or oily substance should be applied until the final rubbing down after the wood is well protected with shellac. We recommend three or more coats of shellac, as may be desired, each coat to be smoothed down with fine sandpaper, while the final coat may be rubbed down with pumice-stone and oil to produce a dead finish, or what is sometimes termed "egg shell" finish. The final coat may be left bright, if preferred, or after rubbing down to a dead finish it may be given a French polish, according to the usual methods.

Cypress will take stains well, but we have never favored the staining of the wood or the use of any color whatever in the finish of it, for it is far too handsome to disguise in any way.

Rosewood

Rosewood (*Dalbergia Nigra*).—It seldom falls to the lot of the ordinary finisher to have to "try his hand" on the genuine wood, but sometimes it *does happen* and it is just as well that he should be armed with the means to wrestle with the work if such is ever thrown in his way. To finish rosewood requires about the same treatment as mahogany, though, as a matter of fact, many pieces of rosewood will be found to have a coarser grain than mahogany, and will require much care in filling. The main thing to be observed is to see that the filling is a shade or two darker than the wood to be filled, before any varnish is laid on. For imitation of rosewood I give below a few recipes:

Take ½ lb. of logwood, boil it with 3 pints of water till it is of a very dark red, to which add about half an ounce of salt of tartar. When boiling hot, stain your wood with two or three coats, taking care that it is nearly dry between each; then, with a stiff, flat brush, such as is used for graining, make streaks with a very deep black stain, which if carefully executed will be very near the appearance of dark rosewood. The following is another method: Stain your wood all over with a black stain, and when dry, with a brush as above dipped in the bright liquid, form real veins in imitation of the grain of rosewood, which will produce, when well managed, a beautiful effect. A handy brush for the purpose of graining may be made by taking a flat brush, such as used for varnishing, and cutting the sharp points of the hairs and making the edge irregular; by cutting out a few hairs here and there the grain may be imitated with great accuracy.

This is suitable to pine, cedar, cypress, whitewood, basswood, while the following should only be used in mahogany, cherry, or birch: Spread on the surface of the material a concentrated solution of hypermanganate of potassa, to act until the desired shade is obtained. Five minutes suffice, ordinarily, to give a deep color, a few trials indicating the proper proportions. The hypermanganate of potassa is decomposed by the vegetable fiber, with the precipitation of brown peroxide of manganese, while the influence of the potassa, at the same time set free, fixes in a durable manner the fibers. When the action is terminated the wood is carefully washed with water, dried, and then oiled and polished in the usual manner. The effect produced by this process in several woods is really remarkable

It has been a mystery to many people why the dark wood so highly prized for furniture is called "rosewood." Its color certainly does not look much like a rose, so we must look for some other reason. It is claimed by some that when the tree is first cut the wood possesses a very strong rose-like fragrance, hence the name. This is the most probable reason for its name. There are about a half dozen kinds of rosewood trees. The varieties are found in South America, and in the East Indies and neighboring islands. Sometimes the trees grow so large that boards or planks four feet broad and ten feet in length can be cut from them. The broad boards are used for the tops of pianofortes. When growing in the forests the tree is remarkable for its beauty, but such is its value in manufacturing as an ornamental wood, that some of the forests where it once grew abundantly now have scarcely a single specimen left.

To repolish old work, such as a rosewood piano or similar articles, the following method may be adopted:

As a rule, polished rosewood pianos are not easily kept in good condition; constant cleaning and an occasional polishing are required, especially in the case of pianos that are faced with genuine rosewood veneer, which has a coarse, open grain, and is of a somewhat oily nature. Sometimes the grain-filler that is used by the polishers will ooze out and cause an uneven surface. Plaster of Paris sometimes forms the basis of a filling, and this is apt to work out white, and becomes more apparent as the dye that has been used to enrich the color of the polish fades away through exposure to strong sunlight. It must not be forgotten that many so-called rosewood pianos are not faced with genuine rosewood veneer; the more correct term to apply to such pianos is "rosewood finish." The method by which this finish is obtained depends largely on the value of the instrument. In most cases the object of the maker is to impart a uniform color (frequently called chippendale) to the wood, and in order to obtain this end much coloring matter is used; such an excessive use of color has a tendency to destroy or imperil the nature of the polish, and accounts for much of the dullness, uneven surface, or variations of color that are more noticeable on some parts of the instrument than on other parts.

Finishing Redwood

Redwood, as a wood to hold its place after worked, has no equal. The shrinkage between green and bone-dry is very little, and after it has been ordinarily seasoned the shrinkage is very little. It does not keep growing a little narrower every year, as a white pine board sometimes does; consequently all tendency to warping and twisting is done away with.

As a finishing wood for interior house finish in the natural color it has no superior among the long list of American woods. It is, however, quite necessary that the work be properly done; the main point to be observed in finishing in natural color is to avoid the use of linseed oil, as it stains the wood a dingy color. The best finishers on this coast invariably use shellac for filler, applied rather thin, so that the wood will absorb it and thereby make a hard surface, which protects the wood from bruising, and for last coat use the best grade of shellac or hard oil.

For an Egg-Shell Gloss.—One coat of orange shellac, sandpapered to a smooth surface, followed by two or three coats of Berry Brothers' (white or light) hard oil finish; rub first coats with hair-cloth or curled hair, and the last coat with pulverized pumice-stone and raw linseed oil.

For a Dull Finish.—Specify that the last coat be rubbed with pulverized pumice-stone and water, instead of oil.

For a Polished Finish.—Specify that the last coat be rubbed first with pulverized pumice-stone and water, and then with pulverized rotten stone and water, and for a *piano finish* specify a further rubbing with Berry Brothers' furniture polish, used with a little pulverized rotten stone, applied with a piece of soft felt or flannel.

If a rubbed finish is not desired, omit the specifications for rubbing the last coat.

White Pine Finishing

Pine (*Pinus Strobus*).—If oak is the king of woods, pine is most assuredly "president," for it is at once the most useful and the most democratic of woods. It is found in the halls of the great and powerful, and in the cottage of the most humble among us. It is strong and vigorous, plain or ornamental, and is not out of place either in the backwoodsman's cabin or in the stately cathedral, and like a true man of the world, it adapts itself to every condition that circumstances may place it in.

Pine can be made to look like any known wood, but is at its best when left natural and finished in clear shellac. There is no wood grows, that will convey so cheerful a feeling to the beholder as yellow or white pine finished in a natural state. Next to being finished in a natural state, is to imitate mahogany or light cherry, which coloring it takes readily.

Where the pine—of any kind—is to be either stained or left natural, it should be "quarter sawed," as it will show a finer grain, shrink less, and last longer. The softness of its texture and its susceptibility to injury may have had some influence in preventing its general use for ornamental purposes, but the wood can be "filled," so that much of this objection is removed.

Most of the stains given under previous heads are applicable to pine. I add, however, a few more, so that the workmen may have a number of recipes to draw from.

For Walnut.—1. Dissolve by boiling 1 part each of Epsom salt and permanganate of potash in about 2 parts of water. This stain may be improved by adding a little eosine, and it works best when applied hot.

2. Catechu broken into crumbs and boiled in about twice its bulk of water until dissolved. To darken to the required depth, add bichromate of potash previously dissolved in about eight times its equivalent of water. If the deep yellow shade peculiar to the Southern walnut be required, add yellow chromate of potash. For the reddish shade of the Northern wood, add more eosine.

3. For oil stain, use Vandyke brown toned up with the siennas, the colors being strictly pure and finely ground in oil, and diluted with turpentine and a small amount of japan.

4. Burnt Turkey umber mixed in the same way as the former.

5. Mix together, by stirring, 1 quart spirits of turpentine, 1 pint asphaltum varnish, 1 pint of japan, 1 lb. dry burnt umber, 1 lb. dry Venetian red; apply with a brush. This stain is transparent, and allows the grain of the wood to show through.

6. Boil 1½ ounces washing soda and ¼ ounce bichromate of potash, in 1 quart of water; add 2½ ounces Vandyke brown. This stain may be used either hot or cold.

7. With a brush apply a thin solution of permanganate of potassa in water, until the desired color is produced, allowing each coat to dry before another is applied.

For Mahogany or Cherry.—1. For mahogany, use a pint of turpentine and an ounce of color known as dragons' blood. Dissolve and shake well before applying. For ebony, use hot liquor from logwood chips, and after dry apply a coat of tincture of steel.

For walnut, use 2 ounces of washing soda, darkened with Vandyke brown in water. Add 2 ounces of bichromate of potash in 1½ pints of water.

2. Mix together, by stirring, 1 quart of spirits of turpentine, 1 pint of varnish, and 1 lb. of dry burnt sienna; apply with a brush, and after it has been on about five minutes wipe it off with rags. This stain takes about 12 hours to dry.

3. Take 1 quart alcohol, 2 ounces of dragons' blood; pulverize the latter along with ¼ ounce of alkanet root; mix, and let stand in a warm place a couple of days. Shake frequently in the meantime. Apply with a sponge or brush. Two or three coats may be required. This makes a fine stain.

For Rosewood.—1. Mix in a bottle ¼ lb. of extract of logwood, 1 ounce salts of tartar, and 1 pint of water; in another bottle, put 1 lb. of old iron in small pieces, and 1 pint of vinegar, which, after standing 24 hours, will be ready for use; make a hard, stiff brush with a piece of rattan sharpened at one end in a wedge shape, pounding it so as to separate the fiber. Mix in 1 pint of varnish ¼ lb. of finely-powdered rose-pink. The materials are now ready, and the first thing in the process is to stain the wood with the logwood stain; give two coats of this, allowing the first to become nearly dry before applying the second; then dip the rattan brush in the vinegar, and with it form the grain, after which give the work a coat of the varnish and rose-pink. There can be no definite directions given for graining, except to study the natural wood and imitate it as nearly as possible. With the above materials skillfully applied, any common wood can be made to resemble rosewood so nearly that it will take a good judge to distinguish the difference.

2. Boil 1 lb. of logwood in 1 gallon of water, add a double handful of walnut shell, boil the whole again, strain the liquor and add to it 1 pint of the best vinegar. It is then ready for use. Apply it boiling hot, and when the wood is dry, form red veins in imitation of the grain of rosewood with a brush dipped in the following solution: Nitric acid, 1 pint; metallic tin, 1 ounce; sal ammoniac, 1 ounce. Mix and set aside to dissolve, occasionally shaking. If carefully executed it will give the appearance of dark rosewood.

For surface stains the following are sometimes used. The colors are all to be mixed with very thin glue size, laid on warm with a soft woolen material, and the wood wiped dry after application. All the colors used in staining should be well pulverized, and before use the liquid should be strained.

Imitation Oak Stain.—Equal parts burnt umber and brown ocher.

Imitation Mahogany Stain.—One part Venetian red, and two parts yellow lead.

Imitation Rosewood Stain.—Venetian red, darkened with lampblack to required shade.

Imitation Walnut Stain.—Burnt umber and yellow ocher, mixed in proportions to give desired shade.

Before leaving the subject of pine, it may be as well to say a few words regarding the long-leaved, or Georgia pine (*Pinus Pulustris*), as a great deal of it is used now in and about the city of New York, Chicago, and other large centers. This wood is very fine, strong and lasting. Some of it is insusceptible of fine finish, but the best success with it is when treated with shellac finish. In all other respects, when used as a finishing material, it may be treated the same as ordinary pine.

The softness of white pine and its susceptibility to injury may have had some influence in preventing its general use for ornamental purposes, but the wood can be "filled," so that much of this objection is removed. Its pure white color—white as compared with other woods—recommends it for purposes for which holly has been heretofore used; and the size of the timber from which clear lumber may be cut is greatly in its favor, boards of a width of sixteen and even twenty inches being not uncommon, with no shade of distinction between sap-wood and heart, and only the faintest perceptible grain.

Some specimens lately examined show a greatly enhanced beauty by very simple treatment—the filling with warm shellac varnish, bleached shellac in alcohol, applied with a brush while warm. Several coats are given, the last coat being rubbed with pumice and rotten stone moistened with water, not oil. A finish of a flowing coat of copal varnish completes the preparation. Thus treated, the wood is of a faint creamy tint, with an appearance of semi-transparency. Beautiful gradations of tone were obtained by panels of this prepared pine, mouldings of holly, and stiles of curly or bird's-eye maple, and fine contrasts were made with the pine and oiled black walnut.

For an Egg-Shell Gloss.—One coat of shellac (white shellac if the natural color of the wood is to be preserved, or orange shellac if the wood is to be stained, or is desired to be darker in tone than the natural color), sandpaper to a smooth surface, and follow with two or three coats of Berry Brothers' (white or light) hard oil finish (specify white hard oil finish if it is desired to retain the natural color of white pine); rub first coats with hair-cloth or curled hair, and the last coat with pulverized pumice-stone and raw linseed oil.

For a Dull Finish.—Specify that the last coat be rubbed with pulverized pumice-stone and water, instead of oil.

For a Polished Finish.—Specify that the last coat be rubbed first with pulverized pumice-stone and water, and then with pulverized rotten stone and water, and for a *piano finish* specify a further rubbing with Berry Brothers' furniture polish, used with a little pulverized rotten stone, applied with a piece of soft felt or flannel.

If a rubbed finish is not desired, omit the specifications for rubbing the last coat.

One of the best ways, though perhaps not the cheapest way, to finish white pine is to see that the work is well sandpapered with the grain, then thoroughly dusted. Give it at least one coat of white shellac varnish and one coat of inside varnish. Should this prove to be too expensive, substitute liquid filler for the shellac. For hard or yellow pine finish apply one coat of orange shellac varnish and one or two coats light hard oil finish, or omit the shellac and apply hard finish instead. A filler is not required for this wood. In every instance, however, whether shellac varnish, liquid filler or hard oil finish is used, care must be taken that the first coat is thoroughly dry and hard before applying the succeeding coat, or the latter is liable to sink in, causing lack of luster.

Maple

Maple (*Acer pseudo platanus*).—This is a close-grained wood and needs no filling; it should always be finished in its own color, and that not darkened but kept as light as possible by the use of white shellac for filling and the whitest ivory varnish to be found. Most manufacturers of varnish make an article from carefully selected gums that is intended for such a use. It goes without the saying and as a matter of course that hard maple takes on the finest polish ot any kind of the woods.

For an Egg-Shell Gloss.—One coat of white shellac sandpapered to a smooth surface, followed by two or three coats of Berry Brothers' or other reliable white hard oil finish; rub first coats with hair-cloth or curled hair, and the last coat with pulverized pumice-stone and raw linseed oil.

For a Dull Finish.—Specify that the last coat be rubbed with pulverized pumice-stone and water, instead of oil.

For a Polished Finish.—Specify that the last coat be rubbed first with pulverized pumice-stone and water, and then with pulverized rotten stone and water, and for a *piano finish* specify a further rubbing with furniture polish, used with a little pulverized rotten stone, applied with a piece of soft felt or flannel.

If a rubbed finish is not desired, omit the specifications for rubbing the last coat.

White and Black Ash

Ash (*Fraxinus excelsior*).—This wood is now used very much by cabinetmakers and house-joiners in place of oak, and I have often seen furniture palmed off to unsuspecting customers as antique oak, and in one instance I knew of an architect who specified oak, and who "passed" a mixture of white and black ash as oak, either knowingly or otherwise. I am not sure that the owners in either case lost anything, for good sound Canadian ash is decidedly better than dosey red oak.

In finishing ash, either black or white, the same methods are adopted as for finishing oak, and similar processes will give similar results. Ingenious stainers and finishers can make ash resemble oak wainscot, in vein and color, so correctly that it is almost impossible for the most experienced connoisseur to distinguish the genuine from the spurious. In order to do this some finishers make a commencement by sketching out, upon certain parts of the ash exterior, the requisite white veins, by means of a camel-hair pencil, with white stain; that done, they coat the veins with thin varnish, and then darken the general ground, dealing carefully throughout. the entire process with the veined portions. Others stain and embody, i.e., French polish, the ash with the ordinary preparation, after which they pursue an operative course termed "hamping"; that is, scratching fancifully, so as to form the veins, upon different parts of the coated surface, before it gets time to harden, with a saturated rag. The former process is, however, the more suitable of the two.

For an Egg-Shell Gloss.—One coat of filler to match the color of the wood, followed by one coat of white shellac sandpapered to a smooth surface, and two or three coats of white or light hard oil finish; rub first coats with hair-cloth or curled hair, and the last coat with pulverized pumice-stone and raw linseed oil.

For a Dull Finish.—Specify that the last coat be rubbed with pulverized pumice-stone and water, instead of oil.

For a Polished Finish.—Specify that the last coat be rubbed first with pulverized pumice-stone and water and then with pulverized rotten stone and water, and for a *piano finish* specify a further rubbing with Berry Brothers' furniture polish, used with a little pulverized rotten stone, applied with a piece of soft felt or flannel.

If a rubbed finish is not desired, omit the specifications for rubbing the last coat.

Other Woods

Cedar, White (*Cupressus thuyoides*), which is really a spruce, and all similar woods, should never be finished in a natural state. Deep stains or surface stains should always be employed on these woods if they are not to be painted.

Beech (*Fagus ferruginea*).—This is one of the unnoticed woods of former years, but is now gradually gaining in favor as a decorative wood. It is cheap and also quite abundant, while the more popular hardwoods are beginning to grow scarcer and higher in price. Beechwood has a fine grain, is quite durable, and can be used in the manufacture of furniture and for decorative purposes generally. The red variety has a handsome appearance and is especially suitable for use where a good imitation of cherry is desired.

If "quarter sawed" it shows a fine grain and has a character distinctly its own which I think has never been properly appreciated. When quartered, properly finished, filled and polished, it looks something like dark leopard wood. It will assume a dark mahogany color if prepared like cherry or birch, or it may be made to appear like walnut if treated with walnut stains and finish.

Elm (*Ulmus Americana*), **Chestnut** (*Castanea vesca*), **Butternut** (*Juglans cinerea*).—These three woods are often used in inferior work, and are very soft and easily dented. The best is perhaps the elm, which does very well for bath-room finish, panels for ash doors and similar work. All require a great deal of "filling," and this should be well rubbed in if a good job is required. All of these woods have a very coarse grain, but if care is taken in selecting the material, very odd and sometimes pleasing effects may be obtained. Any of the stains used on pine will answer for these woods, dependent, of course, on the tints desired. The best result with these woods is derived by giving the work one coat of shellac after filling and staining; then sandpaper well and apply your varnish or oil finish or whatever you purpose finishing in.

Sycamore, or Buttonwood, as it is sometimes called (*acer pseudo platanus*), when quarter sawed and properly finished makes a good appearance, and in many cases is superseding cherry owing to its beauty and cheapness. Heretofore its natural beauty has been destroyed in many cases by staining the wood, and thus preventing the development of many chemical changes which take place and are thrown to the surface when properly treated. When quarter sawed, a light-bodied and light-colored shellac should be used, when by a natural chemical process a beautiful silver leaf is developed and the surface assumes a charming pink hue.

Hemlock (*Abies Canadensis*).—This is rarely used for finishing, owing to its brittleness and splintery nature. Clean boards, however, made into panels or other similar work and then finished in natural color, assume a very handsome appearance. It has a pink tint of the most delicate kind, which improves and mellows with age. It should be finished in the same manner as pine.

I have purposely left unmentioned a number of our finest woods, concerning which I should have more to say, would it not increase the size of this volume beyond reasonable dimensions. The workmen will know, from what has already been said, how these light woods may be treated, and I may add that the various maples, though rather light in color for general purposes, make the most delicate of finish. Gum-wood of late has been used to some extent and is not hard to deal with when to be finished. It should be treated about as cherry and birch, and finished in a similar way, and when done nicely the work looks quite well.

Redwood is getting to be a favorite wood with some builders, owing no doubt to its cheapness, and its easiness to work. It may be classed among the soft woods and requires treating about the same as chestnut, butternut and the cedars. The following formula and directions have been highly recommended as a finish, but for my own part I prefer using Wheeler's filler, as I think better results are obtained. Here is the formula:

> Take 1 quart spirits turpentine.
> Add 1 pound corn-starch.
> Add ¼ pound burnt sienna.
> Add 1 tablespoonful raw linseed oil.
> Add 1 tablespoonful brown japan.

Mix thoroughly, apply with a brush, let it stand, say fifteen minutes; rub off all you can with fine shavings or a soft rag, then let it stand *at least twenty-four hours*, that it may sink into and *harden* the fibers of the wood, afterward apply two coats of white shellac; rub down well with fine flint paper, then put on from two to five coats best polishing varnish; after it is well dried, rub with water and pumice-stone ground very fine, stand a day to dry; after being washed, clean with chamois, rub with water and rotten stone; dry, wash clean, as before, and rub with olive oil until dry.

Some use cork for sandpapering and polishing, but a smooth block of hardwood like maple is better. When treated in this way redwood will be found the peer of any wood for real beauty and life as a house trim or finish. By proper attention, redwood may be made to appear like mahogany or cherry, but **its** softness is very much against it.

SOME GENERAL RECIPES

Ebonizing.—Prepare some shellac varnish by dissolving half a pound of gum shellac in a quart of alcohol; put in a tightly corked bottle, set in a warm place, and shake frequently. When completely dissolved, add sufficient dry lamp or bone black. It will require only about a heaping tablespoonful to half a pint of varnish. Should it be too thick to flow easily from the brush and spread evenly, add alcohol. Give the wood two or three coats of this, which can be done within two days. For fine work give three coats of the black varnish and allow it to dry thoroughly; then take some 00 or 000 sandpaper and rub the work down lightly until the surface is smooth and even, being careful not to rub through to the wood. Then apply two or three coats more, and rub down again with the sandpaper; give two coats more and allow it to dry perfectly hard. Make some rubbers of felt—an old felt hat is good—by tacking the felt on blocks of soft wood of proper shape, which should be flat, concave or convex to fit the work. Apply a few drops of sewing machine oil to the felt and sprinkle on a pinch of pulverized pumice-stone. Rub the work with this, keeping the rubber moist with oil and supplied with the pumice, until the wood shows a perfectly smooth surface, without any gloss. When it has all been gone over, wipe off the surface and rub clean with dry flannel cloths. The result is a fine imitation of ebony. If the shellac varnish is colored with aniline instead of lampblack, the finished surface is smoother and finer.

Others. — 1. Infuse gall-nut in vinegar, in which rusty nails have been soaked; paint the wood with this, polish and burnish when dry. 2. Wash the wood repeatedly with a solution of sulphate of iron, made by dissolving 2 ounces of sulphate in a pint of hot water. When dry, apply a hot decoction of logwood and nut-galls two or three times. When dry, clean with a wet sponge and then polish. 3. Brush the wood with a strong decoction of logwood chips several times. When dry, give it a coat of vinegar in which rusty iron has been placed. Dissolve beeswax in turpentine by setting in a warm place; apply warm with a brush, and rub it till it shines. 4. Wash with a concentrated aqueous solution of logwood several times, and then with a solution of acetate of iron 40° Baume. Repeat till a deep black is produced. 5. Put 2 ounces of logwood chips with 1¼ ounces of copperas in a quart of water, boil, and lay on hot. When dry, wet the surface again with 2 ounces of steel filings dissolved in half a pint of vinegar. When dry again, sandpaper smooth, then oil, then fill it with powdered drop black mixed in the filler. Work to be ebonized should be smooth and free from holes. Give it a light coat of quick-drying varnish, then rub with finely pulverized

pumice-stone and linseed oil until very smooth. **6.**
Boil ½ pound of chip logwood in 2 quarts of water,
and add ½ ounce of verdigris and ½ ounce of copperas, strain, and put in ½ pound of rusty steel filings.
With this go over the work a second time. **7.** A
pound of logwood boiled in 4 quarts of water, add 2
handfuls of walnut shells or peel, boil up again, take
out the chips, add a pint of vinegar, and apply boiling.
Afterwards dissolve 1 ounce of green copperas in a
quart of boiling water and apply hot. **8.** First sponge
the wood with a solution of chlorhydrate of aniline in
water, to which a small quantity of copper chloride is
added. When dry, go over again with a solution of
potassium bichromate. Repeat this twice or thrice.
9. One gallon of vinegar, ½ pound of green copperas,
¼ pound of China blue, 2 ounces nut-gall, 2 pounds
extract of logwood. Boil all these over a slow fire,
and add half a pint of iron-rust. Apply as usual. A
good varnish for ebonized work is made by dissolving
in alcohol some black wax.

STAINS

Many excellent stains for pine may be obtained by
using the ordinary graining colors, Vandyke brown,
raw and burnt sienna, ultramarine blue, etc., applied
with a brush, without previous preparation, and then
wiped off with a cloth—a method that brings out
clearly the grain or marks of the wood, which in pitch
pine, now being extensively used for fittings, are often
extremely beautiful. A better method for general
work—French polish being ordinarily too expensive—
is, where dark oak or mahogany stains are not wanted,
light varnishes, of which two coats are to be applied.
The glue size with which the work is first coated, in

order to fill up the pores of the wood, should not be
too thick, as in that case it is liable to crack.

Logwood, lime, brown soft-soap, dyed oil, sulphate
of iron, nitrate of silver exposed to the sun's rays,
carbonate of soda, bichromate and permanganate of
potash, and other alkaline preparations, are used for
darkening the wood; the last three are specially
recommended. The solution is applied by dissolving
1 ounce of the alkali in 2 gills of boiling water, diluted
to the required tone. The surface is saturated with a
sponge or flannel, and immediately dried with soft rags.
The carbonate is used for dark woods. Oil tinged
with rose madder may be applied to hardwoods like
birch, and a red oil is prepared from soaked alkanet
root in linseed oil. The grain of yellow pine can be
brought out by two or three coats of japan, much
diluted with turpentine, and afterwards oiled and
rubbed. To give mahogany the appearance of age,
lime water used before oiling is a good plan. In
staining wood, the best and most transparent effect is
obtained by repeated light coats of the same. For
oak stain a strong solution of oxalic acid is employed;
for mahogany, dilute nitric acid. A primary coat or a
coat of wood fillers is advantageous. For mahogany
stains, the following are given: 2 ounces of dragons'
blood dissolved in 1 quart of rectified spirits of wine,
well shaken, or raw sienna in beer, with burnt sienna
to give the required tone; for darker stains boil ½
pound of madder and 2 ounces of logwood chips in 1
gallon of water, and brush the decoction while hot
over the wood; when dry, paint with a solution of 2
ounces of potash in 1 quart of water. A solution of
permanganate of potash forms a rapid and excellent
brown stain.

Oak or ash may be stained brown by using linseed oil and benzine half and half, and burnt umber or Vandyke brown incorporated with this. Maple can be stained green-gray by using copperas in water; oak will also be changed to a dark green-blue through the same agency, the effect on ash being various shades of olive green. Ammonia applied to oak produces the bronze olive tint now used so much by architects.

Wash any compact wood with a boiling decoction of logwood three or four times, allowing it to dry between each application. Then wash it with a solution of acetate of iron, which is made by dissolving iron filings in vinegar. This stain is very black, and penetrates to a considerable depth into the wood, so that ordinary scratching or chipping does not show the original color.

A wash of 1 part of nitric acid in 10 parts of water will, if well done, impart a stain resembling mahogany to pine wood which does not contain much resin. When the wood is thoroughly dry, shellac varnish will impart a fine finish to the surface. A glaze of carmine or lake will produce a rosewood finish. A turpentine extract of alkanet root produces a beautiful stain which admits of French polishing. Asphaltum, thinned with turpentine, makes an excellent mahogany color on new wood.

A Method of imparting to any plain white wood the appearance of cedar wood is as follows: Mix 2 parts of catechu, and 1 part of caustic soda, in 100 parts of water (all by weight). The article to be stained should be boiled in this solution for some hours, and is then rinsed in clear water and dried. If the desired depth of tone has not been obtained, a second boiling must be resorted to. This stain is said to sink so deep into the wood that even thick sheets of veneer thus treated will be colored right through; while other wood articles thus stained may be safely manipulated without any fear of the original color of the wood showing through.

For a Brown Stain.—Boil 1 pound of the brown pigment called Terre de Cassel with 4 quarts of water, until it is reduced one-third. Mix 2 ounces (Troy) of white potash with sufficient water to dissolve it, and mix with the Terre de Cassel. This stain must be applied with a brush, two or even three times, according to the depth of the shade required.

Another.—Paint the wood with a solution made by boiling one pot of catechu with 30 parts of water and a little soda; when dry, paint over with another solution made of 1 part bichromate of potash and 30 parts water. By a little difference in the mode of treatment, and by varying the strength of the solutions, several shades of color may be given.

Staining Carved Panels.—First, oil the panels with linseed oil, then mix a little powdered water stain (this is best mixed with rain water), and brush over the stain with a hog's hair brush, using as little stain as possible. When dry, give a coat of button polish, which must be laid on with a camel-hair brush. Care must be taken not to form puddles in the carvings, either with the stain or polish. When the polish is quite dry, the panels will be improved by rubbing with a piece of clean linen rag. By following the foregoing, a good effect is obtained, and, by oiling before staining, the fibers of the wood will not rise.

Staining Spirit Varnish for Furniture, etc.—White hard spirit varnish, as it comes from the makers, is generally much too thick for mixing with stain, and does **not**

distribute evenly. Stained varnishes should be diluted with spirits or turpentine, whichever may be the solvent. Two applications of thin varnish will give far more satisfactory results than one heavy coating of thick varnish. Brown hard spirit varnish with the addition of red stain will give much better results. When the work is streaky, it would be advisable to remove it by softening with spirits or grinding down with pumice-stone powder and water, then using varnish as advised above. Oil varnish, such as church oak varnish, is generally considered too garish for use on furniture. In repolishing old work, the idea of filling up a deep scratch with beeswax and resin is a good one, but it requires considerable practice to get a quite level surface and a perfect match as regards color. The surface that has been disturbed during the operation may be treated by coloring up; that is, bodying up to fill the grain of the wood; then, by blending together suitable colors, mixed in 1 part of polish to 3 parts of spirits, carefully penciling in till a perfect match is secured.

DYEING WOODS

For a Black Dye.—Put 6 pounds of chip logwood into the copper, with as many veneers as it will conveniently hold, without pressing too tight; fill it with water, and let it boil *slowly* for about three hours; then add ½ pound of powdered verdigris, ½ pound of copperas, and 4 ounces of bruised nut-galls; fill the copper up with vinegar as the water evaporates; let it boil gently two hours each day till the wood is dyed through.

Another.—Procure some liquor from a tanner's pit, or make a decoction of oak bark, and to every gallon of the liquor add a quarter of a pound of green copperas, and mix them well together; put the liquor into the copper, and make it quite hot, but not boil; immerse the veneers in it, and let them remain for an hour; take them out, and expose them to the air, till it has penetrated its substance; then add some logwood to the solution, place the veneers again in it, and let it simmer for two or three hours; let the whole cool gradually, dry the veneers in the shade, and they will be a very fine black.

Dyeing wood is mostly applied for the purpose of veneers, while staining is more generally had recourse to, to give the desired color to the article after it has been manufactured. In the one case the color should penetrate throughout, while in the latter the surface is all that is essential.

In dyeing pear tree, holly and beech, take the best black; but for most colors holly is preferable. It is also best to have wood as young and as newly cut as possible. After the veneers are cut, they should be allowed to lie in a trough of water for four or five days before they are put into the copper, as the water, acting as a purgative to the wood, brings out an abundance of slimy matter, which must be removed, or the wood will never be a good color. After this purificatory process, they should be dried in the open air for at least twelve hours. They are then ready for the copper. By these simple means the color will strike much quicker, and be of a brighter hue. It would also add to the improvement of the colors, if, after the veneers have boiled a few hours, they are taken out, dried in the air, and again immersed in the coloring copper. Always dry veneers in the open air, for fire invariably injures the colors.

Fine Blue Dye.—Into a clean glass bottle put 1 pound of oil of vitriol, and 4 ounces of the best indigo pounded in a mortar (take care to set the bottle in a basin or earthen glazed pan, as it will ferment); then put the veneers into a copper or stone trough; fill it rather more than one-third with water, and add as much of the vitriol and indigo (stirring it about) as will make a fine blue, which may be known by trying it with a piece of white paper or wood. Let the veneers remain till the dye has struck through.

The color will be much improved if the solution of indigo in vitriol be kept a few weeks before using it. The color will strike better if the veneers are boiled in plain water till completely soaked through, and then allowed for a few hours to dry partially, previous to being immersed in the dye.

Another.—Throw pieces of quicklime into soft water; stir it well; when settled, strain or pour off the clear part; then to every gallon add ten or twelve ounces of the best turnsole; put the whole into the copper with the veneers, which should be of white holly, and prepared as usual by boiling in water; let them simmer gently till the color has sufficiently penetrated, but be careful not to let them boil in it, as it would injure the color.

A Fine Yellow Dye.—Reduce 4 pounds of the root of barberry, by sawing, to dust, which put in a copper or brass trough; add 4 ounces of turmeric and 4 gallons of water, then put in as many white holly veneers as the liquor will cover; boil them together for three hours, often turning them; when cool, add 2 ounces of aqua fortis and the dye will strike through much sooner.

A Bright Yellow Dye.—To every gallon of water necessary to cover the veneers, add 1 pound of French berries; boil the veneers till the color has penetrated through; add to the infusion of the French berries, the liquid for brightening colors given as stated, and let the veneers remain for two or three hours, and the color will be very bright.

Bright Green Dye.—Proceed as in either of the previous recipes to produce a yellow; but instead of adding aqua fortis or the brightening liquid, add as much vitriolated indigo as will produce the desired color.

Green Dye.—Dissolve 4 ounces of the best verdigris, and of sap-green and indigo ½ ounce each, in 3 pints of the best vinegar; put in the veneers, and gently boil till the color has penetrated sufficiently.

The hue of the green may be varied by altering the proportion of the ingredients; and it is advised, unless wanted for a particular purpose, to leave out the sap-green, as it is a vegetable color very apt to change, or turn brown, when exposed to the air.

Bright Red Dye.—To 2 pounds of genuine Brazil dust, add 4 gallons of water; put in as many veneers as the liquor will cover; boil them for three hours; then add 2 ounces of alum, and 2 ounces of aqua fortis, and keep it lukewarm until it has struck through.

Red Dye.—To every pound of logwood chips, add 2 gallons of water; put in the veneers, and boil as in the last; then add a sufficient quantity of the brightening liquid till you see the color to your mind; keep the whole as warm as the finger can be borne in it, till the color has sufficiently penetrated.

The logwood chips should be picked from all foreign substances, with which it generally abounds, as bark, dirt, etc.; and it is always best when fresh cut, which may be known by its appearing of a bright-red color; for if stale, it will look brown, and not yield so much coloring matter.

Purple Dye.—To 2 pounds of chip logwood and ½ pound of Brazil dust, add 4 gallons of water, and after putting in the veneers, boil them for at least three hours; then add 6 ounces of pearlash and 2 ounces of alum; let them boil for two or three hours every day, till the color has struck through.

The Brazil dust only contributes to make the purple of a more red cast; you may, therefore, omit it, if you require a deep bluish purple.

Another. — Boil 2 pounds of logwood, either in chips or powder, in 4 gallons of water, with the veneers; after boiling till the color is well struck in, add by degrees vitriolated indigo till the purple is of the shade required, which may be known by trying it with a piece of paper; let it then boil for one hour, and keep the liquid in a milk-warm state till the color has penetrated the veneer. This method, when properly managed, will produce a brilliant purple, not so likely to fade as the foregoing.

Liquid for Brightening and Setting Colors.—To every pint of strong aqua fortis, add 1 ounce of grain tin, and a piece of sal-ammoniac of the size of a walnut; set it by to dissolve, shake the bottle round with the cork out, from time to time; in the course of two or three days it will be fit for use. This will be found an admirable liquid to add to any color, as it not only brightens it, but renders it less likely to fade from exposure to the air.

Orange Dye.—Let the veneers be dyed by either of the methods given as above, of a fine deep yellow, and while they are still wet and saturated with the dye, transfer them to the bright red dye, till the color penetrates equally throughout.

Silver Gray Dye.—Expose to the weather, in a cast-iron pot of six or eight gallons, old iron nails, hoops. etc., till covered with rust; add 1 gallon of vinegar and 2 of water, boil all well for an hour; have the veneers ready, which must be hardwood (not too dry), put them in the copper used to dye black, and pour the iron liquor over them; add 1 pound of chip log-wood and 2 ounces of bruised nut-galls; then boil up another pot of the iron liquor to supply the copper with, keeping the veneers covered, and boiling two hours a day, till the required color is obtained.

Gray Dye.—Expose any quantity of old iron, or what is better, the borings of gun-barrels, etc., in any convenient vessel, and from time to time sprinkle them with spirits of salt (muriatic acid) diluted in four times its quantity of water, till they are very thickly covered with rust; then to every 6 pounds add 1 gallon of water, in which has been dissolved 2 ounces of salt of tartar; lay the veneers in the copper, and cover them with this liquid; let it boil for two or three hours till well soaked, then to every gallon of liquor add a quarter of a pound of green copperas, and keep the whole at a moderate temperature till the dye has sufficiently penetrated.

GILDING, SILVERING, BRONZING, AND COMPOSITION

In gilding, the design should be simple and fairly open, so that the gold leaf can be laid in water without too many difficulties. As the particular method of gilding here described requires the whole surface to be burnished, it will be found that a design should be treated in a broad way, as, if the surface is too much broken up, it will, on account of its being burnished, and therefore reflecting light in a high degree, be worrying in its effects, as well as entailing an enormous amount of time to lay the gold leaf in water. The clever craftsman is he who gets his effects by means as simple as possible. That piece of work will be the most satisfactory that fulfills the purpose for which it was designed, however simple the means, so long as the result is lasting.

In the design Fig. 115 now given, the frame is to take a mirror, the sight size of which should be 16⅛ inches high by 13⅛ inches wide, the full size of the plate being 17 inches by 14 inches. The extreme dimensions of the frame are 24¾ inches high, 25⅜ inches wide. The

FIG. 115

plinth will require a piece 20⅛ inches by 3⅞ inches by ⅞ inches thick; the moulding for it will require a piece ¾ inch by ⅜ inch. The pilasters are 3¼ inches by ¾ inch thick. They are tenoned into the plinth, the mortises in which should not be more than 1¼ inches deep, so that they do not come below the marginal line of the carving along it. The top rail, which shows ⅞ inch on the face of the frame, is tenoned into the pilasters; the top of the carving on the pilasters should come on a line with the rail, so as not to weaken

Fig. 116

or cut through the mortises. The hollow moulding is got out of 3⅛ inches by ⅞ inch, and is returned on the sides, as is the moulding on the plinth. The ogee moulding requires a piece 25⅜ inches by 3⅝ inches by ¾ inch; the returns in this are shaped out of the solid at each end of the piece, and it is screwed on the frame from the top.

The design for the pilasters, Fig. 116, is one-fifth full size. It is very important when carving to treat the ground freely; the worker should aim at having the ground somewhat uneven, not in an abrupt and obvious way, but with a soft up and down sort of feeling, which will, when the work is gilded, make it look ever so much more human. The result will be more interesting than if the ground is cut perfectly flat and even. The edges round the carved parts should not be set in, but should slope underneath the forms in an easy hollow. The pilasters should be grounded out a ¼ inch at the base, and more shallow at the top, so that the smaller leaves and flower should be in fainter relief. The plinth should not be grounded out deeper than ⅛ inch. Pine or whitewood may be used to make the frame.

Having made the frame and put it together, we now want to gild it. The way here described is a modification of the old Italian method. First of all, it will be necessary to slake some fine plaster of Paris in water for three weeks (about 1 pound of plaster to 4 gallons of water). It should be stirred frequently the first day to prevent setting. At the end of three weeks the water is poured out, the plaster is put into a cloth, and the water squeezed out; it is then left to dry into a solid cake. When wanted for use, break a piece that will go in a small pipkin, and cover it with water for half an hour. While the plaster is soaking the frame should be got ready. Clear parchment size will now be wanted; it can be had from gilders' material dealers. Some should be melted in a pipkin, care being taken that it does not boil; if it does, its setting property will be destroyed. With a round hog-hair brush give the frame two coats of clear size, using it its full strength; then pour the water off the plaster and pour some warm size, full strength, over it and mix together; it should be mixed to the consistency of cream; warm it up, and strain through muslin, working it through with a brush; warm it again, and give a coat to the carved work with the hog-hair brush, and to the plain parts with a camel-hair mop. Four coats should be given on the carved parts, using the soft brush after the first coat, and six coats given on the plain parts. They should be given as soon as the preceding coat is set, but not dry.

When the coats are quite dry, which should be the next day, the plaster has to be smoothed down. It will be more possible to preserve the shape in the small work if emery cloth is used. When all roughness has been smoothed down, all parts should carefully be gone over with finest sandpaper.

The work has now to be prepared so that the gold

will stand burnishing. Armenian bole, which can be obtained of chemists, will be required, and some pipeclay. Blanc's will do, as it is fine. Three-fifths of bole to two of clay are ground together on a piece of glass with a muller, using some water while grinding. The grinding should proceed for a good half hour, in fact, it cannot be too well ground, as, if it is in the least gritty, it will rub through when burnishing. For the frame in hand, about half a pipkinful will be required.

Melt down some size, and put some water in a pipkin about a quarter full; add some melted size, so that there should be just a bit more size than water. Then put in the ground bole and clay, and mix well together. The mixture should flow easily from the brush, but should not be too thin. Before using all over the frame, it will be as well to try some on the back edge; allow it to dry. If it dries the same color as when put on wet, there is too much size, and it should be weakened with water. If it dries a lighter color, rub it down with D emery paper, wearing down the sharpness of the paper first, as it is too strong if used fresh. If, on being papered, it polishes without rubbing off, it is the proper strength, and may be used. Should it rub off, it is weak, and more size should be added. Having our burnish gold size the proper strength, we give the work four coats all over, using a camel-hair mop, allowing each coat to set, and taking care to take up all pools that may collect in the bottoms. When quite dry, it must be rubbed down all over with D emery paper, and then well bristled with a short hog-hair brush until there is a good polish everywhere. If there be any dull parts, there is something wrong, and the gilding should not proceed until put right, as failure will be the result. The most essential points are that the bole be well ground, and that the size is not too strong.

The frame is then ready for gilding. The water to gild with must have three teaspoonfuls of size to a small pipkin full of water. The gold is laid on in the usual way. The writer will attempt to describe how to lay it; but it is an operation that really requires demonstration. A cushion, a knife, a whole and a three tip (the whole tip to take a whole leaf, the three-tip to take smaller pieces of the leaf), a camel-hair pencil and liner; these should be placed on the same handle—one at each end will be wanted. The plinth had better be laid first, then the pilasters, all the smaller fillets and mouldings next, leaving the hollow and ogee mouldings to be laid last, as the beginner will by then have acquired some facility in the handling of the leaf. It will be better for a beginner to blow out one leaf at a time on to his cushion; it will save waste until he is more expert in the handling. To take out a leaf, hold the book almost perpendicularly, expose a gold leaf, and gently blow it on to the cushion; then take the cushion in the left hand, passing the thumb through the leaf which is underneath; pass the knife very carefully underneath the leaf, lift it up, and spread it open on the cushion. If no corners are folded underneath it, blow gently in the center of it, so that it will be flattened out; then cut the leaf by drawing the knife firmly through the middle of it; then divide the two halves into three pieces, so that the leaf is divided into six pieces 1½ inches by 1 inch. A piece of gold is picked up by the three-tip being placed about halfway on the piece; if it does not adhere to the tip the worker should rub the tip briskly on his hair—a slight oiliness will make

the gold take kindly to the tip. Great care must be
taken to keep the knife clean and free from grease.
The tip with the piece of gold attached to it must be
held between the first two fingers of the left hand, and
the knife by the next two fingers. Take up the pencil,
wet it in. the water and size, and wet the ground
between two of the forms on the plinth. The place to
be gilded must be wet, but pools must be avoided, else
the gold will not reach the ground, or, if pressed
down, the water will burst through the gold and cause
a stain. Holding the pencil and liner in the right
hand, the tip is now taken with the right hand, held
over the place where the gold has to go, and the piece
gently pressed down on it. With the liner the gold is
pressed home, and if the piece is somewhat larger than
the ground, the overlapping gold is turned into the
corners of the ground and ornament with the liner, or
faulter as gilders call it. All the ground should be
gone over in this way; gentleness is required so as not
to break the gold, and smaller pieces should be cut and
used where needed. When all the ground has been
laid over, the leaf is cut in suitable pieces to cover the
forms of the ornament. Great care must be taken in
wetting the former that the pencil does not touch the
parts already gilded, for that will mean a stain. In
laying the fillets and smaller mouldings the gold
should be used the length of the leaf, but cut the width
required to cover the space. It will be better to lay
all the narrowest parts first, going on to the wider and
gaining experience, so as to be able to use a whole
leaf on the hollow moulding. In taking up a whole
leaf with the large tip, the tip must not quite take up
half of the leaf, so as to be able to lay it without
break in the hollow. For wetting the larger parts, the

camel-hair mop should be used. The parts laid should be burnished within two or three hours of the gold being laid. With an agate or flint burnisher sound the part laid first—if it sounds dull, it is not dry enough; if sharp, it is dry and should be burnished at once. The burnisher must be used lightly and across the form. If everything has been done satisfactorily, the burnisher will go very smoothly and softly. The resultant burnish will be the color of the gold, and not dark, as, indeed, one may say black, as all ordinary burnish usually is. When the work has been burnished, the beginner will, no doubt, feel distressed at seeing parts where the gold has not adhered, but that happens to all gilders, more or less, depending on the worker's skill, and all those parts must be faulted, using a smaller pencil to wet the faults. When done, the frame should sparkle with light and shade, full of life and having a depth of color that is absent in the frames gilded in the ordinary way.

Gilding Furniture.—Gold leaf, applied to articles of furniture as a means of decoration, is used in two ways; it is applied over an ordinary varnish or other finish, in which case but . little special preparation is necessary; or, as when used for picture frames, cornices, etc., it is applied to a specially prepared foundation, the basis of which is whiting, mixed with various other ingredients suggested by experience or fancy. In either case, the gold leaf is caused to adhere to the work by size specially prepared for the purpose, recipes for which follow herewith; the size being first applied to the work, and when it has become of the right consistency, the gold is laid upon it. *Oil gilding* and *burnish gilding* are different methods used to obtain certain desired effects, the former principally for articles exposed to the weather, and for heightening the effect of incised carving or engraving, and the latter for picture frames and articles having a specially prepared foundation, whose entire surface is to be gilded. It is intended that the gold shall adhere to the work only in the places to which the size has been applied, but the smallest portion of oil or even a slight dampness may cause the gold to partially adhere to the adjoining surface, resulting in slightly ragged edges; to prevent this, before applying the size to the desired design, the entire surface is covered with a thin film of some substance perfectly free from moisture, and easily removable by water, after completion of the process.

The Requisites.—First, a sufficient quantity of leaf gold, which is of two sorts, the deep gold, as it is called, and the pale gold. The former is the best; the latter very useful, and may occasionally be introduced for variety or effect.

Second, a gilder's cushion: an oblong piece of wood, covered with rough calfskin, stuffed with flannel several times doubled, with a border of parchment, about four inches deep, at one end, to prevent the air blowing the leaves about when placed on the cushion.

Thirdly, a gilding knife, with a straight and very smooth edge, to cut the gold.

Fourthly, several camel-hair pencils in sizes, and tips, made of a few long camel's hairs put between two cards, in the same manner as hairs are put into tin cases for brushes, thus making a flat brush with a very few hairs.

Lastly, a burnisher, which is a crooked piece of agate set in a long wooden handle.

Sizes.—These are of two kinds: oil sizes are those which, when applied, present an adhesive surface, requiring the immediate laying of the gold leaf upon it; of this class is the oil size commonly used in decorating furniture; water sizes are those that are allowed to become dry and hard when applied, and are rendered adhesive when the gold is to be laid, by brushing over with water; for burnish gilding these are always employed, as oil size does not dry sufficiently hard to permit of burnishing.

Oil Size for Oil Gilding.—Grind calcined red ocher with the best and oldest drying oil. When desired for use, add sufficient oil of turpentine to make it work freely.

Parchment Size.—For preparing frames, etc. To half a pound of parchment shavings, or cuttings of white leather, add three quarts of water, and boil it in a proper vessel till reduced to nearly half the quantity; then take it off the fire, and strain it through a sieve. Be careful in the boiling to keep it well stirred, and do not let burn.

Gold Size for Burnish Gilding.—Grind fine sal-ammoniac well with a muller and stone; scrape into it a little beef suet, and grind all wet together; after which, mix in with a pallet knife a small proportion of parchment size with a double proportion of water. When about to use, add parchment size until it will just flow from the brush.

Another.—Grind a lump of tobacco pipe clay into a very stiff paste with thin size; add a small quantity of ruddle and fine black lead, ground very fine, and temper the whole with a small piece of tallow. When ready to use, reduce with parchment size until it will just flow from the brush.

Another. — Grind separately in water, 1 pound Armenian bole, 2 ounces red lead, a sufficient quantity of black lead; mix, and regrind with a small quantity of olive oil. Reduce with parchment size to the proper consistency.

To Prevent Gold Adhering.—Either one of the following methods will prevent gold leaf or bronze from adhering to the surface beyond the outlines of the sizing laid on to receive it:

1. Whiting used dry, and applied by means of a pounce bag.

2. Whiting mixed in water, and applied with a soft brush. When the water has evaporated, dust off the superfluous whiting with an ordinary paint duster. By this method a very thin coating of whiting remains, which is free from any grittiness. One advantage gained by the use of whiting thus applied is, it furnishes a whitish ground over which clear varnish or oil size may be distinctly seen as the striping progresses. After the leaf or bronze has been applied, the work must be carefully washed, so as to insure the removal of the whiting.

3. White of egg reduced with water, and applied with a piece of sponge.

4. A thin wash of starch water, either brushed on with a flat camel-hair brush, or applied with a soft sponge.

5. Take ball liquorice and water, a weak solution, and apply with a soft brush. This may be kept in a bottle ready for use at any time.

6. Cut a new potato in two, and rub over the part to be sized with the raw face exposed, allowing the juice to remain until dry.

It will be observed that any substance which interposes a film over the varnish, itself being free from tackiness and readily removed by water, will answer the purpose.

Oil Gilding.—Applying the gold.—If the wood to be gilded is finished with varnish or otherwise, no additional foundation is necessary upon which to lay the gold leaf; if the wood is not finished, after it has been smoothed and dusted, give it one or two coats of parchment size, after it is perfectly dry and hard, again smoothing the surface with fine sandpaper. That the gold may not adhere to any part of the work except where the size is hard, powder the surface lightly with whiting from a pounce bag, which is a small bag made of material sufficiently loose to permit the powdered whiting to sift through as fine dust; if preferred, any of the preceding recipes for that purpose can be used instead. Remove the surplus whiting with the dusting brush, and the work is then ready for the size. Apply this with a sable or fit brush of the proper size, carefully observing to make the outer lines of the design clear and sharp, that the work may not appear ragged. Let the size remain until it feels tacky, when the gold may be applied. This is the most difficult part of the operation, and experience is necessary before gold leaf can be laid smoothly without a wrinkle or a break. Turn a leaf of gold out of the book upon the cushion; breathe gently upon the center of the leaf and it will lie flat on the cushion; cut it to the proper size by bringing the knife perpendicularly over it, and sawing it gently until divided. Take your tip (a brush used for the purpose) and after drawing it lightly over your hair to remove any particles or dust that may be upon it, breathe upon it gently, which will dampen **it**

sufficiently to cause the leaf of gold to adhere to it; lay the tip upon the leaf of gold and carefully transfer it to the work; blow upon it gently and it will straighten out and adhere. It may be rendered quite smooth by slightly dabbing it with a bit of cotton. In about an hour wash off the superfluous gold from the edges, with a sponge and water. If the article is to be exposed to the weather or much wear, the gilding may be varnished with copal varnish.

Burnish Gilding.—As previously stated, this process requires a specially prepared foundation upon which to lay the gold, and as the preparation of this foundation is a distinct trade, the furniture dealer or cabinetmaker seldom finds it necessary to undertake it, the articles coming to his hand ready-prepared for gilding; but as in repairing picture frames, cornices, mirror frames, etc., it frequently becomes necessary to renew the foundation, a comprehensive description of the whole process is given.

Preparing the Woodwork.—After smoothing and dusting the work, coat the frames in every part with boiling-hot parchment size, as previously described, then mix a sufficient quantity of whiting with size to the consistency of thick cream, and with it by means of a brush, coat every part of the frame several times, permitting each coat to become perfectly dry before proceeding with the next. The wood will thus be covered with a layer of hard whiting nearly or quite a sixteenth of an inch in thickness. The size must not be too thick, and when mixed with the whiting should not be so hot as the preliminary coat of size.

Polishing.—When the preparations are quite dry, clean and polish them. To do this, wet a small piece at a time, and, with a smooth, fine piece of cloth, dipped in water, rub the part till all the bumps and inequalities are removed; and for those parts where the fingers will not enter, as the mouldings, etc., wind the wet cloth round a piece of wood, and by this means make the surface all smooth and even alike.

Where there is carved work, etc., it will sometimes be necessary to bring the mouldings to their original sharpness by means of chisels, gouges, etc., as the preparation will be apt to fill up all the finer parts of the work, which must be thus restored. It is some-times the practice, after polishing, to go over the work once with fine yellow or Roman ocher; but this is rarely necessary.

Applying the Size.—Select the proper gold size from the recipes previously given; add parchment size until it will just flow from the brush; make it quite hot, and apply it to the wood with a very soft brush, taking care not to make the first coat too thick; let it dry and give two or three successive coats, after the last brushing it with a stiff brush to remove any inequalities. The work is then ready for the gold.

Laying the Gold.—The manipulation of the gold leaf has been described under the heading Oil Gilding. In the paint now being described, size used (being water size, which, as previously explained, is permitted to become hard and dry after being applied) must be moistened to cause the gold leaf to adhere to it. For this purpose, with a long-haired camel-hair pencil, dipped in water, go over as much of the work as you intend the piece of gold to cover; then lay the gold upon it in the manner previously explained. Be sure that the part to which the gold is applied is sufficiently wet; indeed, it must be floating, or the gold will be apt to crack. Proceed in this manner a little at a time, and do not attempt to cover too much at once, until by experience you are going to handle the gold with freedom.

Burnishing.—When the work is covered with gold, set it by to dry; there is a particular state or degree of dryness, known only by experience, in which the moulding is in a fit state for burnishing; it will probably be ready to burnish in about eight or ten hours, but it will depend on the warmth of the room or state of the air.

When it is ready, those parts intended to be burnished must be dusted with a soft brush; then, wiping the burnisher with a piece of soft wash-leather (quite dry), begin to burnish about an inch or two in length at a time, taking care not to bear too hard, but with a gentle and quick motion, applying the tool until all the parts of the surface are equally bright.

Matting or Dead Gold.—Certain portions only of the work are burnished, according to the fancy, and the facility with which the burnishing tool can be applied; the remaining parts are now to be deprived of their metallic luster, to make a more effective contrast with the burnishing. The parts thus treated are said to be matted or dead gold. The process is as follows:

Grind some vermilion or yellow ocher very fine, and mix a very small portion either with the parchment size or with the white of an egg, and with a very soft brush lay it evenly on the parts to be dulled; if well done, it will add greatly to the beauty of the work. Previous to matting, the work must be well cleared of superfluous gold, by means of a soft brush.

Finishing.—In elaborate works it is frequently impossible to lay gold leaf into all the intricacies of an elaborate design, and the parts thus left bare must be finished by touching up with a small brush charged with shell gold, or gold powder, mixed with gum. Arabic to the proper consistency. The following recipe describes the preparation of shell gold:

Shelled Gold.—Take any quantity of leaf gold and grind it with a small portion of honey, to a fine powder, add a little gum arabic and sugar candy, with a little water, and mix it well together; let it dry

Silver Size.—Grind pipe clay fine with a little black lead and good soap, and add parchment size as directed for gold size.

Composition for Frame Ornaments.—The ornaments for gilded mirror frames, etc., are usually moulded from some plastic substance that is somewhat tougher and more durable than the ordinary gilding foundation of whiting and size. The proper moulds being prepared, they are thoroughly rubbed upon the inside with sweet oil, and the composition firmly pressed in; after removing the mould the cast may be dried by a gentle heat, or while still plastic it can be applied in its proper place and bent into any position. Following are recipes for composition:

Dissolve 1 pound of glue in 1 gallon of water. In another kettle boil together 2 pounds of resin, 1 gill of Venice turpentine, and 1 pint of linseed oil; mix all together in one kettle, and boil and stir till the water has evaporated. Turn the whole into a tub of finely rolled whiting, and work till it is the consistency of dough.

Boil 7 pounds of best glue in 7 half pints of water. Melt 3 pounds of white resin in 3 pints of raw linseed oil. When the above has been well boiled put them into a large vessel and simmer them for half an hour, stirring the mixture and taking care that it does **not** boil over. The whole, must then be turned into a box of whiting rolled and sifted, and mixed till it is of the consistency of dough.

To Manipulate Gold Leaf.—Get a piece of paper, thin enough to show shadow of gold leaf through, slightly wax it, lay it on gold leaf; the latter will then adhere, and can be easily worked and will come off clean. The paper should be slightly larger than the gold leaf and the fingers passed over the paper to make the gold leaf adhere.

Bronzing.—This is a process for imitating on metal, plaster, wood, or other material, the peculiar appearance produced by chemical action upon the surface of bronze metal. It is accomplished by spreading over the surface of the material to be ornamented a very thin coating of. bronze powder, which is caused to adhere either by applying it directly upon a coating of any of the sizes mentioned in the foregoing pages, or by mixing with a vehicle, such as gum arabic or transparent varnish. The latter is most desirable, as in the other case, being subject to the direct action of the atmosphere, the bronze powder soon tarnishes. In ornamenting furniture, bronzing is generally employed to represent gilding, a variety of bronze called gold bronze being used, which affords an excellent imitation, but is not very lasting. It is usually applied after the completion of the other finishing processes, the ground work being prepared in the manner described under Oi¹ Gilding, and the size likewise applied as there described. A small wad of cotton batting is then dipped in the bronze and passed gently over the sized portions, causing the bronze to adhere. In the other method—that of applying the bronze by means of a vehicle—the preliminaries of whiting the ground and sizing are not necessary, a small quantity of bronze being simply mixed with the vehicle employed to such a degree of fluidity that it will flow easily, and in that condition applied with a fine brush. Many preparations are used as vehicles, such as transparent varnish thinned with turpentine, gum arabic dis solved in water, and gold size reduced with parchment size. There are a variety of colors in bronze powders, and to produce the best effect the size or vehicle should be of a color similar to that of the bronze used; in gold size the coloring pigment is ocher, and in its place, for green bronze, or blue bronze, may be employed respectively verditer, vermilion or Prussian blue, a very small quantity being sufficient. In bronzing on painted work the ground should be as nearly as possible the color of the bronze to be applied.

Banana Solution.—The so-called "banana solution" (the name being derived from its odor) which is used in applying bronzes of various kinds is usually a mixture of equal parts of amyl acetate, acetone and benzine, with just enough pyroxylin dissolved therein to give it sufficient body. Powdered bronze is put into a bottle containing this mixture and the paint so formed applied with a brush to the article to be bronzed. The thin covering of pyroxylin that is left after the evaporation of the liquid protects the bronze from the air and keeps it from being wiped off by the cleanly housemaid. Tarnished picture frames and tarnished chandeliers to which a gold bronze has been applied from such a solution will look fresh and new for a long time. Copper bronze as well as gold bronze and the various colored bronze powders can be used in the "banana solution" for making very pretty advertising signs for use in the drug store. Lettering and bordering work upon the signs can be done with it. Several stiff, very small painter's brushes are needed for such work and they must be either kept in the solution when not in use, or, better still, washed in benzine or acetone immediately after use and put away for future service. It is needless to add that as the "banana solution" is volatile it must be kept well corked.

STAINING WOODWORK WITH ACIDS

For staining wood brown, sulphuric acid, more or less diluted, according to the depth of stain desired, is applied to the wood, previously cleaned and dried with a brush, and when the acid has acted enough its further action is arrested by the application of liquid ammonia.

To age oak artificially, liquid ammonia is laid on with a rag or brush, which does the work rapidly and effectually.

To darken cherry, rub it over with nitric acid of 1.2 specific gravity, and after permitting it to stand for twelve hours, wash and dry thoroughly. Nitric acid gives a permanent yellow stain, which may be converted into dark brown by subsequent application of tincture of iodine.

A hot, concentrated solution of picric acid gives a very fine yellow effect. Aqua fortis, diluted with three times its own weight of rain-water, brushed over the wood, gives a more true yellow effect than the undiluted nitric acid (aqua fortis).

A bright golden yellow stain is made by digesting ¼ ounce of powdered madder for twelve hours in 2 ounces of sulphuric acid and then filtering through cloth. The articles to be stained should be immersed in the fluid for three or four days.

ON HARDWOOD FLOORS

The finish and care of hardwood or parquette floors has been and is now a source of great trouble and annoyance to housekeepers. In many cases where beautiful floors have been laid, they have been left to be finished by persons who have not troubled themselves with finding out the best method of finishing, and the usual way for such persons to do is to treat them with shellac or varnish, says a writer in one of our exchanges. This is all wrong, as a moment's thought will convince any one that a surface that is constantly walked over needs something different from the coating of gum that is left on the surface after the spirit used in dissolving the shellac or varnish is evaporated. This coating then becomes brittle, and is ground up into minute particles by the nails in the boots and swept away, leaving the wood bare, right where it is most exposed to view.

As a matter of course, the beauty of the floor is soon gone, and instead of being an attractive part of the furnishing, the sanitary consideration very often is about all that keeps one from nailing a carpet over the whole floor. Others use linseed oil, and everybody knows that an oil finish is one of the best methods of finishing wood, but the objection is, that each time the oil is applied it darkens the wood, and in a short time the different kinds of wood are of the same color.

Now the question arises, which is the true and only way of finishing floors properly? And the answer is, by the use of hard wax, which, however, must be so prepared that the trouble of applying it and the stickiness attending ordinary beeswax and turpentine are entirely obviated. The wax is treated with special liquids and made into a preparation.

Among the many different things tried, hard wax was found to be the most satisfactory in its results. It is so simple, that when once the floor has been properly filled and finished with it, any servant can renew and keep the floors fresh and bright as long as the wood lasts, and as it does not materially change the color, the wood always retains its beauty. An application about once a year is all that is necessary, if the floors are rubbed over, when a little dull, with a weighted brush or cloth.

In repolishing old floors that have been in use for a length of time and become dull looking, it is only necessary, after they have been cleaned, to rub on a thin coat of the hard wax finish with the brush or cloth, as stated above. If the floors have been varnished and the varnish is worn off in places, as mentioned above, the best way is to have the varnish scraped off, and then a thin coat of the hard wax should be applied and treated as the new wood after it is filled. But if it is inconvenient to have the floor scraped, or the expense too much, the main object being to restore the color in those places which are worn and defaced, the following mixture is recommended: One part linseed oil, 1 part liquid dryer and 2 parts turpentine; a cloth should be dampened with this and applied to the worn and defaced places, which will have the desired effect. After being wiped off clean, it ought to dry twenty-four hours, and then be polished with the hard wax finish. It is very important never to use the wax over oil that is not thoroughly dry, as the floor would invariably be sticky.

Finally, it would be well to mention that hardwood or parquette floors should never be washed with soap and water, as it raises the grain and discolors the wood. After the floors have been properly filled and finished with the hard wax, dirt will not get into the pores, but stays on the surface and consequently can be removed with a brush or cloth, or, if necessary, dampen cloth with a little turpentine. This will take off any stain from the finish.

An excellent method of waxing floors is as follows: Take 1 pound of the best beeswax, cut it up into very small pieces and let it thoroughly dissolve in 3 pints of turpentine, stirring occasionally, if necessary. The mixture should be only a trifle thicker than the clear turpentine. Apply with a rag to the surface of the floor, which should be perfectly clean. This is the difficult part of the work; for if too much or too little is put on a good polish is impossible. The right amount varies, less being required for a hard, close-grained wood, and more if the wood is soft and open-grained. Try a square foot or two at first. Put on what you think will be enough, and leave the place untouched and unstepped on for twenty-four hours, or longer, if needful. When thoroughly dry, rub with a hand brush. If it polishes well, repeat the whole process over the entire floor. If it does not, remove the wax with fine sandpaper, and lay again, using more or less than before, as may be necessary, and continue experimenting until the desired result is secured. If the mixture is slow in drying, add one part japan to six of turpentine.

Birch makes an entirely satisfactory floor for dancing,

as well as for kindred uses. It is easily brought to a smooth surface and a fine polish, and is of a rich amber color of an even shade. In addition, it has that rare elasticity and resiliency that make it alike delightful for walking and dancing. It costs about 10 cents laid, and is in no way a disappointment to those using it.

What is said of birch applies equally well to hard maple, both the white and the red varieties, the white being that chosen for floors, and is the lightest-colored of the woods so used. It is very hard, takes readily a fine polish; the boards are not liable to warp, but, unfortunately, require the very closest care in the drying to prevent shrinkage when laid. It is lasting, and is but little affected by water. Only beech, hickory and white oak approach it in lightness of color. Hickory has sterling qualities, too generally appreciated to need detailed discussion of its intrinsic worth, yet it is sadly neglected when the question of flooring is under consideration. Perhaps this is due to the difficulty with which it is laid. It is an open-grain wood, but takes polish with ease.

Beech makes almost an ideal floor, light-colored and hard, and has the rare quality of wearing smoother with age; at times it is found beautifully bird's-eyed. In the Southern States it grows in the greatest profusion in the swamps and lower woods, but is unappreciated, only enough being preserved for use in making plane stocks and other tools requiring a hard, durable wood that does not shrink, warp or split. It could be laid for 20 cents per foot. And along with it goes apple, which polishes to a rich, delicate amber color; the cost being about the same as beech, but the apple wood has the tremendous disadvantage of not being obtainable in large boards

The laying of a hardwood floor requires not only a good carpenter, but an expert judge of woods, and of the individual boards, because only by carefully selecting and placing like planks can we get a permanently even surface. Suppose a plank of heart and one of sap should be placed side by side; no matter what the wood, when a rainy season may come the sap will swell more and rise above the heart. Even when they come from like relative positions in two like trees, their texture may differ so widely as to make them undesirable companions. In spite of the nicest workmanship and the best judgment in selecting, some inequalities of surface will be present till removed by the most thorough sandpapering. This should be done with enough care to avoid scratching; then comes the polishing.

To get the best results, hardwood floors should be laid after the building is thoroughly dry, and in case of new building it should be the last work done.

Care should be taken that the surface on which the floor is laid is clean and smooth. Drive the flooring well up and be careful not to break the tongue.

Seven-eighths-inch flooring should be nailed with 2½-inch special flooring nail. For ⅜-inch flooring 1¼-inch finishing nail, No. 15, will be found about right.

An oak floor after being laid should be evenly cleaned off and sandpapered until perfectly smooth. It must then be filled with what is known as "wood filler," and allowed to stand for six to ten hours. This filler can be made any shade desired.

If a wax finish is desired, apply two light coats of white floor shellac. Let the first coat stand one hour before putting on the second. After the second coat has stood for two hours, sandpaper with No. 0 sand-paper and the floor is ready for the wax, an article made expressly for this purpose and ready for use.

Put the wax on as thin as possible and let it stand for half an hour, then with a rubbing brush rub across the grain of the wood and again lengthways until the

Fig. 117

brush slips easily, then take a piece of soft carpet and rub until the desired polish is obtained.

For maple, birch, or other close-grain woods, use the same process, omitting the "wood filler "

Estimate of Material Required.—For laying and finish-ing ⅜ flooring per 100 feet surface: 100 feet ⅜ floor-ing, 2½ pounds finishing brads No. 15, 3½ pounds wood filler (for oak only), 3 pints shellac, ½ pound

floor wax. For ⅞ flooring, 6 pounds 2½-inch flooring
nails will be sufficient per 100 feet.

A weighted brush with a long handle is generally
employed for polishing a wax-finished floor, similar to
the one shown in Fig. 117. The wax is applied with a
rag or brush, after the filler has been properly rubbed
down and all is hard and dry. The weighted brush is
then rubbed over the surface to and fro until the
desired polish is attained.

Stained Floors.—A floor stained to represent dark
old oak is preferred by many. The mixture for
accomplishing this is sold at all paint shops, and
comes in grades 1, 2, 3, and 4, varying from light to
dark. If the boards are smooth and fine-grained, a
satin wood or pitch pine stain or polish is preferred;
but if the floor is old or rough it is folly to attempt
any stain except that of dark oak or dark mahogany.
Some of the mixtures used for this can be put on with
a rag, although a brush is better. Pour the liquid into a
saucer, dip the brush in, saturate thoroughly, rub evenly
over the wood, and dry instantly with a soft cloth.

For the ultra-fashionable floor, which is of a pale
shade of oak, sized and varnished, buy the desired
amount of raw sienna powder; mix with water, and
rub into the boards as directed above. Mahogany
staining: Make a mixture containing ½ pound of
madder, 2 ounces of logwood chips, boiled in 1 gallon
of water; brush this over the wood while hot. When
dry, go over this with a solution of pearlash, 2 drachms
to 1 of water, size and polish. If a redder shade is
required, it can be produced by smearing the surface
with a strong solution of permanganate of potash,
which is left on for five minutes. The wood is then
carefully washed, dried and polished.

A good cheap oak stain is made of equal parts of potash and pearlash, 2 ounces of each to a quart of water. As potash is a solvent, care must be taken to keep it from the hands; and an old brush should be used.

For other stains and methods of applying them, see recipes described in previous pages, where stains for nearly all purposes are given.

MISCELLANEOUS MATTERS

Floor Polish.—Cut beeswax into small pieces, or else grate it up; add turpentine, and allow the mixture to stand for twelve hours; then heat it over the fire till it dissolves. Care must be taken not to heat the mixture too hot, and also the flame must not come too near, for explosive vapors are generated, which are liable to catch fire.

Dull Polish on Stained Whitewood.—The dull polish that is seen on most furniture is obtained by partly French polishing the article, and then removing any apparent shine or gloss by well brushing the surface over with medium grade pumice-powder or fine emery; or the stained wood might be coated with spirit varnish. In the absence of details as to the purpose for which the stained wood is to be used, no other procedure can be suggested. Stained floor-boards, for instance, would not require French polishing, nor even spirit varnishing, because a suitable polish can be readily obtained by using beeswax dissolved in turpentine, applied with a weighted brush. On the other hand, on furniture goods French polish serves a double purpose; the polish partly fills the grain or pores of the wood, and gives a hard surface that can be dulled without rubbing off the stain.

Refinishing Oak Doors that are Badly Weather-Stained.—If possible, take the doors off the hinges and lay them down flat on some trusses or boxes, and remove the old varnish with ammonia or a mixture of 2 parts strong ammonia and 1 part of turpentine and benzine, using a stubby brush to get into the cutwork and about the mouldings. When all the varnish has been removed, dope over stained portions with a strong oxalic acid solution, and see whether you cannot bleach the wood by that operation. If this will not work, you have to resort to staining. Use raw sienna for light effect, and, after staining, use paste wood filler, colored to match the stain. Then proceed as you would on new work. If the light stain does not hide the weather stains, you will be obliged to use a darker stain and darker filler.

Coloring Wood Clear Through.—All the sap is expelled and the log is then treated with chemicals, and the color or colors are pressed into the wood. Any shade desired can be obtained, and, in fact, several colors can be merged one into the other, producing a very beautiful effect. On cutting up the samples we received, we found that the color was evenly distributed all through the fibers, the grain of the wood giving a very pleasing effect, especially when polished. The wood, it is claimed, dries sooner than by ordinary seasoning, and it can also be rendered fireproof by adding special chemicals. Of course, painting is done away with, so that the natural structure of the wood is seen to better advantage than when painted in the ordinary way. The coloring is, we understand, free from arsenic and quite harmless; the colors do not fade, and, of course, cannot be worn off by rubbing, etc.

Cleaning Polished Wood.—A good encaustic, which will clean and polish at the same time, may be made from wax, sal soda and any good soap. The wax and soap should be shaved and dissolved in boiling water. Stir frequently and add the soda. Put the mixture in something which may be closely covered, and stir constantly until cool. This may be applied to floors, furniture, marbles, tiles, bricks, etc. It will remove ink from polished surfaces. The French use white wax on white marbles, but this is not absolutely necessary.

Finishing Hardwood.—If it is open-grained wood I should first fill it with paste filler, then I would give it a coat of shellac, and after that I would bring it up with a first-class varnish.

It would be all right to finish it all in shellac if it could be kept from moisture, but wherever a drop of water touches a shellac finish it will turn white. And just as like as not the mistress will set the servants to wiping up the hardwood finish with a damp cloth. Now a good varnish will stand it, but shellac won't. But the best way to clean furniture and hardwood work is to use crude oil—only a very little of it—and then wipe it off thoroughly with cotton waste or cheesecloth. The latter is preferable because it has no lint to catch on the woodwork, although if you rub it dry enough with cotton waste you can rub off any lint that may be left. The crude oil acts as a varnish renewer as well as a cleaner. But if it is not thoroughly wiped off with plenty of elbow grease it will catch the dirt and look pretty bad. Crude oil is a good thing, provided you don't use too much of it, and then, again, provided you don't leave it on.

Making Paste Wood Fillers.—Paste fillers for hard woods are made from any of the following materials, or a combination of these: silex or silica, terra alba, whiting, china clay, starch, rye flour, and sometimes barytes. Silex or terra alba will, on drying, give th. least discoloration to the wood. The pigment should be of impalpable fineness and intimately mixed to a stiff paste with one-third each of pale linseed oil, pale gold size japan and turpentine. This paste may be either run through a mill or be given a very thorough mixing, and to test it for quality it should be thinned with turpentine to the consistency of a varnish, applied with a varnish brush to open-grained wood, preferably oak, allowed to set for about twenty to thirty minutes, and the surplus filler removed by wiping across the grain in the usual manner. After twenty four to thirty-six hours, the surface should be lightly sandpapered and a good, flowing coat of rubbing varnish applied, which, when fairly well set, should not show any pitting or pin holes. Should it pit, however, or show pin holes or needle points, the filler is defective in binding properties, and the portion of japan should be increased, with a corresponding decrease in the proportion of turpentine. The linseed oil and the gold size japan must be of good body, and if cornstarch or rye flour is used in connection with silex or silica, the proportions should be about one of the former to five of the latter by weight.

Filler for White Ash.—As white ash is a very porous wood, it should be treated with an extra light mineral paste wood filler, made from clean silex, mixed with 2 parts bleached linseed oil, 3 parts pale japan gold size and 1 part turps, to stiff paste and thinned for use with turpentine to the consistency of medium-bodied varnish. When dry and hard the surface should be smooth sandpapered and given a coat of white shellac varnish, after which it may be finished with rubbing varnish, that may be rubbed and polished in the ordinary way.

Good Wood Finish.—Richness of effect may be gained in decorative woodwork by using woods of different tone, such as amaranth and amboyna, by inlaying and veneering. The Hungarian ash and French walnut afford excellent veneers, especially the burs or gnarls. In varnishing, the varnishes used can be toned down to match the wood, or be made to darken it, by the addition of coloring matters. The patented preparations, known as "wood fillers," are prepared in different colors for the purpose of preparing the surface of wood previous to the varnishing. They fill up the pores of the wood, rendering the surface hard and smooth. For polishing mahogany, walnut, etc., the following is recommended: Dissolve beeswax by heat in spirits of turpentine until the mixture becomes viscid; then apply, by a clean cloth, and rub thoroughly with a flannel or cloth. A common mode of polishing mahogany is by rubbing it first with linseed oil, and then with a cloth dipped in very fine brickdust; a good gloss may also be produced by rubbing with linseed oil, and then holding trimmings or shavings of the same material against the work in the lathe. Glass-paper, followed by rubbing, also gives a good luster.

There are various means of toning or darkening woods for decorative effect, such as logwood, lime, brown soft soap, dyed oil, sulphate of iron, nitrate of silver exposed to sun's rays, carbonate of soda, bichromate and permanganate of potash, and other alkaline preparations are all used for darkening woods. The last three are specially recommended. The solution is applied by dissolving 1 ounce of the alkali in 2 gills of boiling water, diluted to the required tone. The surface is saturated with a sponge or flannel, and immediately dried with soft rags. The carbonate is used for dark woods. Oil tinged with rose madder may be applied to hardwoods like birch, and a red oil is prepared from soaked alkanet root in linseed oil. The grain of yellow pine can be brought out by two or three coats of japan much diluted with turpentine, and afterwards oiled and rubbed. To give mahogany the appearance of age, lime water used before oiling is a good plan. In staining wood, the best and most transparent effect is obtained by repeated light coats of the same. For oak stain a strong solution of oxalic acid is employed; for mahogany, dilute nitrous acid. A primary coat, or a coat of wood fillers, is advantageous. For mahogany stains the following are given: 2 ounces of dragons' blood dissolved in 1 quart of rectified spirits of wine, well shaken; or raw sienna in beer, with burnt sienna to give the required tone; for darker stains boil ½ pound of madder and 2 ounces of logwood chips in 1 gallon of water, and brush the decoction while hot over the wood. When dry, paint with a solution of 2 ounces of potash in 1 quart of water. A solution of permanganate of potash forms a rapid and excellent brown stain.

Easy Method of Finishing Woodwork.—French polishing as a means of finishing furniture and woodwork is generally regarded as a most tedious operation, owing to the number of solutions to be used on work that is built up of various kinds of wood, in bringing it up to uniform color, and in polishing it so as to bring out and reflect to the fullest extent the markings or figure of the wood. On high-grade goods, with a bright, lustrous, level finish this is so. Yet much furniture is not of high-grade finish, so far as the polisher is concerned; for instance, bedroom furniture that is stained green is rarely finished out extra bright, and the same may be said of fumed oak goods and many American organs. In fact, some goods look far better with a faintly lustrous polished surface than if finished out very bright, especially if the surface is at all uneven or badly cleaned up. A process of finishing known as "dry shining" strikes a medium between high-grade finish and simple spirit varnishing. In the crudest form of this process the work is simply oiled and a wet rubber of polish applied all over, not sufficient being used to fill the grain, but just enough to kill the oil. This treatment is generally considered good enough for the insides of drawers, cupboards, etc., the object being to remove an unfinished appearance and to prevent the surface getting as dirty as it otherwise might. From this better degrees of finish may be reached. , The work may be oiled, filled in, one or more rubbers of polish laid on just to fill up the grain, and then an even coat of spirit varnish applied. If the articles are of white wood, they may be stained to imitate some choicer wood before oiling; and if the goods are likely to be subject to hard wear, the coating of spirit varnish may be omitted, the polish being worked out fairly dry to ensure the removal of all oil; then apply a coat of oak or painter's varnish, which, however, gives a bright surface when dry, and is merely mentioned as a means of obtaining a bright finish with the minimum of trouble.

Egg-shell finish also does not require the troublesome operation of spiriting out. Here the work is brought up to a stage nearly approaching that for spiriting, but the surface of polish when hard is dulled bv rubbing or brushing with fine-grade pumice-stone powder or flour emery, in which condition it may be left. If a gloss instead of a shine is preferred, the wood should have a smart rubbing of beeswax and turps. Black work has a specially chaste appearance thus finished, and the black stain of logwood and iron solution may be used, aniline spirit black being employed for imparting density of color to pale shellac polish. If it is not convenient to use varnish, and a simple solution of shellac in spirits (4 ounces orange shellac dissolved in 1 pint methylated spirit) is the only solution at hand, a passable finish may still be gained by enclosing the pad in a piece of soft rag and finishing out by working it in straight lines, after a body has been put on without a covering. When the articles must be stained, it will be found more economical to buy the stains ready-made if only a small quantity is required. Dry shining has at least the merit of building up a surface that can be taken in hand again and French polished.

Metallization of Wood.—Some artisans in Germany have succeeded in turning to practical account the recently devised process by which wood is made to take on some of the special characteristics of metal, that is, the surface becomes so hard and smooth as to be susceptible of a high polish, and may be treated with a burnisher of either glass or porcelain; the appearance of the wood being then in every respect that of polished metal, having, in fact, the semblance of a metallic mirror, but with this peculiar and advantageous difference, namely, that, unlike metal,

it is unaffected by moisture. To reach this result the
wood is steeped in a bath of caustic alkali for two or
three days, according to its degree of permeability, at
a temperature of between 164° and 197° Fahr.; it is
then placed in a second bath of hydrosulphate of
calcium, to which a concentrated solution of sulphur is
added, after some twenty-four or thirty-six hours; the
third bath is one of acetate of lead, at a temperature
of from 95° to 122°, and in this latter the wood is
allowed to remain from thirty to fifty hours. After
being subjected to a thorough drying it is in a condition for being polished with lead, tin or zinc, as may
be desired, finishing the process with a burnisher, when
the wood apparently becomes a piece of shining,
polished metal.

How to Tone Down New Mahogany, Oak, etc.—In
making repairs to furniture, it usually happens that
the new wood is considerably lighter in tone than the
old, and ordinary stains will not match it so as to give
satisfaction. This can be done easily, however, by
means of a solution of bichromate of potash. To
make this, purchase a cent's worth of the chemical,
and placing it in an ordinary medicine bottle, fill up
with water and shake until dissolved. To use the
solution, rub a small quantity on the wood to be
darkened, and await results. If not dark enough, give
another coat. It dries in a few minutes, and can be
sandpapered after, as it is not a surface stain, but a
chemical one. By a judicious use of the above
solution it is easy to match old work of any description,
so that the new and old cannot be distinguished from
each other.

Spirit Varnish for Violins.—Spirit varnish is difficult
to apply evenly, owing to its drying so quickly. The

color generally appears streaky. In any case, no shellac should be used in the varnish, as shellac is too hard. A good spirit varnish is made as follows: First size the violin with a mixture of 3 parts of best copal varnish and 1 part of turpentine, applied hot with a rag, and well rubbed in. Color ½ pint of alcohol with turmeric and a little red sanders added to take away the greenish tinge. Dissolve 2 ounces of gum sandarach (juniper) in ½ pint of alcohol. Put the two half-pint mixtures together, and add 2 tablespoonfuls of Venice turpentine and 2 ounces of white shellac. When dissolved, filter through cotton wool.

Putting Transfers on Coach Panels.—The method of transferring crests and monograms to the panels of coaches, etc., is as follows: Cover carefully the face of the design (that is, the colored or printed side) with a thin, smooth coat of gold size mixed with two or three drops of varnish, being careful to cover all parts that are to be transferred. Let the gold size coating become thoroughly tacky or sticky, then lay the design face downward on the panel to be decorated, and roll it down smoothly with a rubber roller, pressing out all air bubbles. When the adhesive has got quite dry, thoroughly soak the paper with water by means of a sponge, then gently peel off the paper from one corner. Sponge the surface composition off the panel, and when the design is quite dry, apply a finishing coat of varnish. Transfers can also be applied without coating them with gold size, if the panels have been recently varnished, and have a good tack (that is to say, when the varnish is sticky , as the design will then adhere by gentle pressure.

Paint for Blackboards.—The best blackboard paint is made by moistening 4 ounces dry lampblack with alcohol, rubbing it out with a spatula, gradually adding 1 quart of shellac varnish, and stirring into this 3 ounces flour of pumice and 3 ounces finely pulverized rotten stone; then straining through a fine sieve or strainer to break up any lumps that may have formed. This is applied quickly to the bare wood, so that no laps are formed, and in a day or so a second coat may be applied, and after standing a day or two longer may be haired or mossed.

Ebonizing.—Apply to the wood, by means of a brush or sponge, a solution of hydrochloric aniline dissolved in water, to which has been added a little protochloride of copper. When this coating has dried, apply similarly a solution of bichromate of potash dissolved in water. After this process has been repeated two, or at the most three, times, the wood will assume a clear, full, durable black color, which is affected neither by the action of light nor dampness.

Polishing Boxwood Draughtmen. —The cheaper class of draughtmen are simply coated with a good quality spirit varnish, but high-grade goods are polished in the lathe. The polish that is used and the method of applying the polish differ slightly from the method that is employed in polishing flat surfaces. A bright finish on both sides and edges is only obtained after several handlings, the chief difficulty being the manipulation in the early stages, such as the provision of suitable chucks, the avoidance of the use of glass-paper, and the knack of using the polish so that it will not clog up the finer grooves. If ordinary French polish is used, it should not be applied with new wadding; a wad made from a rubber that has been used on other work should be employed, so that there may be less risk of loose fluff sticking to the work while the polishing is being done. The wad would not require the rag covering that is usual on flat surfaces. If a lathe is not available, very good results could be obtained by using polish for sealing up the pores of the wood and forming a smooth foundation, and then applying carefully a coating of good quality clear spirit varnish. Black goods should be stained first with French black water stain, and the polishing done with black polish. White polish made from bleached shellac, or a transparent polish, should be used in preference to polish that is made from orange or lemon shellac.

Softening Putty.—To soften putty that has become hard by exposure, so as to remove it easily from a sash, take 1 pound of pearlash and 3 pounds of quick-stone lime; slake the lime in water, then add the pearlash, and make the whole of about the consistency of paint; apply it to both sides of the glass, and let it remain for twelve hours, when the putty will be so softened that the glass may be taken out of the frame with the greatest facility.

Bruises in Wood.—To take out bruises in furniture, wet the part with warm water; double a piece of brown paper five or six times, soak it, and lay it on the place; apply on that a hot flatiron till the moisture is evaporated. If the bruise be not gone, repeat the process. After two or three applications, the dent or bruise will be raised level with the surface. If the bruise be small, merely soak it with warm water, and apply a red-hot poker very near the surface; keep it continually wet, and in a few moments the bruise will disappear.

Wood Stains.—The following have been published by a German paper as formulæ for some wood stains, which may be put up in a dry form, and when wanted for use may be readily dissolved in water: Oak wood: 5 kg. of Cassel brown, .5 kg. of potash, and 10 kg. of rain-water, boiled together for an hour, the whole strained through a linen cloth, and the clear, dark-colored liquid boiled to a syrupy consistency.   Walnut wood: A decoction of Cassel brown, 3 kg.; potash, .3 kg.; and water, 7 kg.; the whole strained through linen, and during evaporation to syrup 2.5 kg. of extract of logwood added.   Mahogany: A decoction of extract of Brazil wood, 3 kg.; potash, .25 kg., and water, 3 kg.; to which, before evaporating to syrup, 150 gr. of eosine are added.   Ebony: 5 kg. of extract of logwood, boiled with 11 kg. of water, and, when near the syrupy state, 300 gr. of iron nitrate added; evaporated to a syrup under constant stirring.   All the above stains are brought into a dry condition by running the respective syrups into trays of sheet iron, with low rims, in which the syrup hardens, and is afterward broken up and ground.

It is often desirable to retain the grain of the natural wood exposed to view, at the same time to preserve its surface from decay and give it a more beautiful appearance; this is done either by polishing or varnishing.   To varnish such woods a little skill is required to obtain a really good gloss, smooth as glass, upon its surface.   All roughness should be carefully removed, being particular not to leave any marks, especially across the grain, of the sandpaper or other material used in smoothing, and the work should be afterwards well sized, either with gelatine or good glue size.   This size is to prevent the absorption of the varnish in soft places, and to obtain a more even gloss.   Sizing sometimes has a tendency to raise the grain of the wood, more particularly of soft wood, especially if applied warm. Use oak varnish.

Aniline Dyes.—Aniline dyes are of two kinds, one dissolving in water, the other in spirits. As they have a tendency to fade in the light, the water dyes are preferable, as they can be mixed with a little vinegar, this greatly hindering the fading out process. To dissolve in spirits, use a spirit varnish, such as painters use. No definite amount necessary to stain varnish can be given, and it will be necessary to experiment with it.

HARDWOOD FINISHER.

The student will be expected to read carefully these papers before doing any work. His name and address will require to be given on each paper. He will be expected to write up the questions in a neat and intelligent manner, using his own language and style, representing the answers in such a manner as will be intelligible, make all drawings as clear as possible, and wherever it can be done render them in India ink. Let each answer be original, do not copy either from the instruction papers nor from any other source. The paper used may be of any kind, provided that it is clean and durable. Do not attempt an answer until you have thoroughly grasped the subject.

QUESTIONS.

1. Give a description of the different kinds of wood that used to be in vogue about thirty or forty years ago, but are now reckoned inferior in the manufacture of furniture.

2. Whether have dark or light colored woods the preference from an æsthetic point of view?

3. Mention some of the valuable qualities to be found in white oak.

4. Mention other two kinds of wood that are frequently used for high-class work, and well adapted for finishing purposes.

5. Whether is it preferable a finish in hardwood or a finish in pine?

6. Is there any difference in cost between a finish in the best clear pine and the best selected hardwood?

7. What is essential in the choice of all kinds of hardwood for finishing purposes?

8. What are the characteristic features in hardwood that recommends it above others?

9. What class of work is pine peculiarly adapted for?

10. What other kinds of soft wood are fairly good for finishing purposes?

11. Mention the names of some of the woods that have all coarse grain, and that are not so suitable for tasteful work.

12. What has been the result of introducing the modern methods of polishing finished woodwork?

13. Give a description of the process termed "French polishing" and for what purpose it is best adapted.

14. Give an account of the organic tissue in woods, also the variable organic elements associated with it, and examples illustrating same.

15. Give a description of the exterior characteristics of woods, and their subdivision into two classes, also the names of some of the woods in each class.

16. Give a description of the different ways in the consideration of the density of wood.

17. Whether is the density of the harder or softer woods more preferable and popular with wood finishers, and state the reasons for preference?

18. Give a description of the qualities of "walnut" wood.

19. Give a description of the qualities of the "mahogany" wood, and the several kinds.

20. Give a description of the qualities of the "cherry" wood.

21. Give a description of the qualities of the "black birch."

22. Give a description of the characteristic features to be found in the different varieties of oak.

23. Give a description of some of the qualities to be found in the "butternut."

24. Give a description of the qualities to be found in "rosewood."

25. Give some of the characteristics that are to be found in the "apple" wood.

26. Give a description of some of the qualities to be found in the "maple" wood.

27. Give a few of the characteristic qualities to be found in the "chestnut" and "ash."

28. When does it seem superfluous to have complex decoration in the finishing of hardwoods?

29. What wood is made most use of for interior finish, and what are some of the articles for which it is well adapted?

30. Describe the difference between the working of oak, particularly in the framing up of panel work, from ordinary pine or other soft wood panel work.

31. Give a description which shows the method of setting out the twist or spiral for a column, pillar or spindle.

32. Give a description of the method of making properly a dovetail joint.

33. Give a description of secret lap dovetailing, and for what purposes it is well adapted.

34. What is the difference between secret and plain lap dovetailing?

35. Give a description of what is mean by the process "miter dovetailing.

36. Give a description of what is meant by the process "bevel or splay dovetailing."

37. Give a description of the method adopted in the manufacture of veneered doors, when a number of them are to be made at one time.

38. What should be done in the manufacture of first class doors before they are veneered?

39. What equipment is required aside from the usual door-making machinery?

40. Give a description of the preparatory work of the materials previous to their construction.

41. Give a description of the process of construction in the manufacture of doors and particulars regarding the veneers and process of veneering.

42. Give a description of the advantages derivable in the construction of "dowel" doors.

43. Give a description of the best method whereby to test the quality of glue.

44. Give a description of the best way in which to prepare glue for use.

45. Give a description of the process in applying the glue to the purposes for which it is intended.

46. Give a description of the kinds of wood suitable for veneering purposes, and the preparatory processes necessary.

47. Give a description of the process of "jointing" in veneering.

48. Give a description of the process of "veneering by caul."

49. Give a description of the process of "veneering round and tapering columns."

50. Give a description of veneering small work by

using the cauls, such as in making picture frames, clock stands or similar work.

51. Give a description of what should be done preparatory to the process of polishing.

52. Give a description of "the scraper," for what purposes it is employed, and the method of its manipulation.

53. Give a description of the proper method of sharpening scrapers.

54. Give a description of the method of using sandpaper.

55. Give a description of "rasps and files" and their uses and modes of manipulation.

56. Give a description of the different kinds of saws for working hardwood, and how to manipulate them.

57. Give a description of the method of sharpening tenon saws.

58. Give a description of planes in general, and the methods of manipulating them.

59. Give a description of the grain direction for planes.

60. Give a description of the proper method of setting an iron in a plane.

61. Give a description of oilstones for sharpening plane irons, and method of manipulating the iron during the process of sharpening.

62. Give a description of the process termed "secret or blind nailing."

63. Give a description of what the term "wood fillers" means, and the methods of their application.

64. Give a description of the preparatory work necessary before commencing the process of "filling in."

65. Give a description of the principal fillers used in the trade.

66. Give the description of a walnut filler for medium and cheap work.

67. Give the description of a walnut filler for imitation wax finish.

68. Give the description of a walnut filler for first class work.

69. Give the description of a filler for light woods.

70. Give the description of a filler for cherry wood.

71. Give the description of a filler for oak wood.

72. Give the description of a filler for rosewood.

73. Give a description of the operations to be employed when the work with the filler is done.

74. Give a description of the method in applying "luxeberry" to the wood.

75. Give a description of the process of wood stain ing in general, stating some of the varieties, and the best woods that are well adapted for their application.

76. Give the reason why French polishing is employed in finishing first class work.

77. Give a description as to the time and temperature in which the varnishing should be done, in order to be of durable character and produce beautiful work.

78. Give an example of how to treat cabinet work during the process of varnishing.

79. Give a description of how to manipulate the brush while varnishing, and the best kind of brush for the purpose.

80. What should always be considered before beginning the process of varnishing.

81. Give a description of the preparatory work necessary for the process of French polishing.

82. Give a description of the "pad or rubber" with which the polish is applied, and the best kind of material of which it should be made.

83. Give a description of the amount of polish to be applied to the "rubber," and the manner of manipulating the latter.

84. Give a description of what should be done with the old "rubber" when the job is finished upon which it was used.

85. Give a description of the time to be allowed for the polish to sink, and the process to be employed before commencing to polish again.

86. Give a description of the ingredients that compose a good all-round polish that can be relied on.

87. Give a description of how to use the material for bodying.

88. Give a description of what should be done when the rubber dries.

89. Give a description as to how long the first bodying-in process should be continued.

90. Give a description as to the number of times the work will require to be bodied.

91. Give a description of how to proceed before beginning to work a fresh body on a previous one.

92. . Give a description of what should be observed by polishers when bodying up.

93. Give a description of the important matter regarding how to dry the rubbers.

94. Give a description of the final operation in French polishing, by which the gloss is put on the body previously applied.

95. Give a description of the process known as wax polishing.

96. Give a description of the class of wood upon which wax polishing is often applied, and the characteristic features it imparts in comparison with French polish.

97. Give a description of the appearance that wood stained black has after it is wax polished.

98. Whether upon coarsely grained woods or light woods of close texture, is wax polish better to be applied?

99. Give a description of the ingredients in the composition of wax polish, and the process of their admix ture.

100. Give a description of the process of oil polishing, for what purposes it is best adapted, and the characteristic features in its favor.

101. Give a description of the process known as "dry shining," the method of its adaptation, and the chief advantages in connection with it.

102. Give a description of repolishing and reviving old work, and the various processes that should be adopted in the class of work to be operated upon, so that the best results may be produced.

103. Give a description of how to renovate the polish on German pianos, and the different ingredients and method of admixture that are applied to render the operation effective.

104. Give a description as to matching up satin walnut.

105. Give a description of how the wavy appearance of some woods may be given, and how veins, either black or red, may be produced in matching.

106. Give a description of the operation entailed in the final stage, when finishing off repolished work.

107.   Give a description of the utility of dry colors, known as pigments, in the polisher's operations.

108.   Give a description of the preparation of a mixture which is used in making an imitation marble which wears well, and its effective appearance when produced.

109.   Give a description of the manner of finishing oak in general.

110.   Give a description of how to produce the effect of a good imitation of antique oak.

111.   Give another description of how a very clever imitation of the general antique can be obtained.

112.   Give a description of how oak may be fumigated, stating the liquid used, and the method of procedure in the operation.

113.   Give a description of how to darken oak.

114.   Give a description of the different styles of oak finishes, namely, "bog oak," "weathered oak," "Antwerp oak," "black Flemish oak," "brown Flemish oak," "Malachite," and "Tyrolean oak."

115.   Give a description of how to obtain a good "golden oak" finish.

116.   Give a description of cherry wood and the best method of making it look like mahogany.

117.   Give a description of black-birch, and what woods it can be easily stained to resemble.

118.   Give a description of mahogany, and the excellent qualities it possesses, also what may be done to darken the reddish hue which newly wrought mahogany presents.

119.   Give a description of the process in repolishing and reviving old mahogany work.

120. Give a description of walnut and how it may be treated in the finishing, also mention some of the woods that may be stained to resemble it.

121. Give a description of the cypress wood, and its adaptability for the process of finishing, also the names of several of the varieties.

122. Give a description of rosewood and how it may be treated in the process of finishing.

123. Give a description of the maple wood, and its adaptability for staining purposes, stating some of the imitations that may be obtained.

124. Give a description of the maple wood, and its adaptability for finishing, also the method of. obtaining an "egg-shell" gloss, "a dull finish," and "a polished finish."

125. Give a description of white and black ash, and its adaptability for finishing, also the method of obtaining an "egg-shell" gloss, "a dull finish," and a "polished finish."

126. Give a description of dyeing wood, and for what purpose this process is mostly applied.

127. Give a description of the process termed "gilding" and the characteristics of the design upon which it is employed.

128. Give a description of the process known as "burnish gilding."

129. Give a description of the process termed "bronzing" and how it may be accomplished.

130. Give a general description of the "metallization of wood," and the process by which it may be obtained.

HARDWOOD FINISHER

INDEX TO PART ONE

INDEX TO PART ONE

HARDWOOD FINISHER

INDEX TO PART TWO

SIGN WRITING

Italian, Large and Small.

ABCDEFGHIJKLN
MPQRSTUVWWXYZ

abcdefghijklmnopqrs
tuvwxyz

Old English Analytical, Small.

abcdefghijklmnopqrs
tuvwxyz

1234567890

A B C D E F G H I K
L M N O P Q R S T
U V W X Y Z

11 th Century   From MS   Munich

A B C D E F G

H J K L M N O P

Q R S T U V W

X Y Z &

13th Century. Henry the Third. Westminster Abbey.

ABCDEFGHIJKLMNOPQRSTUVWXYZ

Roman Analytical, Small.

abcdefghij klmn opq

rstuvwxyz

1 2 3 4 5 6 7 8 9 0

13th Century. From Latin MS.

Old English Analytical, Large.

A B C D E F G H I J K L M N O P Q R S T U V W X Y Z

ABECOE F E C h O J
K L M N N O P O R S T
U X X Y Z Æ Œ
A A

Italic Shaded.

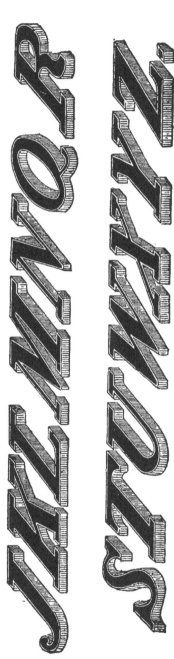

11th Century, and Numerals.

14th Century. British Museum.

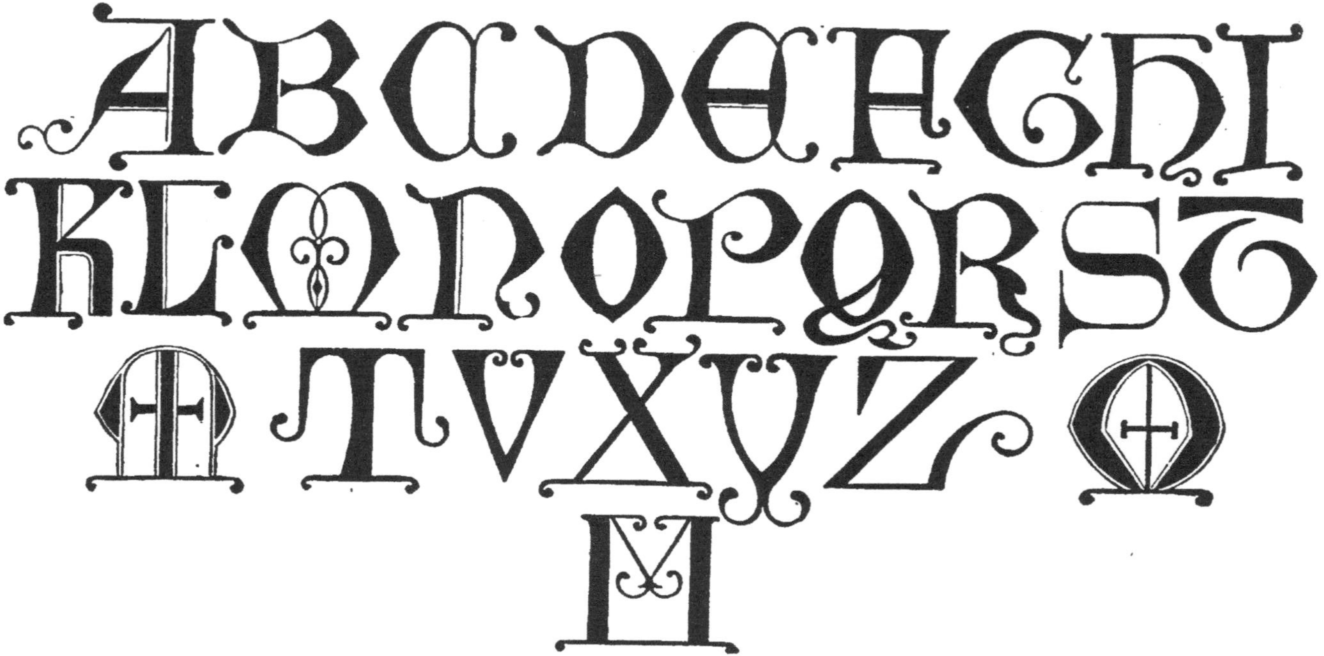

8th and 9th Centuries Anglo-Saxon

8th Century. British Museum.

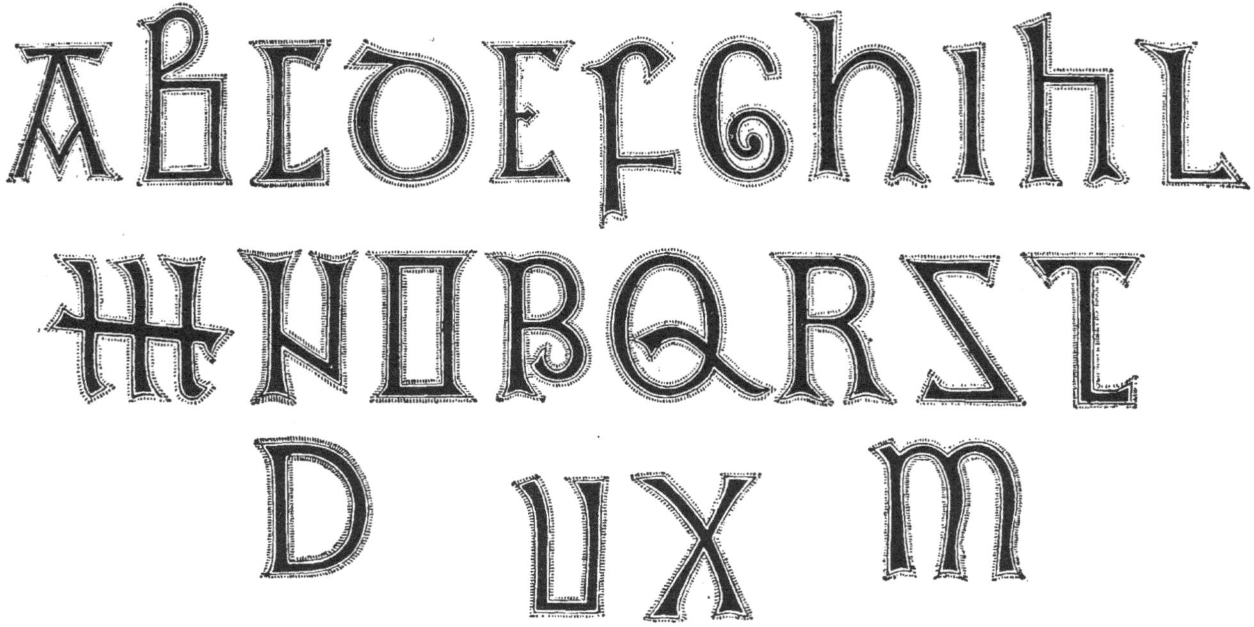

Tuscan.

A B C D E F G H I
K L M N O P Q R S
T U V X Y Z

CYCLOPEDIA

—OF—

Bricklaying, Stone Masonry, Concretes,

Stuccos and Plasters

Covering Everything Connected with the Allied Trades

By FRED T. HODGSON.

———

Three volumes in one. 840 pages. Fully illustrated. Bound in silk cloth. Special, Exclusive Edition. Printed by Frederick J. Drake & Company expressly for Sears, Roebuck & Company. Contains:

THE TWENTIETH CENTURY BRICKLAYER'S AND MASON'S ASSISTANT. By Fred T. Hodgson. Retail price $1.50.

CONCRETES, CEMENTS, MORTARS, PLASTERS AND STUCCOS. How to Make and How to Use Them. By Fred T. Hodgson. Retail price $1.50.

DIAGRAMS AND PLATES. Retail price $1.50. Bricklaying—Stone Masonry—Concretes and Cements—Mortars, Plastering and Stucco Work. There are 1,000 Illustrations and Diagrams.

No. 3R9130 CYCLOPEDIA OF BRICKLAYING, STONE MASONRY, CONCRETES, STUCCOS AND PLASTERS.

OUR SPECIAL PRICE $1.62.

If by mail, postage extra, 21 cents.

———

SEARS, ROEBUCK & COMPANY,

Chicago, Ill.

Lightning Source UK Ltd.
Milton Keynes UK
UKOW06f0255010815

256205UK00013B/264/P